Cosmopolitanism, Migration and Universal Human Rights

Mogens Chrom Jacobsen · Emnet Berhanu Gebre · Drago Župarić-Iljić
Editors

Cosmopolitanism, Migration and Universal Human Rights

Nordic Summer University

Springer

Editors
Mogens Chrom Jacobsen
Nordic Summer University
Copenhagen, Denmark

Emnet Berhanu Gebre
University Toulouse I Capitole
Toulouse, France

Drago Župarić-Iljić
University of Zagreb
Zagreb, Croatia

ISBN 978-3-030-50647-6 ISBN 978-3-030-50645-2 (eBook)
https://doi.org/10.1007/978-3-030-50645-2

This Springer imprint is published by the registered company Springer Nature Switzerland AG
The registered company address is: Gewerbestrasse 11, 6330 Cham, Switzerland

Cosmopolitanism, Migration and Universal Human Rights: Introduction

This collection is the result of activities carried out within the Nordic Summer University (NSU). NSU is a nomadic university established in 1950. It is an independent and international-oriented academic institution organising symposia across disciplines in the Nordic and Baltic regions (http://nordic.university). The activities of the NSU are organised in thematically structured study circles. The great majority of the contributions were presented within circle 5—International Relations and Human Rights—during its winter session in Tallinn, Estonia (11–13 March 2016). Circle 5 was a joint venture between NSU and the European Humanities University, Vilnius, Lithuania, and it was co-coordinated by Oleg Bresky and Mogens Chrom Jacobsen. We warmly thank the School of Governance, Law and Society at Tallinn University and Abel Polese for their help in organising this session. Some of the contributions (Chaps. 8 and 16) come from circle 1—Understanding Migration in Nordic and Baltic Countries—and we thank the coordinators, Stéphanie Barillé and Bremen Donovan, for allowing us to publish these contributions here.

The special focus of the NSU meeting taking place in Tallinn in March 2016 was Human Rights and Migration, and it was largely inspired by the ongoing events at the time: 2015 had seen a large number of refugees and other forced migrants coming to Europe—more than a million, according to the International Organization for Migration (IOM 2016). These events created a stir at the time, but seen in the larger historical perspective the event should be relativised. It seems as if humanity has always been on the move since the movements out of Africa from the Rift Valley, the seasonal movements of our hunter-gatherer ancestors, the 'Barbarian Invasions' in the first millennium and European immigration to other parts of the world to mention just a few (Muséum Manifesto 2018). This would indicate that migration is the rule rather than the exception, even though the UN indicates that only 3.5% of humanity are currently international migrants (UN DESA 2019), together with more than 70 million forcibly displaced people worldwide (UNHCR 2019, 2). Seen from the perspective of the individual European countries, these movements seemed, however, overwhelming; the media coverage, at least, tried to give this impression. Governments and public personalities (some faster than others) thus tried to find or enhance the means of circumventing international obligations and argue against them, while others embraced the other extreme by advocating open borders. This prompted the idea of trying to take stock of the present situation of cosmopolitanism: both to highlight the challenges facing cosmopolitanism and gauge the proper scope of cosmopolitanism and its potential 'darker sides'.

What we would like to present to readers in this volume as its editors is not a unitary, exhaustive and fully integrated work ordained uniformly according to a preconceived theoretical perspective and outlined as a unique argument with premises and conclusion. This is not at all the ideal we pursue here. The hallmark of the NSU is the interdisciplinary approach. Inherent in this approach is the coming together of different perspectives and methods. Disciplines have different historical roots, different assumptions and perspectives, approach problems differently, and often they even see different problems. To impose a common theoretical framework, common epistemological positions or even a common formulation of the problem would be contrary to the interdisciplinary endeavour we undertake here. A unitary approach could very well exclude interesting, complementary or conflicting paradigms and disregard individual researchers' appreciation of what is the most urgent matters of the moment. What is interesting about the interdisciplinary approach is to confront one's own assumptions and perspectives with an approach foreign or less familiar to our own discipline. This could inspire new ways to look at our own discipline, enlarge our own perspective(s), prompt us to reconsider our problem, envisage combined ways to deal with some subject matter or question our assumptions. This process can be challenging yet a fruitful one.

The theme chosen here is vast, and we have privileged new and original contributions rather than exhaustiveness. We have decided to give room for researchers' commitment and dedication to their subject and their perception of where the real problems are, rather than obliging them to fit into a preconceived framework. As a consequence, the length of chapters can vary according to the concerns and styles of the different authors and we have thus abstained from uniformity for the sake of uniformity. This will leave the reader with a variegated picture that points in many directions. This openness is exactly what is interesting and luring in the interdisciplinary venture, opening the floor for reflection and discussion of various yet complementary theoretical and empirically funded contributions. Chapters based on empirical field case studies, for example, are thus an essential part of the overall purpose of this volume, namely, to embed discussion on human rights, migration and cosmopolitanism as well as legal and philosophical concepts into the experienced world of social facts, institutions, actors and processes.

As editors, we did not feel it was appropriate to make a conclusion in the end. What the reader will take away from this volume will vary according to background, concerns and preoccupations, and we did not find that we should conclude on their behalf. The aim of this book, taken as a whole, is not to argue any specific point, but to present a panoply of approaches and in this way taking stock of the present situation of cosmopolitanism, and its interconnectedness with human rights and migration. The purpose of this introduction is therefore to situate the theme conceptually and historically, to summarise the findings and suggest possible interrelations between the contributions.

Relationship between Human Rights and Cosmopolitanism

This volume assumes that human rights are an integral part of cosmopolitanism, even though this view does not command universal consensus. We would think, however, that this view is the one challenged today and, therefore, the proper object of our stocktaking. In fact, cosmopolitanism became popular in the wake of the fall of the Berlin Wall in 1989. During the 1990s, voices came forward to argue that democracy could no longer be confined to the limits of the nation-state. They asserted the need for a new cosmopolitan political order extending democracy and political community beyond the territorial limits of the state (Chandler 2009, 54). Should we conclude from this that cosmopolitanism basically means democracy extended to the international level with the human rights regime defining the fundamental rights of the cosmopolitan citizen? There is a different view held by our lead author Yves Charles Zarka. According to him, cosmopolitics should regulate politics and not substitute itself for it. Global democratic institutions would belong to the particular historical developments within the political sphere, and they would not be a necessary part of cosmopolitics. However, such a view would not sever the connection between cosmopolitanism (cosmopolitics) and human rights. Human rights are cosmopolitan rights, and, as such, they should be inscribed in politics (Zarka *in this volume*).

Both of these versions of cosmopolitanism would thus emphasise the connection between human rights and cosmopolitanism. Human rights, as it were, are the fundamental rights of world citizens. Since global democratic institutions are embryonic at the most, challenges would naturally concentrate on the human rights part, and that is also where our emphasis will be. In fact, the original use of the term *cosmopolis*, in ancient Greece, did not imply the idea of a world government. As noted by both Carsten Friberg and Adam Diderichsen, the fourth-century BC philosopher Diogenes of Sinope claimed to be a citizen of the world, but this seemed to be a wholly negative claim protesting against life in particular political communities and conventional morality (Friberg; Diderichsen; *in this volume*). Membership of the city-state was, however, inserted into the larger community of Greeks, the counterpart of which was the *ethnos* or *ethnikos,* which were commonly used to describe those who were non-Hellenic, barbarians, pagans (Malešević 2004, 1). The Stoic version of cosmopolitanism transcended these distinctions, having a positive moral content for those who were able to live according to nature, but it did not, as such, imply a world government, even though it was at some point associated with the Roman Empire. Ancient cosmopolitanism being essentially of the moral kind, the legal aspect is fuzzy or non-existent, and here Immanuel Kant was an innovator (Kleingeld and Brown 2014).

Kant is clearly an important inspiration for modern cosmopolitanism, and this is clear both from the contributions of Zarka and Rebecka Lettevall. They both insist that cosmopolitan rights, according to Kant, are genuine rights and not a mere question of philanthropy, but with Kant, there seems to be only one such right, namely hospitality. Hospitality means that a peaceful stranger cannot be treated with hostility, but such a stranger can be turned away if it can be done without mortal danger (Zarka; Lettevall; *in this volume*).

Modern cosmopolitanism would, of course, go far beyond Kant both on cosmopolitan rights and human rights, whatever their relation. David Beetham, reflecting on what human rights have to offer as a model for cosmopolitan democracy, considers that 'the human rights covenants taken together provide much of what is required for the foundation of a global democratic citizenship' (Beetham 1998: 58, 66).

Downsides and Criticisms of Cosmopolitanism

Proclaiming a right to hospitality, Kant draws on ideas dating back to the late Middle Ages. Adam Diderichsen introduces us to the works of Francisco Vitoria and their historical context. This context was the discovery of the Americas and considerations about how Europeans could approach these lands. Vitoria considered all arguments carefully on the matter and concluded that Europeans had a right to settle when no harm is done, to trade and to preach the Gospels (Diderichsen *in this volume*). The right to visit or to travel was important for different imperial and colonial ventures, and Diderichsen suggests that cosmopolitanism is stained by original sin, even though a cosmopolitanism which then allowed extensive colonisation now seems to justify movements in the opposite directions.

Jeremy Bentham's criticism of human rights was nearly contemporary with the development of the human rights idea. Bentham thought that the vague principles of the declarations would be inoperative and foment anarchy. Jean-Pierre Cléro, in his re-reading of Bentham's arguments, acknowledge that somehow it was possible to have a functioning human rights jurisdiction since we have one today in the form of the European Court of Human Rights and the UN's human rights system. Anarchy did not ensue, but Cléro raises another question dear to Bentham, namely regarding the sovereignty of the people. According to Cléro, human rights risk killing politics by posing them as external standards outside of ordinary politics and by confiding decisions about them to unelected judges. With Cléro's striking expression, the French revolutionaries merely relocated 'the tyranny they claimed to fight' (Cléro *in this volume*).

One could object to Bentham's focus on popular sovereignty, considered as the sovereignty of a particular identifiable people organised in a state, on the grounds that it is difficult to restrict his own principle, utilitarianism, to a particular people rather than applying it to humanity as a whole or maybe beyond. On this conception, the burden of proof lies on those who want to limit the application of the principle to a particular group, and arguing for this is generally an uphill venture (Jacobsen *in this volume*). This can be seen from Irina Ivankiv's treatment of visa regimes. If we accept maximising economic growth as an indicator of maximising utility, it would seem that the existing visa regimes would not survive the application of Rawlsian, utilitarian or related conceptions (Ivankiv *in this volume*). This would suggest yet another kind of 'cosmopolitanism' advocating open borders. This kind of 'cosmopolitanism' is different from the one defended by Zarka and generally held by many, which is in no way incompatible with borders and visa regimes. Respect for human rights and the 1951 Convention Relating to the Status of Refugees do not imply open borders.

That the relationship between cosmopolitanism, the state and different versions of nationalism is a complex one is clear from Barbara Gornik's empirical study (Gornik *in this volume*). By examining the public opinion on refugees, she poses a seemingly contradictory question: whether cosmopolitanism and nationalism, with all its possible exclusionary practices, might be antagonistic, yet compatible and complementary worldviews. When it comes to attitudes of the local Slovenian population, it appears that their endorsement of refugee rights could at the same time be driven by cosmopolitan and nationalistic predispositions. Thus, on the abstract level, cosmopolitanism and nationalism seem quite compatible in people's minds, and here Rebecka Lettevall's findings on the history of 'cosmopolitanism' and 'patriotism' in Sweden is illuminating. The attachment to one's country or territory was formerly seen as a complement to a cosmopolitan attitude. Today 'patriotism' is little used, and when it is, it is often conflated with nationalism (Lettevall *in this volume*). Some forms of nationalism are clearly incompatible with all versions of cosmopolitanism. Nationalism, ethnically defined, denying the existence of human rights and refusing refugees their rights according to the UN convention, would be in opposition to cosmopolitanism. In Gornik's work, we can get a glimpse of the cracks in the abstract ideals of cosmopolitanism, but at the same time make out the possibilities for a different kind of nationalism or patriotism according to Lettevall's findings.

Rights, Spaces and Citizenships

The contributions of Oleg Bresky, Leif Kalev and Mari-Liis Jakobson emphasise the differences between the post-Soviet experience and traditional conceptions of democracy and citizenship in the West. Citizenship conceptions in Eastern Europe are much more instrumental and more like a bargaining chip to negotiate social benefits. The authors warn us that the same kind of attitude is spreading to Western Europe. Traditional conceptions in the West emphasise the autonomous individual, the identification with the role of citizens, substantial participation and equal rights for all citizens, among other things (Bresky; Kalev and Jakobson; *in this volume*). These are challenged today, and Kalev and Jakobson consider the possibilities for maintaining or enhancing the traditional concept in a contemporary context. The authors remind us that the reproduction of citizenship through social context and daily activities of the citizens, embedded meaningfully in social practices, will not come without tensions regarding interactions between state, citizens and migrant non-citizens (Kalev and Jakobson *in this volume*). Carsten Friberg is interested in the same question, but from a rather different perspective. Considering the conditions and embedding of democracy, the focus is often on legal regulation, institutions and attitudes, but the way these are embedded in and influenced by our built environment is often neglected. Friberg considers how human rights and citizens' relations interact with the environment. The keyword for him is 'ambiance', which crystallises these interactions in its concept and indicates a complex context for the implementation of abstract principles (Friberg *in this volume*).

Implementation of human rights is, in fact, a very complex process, but it also has a complex relation to citizenship. Mogens Chrom Jacobsen argues that the eighteenth-century declarations of human rights distinguished sharply between human rights and citizen rights. This becomes much murkier with the Universal Declaration of Human Rights (1948). In this declaration, citizenship and political participation become a part of human rights. This means that everybody has a right to be a citizen somewhere (but not necessarily where they are actually living). This view is not followed, however, by the Convention on Civil and Political Rights (ICCPR) (Jacobsen *in this volume*). In both cases, though, there is a dichotomy between citizens and non-citizens.

Bresky demonstrates, however, that such a strong dichotomy is not a useful approach. People staying or living in a territory have various kinds of rights. Some membership rights will not be human rights yet others will, while others again will stem from international treatises, EU law or some other source. This will yield a conception of citizenship as a continuum of various degrees of membership rights (Bresky *in this volume*). This opens up new perspectives for the management of a much more variegated situation. The challenges that migration of different kinds as well as post-migration phenomena pose can thus be attenuated and absorbed within a form of cosmopolitanism deploying graduated membership rights.

These could, to some extent, accommodate concerns that migration, identity and citizenship are exclusive, as migrants are excluded from a given community according to criteria related to identity and citizenship. Just like migration, identity and citizenship are elements that continue to fluctuate through expansion or shrinkage as political ramifications occur. In her well-known writings, Shachar (2009) sees birthright entitlements to citizenship as too arbitrary criteria for securing membership into some/any political community. Shachar argues that if we see citizenship on the blood-and-soil principle as a capital or a property inheritance, it will only help to sustain and reproduce the inequalities of opportunity. Thus, new post-national models of citizenship that would transform or maybe only add to the known binary understanding of ethnic vs civic citizenry have not yet been seen as occurring in political realities of nation-states, apart from limited cases of multiple citizenship or sovereign-state principles of residence or protection statuses (cf. Bresky *in this volume*). Of course, transnational social spaces and activities of transmigrants (including refugees) add to legal, social and political complexity, and this must not be forgotten. However, their positions are still bounded by the concept of possessing nation-state citizenship as a guarantee of their status and their residence/jobs/protection permits.

Having thus outlined the conceptual map of cosmopolitanism, human rights and citizenship, we must consider the actual challenges to the cosmopolitan order outlined above. For this purpose, migration is a particularly effective test case, since the concern for people not belonging to the national community is at the heart of cosmopolitanism, and both legal and empirical research evidence the ways cosmopolitanism is sidestepped, chipped away, eroded or simply ignored.

Relationship Between Migration and Human Rights

The link between migration and human rights is multifaceted. One may say that they have a quite ambiguous relationship. It must be recalled that migration can be both beneficial and detrimental to human rights. Engaged in an orderly and regular manner, migration can be a vector of human development. Individuals migrate for many reasons: from education and work, to family reunification, health and lifestyle or simply for leisure purposes, they are given an opportunity to exercise and enjoy several freedoms. People fleeing persecution, violence, human rights abuse and other life-threatening circumstances also migrate to leave their country of habitual residence for a safe haven (Collier 2013).

In contrast, when engaged in irregular channels, migration across borders can present multiple threats to human rights. Smuggled and trafficked individuals face highly hazardous situations to reach the European continent, including life-threatening or exploitative circumstances ranging from precarious and/or forced labour to slavery. By increasing their vulnerabilities, it is a truism that the exercise of the most fundamental rights of migrants is thus undermined.

As migration constitutes a long and costly journey, its link with human rights is a continuous process since the challenge for migrants continues even after they have successfully reached their final destination in the post-migratory phase. The right to obtain a status that will enable the migrant to remain within the territory of the state is a right for which non-citizens have to fight for administratively.

We understand the term 'migrants' as referring to multiform and diverse categories which encompass different kinds of group of persons: temporary residents, permanent residents, students, circular migrants, short-term workers, sojourners, asylum seekers, refugees, irregular and undocumented migrants and many others. Considering this diversity, all these categories of persons do not necessarily have the same legal status and, accordingly, the same rights to enter and remain in the territory of the host country.

While a person fleeing persecution, violence or war can, in theory, be entitled to refugee or subsidiary protection status, the vast majority of migrants fall outside the scope of international protection (Becker 2019). Even the former nowadays face more and more difficulties persuading the authorities that they are worthy of protection. Facing discrimination, non-citizens encounter rejection and are excluded from the enjoyment of a wide range of human rights, some arguing that states' obligations only exist vis-à-vis their citizenry (Berlingske 2019). From a legal perspective, states have a duty to respect, protect and fulfil fundamental rights to all persons who are under their jurisdiction. While ensuring economic and social rights for migrants may give rise to debate, the state cannot deprive a migrant, even in an illegal situation, of the enjoyment of fundamental rights guaranteed for all human beings by international law. As Louise Arbour, United Nations Special Representative for International Migration, stated, 'the fundamental principle of the universality of human [rights] means that those individuals deemed irregular migrants also have rights. While irregular entry and stay may constitute administrative offences for non-refugee migrants, they are not crimes per se against persons, property or national security. And while states retain the sovereign prerogative to order their removal, the very presence of such migrants under their jurisdiction places certain obligations on national authorities' (Arbour 2017, 2).

Migrants have incontestably gained a claim to rights through international law, which has contributed to democratising human rights in a way that individual rights are guaranteed to all as human beings and not as citizens, regardless of their belonging to a nation-state. Universal personhood undergirds the expansion of rights and rights claims and surpasses the sole identity of a person. This has constituted a paradigm shift as the nation-state system, which by nature was territorial, conditioned the enjoyment of rights since membership of a national community, or, more specifically, a political membership has been the criterion. With the advent of international law proclaiming equal and universal rights, transnational migration challenges the nation-state model.

This shift has been operated progressively and only on a sectoral basis. In the aftermath of the Second World War, refugees were recognised and provided with the right to asylum by the Universal Declaration of Human Rights (1948) and the Convention Relating to the Status of Refugees (1951) and its Protocol (1967). Later on, under the auspices of the International Labour Office, labour migrants became protected under a series of international conventions which guaranteed a wide range of human rights ranging from non-discrimination in the enjoyment of economic rights to social and cultural rights, such as the International Convention on the Protection of the Rights of All Migrant Workers and Members of Their Families (1990).

However, even though national membership cannot be cited as the sole status that underpins the enjoyment of human rights, it constitutes an identity that does not lose its relevance: in practice, there is a 'political culture in which universal personhood continues to be subordinated to citizenship as a basis for rights' (Hill Maher 2002, 21). Many rights remained as an entitlement exclusive to citizens. The exclusion of migrants particularly those from the developing countries from the enjoyment of the right to immigration is also one of the compelling examples. In the light of the racial violence and the discriminatory policies migrants encounter, 'identities still matter to rights claims and that human rights are not hegemonic norms' (Hill Maher 2002, 25). Claims to rights based on universal personhood are progressively weakened in the face of restrictive immigration policies.

The exclusion of migrants from the right to immigrate into a foreign state founds its roots in the liberal tradition pertaining to the notion of contract and consent in so far as their inclusion into the host community depends on the consent of the members of the latter, assuming that the former has already expressed the will to join the community. The state policy on immigration and its will (or absence of will) to welcome newcomers is presumed to be the reflection of its citizens.

Freedom of Movement: A Human Right?

As shown in Zarka's chapter (*in this volume*), while the absence of a right to immigration in positive law is well established, whether or not this right exists from a philosophical perspective and whether it is compatible with cosmopolitanism can be considered a debatable issue (Jacobsen *in this volume*).

The proponents of an open border policy consider freedom of movement to be a fundamental human right. From a legal point of view, the controversy lies mainly on the duality of freedom of movement as guaranteed by international conventions since the right of emigration and the right of immigration are not guaranteed in the same terms. These rights entail different duties on behalf of different entities operating on different geographic spheres. By virtue of Article 13 of the Universal Declaration of Human Rights: '(1) Everyone has the right to freedom of movement and residence within the borders of each state. (2) Everyone has the right to leave any country, including his own, and to return to his country'. An individual has, therefore, the right to leave his country without having the guarantee to be received in another country. This asymmetry has resulted in different duties on behalf of different entities operating on different geographic spheres.

If one is not persuaded by legal, moral and philosophical arguments for open borders, one could try to convince a state to open its borders and welcome foreigners into their territory based on economic arguments. The liberalisation of visas, along with freedom of movement for all, could have beneficial effects for their economies (Ivankiv *in this volume*). There is, however, a contradiction because states might tend to refuse entry on account of limited resources arguing that unlimited immigration policy would put an 'unreasonable' burden on their welfare system, while Ivankiv argues that an open border policy will rather have favourable impacts on the same welfare system.

Economic considerations are probably also the reason for the discriminatory visa regime, which exempts or at least facilitates the visa process for the citizens of wealthy countries and burdens those from developing countries. Some may justify this by saying it is 'the fear of others'; however, representing all foreigners as 'others' seems quite simplistic because even if the visa system can be considered discriminatory, it mostly disfavours the 'poor'. The 'fear of the poor' is what really justifies the established restrictive immigration policies as rich individuals from developing countries still have the opportunity to travel for touristic, educational, business, amenity and many other purposes.

This discrepancy in the discriminatory visa regime and mechanisms for refugee protection pinpoint the known fact that those in need of protection are not able to travel to desired destinations but stay mostly inside the borders of their own country or immediately surrounding states. It is a rather Eurocentric perspective to forget that 80% or more of forcibly displaced populations follow this pattern. In this light, Lars Erslev Andersen's chapter on Palestinian refugees in Lebanon becomes particularly salient, relativising what happens in Europe. According to EU numbers, refugees make up 30% of the Lebanese population (EU 2019). Erslev Andersen analyses the situation of the Palestinian refugees in Lebanon and how the Syrian 'refugee crisis' affected their livelihood, considering what perspectives there are for them in the future. Being in a very vulnerable position, with a protection gap that cannot be one-sidedly bridged, with dim and slim chances of return to their homes, they often feel themselves to be victims of regional politics and the impotence of international politics to help them with any possible durable solutions whether this would be the desire to return or local integration outside camps and informal settlements. Acknowledging and exercising their rights remain a difficult task, yet is the only possible course to pursue, when the endorsement of their human rights and their social rights stands contrary to their stateless status in the host country (Erslev Andersen *in this volume*).

Rejection of Asylum Seekers and Refugees: Contravention of Cosmopolitanism?

It must be recalled that once migrants, whether legally or illegally, have entered the territory of a state, the latter has a duty to respect their fundamental human rights and treat them with dignity. Criminalisation of migration in the political discourse and also in public opinion has become a common phenomenon. The migrant is 'constructed' not only as the undocumented worker who does not pay his taxes and contributes to the lowering of social standards by accepting to work for low wages and social protection, but also the alien engaged in criminal activities ranging from drug dealing to terrorist activities. This biased Manichean perception tends to have 'complex repercussions in terms of popular sentiment, future public policy and the potential for migrants to make human rights claim' (Hill Maher 2002, 29). Public opinion reveals a sentiment of rejection and fear towards migrants who are often perceived as not deserving of rights.

While Christianity has contributed greatly to the very idea of non-discrimination and has promoted a welcoming culture towards newcomers, during the so-called refugee crisis, the Catholic Church and believers in Poland seemed to have moved away from the principle that constitutes the foundation of their faith. Anna Wilczyńska and Karol Wilczyński have demonstrated that despite the very low number of refugees in Poland, the Catholic Church did not play its role in fostering a positive attitude towards refugees among its faithful, whether through its silence (as in the case of Croatia) or negative rhetoric on the refugee crisis. Presently, the Catholic Church's influence on the opinion of Polish society seems to have declined as the Church has lost its authority over the years (Wilczyńska and Wilczyński *in this volume*).

The sentiment of rejection and fear observed towards migrants and refugees should not overshadow all the solidarity initiatives that were engaged in favour of migrants. As Drago Župarić-Iljić explained, many faith-based actors became highly involved during the period of the Balkan corridor and afterwards in the process of fostering solidarity towards newcomers. Their mandate evolved to an extent where they also became actively engaged in human rights and refugee rights advocacy activities. Despite the remaining challenges, including overall securitisation and criminalisation of migration and of citizens' solidarity, faith-based actors strive to promote a humanitarian approach shifting progressively from the provision of emergency assistance to long-term integration solutions. These were among many other humanitarian, solidary, civil society and pro-refugee rights actors, initiatives or grassroots movements active during the 'long summer of migration' (Kasparek and Speer 2015) and in its aftermath.

Analysing volunteer networks supporting refugees in Copenhagen and Berlin, Kirchner and Steen Bygballe Jensen come up with a challenging idea that these networks for refugees could serve as alternative structures for political participation and ways of belonging. Volunteers and refugees working and cooperating actively together may overcome the separation due to national legal borders (citizen–non-citizen divide) and create a sort of transborder citizenship, understood as everyday negotiation and practising of refugee rights counteracting the mistreatment of newcomers.

Various campaigns denouncing the treatment of migrants have been undertaken. But far from pressuring the European Union to take positive actions towards migrants, it drove the EU to legislate against the activism geared towards the support of migrants by criminalising the assistance of illegal migrants and targeting all those who offer humanitarian aid (Council Directive 2002/90/EC of 28 November 2002 and Council framework Decision of 28 November 2002). As a result, multiple lawsuits were brought against citizens, politicians and even medical professionals and NGOs working in the field of humanitarian aid.

Beyond the debate pertaining to migrants, there are indicators that the European states are progressively closing more and more their borders and 'building walls' (Zarka *in this volume*), notably by lowering protection standards even for categories of forced migrants already protected by international law (i.e. refugees, asylum seekers). The sole reason for fear of persecution is not always sufficient for protection to be afforded as per the terms of the 1951 Convention Relating to the Status of Refugees. Asylum is rather granted on the basis of 'humanitarian grounds' thanks to the goodwill of the states. One may think this could potentially extend the list of beneficiaries of international protection as it goes without saying that more humanity in the management of migration flows is always welcomed. The reality is far from this as a shift from a right-based approach to vulnerability-based approach has been operated. Asylum seekers cannot be trusted solely on the basis of the story they tell: a strong suspicion and mistrust are expressed towards them; as their fear of persecution in their country of origin cannot be measured, their stories are often presumed fraudulent. Since these individuals are perceived as a burden, the authorities regard them as 'abusive migrants'.

If an individual aspires to get refugee status, he or she must manifest visible and scientifically measurable signs of vulnerability: serious physical or mental illness is one of those situations that can render an individual eligible to remain in the territory of a given state. Camille de Vulpillières discusses how migrants are seen as biological rather than social human beings, whose human rights in the perspective of the state rely on humanitarian grounds that basically strip them of their agency. The administration, legal procedures and humanitarian reasoning might thus reduce human rights and people's destinies to bare reification of suffering, vulnerability, passivity and dependency (de Vulpillières *in this volume*). The story of a young asylum seeker who started a hunger strike after his asylum claim was rejected is a compelling example. His health condition declined so severely that he received the right to stay as a 'suffering body'. This could seem rather strange as the individual would not have been in this situation if he had been heard in the first place. After their asylum claim was rejected, others experienced a great deal of suffering and distress due to the fear of returning back to their country of origin and had to be recognised as psychiatric cases. While the story behind this trauma was not considered veracious, the mentally ill man was recognised as eligible for protection on humanitarian grounds (Dubois-Girard 2011, 4–5).

It seems as if supranational institutions, to whom the responsibility to ensure the proper application of human rights standards has been given, are staggering in the face of state parties' protective tendencies of their national sovereignty with regard to immigration matters. The European Court of Human Rights, indisputable champion of the protection of human rights, tends to adopt a restrictive approach when dealing with immigration matters and access to international protection for foreign claimants, thus leaving the impression that state sovereignty punctuates the level of protection the court is willing to afford to foreigners. Two revealing examples are provided in this book: the situation of women asylum seekers and individuals accused of terrorism who potentially face *refoulement* to countries where their life is at great risk (Petropoulou; Gebre, *in this volume*).

As far as women asylum seekers are concerned, Athanasia Petropoulou shows that the Court of Strasbourg does not place their claims of asylum in a broad structural, institutional and social context while examining the existence of ill-treatment under Article 3 of the Convention, overly focusing on the individual characteristics of the applicant. In cases concerning sexual orientation and gender identity, it seems that the court sets a double standard when applying the safeguards of the Convention. Foreign victims of criminalisation of homosexuality, and often of gender-based violence in general, do not receive the same level of protection when they seek international protection as European homosexuals victims of discrimination because of their sexual orientation.

Emnet Berhanu Gebre discusses the same point regarding the application of the principle of *non-refoulement* to persons convicted for terrorism. The European Court of Human Rights is more or less resisting the pressure of the states which mangle the principle of *non-refoulement* in the name of the fight against terrorism. This issue is at the crossroads of states' obligation to protect their population along with the prerogative to oversee their sovereignty in deciding who is entitled to remain on their territory and the right of a person not to be sent to another country where his life is in danger. Gebre (*in this volume*) contends there are signs in the jurisprudence of the court that presage that the absolute character of the right to be protected against ill-treatment can be eroded in the face of growing security concerns.

From the European Union side, the states of the Visegrad group pose a challenge to the legal order of the EU, notably to the European legal cosmopolitanism developed by the European Court of Justice and the Commission. As emphasised by Joseph Krulic, despite their favourable past towards the right of asylum, these countries have recorded systematic failure in matters of asylum rights either by refusing to take responsibility in the processing of asylum applications or to accept the rule of law model. This conflict between the two represents the epitome of the debate between the sovereign right of the state and the supremacy of transnational rights recalling 'the rift between Hans Kelsen and Carl Schmitt, Grotius and the raison d'Etat' (Krulic *in this volume*).

The Challenges of the Post-migratory Phase

Lack of political will on the part of political elites and policymakers of asylum and integration policies may curtail the chances of obtaining adequate protection and proper implementation of both human rights and refugee rights. However, the inclusion of refugees into the education system and the labour market, as well as their participation in the social life of the destination/reception country, depends not only on the political will and the legislative and institutional capacities but also on the social climate that enables interaction between local hosts and newcomers. Župarić-Iljić and Gregurović (*in this volume*) tackle those security discourses used by politicians and the media that have caused the gradual deterioration of human rights and refugee rights in the post-Balkan corridor period. This has, to some extent, downgraded the trust that the local Croatian population has in refugees. The public perception of asylum seekers and refugees and of their rights seemingly reaffirms symbolic (non)citizen borders between cosmopolitan inclusiveness and ethno-national exclusiveness.

In the context of another Central East European country, focusing on exploring the attitudes of youth in Belarus towards civil and political rights, Olga Breskaya scrutinises different modes of political culture, and she equally emphasises the importance of the migrants' context when it comes to the endorsement or rejection of human rights. From a societal perspective, positive attitudes towards pluralism and especially multiculturalism, in combination with critical stances towards governing institutions, could help to explain the positive perception of refugee rights (Breskaya *in this volume*).

One could also wonder whether yesteryear's immigrants are becoming accepted parts of society at the same pace in states with a more ethnic-based citizenship model (such as Germany) compared with those with a civic/citizen-based citizenship/nationhood (such as France). However, there is also a contrary tendency that we might have witnessed on the eve of the EU enlargement's cycles to countries of Central Europe and the Baltic states, where whole ethnic populations of yesterday's neighbours are becoming 'strangers' without moving, yet in the early 1990s borders were transformed in the geopolitical space and consequently made 'de-citizen-isation' and other exclusionary administrative practices towards 'new minorities' possible.

As a result of a formal naturalisation process or status regularisation in national programmes or even after a political construction (e.g. the introduction of EU citizenship) yesterday's migrants become the citizens of the present after the newcomers and the host community expressed their will for this political inclusion to become possible. This was the case during the establishment of the European Union, which resulted in the creation of European citizenship encompassing progressively 27 member states today. Since the economic and political integration was done gradually, citizens of the member states did not all acquire the same rights associated with their status at the same time. On the contrary, individuals that were part of a given community and considered as citizens can become migrants after they expressed collectively the will to withdraw themselves from it and accordingly lose some of the entitlements related to their previous status. This second case scenario arises from the ramifications that resulted from Brexit.

Conclusion

Cosmopolitanism, as we understand it here, is essentially moral and focused on the international human rights regime. Cosmopolitanism, in this sense, is challenged by proponents of open borders and utilitarianism on the one side and nationalism with its cortège of xenophobia and racism, chauvinism, authoritarianism and fundamentalism on the other. Being once associated with patriotism, it has now conceded it to nationalism. It drags behind itself memories of colonialism, which still haunt it today. The main challenge is, however, the one coming from different forms of nationalism gaining influence on the state apparatus and to some extent dragging the courts with them. Attempts to transform rights to humanitarian action circumvent the principle of *non-refoulement* and indiscriminate protection against ill-treatment, refusing asylum rights altogether, ignoring the structural, institutional and social context of asylum claims. These phenomena also express changes in people's perceptions. Even though some elements of nationalism can coexist with cosmopolitanism, other elements make this coexistence illusory. It seems that attitudes to pluralism and multiculturalism are decisive in this respect. The elements of a more ethnic nationalism are, in turn, reinforced by security discourses and internal power struggles.

Religion can both be a challenge and a reinforcement of cosmopolitanism since it has remained silent or embraced nationalist rhetoric in some places, while religious organisations have supported the rights of refugees in other places. There is, however, a wider context of embeddedness both institutionally and in our built environment, which is important for the respect of human rights, democratic procedures and attitudes towards migrants. Authors of this volume have pointed to the notion of ambiance and the autonomous and participating citizen. A wide range of populations are feeling they are not being represented or account is not taken of their voices even when they express anti-migrant and anti-refugee views. Cosmopolitanism is being depoliticised in the public sphere (moved out of the mainstream) and transferred to the cultural domain as an arrogant, self-righteous and moralising position on the issue of human rights. Cross-cutting migration and human rights issues within the virtual, digital sphere, in post-truth politics, could be reasons for the polarisation of society. There is a dangerous tendency for democracy to become a bargaining chip for social benefits, and this will not bode well for the respect of human rights and thus for cosmopolitanism. There are, however, some reasons for optimism. Transborder grassroot movements and more gradual conceptions of citizenship could ease or contravene these tendencies.

Emerging challenges, however, related to all phases of migration, cannot be addressed only with declaratory efforts within the particular political sphere of the nation-state members of the United Nations system. Yet, as we have seen in many cases, the sovereignty principle acts against the legal and institutional attempts to manage human movements within a global intergovernmental policy. And then we end up in the so-called broken refugee system (Betts and Collier 2017), where we, in the case of Europe and the reactions during the so-called refugee crisis, witnessed that not every national political actor is committed to following elementary provisions of international and European regulative mechanisms (charters, conventions, principles, laws, bylaws, protocols) regarding respect of human rights in general and migrants' and refugees' rights in particular. This could potentially not only lead to the undermining of the commonly developed asylum and migration system but also jeopardise the very basic ideas of common values and dedication to the protection of human rights at no matter what cost. Otherwise, the cosmopolitan idea(l) of a global community that could strive towards more global justice will remain a prerogative of a few rich OECD countries, or, to be precise, a particular stratum of cosmopolites within these countries.

We are aware that nation-states are not the only actors within the migration and human rights regime. Other proponents, such as supranational institutions and international organisations, take a larger and larger share in the processes of regulating the drivers and consequences of migration and especially advocating and/or enabling protection for displaced persons. In the aftermath of the mass arrival of Syrian and other refugees and migrants in 2015 and 2016, we have witnessed the development of a new UN instrument—the New York Declaration for Refugees and Migrants that seeks commitments from member states to strengthen the national mechanisms for protecting all types of migrant and refugee movements. States are obliged to respect the human rights of migrants and refugees with greater solidarity and responsibility. Yet again, the promise of more global governance is endangered because not all states of the UN have agreed to the provisions of the two new global compacts—Global Compact for Safe, Orderly and Regular Migration (GCM) and Global Compact on Refugees (GCR). However, as pointed out by Guild et al. (2019, 1), 'while the GCM is not legally binding, the human rights obligations of states which underpin the GCM are. The application of international human rights law to everyone, including migrants, has led to frictions in the intergovernmental negotiation process, with some states declining to sign the GCM. States cannot relieve themselves of the human rights obligations to which they are already, voluntarily, bound by refusing to sign the GCM'. The future will tell us how the operationalisation and the implementation of these compacts' objectives regarding human rights will be met in the political arena characterised by (national) fragmentation of the migration governance system, and how that will affect the cosmopolitan approach to it. Although—and we cannot stress this too much—the evocation of any sort of 'global migration/refugee management regime(s)' is to advocate a Janus-faced politics of population control and surveillance, as well as often a purely technocratic and social-engineering solution to such diverse and multifaceted phenomenon as human mobility.

It seems that there are many other challenges ahead. One could be possible violations of human rights and derogation from them that we cannot yet foresee. Some of them relate to assessments that are already present, like the dire effects of economic instabilities and political atrocities, together with the current global health crises. Other challenges have to do with future consequences of climate change that will not only have devastating effects on people's livelihood, on their vulnerability and their adaptation potential, but could also threaten democracy and the guarantees of human rights, pushing humanity into a state of 'climate apartheid' (UN OHCHR 2019). One could pose a challenging yet unavoidable question: will human rights of people on the move because of the climate and environmental reasons be recognised as a legitimate ground for granting them some sort of protected status and when would that be? Some future mass forced migration will most likely be motivated by intertwined macro-structural reasons such as poverty, wars, hunger, climate disasters, overpopulation and others. Whether, in such a world, there would be any form of post-national cosmopolitan membership able to create a more just and equal ground for protection, a chance for a secure and prosperous life, including the respect for human rights and participation in society and politics at their destinations, remains to be seen.

Mogens Chrom Jacobsen
Emnet Berhanu Gebre
Drago Župarić-Iljić

References

Arbour, L. (2017). First informal thematic session on human rights of all migrants, social inclusion, cohesion and all forms of discrimination, including racism, xenophobia and intolerance 8–9 May 2017, pp. 1–4. https://refugeesmigrants.un.org/sites/default/files/ts1_srsg_opening.pdf. Accessed 25 November 2019.

Becker, U. (2019). EU 'asylum system'—elements, failure and reform prospects. In: E. Wacker, U. Becker & K. Crepaz (Eds.), *Refugees and forced migrants in Africa and the EU: Comparative and multidisciplinary perspectives on challenges and solutions* (pp. 37–68). Springer.

Berlingske, T. (2019). DF mener, at Grundloven kun er til for danske statsborgere—men en afdød professor og tre nulevende eksperter er dybt uenige. 03/06/2019. https://www.berlingske.dk/politik/df-mener-at-grundloven-kun-er-til-for-danske-statsborgere-men-en-afdoed Accessed 26 November 2019 (in Danish).

Betts, A. and Collier, P. (2017). *Refuge: transforming a broken refugee system*. UK: Allen Lane

Collier, P. (2013). *Exodus: How migration is changing our world*. Oxford: Oxford University Press.

Chandler, D. (2009). Critiquing liberal cosmopolitanism? The limits of the biopolitical approach. *International Political Sociology, 3*(1), 53–70. https://doi.org/10.1111/j.1749-5687.2008.00063.x.

Council Directive 2002/90/EC of 28 November 2002 defining the facilitation of unauthorised entry, transit and residence, OJ L 328, 5 December 2002.

Council of the European Union (2002) Council framework Decision of 28 November 2002 on the strengthening of the penal framework to prevent the facilitation of unauthorised entry, transit and residence, 2002/946/JHA, OJ L 328, 5 December 2002.

Dubois-Girard, C. (2011). *La maladie comme ultime recours, le droit d'asile pour raison humanitaire*. Vivre Ensemble Education, pp. 1–8. https://vivre-ensemble.be/IMG/pdf/2011-04-droit_d_asile_humanitaire.pdf. Accessed 25 November 2019.

EU (2019). European Civil Protection and Humanitarian Aid Operations. Factsheet Lebanon. https://ec.europa.eu/echo/where/middle-east/lebanon_en Accessed 26 November 2019.

Guild, E., Basaran, T. & Allinson, K. (2019). From zero to hero? An analysis of the human rights protections within the global compact for safe, orderly and regular migration (GCM) (prepublished version) https://doi.org/10.1111/imig.12609.

Hill Maher, K. (2002). Who has a right to rights? Citizenship's exclusions in an age of migration. In: A. Brysk (Ed.), *Globalization and human rights* (pp. 19–43). Berkeley, Los Angeles, London: University of California Press.

IOM—International Organization for Migration (2016). *Global Migration Trends Factsheet 2015*. IOM's Global Migration Data Analysis Centre GMDAC. https://publications.iom.int/system/files/global_migration_trends_2015_factsheet.pdf. Accessed 26 November 2019

Kasparek, B. & Speer, M. (2015). *Of hope. Hungary and the long summer of migration*. Boredrmonitoring.eu, February 9, 2015, http://bordermonitoring.eu/ungarn/2015/09/of-hope-en/. Accessed 15 February 2019.

Kleingeld, P. & Brown, E. (2014). Cosmopolitanism. In: E. N. Zalta (Ed.), *The stanford encyclopedia of philosophy* (Fall 2014 Edition), https://plato.stanford.edu/archives/fall2014/entries/cosmopolitanism/.

Malešević, S. (2004). *The sociology of ethnicity*. London, Thousand Oaks, New Delhi: SAGE Publications.

Muséum Manifesto (2018). *Migrations*. Paris: Reliefs Éditions.

Shachar, A. (2009). *The birthright lottery: Citizenship and global inequality*. Cambridge and London: Harvard University Press.

UN (1990). *International Convention on the Protection of the Rights of All Migrant Workers and Members of Their Families*. General Assembly resolution 45/158 of 18 December 1990.

UN DESA (2019). The number of international migrants reaches 272 million, continuing an upward trend in all world regions, says UN. 17 September 2019, New York, Unite Nations—Department of Economic and Social Affairs, https://www.un.org/development/desa/en/news/population/international-migrant-stock-2019.html. Accessed 12 November 2019.

UN OHCHR (2019). UN expert condemns failure to address impact of climate change on poverty. 25 June 2019. United Nations Human Rights Office of the High Commissioner. https://www.ohchr.org/EN/NewsEvents/Pages/DisplayNews.aspx?NewsID=24735. Accessed 12 November 2019.

UNHCR (2019). *Global Trends: Forced Displacement in 2018*. 20 June 2019. https://www.unhcr.org/5d08d7ee7.pdf. Accessed 12 November 2019.

Contents

Part V Facets of Citizenship and Border Regimes

Editors and Contributors

About the Editors

Mogens Chrom Jacobsen is cand. mag. in philosophy and political science from Copenhagen University. His Ph.D. thesis on *Jean Bodin et le dilemme de la philosophie politique moderne* was published at the Copenhagen University Press in 2000. His habilitation thesis, *Three Conceptions of Human Rights*, was published at the NSU press in 2011 (second edition, *A Different History of Human Rights*, Les politiques 2017). He is specialised in political philosophy and human rights.

Emnet Berhanu Gebre defended her Ph.D. thesis in Public Law at the University of Toulouse 1 Capitole on the International Protection of Displaced Persons by Climate Change (2016). After working as a research and teaching fellow at the University of Toulouse 1 Capitole and the Catholic Institute of Toulouse (2010–2018), she is currently working as an international consultant in the field of migration, focusing notably on migrant protection and assistance issues.

Drago Župarić-Iljić, Ph.D. is a sociologist, working as an Assistant Professor at the Department of Sociology, Faculty of Humanities and Social Sciences, University of Zagreb. He has published articles and chapters within the interdisciplinary fields of forced migration, asylum, ethnicity, population and environmental studies, focusing on various structural causes and drivers of migration, mobility and post-migration phenomena, with a special interest for the Central East European region.

Contributors

Olga Breskaya University of Padua, Padua, Italy

Oleg Bresky Vilnius, Lithuania

Line Steen Bygballe European Ethnology, University of Copenhagen, Copenhagen, Denmark

Jean-Pierre Cléro University of Rouen, Rouen, France

Camille de Vulpillières Paris-Nanterre University, Sophiapol - Paris 1 Panthéon-Sorbonne, Iredies, ICM Migration Fellow, Paris, France

Adam Diderichsen University College Copenhagen, Copenhagen, Denmark

Lars Erslev Andersen Danish Institute for International Studies, Copenhagen, Denmark

Carsten Friberg Independent Scholar, Copenhagen, Denmark

Emnet Berhanu Gebre University of Toulouse 1 Capitole, Toulouse, France

Barbara Gornik Science and Research Centre Koper, Koper, Slovenia

Margareta Gregurović Institute for Migration and Ethnic Studies, Zagreb, Croatia

Iryna Ivankiv National University of "Kyiv-Mohyla Academy", Kyiv, Ukraine

Mogens Chrom Jacobsen Nordic Summer University, Copenhagen, Denmark

Mari-Liis Jakobson Tallinn University School of Governance, Law and Society, Tallinn, Estonia

Leif Kalev Tallinn University School of Governance, Law and Society, Tallinn, Estonia

Lydia Maria Kirchner European Ethnology, University of Copenhagen, Copenhagen, Denmark

Joseph Krulic The National Court of Asylum, Montreuil, France

Rebecka Lettevall Malmö University, Malmö, Sweden

Athanasia Petropoulou University of Paris I, Paris, France

Anna Wilczyńska Krakow, Poland

Karol Wilczyński Krakow, Poland

Yves Charles Zarka University of Paris, Paris, France

Drago Župarić-Iljić University of Zagreb, Zagreb, Croatia

Part I
Cosmopolitanism and the Freedom of Movement: Hopes and Challenges

Chapter 1
Cosmopolitanism and Politics: The Foreigner, the Migrant, the Refugee

Yves Charles Zarka

Abstract Human rights are cosmopolitan rights while migration belongs to history and politics. What confronts us now with full force is the contradiction between cosmopolitics and politics. Politics is essentially tied to frontiers. Frontiers preserve the world's diversity and have a positive function, but they can be misused. I will show how cosmopolitical regulation of politics should give us the means to determine what we have to do, and what we have to resist nowadays.

Keywords Cosmopolitanism · Politics · Migration · Refugees · Foreigners · Human rights

1.1 Introduction

The relationship between human rights and migration, which is at the heart of our meeting, involves the relationship between cosmopolitanism and politics very directly. Why? Because human rights are cosmopolitical rights, i.e. both universal and natural. Universal, in that they concern all human beings as such, as citizens of the world or belonging to the human world, and not in any way as political citizens of this or that country, nation or state. Of course, the effectiveness of human rights can only be achieved on the political level once they are inscribed in the positive legislation of a state or in its constitution. This is the case in democratic states. Indeed, what defines a democratic state is that its fundamental goal is to protect and guarantee human rights, i.e. private and public freedoms, equality, security, etc.

When this is so, it can be said that cosmopolitical rights are inscribed in politics. But as we know, this is not always the case, far from it. Most commonly, human rights are violated on the political level, either by totalitarian states or, more simply, by authoritarian or despotic states. They can also be violated in times of war, when destruction reaches civil populations considered to be military objectives. They can be violated, too, in cases of land expropriation by corrupt political leaders with a

Y. C. Zarka (✉)
University of Paris, Paris, France
e-mail: yczarka@gmail.com

M. C. Jacobsen et al. (eds.), *Cosmopolitanism, Migration and Universal Human Rights*, https://doi.org/10.1007/978-3-030-50645-2_1

view to their personal profit, and for the even greater profit of capitalist-type national and international companies. It is precisely because human rights are cosmopolitical, and not merely political, that it is possible, in their name, to denounce those who violate them. The cosmopolitical human is transcendence in relation to politics.

In their name, we can denounce those who do not respect them. It is only in democratic states that cosmopolitical rights become immanent to politics, in a more or less precarious or adequate way, and even in this case it is possible to measure the degree to which they are put in place and respected.

The cosmopolitical meaning of human rights has to be well understood. Since they were first systematically formulated in the 'Déclaration des droits de l'homme et du citoyen' on 27 August 1789, right up to the 'Universal Declaration of Human Rights' on 10 December 1948, human rights have only been the subject of simple enumerations. Admittedly, we know that there were earlier forms of declaration or recognition of human rights for this or that population in this or that situation, before the 1789 declaration, from Magna Carta in the thirteenth century, via the 'Bill of Rights' in 1689, American declarations of rights such as that in Virginia in 1776, and elsewhere. We also know that after the universal declaration of 1948 there was the 'European Convention for the Protection of Human Rights and Fundamental Freedoms' in 1950, the European Union's Charter of Fundamental Rights in 2000, and others. But in all these cases, human rights are simply enumerated; they are never truly deduced from a fundamental principle such as human dignity, for example. Now this simply enumerative character of fundamental rights explains, on the one hand, that they have been the subject of radical criticism, and on the other that these different declarations contain various rights, not always identical. In these declarations we even find rights which are held to be human rights but absolutely are not. So, for example, in the 1948 declaration, Article 15 states that 'Every individual has the right to a nationality'. As if nationality, belonging to a nation, was a matter of human rights as such, which was obviously not in any way the case.

Nationality is a matter of politics, not cosmopolitics. It is always acquired by virtue of history and specific legislation, and in no way transcendent in relation to them. Better yet, Article 2 of the 1789 declaration mentions property under the heading of human rights. But property is not a human right in the strict sense. Property is certainly not a cosmopolitical right; it is equally a matter of history and politics, and no doubt also of economics. The cosmopolitical perspective should enable us to get away from simple, more or less random enumerations of various rights, with a view to defining their essence and providing a deduction.[1]

Human rights have another characteristic: the fact that they are natural, not conventional. As such, they are not attributed by anyone (individuals, powers, states), nor can they be taken away by anyone. They are original rights which we have simply because we are human beings. So it can be seen in what sense human rights are universal and natural, and therefore cosmopolitical. We possess them as citizens of the world, not merely as political citizens. Migrations, however, are entirely a matter of history and politics. There are migrations because of famines, wars, oppression,

[1]For an outline of this deduction, see Zarka (2014).

persecutions, even attempts to exterminate populations. Nowadays, there are also migrations due to climate change. People leave the land of their birth, or simply the land where they live, to go to another place, another country, another state, in order to escape from these calamities and strive towards a life worthy of being lived. Migration is exile towards an uncertain elsewhere. There is no such thing as cosmopolitical exile, outside the world of humanity. So there is migration when politics is engaged in a dynamic which opposes it to cosmopolitics. When the humanity of man (human rights) is no longer respected, when it is violated in a particular historical-political context, individual citizens of the world migrate towards another, more hospitable place in the world. It is this contradiction between politics and cosmopolitics which now confronts us with full force. Far from regulating politics, cosmopolitics is being denied by politics. Please do not misunderstand: I am not saying that cosmopolitics should be substituted for politics in any way. Such a conception would not only be false, but would also be radically harmful. We can show this with a particularly important point: that of frontiers. I shall return to this at greater length, but it suffices to say for now that cosmopolitics knows of no frontiers. The earth is the common world of the whole of humanity. By contrast, politics is essentially tied to the existence of frontiers by which communities, peoples, nations identified by a language, customs, institutions and forms of government are distinguished. Now these frontiers are not walls. They have a positive aspect. They preserve the world's diversity. If frontiers were abolished, all human beings would be conceived as being interchangeable, without specificity, without identity, as if denuded of any specific history or culture. To abolish frontiers would be to lose the diversity which is the wealth of the world. If we ask ourselves about the strongest attempt today to abolish frontiers, we shall see that it is powered by the capitalist economy. That economy dislikes frontiers; it would like the world to be an even, limitless space with no obstacles to production, exchange and consumption. A world, that is, of free movement of goods, for the greatest profit of a small minority against the immense majority.

Globalisation is exactly that: the world transformed into a homogenous, undifferentiated space. But such homogenisation is a betrayal of cosmopolitics, not in any way its fulfilment. It is absolutely not a matter of substituting cosmopolitics for politics, because that substitution would be a betrayal. On the contrary, cosmopolitics should regulate politics—that is, it should provide principles which ought to constitute regulating ideals in the Kantian sense. In no way does that mean conferring a purely utopian dimension on cosmopolitics. On the contrary, cosmopolitanism should make it possible to change the course of things in politics, to resist oppression in all its forms, or at least to call any negation of human rights into question.

Here I would like to show how the cosmopolitical point of view makes it possible to change the way we look at politics, with regard to the status of the foreigner, the migrant and the refugee, as well as that of the terrorist. This cosmopolitical regulation of politics should give us the means to determine what we have to do, and what we have to resist nowadays.

1.2 The Foreigner

I have just referred to Kant, and I shall explain my relationship with Kant's cosmopolitanism later. However, I think one of the main roles of cosmopolitical law in Kant is to change the status of the foreigner. Why this change? Because, on a political level, the foreigner has often been thought of as a figure of the enemy. In the modern era there are essentially two figures: either someone who is outside the legislation of the state and who is therefore in a state of war, or someone within the state who explicitly denounces their membership of the state and becomes an internal public enemy, a rebel. To be, or become, a foreigner is to be or become a potential or actual enemy of the republic and therefore a public enemy. This is the status of the foreigner in Hobbes, for example.

Cosmopolitical law has to define a different status for the foreigner within the horizon of a world governed by law: '… hospitality (hospitableness) means the right of an alien not to be treated as an enemy upon his arrival in another's country' (Kant 1983, 357–358). Cosmopolitical law must thus shift us from *hostility* to *hospitality*, as much on the individual level as that of peoples. To achieve this, Kant founds hospitality, not on virtue, but on a right, an original right, a right from before there were any positive rights or differences between individual states. This right is the one which derives from the undivided property of the earth, which is the foundation for the community of humanity:

> … but the right to visit (*sich zur Gesellshaft anzubieten*), to associate, belongs to all men by virtue of their common ownership of the earth's surface; for since the earth is a globe, they cannot scatter themselves infinitely, but must, finally, tolerate living in close proximity, because originally no one had a greater right to any region of the earth than anyone else. (Kant 1983, 358)

Three cosmopolitical principles result:

1. Whatever the distance between different parts of the earth, maritime or land communications make it possible to connect them. So it can be seen that—virtually, at least—individuals and peoples can move and meet each other all over the earth's surface. On the cosmopolitical level there is no part of the earth which is for the exclusive use of anyone, even if it is isolated or distant.
2. More fundamentally, still from the cosmopolitical point of view, no individual nor any people has an original right over a particular piece of land. Territories and states, their frontiers, are historical and have nothing to do with natural law. Originally, there was only the human race's right to benefit from the whole surface of the earth. Consequently, the hospitality required by cosmopolitical law has a more original foundation than political citizenship or nationality.

   Kant says that hospitality comes from a right of nature: 'In this way distant parts of the world can establish with one another peaceful relations that will eventually become matters of public law, and the human race can gradually be brought closer and closer to a cosmopolitan constitution' (Kant 1983, 358).

3. Yet there is no weakening of the right to property, or the use by a people of a particular territory, as a result. In §62 of his *Science of Right*, Kant radically questions all those who would seek to transform hospitality into usurpation, i.e. to transform the right to visit into a right to settle where one arrives, denying the reality of the inhabitants' property. This is how Kant attacks European state colonialism:

> Compare this with the inhospitable conduct of civilized nations in our part of the world, especially commercial ones: the injustice that they display towards foreign lands and peoples (which is the same as conquering them), is terrifying. When discovered, America, the lands occupied by the blacks, the Spice Islands, the Cape, etc., were regarded as lands belonging to no one because their inhabitants were counted for nothing. Foreign soldiers were imported into East India under the pretext of merely establishing economic relations, and with them came subjection of the natives, incitement of various nations to [359] widespread wars among themselves, famine, rebellion, treachery, and the entire litany of evils that can afflict the human race. (Kant 1983, 358–359)

So Kant denounces colonial wars and imperialism, as well as the false justifications on which they usually found their undue pretensions.

In order to think of hospitality, we need to hold three principles together: (1) the original community of the ground, all over the surface of the earth, of all individuals; (2) this community does not consist of a juridical community of property—such a community is positive and belongs in each case to a particular people; (3) there is a right to move, visit and trade with all the individuals or peoples of the earth, however distant they are from one another. As these rights are reciprocal, they can be thought of in terms of possible reciprocal physical actions. These principles define the conditions of hospitality, i.e. a world of peoples and states where the foreigner, the one who comes from elsewhere in order to move through, to visit, to trade or to settle (under certain conditions) is not treated as an enemy:

> The rational idea, as discussed above, of a *peaceful* (if not exactly amicable) international community of all those of the earth's peoples who can enter into active relations with one another, is not a philanthropic principle of ethics, but a principle of *right*. (Kant 1991: §62 172)

Cosmopolitical law for Kant derives its meaning, strength and philosophical scope from the fact that it enables a conception of a juridical-political world order where hostility is overturned or, more exactly, turned into hospitality. Over and above state law and civil citizenship, there is a citizenship of the original world: a natural, universal citizenship which founds the idea of a community of humanity and obliges hospitality.

In this way, cosmopolitical law, as it becomes the regulator of politics, does not suppress the differences between peoples, nor does it dispute their ownership of the land on which they live, nor even the political sovereignty they possess, but opens the horizon of a pacific relationship between them. Likewise, the figure of the foreigner is not abolished, yet it is totally dissociated from that of the enemy, and associated with the figure of the one whom one receives because he has the right to be received by virtue of a right more original than state rights, the original cosmopolitical right bound up with belonging to the human world.

1.3 The Migrant and The Refugee

Kant distinguished the right to visit (*Besuchsrecht*) from the right to stay (*Gastrecht*) and limited hospitality to the former, so as to contest all forms of colonisation. But today the huge migrations we are witnessing, due to the wars ravaging in certain parts of the world (the Middle East in particular) or to poverty, as well as the even greater migrations which will probably come as a result of climate change, raise the question of the right to stay and settle in the receiving country. To what extent can cosmopolitical law found a right to stay, even to settle?

Note, first of all, that migrations concern a directly political problem which is only indirectly cosmopolitical. From the latter point of view in fact, there are no migrations because in a certain way all human beings are migrants, none of them having a more original right than another over a particular part of the earth. Differences between peoples, territories and nations are a matter of history and politics. The question, then, is this: How can cosmopolitics change our political view of this major question of migrations and modify the course of events?

Huge current migrations coming from Syria, Iraq, Libya and elsewhere raise political questions about the capacity of European states to integrate migrants, given their economic difficulties and their different traditions. Cosmopolitical principles of humanity that urge welcome and hospitality by residents would appear opposed to political requirements touching on the concrete possibilities of receiving migrants, given the social, economic, political—even cultural and religious—difficulties in the receiving states. This situation gives rise to two extreme positions which are opposed in every detail: some want frontiers abolished, others want them sealed. But neither of these two extreme positions is valid. They are both based on a confusion—although in opposing senses—between cosmopolitics (the citizen of the world, who knows no frontiers and is at home everywhere) and politics (the citizen of a state who is only at home within the frontiers of that state, and nowhere else), instead of thinking of the former as the regulator of the latter. What I mean is that the principle of hospitality for refugees, their right to be received, as well as the possibility for them to demand the right of asylum have to be guaranteed. This is not only by virtue of international conventions, but even more because of the original cosmopolitical law, mentioned earlier, which confers cosmopolitical, and thus original, legitimacy on those conventions.

Cosmopolitical law, which in the last resort founds human rights, carries a double principle as I tried to show with Kant but also beyond him,[2] a principle of original common belonging to the human world and a normative principle, no less original, of responsibility for humanity. This cosmopolitical responsibility for humanity enjoins us to give refuge, residence and asylum to those whose lives have been put in danger.

---

[2]Cf. Zarka (2013, 2014). These two works attempts to rethink cosmopolitanism after and beyond Kant. The essential notions are the principle about the inappropriability of the Earth and the responsibility entrusted to humanity for humanity and the entire living world.

But these rights, which derive from a concern for humanity, must not be instrumentalised for other objectives. The cosmopolitical idea must not become a mask for other, hidden objectives deriving from quite different intentions. The right to be welcomed and to stay in the receiving country must therefore be linked to two political conditions: that refugee status be established with maximum probability, and that reception be subject to a commitment on the part of the refugee to respect the customs and culture of the reception country where they wish to settle. Cosmopolitical law would then regulate politics without denying its specificity.

In order to look more closely at the concrete situation in the European Union today, we should return to the crucial question of frontiers. In the history of nation states, territorial sovereignty was bound up with control of frontiers. Frontier surveillance, indeed, was seen as one of the attributes of sovereignty; this was the case in Kant's time. But today in the European Union sovereignty rests for the most part with member states, whereas frontiers have come down within the Union and also to a certain extent at its exterior. On this last point, remember that the EU does not see itself as in any way restricted to the current 28 members, and the possibility of other countries joining the Union is currently under consideration.

Not only has Europe lost its sense of frontiers, but it also lacks the means to control the frontiers of states currently on its edges. In fact, as they cannot be controlled by what would be a European sovereignty—which quite evidently does not exist—their control is devolved to those border states. But the problem is now completely different from that which prevailed in a configuration of entirely independent nation states, in that the frontiers of Europe are considerably larger than those of the states involved. What can be done to control the frontiers of a space which is considerably larger than that of individual states? Setting up controls using electronic and information technology, which exist in other parts of the world, raises specific questions here. The use of these technologies cannot be devolved to the sovereignty of individual states, as the control has to extend well beyond their territory, but nor can they be under the control of a European sovereignty, since it does not exist. So we can see the problem of frontiers which arises in Europe today. And it is precisely when frontiers are no longer secured or controlled that walls get built.

By contrasting frontiers with walls, I want to emphasise that there is a difference in nature between the one and the other. The characteristic of a frontier is, first of all, that it concerns not only people but also law, goods, works, languages, cultures, etc., whereas the sole function of walls is to prevent people judged undesirable from getting across. What is more, although frontiers make controls possible, they have none of the unilateral, closed-in character of walls.

In the history of humanity, the function of walls and fences has been to prevent invasion by enemy armies, expansions, the influx of populations considered undesirable—and also to oppose the arrival of desperate populations in countries of real or imagined abundance. Apart from the fact that they are usually ineffective, walls solve nothing. Certain European states are building walls because of Europe's uncertainty concerning its own frontiers.

Building walls to keep refugees and asylum seekers out is a contravention of cosmopolitical law, and therefore the neglect of the responsibility for the whole of the human world. This is how politics enters into the logic of hostility, opposed to the cosmopolitical right of hospitality, against the right to refuge and asylum. But it should be added that this cosmopolitical right cannot be unconditional, as Derrida wished, because then the cosmopolitical idea could become the instrument of other ambitions, quite different from—even opposed to—the quest for refuge. The distinction between the two orders, cosmopolitical on the one hand and political on the other, has to be respected. The former must be the regulator of the latter, not its negation.

Bibliography

Kant, I. (1983). *Perpetual peace and other essays, hackett classics*. Indianapolis: Hackett Publishing Company Inc.

Kant, I. (1991). *Political writings*. Cambridge Texts in the History of Political Thought. Cambridge: Cambridge University Press.

Zarka, Y.-C. (2013). *L'inappropriabilité de la Terre*. Paris: Armand Colin.

Zarka, Y.-C. (2014). *Refonder le cosmopolitisme*. Paris: PUF.

Yves Charles Zarka is Professor Emeritus at the University of Paris in political philosophy and Global Professor at Peking University. He also teaches at New York University, at the Ca' Foscari University in Venice, at La Sapienza University in Rome and in several other universities throughout the world. At the University of Paris he founded the PHILéPOL (Philosophie, épistémologie et politique) team dedicated to the study of the profound changes in contemporary societies and to the construction of the concepts susceptible of explaining them. He is further the director of the journal *Cités* (PUF). His recent publications include *Repenser la démocratie* (Paris, Armand Colin, 2010), *Démocratie, état critique* (Paris, Armand Colin, 2012), *Le monde émergent* (Paris, Armand Colin, 2010), *Pour un monde habitable* (Paris, Armand Colin 2014), *L'inappropriabilité de la Terre* (Paris, Armand Colin, 2013), *Refonder le cosmopolitisme* (Paris, PUF, 2014), *Machiavel le pouvoir et le peuple* (with Cristina Ion, Milan, Mimésis, 2015), *Critique de la reconnaissance* (Milan, Mimésis, 2015), *Métamorphoses du monstre politique* (Paris, PUF, 2016), *L'Union européenne entre implosion et refondation* (with Pascal Perrineau and Alain Laquièze, Milan, Mimésis, 2016), *Jusqu'où faut-il être tolérant ?* (Paris Hermann, 2016), *La démocratie face aux enjeux environnementaux* (Milan, Mimésis, 2017), *Les révolutions du XXIème siècle* (Paris, PUF, 2018), *Points névralgiques de la philosophie* (Paris, PUF, 2018) and *La phénoménologie et la vie* (with Avishag Zafrani, Paris, Cerf, 2019). Within the history of political philosophy, he is the general editor of the French translation of the work of Hobbes at the Éditions Vrin (seven volumes) and he has recently published *Liberté et nécessité chez Hobbes et ses contemporains* (Descartes, Cudworth, Spinoza et Leibniz, Paris, Vrin, 2012) and *Hobbes et le libéralisme* (Paris, Vrin, 2017). His books *La décision métaphysique de Hobbes: conditions de la politique* (Paris, Vrin, 1987) and *Hobbes et la pensée politique moderne* (Paris, PUF, 1995) are now classics within Hobbes studies. Some of his works are translated into English, including *Hobbes and Modern Political Thought* (Edinburgh University Press, 2016), *How Far Should Tolerance Go?* (Mimesis International, 2018).

Chapter 2
Could We Apply Bentham's Critical Examination of the 1789 and 1795 Versions of Human Rights to Contemporary Versions?

Jean-Pierre Cléro

Abstract Cosmopolitanism, giving rights to foreigners and, first of all, the right to immigrate in order to flee from the tyranny of the state from which he originates, hunger, unemployment or war, ordinarily leans on human rights in order to do so. However, are human rights a stable, solid and irreproachable foundation to the extent that no more questions are possible? One would say that they were able to resist the impact made by the criticisms of utilitarians such as Bentham and those of Burke at the time of the French Revolution, but what was the precise nature of this criticism? After having recalled Bentham's main criticisms against human rights, as they were settled in his time, I would like first to establish that they would be equally applicable to contemporary versions of them; secondly, I would like to explain one reason for the persistently powerful appeal of human rights in spite of the ambiguity of their wording which forces a sort of hypocrisy upon whoever reads them; and thirdly, I want to emphasize that, far from being the unconditional guarantors of democracy they pretended to be, the articles of the manifold versions of human rights may promote non-democratic powers and practices.

Keywords Cosmopolitanism · Immigration · Bentham · Human rights · Democracy · Universal declaration of human rights · Dworkin

> *Good sense.* They are forced to say: 'You are not acting in good faith […].' How I love to see this proud reason humbled and suppliant!
>
> (Pascal 1995, Laf. 52, Brunsc. 388).

2.1 Introduction

When Bentham criticises, in a hundred pages entitled *Nonsense upon Stilts or Pandora's Box Opened* (Bentham 2002), with the epigraph *Right the child of Law*—but not the reverse—he unveils from the beginning the message that will be hammered

J.-P. Cléro (✉)
University of Rouen, Rouen, France
e-mail: jp.clero@orange.fr

M. C. Jacobsen et al. (eds.), *Cosmopolitanism, Migration and Universal Human Rights*, https://doi.org/10.1007/978-3-030-50645-2_2

home in, on the one hand, his commentary on each of the 17 articles written by the Revolutionaries of the *Constituante* in 1789 (reiterated as the preamble of the *Constitution* of 1791), and, on the other hand, though more briefly, in his commentary on Abbé Sieyès' Declaration of the Rights and Duties of Man and of the Citizen from 1795. If Bentham was neither the first nor the only critic desirous of combatting such declarations, and whatever the quality of his destructive arguments, there is no other choice than to accept that he has lost the battle, considering the countless versions of human rights adopted by states today, whether as preambles to their own constitution or as a premise to their association with other states—as in the European Union—or inside the United Nations, thus binding them all. It is paradoxical that, apart from some enthusiasts, everybody knows the defects of these texts, which are used as preambles for laws or directly as laws; and yet most men believe in their value, or they feign at least to believe in them because they fear that criticising or dismissing them out of hand runs the risk of being labelled as bad citizens and bad human beings, with whom nobody wants to be associated and to whom nobody wants to listen. It seems that the rejection of human rights means endorsing, or at least opening the door to torture, genocide, war crimes, crimes against humanity, ethnic cleansing and so on.

After having recalled Bentham's main criticisms against human rights, as they were settled in his time, I would like first to establish that they would be equally applicable to contemporary versions of them. Second, I would like to explain one reason for the persistently powerful appeal of human rights in spite of the ambiguity of their wording which forces a sort of hypocrisy upon whoever reads them; and, third, I want to emphasise that, far from being the unconditional guarantors of democracy they pretended to be, the articles of the manifold versions of human rights may promote non-democratic powers and practices.

2.2 How to Go from Principles to Rules: An Unconscious or Deliberate Hypocrisy?

Certainly, the versions of human rights known today, to begin with the Universal Declaration of the United Nations, proclaimed in 1948 by the General Assembly (United Nations 1958), do not refer directly to natural rights that would stand above the positive rights of states or organisations of states, and do not claim to judge them or do at least not appear to do so; except perhaps in article 16 of the Declaration where the family is entitled to certain rights (protection by society and the state) as it is 'the natural and fundamental group unit of society'. However, the reference to men as 'members of the human family' is given without further precision—I mean: as if there was only one family and only one type of family. Furthermore, it locates the foundation of human solidarity in the ambiguous notion of brotherhood from the very beginning. It is as though it was necessary, in order to establish one's rights, to recognise between human beings bonds to I do not know which father, which mother or which brothers with no relation to these rights, who nonetheless appear or pretend to be their underpinnings.

Indeed, it is impossible to read any declaration of human rights without feeling one's breast expanding, one's heart beating with emotion, one's head lifting up high, as if one's humanity does recognise itself in them. But one must be careful not to be fooled by this theatrical emotion that never seizes anybody when he reads the codes of positive law, even if they are often preceded by declarations that excite the passions. One may rightfully ask oneself what is the style of writing moving the reader and the hearer of this sort of text. Certainly it is neither the style of a *metaphysician*, because the points of view from which every article is written change without warning and because those who are in favour of them never stop trying to justify them; nor it is the style of a *lawyer*, because the wording, in respect to the form it has, is absolutely ineffective and gives no indication of any precise procedure. It will be objected that, in legal matters, the order of the rules must be distinguished from the order of the principles. The rule implies a real operativity, whereas the use of principles is necessarily vaguer: a principle may never be completely and definitely opposed to another principle, while a rule may be accurately countered by another rule. It is often claimed by sharp wits that the use of rules implies principles which would be their 'soul' or their 'spirit', but this kind of 'schöne Seelen' never descends to the task of showing us the way to pass from principles to rules and leaves it to intuitions and feelings to convince us that this passage is indeed possible or rather that it has already been achieved.

But this legal drowsiness is not only a laziness that slows down the passage from principles to rules; it misleads us into confused notions and to strategic contradictions. Confusions stem from the theatrical grandiloquence of the quantifiers of the subjects and from the adverbs of time—*all, everyone, no one, never, always*—without any careful limitation regarding their inevitable qualifications; the unceasing variations of the subjects by turns—*human beings* (preamble, art. 1), *person* (art. 2-2, 3, 6), *human person* (art. 5), *man* (preamble, art. 3), *men and women* (art. 16-1), *the people* (operative paragraph, art. 21-3), *personality* (art. 22, 26-2, 29-1), *subject* (art. 29-2), *the community* (art. 29-1), *individual* (operative paragraph), *mankind* (preamble, art. 3)—as if it were of no importance to move from one of these designations to the other. Finally, in respect to time, there is the sleight of hand in switching between auxiliaries and defectives, in the present or in the future, that leads the authors to assert that 'all human beings *are* born free and equal in dignity and right', while they mean that every man *must* act and *should* act—as we are told in the second part of the first article—so as to progress towards the day when all human beings *will be born free* and *will enjoy* equal dignity and right; or that leads them to proclaim that 'everyone *has* the right to life, liberty and security of person', instead of 'everyone *should have* the right to life, liberty and security of person' (art. 6-8). This 'language of daggers'—as Bentham called it—settles a certain type of being (whether it were the being of *nature* or of *natural right* or of any other authority) above the discourse of 'ought to' and of 'may', 'can', 'shall' or 'should'; above a discourse of interdiction and impossibility, and thus leaves the way open for the passage from one to the other. To take one example, why is article 9 worded 'No one shall be subjected to arbitrary arrest, detention or exile' rather than 'no one is subjected to arbitrary arrest, detention or exile'? Such constructions are typical of the prose with which the lawyer can make no assertion capable of being reasonably defended.

Indeed, the logicians of law texts have taught that laws could be expressed in the present indicative and that Hume had largely misled nomography when he pretended to distinguish too crudely the 'to be' from the 'ought to be', begging us to restore systematically the 'ought to' ordinarily hidden behind the 'is'. But there are places where the authors write 'is' and 'are', though they think 'ought to' and they can neither think otherwise nor make others think otherwise. Why this hypocrisy? And why drag the reader down to this level of deliberate duplicity, precisely when the reader may be seized by the enthusiasm of the heart beating for mankind only because he considers a single meaning where many are possible?

2.3 Bentham's Two Explanations for this Perplexity

Following Bentham, this deception has two explanations; these two explanations make a distinction between the import of human rights in revolutionary circumstances at the end of the eighteenth century and the meaning they now have in the eyes of a 21st-century man. The *first explanation* is that it was necessary, in order to justify revolution, to establish an authority above the existing laws and even above the state sovereignty that gives them. This places the citizen in an uncomfortable and dangerous situation which was already denounced by Hobbes (1998) when he analysed the fatal risk taken by politics if it should admit to being dominated by any authority, whatever it may be, religious or not. Strangely enough and because of their religious spirit in spite of their hatred for God, the French revolutionaries ran the risk of killing politics. The *second explanation* emerges from the manner in which Burke and Bentham—who agreed this time—denounced the cunning of the French who, through their formulations of pretended rights as universally valuable for all peoples and their penning of constitutional preambles valuable for all the nations, thus secured for themselves a supremacy, first symbolic and then real and military, over all peoples and all nations that had neither real government nor any real constitution and consequently only had the pretence of being governed by laws. This normative claim allowed the French to assume the right to interfere in the affairs of other countries with a view to impose, under the veil of liberty, their own conception of international order. If the latter reason leaves us with a smile today, though it was a justification for the adventure of the revolutionary wars, it is because the problem should not be stated in these terms, especially inside European politics.

To return to the *first explanation*, it appears to us, as Europeans, now used to living in a community with other states—though we cannot know for how much longer!—that this explanation is rather too 'sovereigntist' and 'republican' to be fully convincing, as well as somewhat outdated and anachronistic. In the same way that Americans have been living for more than two centuries with a double law, we have learned in Europe to live—not without occasional rough patches—with a national law that attempts to mesh with a Community law having primacy. Now if Community law consists of something more than natural laws expressed in mere assertions of principles, and it yields as many constraining rules as national law, it is nevertheless a fact that while Community law often has the hard task of reconciling the different rules coming from the different systems of laws which it is charged with uniting, its own rules tend to become principles that must be composed together to conceptualise and govern the particular situations that arise in history. In fact, a principle cannot simply be bolted on to another in the same way that a rule may be linked to another rule. Whereas rules are applied according to a principle of all-or-nothing, that is to say without leaving room for the contrary rule, principles do not operate in the same way and none of them is compromised by the appeal to other principles, even though they might be contrary to it in certain given circumstances. In some situations one of them seems to be promoted; in others, it is another that is elected whereas the others are not.

In consequence, the characteristic that Bentham feared and denounced in natural rights—that of being unable to yield or even to inspire true jurisdictions (Bentham 2002)—has been contradicted by the facts. There exist Courts in Europe (The European Court of Human Rights, the Court of Justice of the European Communities) and in the United States (The Supreme Court) that, relying on human rights, are able to adjudicate not only on disagreements between citizens in the same state, but also on deeper controversies between the laws of different states or between the laws of a state and the laws of the federation of which it is a member. In cases where there is no pre-existing rule for settling disagreements between one system of rules (in a state) and another (in another state), it is unavoidable that the practice and procedure of these courts resorts to principles of guidance. So it is necessary to generate the rules that will permit the resolution of such problems and people conceive that human rights supply, by force of the circumstances (for what else can do it?), the principles necessary to write the rules or, at least, to generate the illusion that they have been written. But who, then, is responsible for their generation?

Moreover, the situation is not unique to Europe or North America; the United Nations, in as far as it claims to found itself on human rights, operates in the same way towards every nation between which it organised the entente.

2.4 Ronald Dworkin and Judicial Law Making

The question concerning the authors of the rules is crucial because the community that must and will settle its disagreements does not have at its disposal the legislative and executive powers necessary to allow it to resolve any controversy by enacting clear and precise rules and enforcing them. Since the means of government are not available, man must rely on the judgments of courts and almost on the government of courts. But one must face another problem to which R. Dworkin draws our attention (Dworkin 1977), perhaps against his will.

Indeed, if neither the legislative power nor the executive power is capable of bearing the burden, it remains only for the power of judges to do so. But, in such circumstances, the judicial power consists not only of applying and upholding the law in contentious issues: it goes so far as to create the missing rules, and even to contradict and thwart, with the force of law, the existing rules so that they lose all authority. The trouble lies in those rules which are declared null and void, even though they were discussed and decided by elected assemblies (which is possible when the states that issue them are members of some particular community, such as the European Union, for instance) and even though they had never been abrogated by these assemblies or by others with similar mandates.[1] We see the authority of these rules demolished by authorities which are not always elected and which can be justified in exerting their discretionary power, free from all democratic constraint or guarantee, only by their own legal knowledge.

We do not mean to say that the decision of the judge is always arbitrary, but, if there are many solutions to a political or economic problem, would it not then be worth making an inventory of those problems in a legislative framework and seeking to resolve them only after a full democratic discussion of them? Such an approach might yield the same decision as the judges, in which case the decision would have a more democratic basis than a decision made by a discretionary power. And even though an assembly might not find any agreement between its members on some point, would it not be more likely that the choice made by an assembly would always be better than the choice of a single man, even if he is taken for or claims to be an expert?

Certainly, Dworkin attempted to argue that the judge, as a modern hero, invents the law he needs to settle disagreements between rules or conflicts between the behaviour of citizens and the rules in force.[2] However, is his solution not just a mere sign of a deficiency in democracy? In that case, Bentham's arguments against natural rights as the midwives of anarchy, which merely relocate the tyranny they claimed to fight, could still be applied today, even though they were drafted to explain and denounce the revolutionary movement arising in France at the end of the eighteenth century, and they can thus be applied on a longer-term basis, for some further decades. The problem is far from being insignificant and the Pandora's box is opened when judges are established for the abuse of authority, defending, for example, the right to property that some states attempt to limit or alter, and when it is so easy for transnational economic powers to exploit their presence on both sides of particular frontiers and effectively to influence and press the legislation that meets their interests just as if

[1]Dworkin is faced with this problem in *Taking Rights Seriously* "In most American jurisdictions, and now in England also, the higher courts not infrequently reject established rules. Common law rules—those developed by earlier court decisions—are sometimes overruled directly, and sometimes radically altered by further development. Statutory rules are subjected to interpretation and reinterpretation, sometimes even when the result is not to carry out what is called the 'legislative intent'". If courts had discretion to change established rules, then these rules would, of course, not be binding upon them, and so would not be law on the positivists' model' (Dworkin 1977, 7).

[2]We refer here to Chap. 4 of *Taking Rights Seriously*, named 'Hard cases' in which the judge is compared to Hercules.

they were buying any other service or good. The danger posed to the sovereignty of states by the modern *homo oeconomicus* is certainly worse than the danger posed by the *homo turbulentis* of earlier ages.

But the paradox is that, for the hopeless deficiencies of human rights (which, bringing themselves forward as principles rather than as rules, do not formally stand in need of any validation by the democratic process which seems implied by their substance), people prefer to 'blame themselves' rather than renounce those principles; they seem to ignore that, by this 'absurd humility'—as Pascal said (Pascal 1995, Laf. 33) —they have become accustomed to believe that law is law by virtue of its connection to human rights, even though this is untrue and that human rights, on the contrary, draw their illusory justice from the interference with positive rights. That belief is, in any case, useful for those who attempt to hide their power of creating law behind the agreeable idea that men have moral rights against their states. Far from underpinning and legitimising law, do principles rather not work like a machine for transforming questions of policy, which could have been resolved by the consistent application of democratic decision-making, into questions of justice, resolvable only by a judge?

2.5 Conclusion

It is well known that the musician R. Schumann wrote between the two main lines of some of his scores for the piano—as in *Humoreske* in *Klavierwerke IV*—what is called in German 'eine innere Stimme', at a time when physics and astronomy had largely developed the idea of law as a chart or as a contract between researchers, in such a way that Newtonian law, for instance, existed merely through the analytical variations that the nineteenth-century scientists gave of it. We might wonder whether the many declarations of human rights are not the awkward writing of some 'innere Stimme' or of some charter, which exists really only by the interference of the many interpretations that the constitutional spheres, in Europe for instance, give of the historical circumstances. That is the way J. Weiler praises 'the current constitutional architecture, which encapsulates one of Europe's most important constitutional innovations', the 'Principle of Constitutional Tolerance' (Weiler 1999). This renouncement of every constitutional sphere's narcissism in dialogue with other constitutional spheres cannot make us forget how much the pretended harmonious dialogue is nothing but a metaphorical and fictional figure, when it does not prevent the intervention of the judge, who, far from entering into dialogue, signals the end of the dialogue, because 'he must make his decision that terminates the litigation brought up before him'.

Bibliography

Bentham, J. (2002). Nonsense upon Stilts or Pandora's Box Opened, or The French Declaration of Rights prefixed to the Constitution of 1791 laid open and exposed—with a comparative sketch of what has been done on the same subject in the Constitution of 1795, and a sample of Citizen Sieyès. In P. Schofield, C. Pease-Watkin, & C. Blamires (Eds.), *Rights, representation, and reform: Nonsense upon stilts and other writings on the French revolution* (pp. 317–401). Oxford: Clarendon Press.

Dworkin, R. (1977). *Taking rights seriously.* Cambridge Mass: Harvard University Press.

Hobbes, Th. (1998). *Philosophical elements of a true citizen.* In *The collected works of Thomas Hobbes*, W. Molesworth (Ed.), Routledge: Thommes Press, London, 1992, vol. II. Chapitre II, §§ 20, 21, 22, 23, (p. 27–8) ; Chap. III, § 33, (p. 49–50) ; Chapitre VI, § 11, note (p. 78–9).

Pascal, B. (1995). *Pensées.* London: Penguin Books.

United Nations. (1958). *The universal declaration of human rights.* New York.

Weiler, J. H. H. (1999). *The constitution of Europe: "Do the New Clothes Have An Emperor?" And other essays on European integration.* Cambridge: Cambridge University Press.

Jean-Pierre Cléro is Professor of Philosophy at the University of Rouen, France. He also teaches at the Science Po, where he is director of the Bentham Center. He specialises in David Hume and the Anglo-Saxon utilitarians. He also takes an interest in the philosophy of mathematics and Jacques Lacan. His publications include *La Philosophie des passions chez David Hume* (Méridiens-Klincksieck), *Les Raisons de la fiction. Les philosophes et les mathématiques* (Armand Colin), *Bentham. Philosophe de l'utilité* (Ellipses), *Le vocabulaire de Lacan* (Ellipses) and *Lacan, y a-t-il une philosophie de Lacan?* (Ellipses).

Chapter 3
The Right to Travel: Cosmopolitanism as Imperial Ideology

Adam Diderichsen

Abstract After a short discussion of cosmopolitanism and empire in ancient Stoicism, the chapter focuses on the role of cosmopolitanism in early modern political philosophy. I show that cosmopolitanism in general and the right to travel in particular played an important role in justifying Spanish and other European colonial conquest. At the same time, many early modern philosophers argued against empire and universal monarchy, which they saw as inherently despotic. The end result was a vision of free trade and the state of nature as a kind of empire without an emperor. In the final part, I show that this historical background is important for understanding Kant's republican cosmopolitanism, and I argue that the dilemmas and paradoxes created by the early modern use of cosmopolitanism to justify empire are important for understanding present-day criticism of the international order.

Keywords The right to travel · Cosmopolitanism · Imperial ideology · Vitoria · Grotius · Pufendorf · Kant

3.1 Introduction

A prominent feature of contemporary politics and law is a broad and massive backlash against the liberal world order and the cosmopolitan values that allegedly support it. From the presidential election of Trump, over Brexit to the spread of right-wing nationalism across Europe, the political challenges to the liberal order have been mounting.

In the present-day context, the backlash typically presents itself as a defence of national sovereignty against an international order, which is seen as encroaching on the legitimate right of nations to decide their own political destiny. In an earlier stage, more dominated by left-wing 'anti-globalism', the liberal world order was criticised as a type of empire, i.e. a new type of political power fundamentally different from the nation state (Hardt and Negri 2000). The two types of critique are, however,

A. Diderichsen (✉)
University College Copenhagen, Copenhagen, Denmark
e-mail: addi@kp.dk

M. C. Jacobsen et al. (eds.), *Cosmopolitanism, Migration and Universal Human Rights*, https://doi.org/10.1007/978-3-030-50645-2_3

closely related and both present the liberal order as illegitimate and oppressive, and dominated by either capital interests or the international elite (which, in the eyes of the international order's opponents, would amount to the same thing).

In this chapter, I shall argue that the present political conflicts have (some of) their historical roots in the way that the relation between universal rights and imperial power was conceptualised in early modern natural law jurisprudence. Picking up on the connection between international law and empire, I shall argue that early modern natural right is characterised by an inherent conflict between ethical universalism and a sceptical attitude towards, or criticism of, the imperial ambitions of the various European powers. On the one hand, universalism seems naturally to lead to the claim that all of humanity should be united in one common state or political community. On the other hand, empire and universal monarchy seem inherently despotic and incompatible with liberty.

More precisely, I shall discuss the connection between cosmopolitanism and imperial power. I focus in particular on the right to travel, which is today probably the most controversial among the list of rights ascribed universally to all human beings. This is the case if we interpret the right to travel as a political or ethical right, as is clearly illustrated by the heated controversies that the right to asylum gives rise to, including in particular the question whether and to what extent this right can be limited or curtailed. And this is the case if we give the right to travel an economic interpretation in the sense of free movement of labour, which is perhaps the most politically controversial aspect of the European internal market, as exemplified by the debate leading to the British referendum on Brexit.

In the present context, I will try to shed some light on the tensions implicit in the notion of a right to travel. I will do this by returning to the historic period in which the controversy concerned the (alleged) right of Europeans to travel to, trade with and settle in other parts of the world—rather than the right of non-Europeans to seek asylum in Europe. As we will see, the right to travel has often been used to legitimise various forms of imperial power in general and European colonialism in particular; a line of argument that draws on the more general connection between imperial power, on the one hand, and political, ethical and legal universalism, on the other. However, for the same reason, the right to travel has often been held to be politically problematic, precisely because it could be used to legitimise imperialism and therefore potentially undermine national autonomy. The right to travel thus contains a fundamental tension, because, on the one hand, we seem to have strong universalistic ethical grounds for holding that individuals have the freedom to travel to, trade with and perhaps settle in foreign nations. But, on the other hand, the right to travel implies that individuals have claimable rights against foreign nations, and therefore also at least suggests the idea that we need a common state power that can enforce these rights.

In the following, I will show how this tension runs through early modern discussions of the right to travel. Thus, it turns out that the interpretation of the right to travel is systematically linked to differing imperial strategies on the part of the various European powers. The right to travel initially came to the forefront in connection with the Spanish conquest of America. Later, however, the right to travel was used as an ideological weapon turned against the Spanish and Portuguese in East Asia in a Dutch attempt to justify a new type of mercantile empire. This again leads to the notion of free trade as a kind of limited universalism based on narrow self-interest, but nevertheless having a civilising effect. I conclude by discussing another attempt to resolve the tension in the right to travel—another way of loosening the bond between universalism and imperial power—namely Kant and his vision of a future cosmopolitan international order based on voluntary cooperation rather than coercion. Both the notion of free trade as a form of liberty and the Kantian vision of the cosmopolitan are, however, quite difficult to reconcile with the realities of the modern regulatory state.

3.2 Cosmopolitanism and Empire

By a peculiar irony, many of the central concepts, which we use today to limit and civilise the exercise of political power, derive historically from attempts to legitimise imperial rule. It is true to a large extent of human rights, which may, on further reflection, not seem surprising, given that imperial rule is characterised by the need to rule over a large and heterogeneous group of people; imperial rule must therefore be legitimised in universal terms, which does not draw directly on any particular trait characterising a specific nation or group of people. And it is true of cosmopolitanism, which is often today, especially in its Kantian form, used as a basis for arguing for a strong political universalism, which derives historically, however, from the close connection between ancient Stoicism and the legitimisation of empire.

The first to actually use the term 'cosmopolitan' may have been the Cynic philosopher Diogenes of Sinope, who, on being asked where he came from, replied that 'I am a citizen of the world (κοσμοπολίτης)' (Diogenes Laertius 2005, 6:63). Diogenes's comment was probably intended as a rejection of culturally dominant customs, norms and values; it occurs in a passage depicting him behaving oddly while challenging or refusing commonly accepted norms of politeness, religious practice and hygienic standards, and probably serves the more general purpose of underlining that Diogenes, preferring the Cynic life in accordance with nature, owed no particular allegiance to Sinope or any other particular political community. We may perhaps say that Diogenes's cosmopolitanism is mainly negative in the sense that it amounts to a rejection of a particular political community and its conventional morality (Kleingeld 2012, 2).[1]

[1] It is also a version of cosmopolitanism that corresponds quite well to the often-voiced criticism of cosmopolitanism as being rootless and lacking in (personal, ethnic, political) identity – and therefore as potentially ethically and politically problematic in its denunciation of conventional morality. We find a contemporary statement of that view in Theresa May's (in)famous comment at the 2016 Tory Party Conference that 'if you believe you're a citizen of the world, you're a citizen of nowhere. You don't understand what the very word "citizenship" means' (May 2016). In my view, the best reply to the rootlessness objection remains Isaac Deutscher's famous aphorism that 'trees have roots; Jews have legs'.

In Stoicism, we find a more positive conception of cosmopolitanism, built on a strong universalistic morality. In this view, world citizenship is not so much a question of rejecting the values and norms of a particular political community, but rather of accepting the fundamental kindredness of all human beings and the universal (natural) moral laws to which it gives rise. The Stoic version of world citizenship was, however, closely linked to a new political reality, namely the empire. It is, of course, impossible to decide exactly to what extent the philosophical ideal of world citizenship was inspired by empire as a political reality and to what extent the philosophical ideal and Stoic philosophy more generally were enlisted as ideological support of the political project. It is, however, likely that Zeno, the founder of Stoicism, had the empire of Alexander the Great in mind, when claiming that 'all the inhabitants of this world of ours should not live differentiated by their respective rules of justice into separate cities and communities [...] we should consider all men to be of one community and one polity, and [...] we should have a common life and an order common to us all, even as a herd that feeds together and shares the pasturage of a common field' (Plutarch 1989, 329B). Moreover, Plutarch, the source of Zeno's saying, clearly drew the connection between Stoic cosmopolitanism and Alexander's empire (Pagden 2015, 7). As Plutarch notes, Zeno's writing gave 'shape to a dream or, as it were, shadowy picture of a well-ordered and philosophic commonwealth; but it was Alexander who gave effect to the idea [and bade men everywhere] consider as their fatherland the whole inhabited earth' (Plutarch 1989, 329B-C).

During Roman times, the connection between cosmopolitanism and empire became even more pronounced. Cicero argues that Roman law is a partial realisation of the Stoic doctrine of natural law (Cicero 1999), just as his version of a universal ethics combines particular duties towards one's family and political community with duties towards humanity in general (Cicero 1991). Later Roman writers were even more explicit in their identification of the Roman Empire with the Stoic *Cosmopolis*, as was perhaps most clearly illustrated by Marcus Aurelius, who personally combined the persona of a Stoic philosopher with the political figure of the Roman emperor and thus came close to realising the ideal of a unified political order reflecting the rational nature of the universe.

3.3 Cosmopolitanism and the New World

The close connection between cosmopolitanism and imperial power reappeared in the early modern period, when arguments inspired by ancient Stoic cosmopolitanism were advanced in support of European colonial expansion. Shortly after Columbus's first voyage, a series of papal bulls gave the Spanish Crown legal control over the newly discovered territories and obliged the Spanish to evangelise the inhabitants of the New World. Furthermore, Spain and Portugal signed the treatise of Tordesillas, which was sanctioned by the pope and divided the world beyond the oceans between the two nations. This way of legitimising Spanish rules raised at least two questions: first, whether and to what extent the Amerindians are capable of being evangelised;

second, whether the pope has the right to grant control of newly discovered territories to secular princes, a point that did seem particular doubtful after Lorenzo Valla had proved the Donation of Constantine a forgery.[2]

It is important to note that the newly discovered world was fundamentally different from the territories targeted by earlier European or Christian expansions. The Spanish Reconquista and the Crusades were in principle defensive wars, because they were attempts to reconquer areas that had earlier been under Christian rule. The inhabitants of the New World were, however, clearly not Christians and had never been (although some early European travellers and missionaries to the New World did believe that they had found evidence of earlier evangelisation attempts). It is, however, difficult to justify an offensive war within the European legal and philosophical tradition, since the whole 'just war' tradition is based on the assumption that only defensive wars (including reconquests) are permissible (Pagden 2015).

Furthermore, the question of how to legitimise the Spanish transatlantic empire quickly became entangled in the internal power struggles between different institutions and persons vying for control over the newly conquered territories. Seen from the perspective of the Spanish Crown, using the papal bulls as legitimation carried the political risk of making Spanish control over the New World dependent on the good will of the pope, which in turn meant that royal authority in the Indies would be subjected to the Church. Another option would have been to argue from the right of discovery and the fact that a large part of the New World actually was in the possession or under the control of the Spanish monarchs. Moreover, such arguments could have found at least some support in Roman law and the natural law tradition, for instance in the provisions regarding the taking into possessions of a thing that does not yet belong to anyone (*res nullius*). Although such arguments were occasionally made, they carried another political risk, namely of making the royal dominion dependent not on the Church but on the conquistadores, who were, of course, the actual discoverers and often also the only Europeans who could be said to have taken the New World into possession in a literal sense.

Yet another option, at least after the ascension of Charles V, would have been to argue that the Spanish conquest was legitimate, because the Spanish king was also Roman emperor, and could therefore claim, as his ancient counterpart had done, to be the ruler of the whole world. In other words, the Spanish conquest could be justified in terms of universal monarchy, which in turn could be justified in cosmopolitan terms. Since every human being is a citizen of the same world or cosmos, subjected to the same rational and eternal law, it is just that the same monarch should rule over the whole world, in the same way that the one and true God rules the whole universe. However, although the argument later made a reappearance in the work of Tommaso Campanella (Pagden 1990), it never played any major role in the Spanish debate concerning the New World. In particular, it was rejected by Vitoria (Vitoria

[2]The so-called Donation of Constantine is a forged decree by Constantine the Great, in which he (supposedly) gives the Western Roman Empire to the Catholic Church. In his *De falso credita et ementita Constantini Donatione declamatio* (1442), Valla argues from philological and historical grounds that the document must be a forgery, thereby undermining one of the main (although contested) arguments for papal temporal power (cf. Valla 2008 for a modern translation).

1997, *De Indiis* II.1) the founder of the School of Salamanca, on the grounds that universal monarchy cannot be justified in terms of either natural or Divine Law, or positive human law. More generally, Thomistic philosophy does not accept the Stoic claim that all human beings are inhabitants of the same universal city.

Nor would it be possible to justify the Spanish conquest directly in terms of the Christian faith, since it is also a defining feature of Thomistic political theory that it rejects the suggestion that the legitimacy of a political rule depends on a divine grant of the right to rule or on the personal faith of the ruler. Political authority is founded on God's law, not on his grace. So the rule of a heathen ruler may be just as legitimate as that of a Christian. This means in particular that the political institutions of the Americans were fully legitimate before the Spanish invasion. More specifically, Vitoria argues that the fact that the Indians are sinners and heathens does not mean that they did not have full *dominium* over both themselves and their lands before the arrival of the Spanish. Even sinners are created in the image of God, and they are therefore capable of *dominium* over themselves and the things of the world (Vitoria 1997, *De Indiis* 1.2, cf. 1.3).

Vitoria thus rejects that the Spanish rule could be justified directly in cosmopolitan terms. However, when he turns his attention to the valid arguments for Spanish rule, he does strike a guarded cosmopolitan chord. He first argues that the Spanish have a right to natural society and communication with the Indians. More precisely, this right of communication (*ius communicationis*) means that the Spanish have the right to travel (*ius perigrinandi*) and settle in the new lands, when this can be done without harm to the barbarians, just as they also have the right to trade with the barbarians, again on the condition that this can be done without harm to them. Furthermore, the Spanish also have a right to preach (*ius praedicandi*) the Word of God to the Indians. This follows both from the right to human communication and from the fact that the Indians are human beings and therefore part of God's plan of salvation, which in turn presupposes that his words can be preached to them.

Vitoria's somewhat guarded defence of Spanish colonialism was immensely important for both international law and later attempts at legitimising various European colonial enterprises. It would, however, be wrong to see Vitoria as the chief ideologue of the Spanish empire, as is clearly illustrated by the fact that Charles V forbade the printing and diffusion of Vitoria's *relectiones* in Spain. We may suspect that Charles's reaction was motivated by the fact that the right of communication could also be used to argue in favour of the rights of other European nations to travel to the Americas. As we shall see, it may not be a coincidence that Vitoria's *relectiones* was printed in Lyon in 1557 (Gliozzi 2000, 266).

3.4 Trade: Empires of Liberty

The political, economic and military competition and conflict between the major European powers for control over the New World led to an ideological struggle between various ways of conceptualising and legitimising empire. At the same time, the Spanish conquest of America quickly lost legitimacy in the eyes of other Europeans as tales of their mistreatment of the American Indians spread. Moreover, the question of the legitimacy of Spain's transatlantic empire became entangled in the wider ideological struggle between Catholicism and Calvinism, as Huguenot writers, such as Theodor de Bry[3] and Urbain de Chauveton,[4] connected the Spanish massacre of the Indians with their crimes in Europe (see Lestringant 2004 for more on the ideological use of America during the French wars of religion).

This led to the ambition of creating another and more just type of relation between Europeans and the inhabitants of the New World. French writers such as Léry, Chauveton and Montaigne thus argued that France should establish a relation based on trade and mutual interest rather than imperial conquest, and that such a relation would be not only more legitimate and just but also in France's long-term national interest (cf. Lestringant 2004, Postface II, 449–462). Moreover, the French writers taught the Spanish a lesson in the logic of universality: the trouble with adducing strongly universalistic arguments in favour of your own position is that the same arguments can, by their very nature, be used by everyone else. And that is exactly what happened with Vitoria's *naturalis societas et communitas*, which could be used both for criticising Spanish colonialism and for imagining a more positive relation to the natives. Montaigne thus invites us to imagine what would have happened if the Europeans had presented the Americans with a model of virtue to be imitated and had created 'a fraternal society and mutual understanding' (Montaigne 1962, 888). We find the same line of argument in other French writers of the period such as Bodin and La Popilinière, who also uses the free communication between human beings as a starting point for attacking Spanish exclusion of other European powers from the New World, and as a source of inspiration for elaborating alternatives to the militaristic Spanish colonial strategy (Gliozzi 2000, 179, 265–266).

The same argument was also used to much the same effect by the Dutch natural lawyer Hugo Grotius, who, in his short book *On the Free Sea*, draws extensively on Vitoria and argues that every nation has a right to travel to any other nation and trade with them (Grotius 2004, 7). This time, however, the argument was directed towards Portugal's attempt to control the trade routes to the Far East. So Grotius is once again deploying the argument in favour of an imperial project; only this time it is the Dutch project of creating a trade empire in East Asia. It is therefore not surprising that the right to preach is missing from Grotius's version of the argument; clearly, he had no use for it.

According to Grotius, the Portuguese adduced, or could adduce, four possible 'titles' in support of their dominion over the Asian trade, namely (1) Papal donation; (2) just war; (3) the right of discovery; (4) prescription or custom. Drawing on Vitoria and his *De Indiis*, Grotius rejects all four possible titles, and argues that the right

[3]Cf. the illustrated edition of Las Casas's *Short Account of the Destruction of the Indies* by de Bry and his sons (Casas 1598), which leave the reader in little doubt as to the criminal nature of the Spanish conquest.

[4]Cf. Chauveton's French edition of Benzoni's *Historia del Mondo Nuovo*, to which he added Nicolas Le Challeux's short account of the Spanish massacre of the French colony in Florida (Chauveton 1579).

to travel and trade cannot be 'conquered' (Pagden 2015). More precisely, Grotius's use of Vitoria is predicated on his own theory of property rather than on a theory of human nature or universal monarchy. Thus, Grotius holds that the things of the Earth were originally held in common in the negative sense of belonging to no one in particular. Property is then established by the act of taking them into possession. This can also be done with smaller bodies of water, such as lakes, rivers and coastal areas, by fortifying them or controlling them with a fleet. The ocean, however, is simply too large for any single state to control it and therefore remains in the original state of common property.

The Dutch commercial empire in East Asia thus legitimises itself as an expression of natural human freedom rather than as an empire in the literal sense, i.e. a coercive political power. In stark contrast to Spanish colonialism, the Dutch do not attempt to conquer foreign nations and subjugate them under a morally questionable European rule, but merely let people enjoy their right to communication and the pursuit of their self-interest. The commercial empire is, as it were, an empire without an emperor (except God, who serves as the lawgiver in the state of nature). Cosmopolitanism and the right to travel no longer serves to justify empire, but to define an empire of liberty under God, but not under the rule of man. Note also that Grotius was defending the *private* commercial empire of the Dutch East Asian Company rather than an empire in the traditional public and political sense.

We also find the connection between a critique of imperial power and a defence of free trade in Montesquieu. Perhaps the most persistent and important theme in Montesquieu's political thought is the critique of empire and the imperial ambitions of the European great powers, in particular the imperial ambitions of Philip II's Spain and Louis XIV's France. But while Montesquieu criticises imperialism for its tendency to degenerate to despotism, he also presents a more positive image of another type of international relation, namely trade or 'doux commerce' (Larrère 2014). Trade thus has a tendency or capacity to render people gentle and make customs and moral norms more accommodating to foreigners. For Montesquieu, free trade is not so much a natural or universal right as a way of building mutual understanding and civilised manners.

Trade thus functions as a positive counter-image to the despotic regime with its subjugation of human freedom through fear, crippling both human nature and economic development along the way. Moreover, despotic regimes have a tendency to isolate themselves and to extend their borders through warfare until they reach natural boundaries such as deserts or mountains, because these regimes are unable to establish a trusting relationship with their neighbours (Montesquieu 1989, 5, 14; 9, 4). Whereas Vitoria tried to justify empire on the ground of human communication, empire thus tends to undermine and disrupt human communication in Montesquieu. In contrast, human communication is for Montesquieu indissolubly tied to freedom and therefore also to trade; he even goes so far as to identify the history of trade with the history of human communion: 'The history of commerce is that of communication among peoples' (Montesquieu 1989, 5, 14; 9, 4).

3.5 Free Nations or Free Trade

Grotius's natural jurisprudence thus opens a conceptual space, where trade is associated with freedom and civilisation, whereas imperial rule is associated with despotism and lack of economic and cultural development.

The ideal of free trade did not, however, remain unchallenged for long. Thus, the German-Swedish natural lawyer Samuel Pufendorf rejects both Grotius's account of the open sea and the more general argument from human communication. In stark contrast to Grotius, Pufendorf argues that the ocean can, at least in part, be taken into possession. Originally, the sea was, of course, common property and everybody had a right to use it. Nevertheless, private property may be justified. Since uses of the sea, which draw on exhaustible resources, such as fishing, may cause conflicts to arise, a community may be justified in taking the sea into possession in order to regulate its use or reserve it for itself. Furthermore, free passage may cause military concerns that justify patrols and coastal fortifications, which in turn amounts to a de facto property by occupation.

As for human communication, Pufendorf is himself, or so he claims, a Stoic, and his theory of duties include a category of duties, which we owe to all other persons in virtue of the general friendship between men. Significantly enough, the rights of free passage and trade are not among them. Pufendorf lists a whole catalogue of particular duties deriving from the general duty to make ourselves useful to other persons. These duties can be divided into *indefinite* and *definite*. The first group encompasses the duty to train your body and mind in such a manner as to render yourself useful to society. The second group encompasses a rather diversified set of duties to help others in particular situations, as opposed to a general duty to be a useful member of society. This includes the duty to give to others what can be given at no cost to us, such as good counsel or water from a river (Pufendorf 1998, III.3.3). It also includes granting strangers free passage—excepting, however, large armies—and permitting them to seek harmless profit through trade (Pufendorf 1998, III.3.5).

Being in this respect a child of the age of mercantilism, Pufendorf limits the latter duty to goods, which are necessary for supporting the lives of recipients (Pufendorf 1998, III.3.6), whereas we have a right of restricting trade in other goods, just as we may, in a condition of scarcity, restrict trade in necessities, if we are required to do so in order to secure our own survival (Pufendorf 1998, III.3.11). This also means that we have the right to demand toll and custom and enter into trade agreements, including such that assign monopoly to one specific trade partner (Pufendorf 1998, III.3.6–7).

Furthermore, the duty to sell does not include a duty to buy, which is why Vitoria is wrong in claiming that the Indians had a duty to accept Spanish traders, since they, being under no obligation to buy Spanish goods, had the right to restrict access to their lands (Pufendorf 1998, III.3.12). Vitoria is also wrong when he claims that the Spanish have a natural right of travelling to and settling in the lands of the Indians, based on the natural duty to receive strangers and the natural right to society and communication. Clearly, we do have a duty of hospitality. It is, however, limited to persons of integrity, who travel on necessary or honest business, and only applies in situations where appropriate lodging cannot be had for money. It also excludes persons who travel out of mere curiosity, since such travels may raise suspicions about their motives and therefore jeopardise our own security, although it does include survivors from shipwrecks and other persons in dire necessity. This again shows that Vitoria is wrong in using the right of natural communication to legitimise the Spanish conquests in America (Pufendorf 1998, III.3.9). Completing the list of duties, Pufendorf adds that a prince must allow marriages between strangers and his subjects, just as every person who receives benefits from another is under a duty to express gratitude (Pufendorf 1998, III.13.15).

As noted by Boucher, Pufendorf's rejection of the right of free passage may perhaps be explained by the fact that his theory of natural law is not tied to European colonial interest in the same way that those of Vitoria, Grotius and Locke were tied to Spanish, Dutch and English colonial enterprises and trade interests, since Sweden and the German principalities were not involved in colonial adventures, at least not to the same extent (Boucher 1998, 247–9). However, the rejection also reflects a more philosophical difference between a cosmopolitan and a national perspective; a difference that would continue to be of central importance for later German political thought.

3.6 Cosmopolitanism and Free Nations

I now turn to Kant and his attempt to formulate a cosmopolitan political project. Kant's cosmopolitanism is among the most controversial aspects of his later ethical and political thought and is often seen as somewhat incoherent. At least Kant seems to have changed his mind on a number of important issues. In earlier texts, in particular the *Idea to a Universal History*, he argues in favour of a strong federation of peoples, which would have the capacity to enforce international law and coerce individual states. In his later writings, especially *Toward Perpetual Peace*, he seems to have changed his mind, arguing instead that since states would never accept surrendering their sovereignty to an international federation, the international order should instead be based on a looser and more voluntary international league with no coercive powers. This line of thought may seem to reflect a willingness to compromise with political reality, which is not only somewhat unusual for Kant but also contradicts his rejection of a division between (ethical, political) theory and practice (cf. Kant 1996b). It seems likely, however, that Kant's change of mind should be seen as a way of distancing himself from the more radical elements in French revolutionary thought that sought to export the French Revolution and establish an international state by means of warfare (Kleingeld 2012). In other words, Kant's later preference for a voluntary international league is an attempt to disentangle cosmopolitanism from any actual coercive power that would be able to claim the authority of international law or cosmopolitan right.

Nonetheless, the right to travel still plays a central role in Kant's version of cosmopolitanism, since he takes the right to hospitality to be the core of cosmopolitan right. Furthermore, Kant also draws support for his cosmopolitanism from free trade and the claim that it tends to create peaceful relations between nations. However, Kant limits the scope of the right to hospitability in much the same way as Pufendorf. So it does not include the right to actually enter a foreign nation, unless one is in danger of perishing; nor does it give a right to trade with or visit foreigners. It only gives a newcomer the right 'to *seek* commerce with the old inhabitants' (Kant 1996b, 8:358, quoted translation p. 329) of a foreign country. The inhabitants of the foreign nation on their part are under no obligation to accept commerce with the newcomer or allow her to enter. Kant thus reinterprets early modern cosmopolitanism in a manner that respects the political autonomy of individual nations and the existence of a plurality of nation states. Just as the league of nations is a voluntary association assembling the free republican nations of the world, so the foundation of cosmopolitan right, namely the right to hospitality, is strictly limited so as to not undermine the political autonomy of foreign nations.

3.7 Conclusion

As we have seen, the Enlightenment revival of cosmopolitanism and the right to travel gave rise to two different and competing visions of the international order: on the one hand, the ideal of an international capitalist order based on free trade and the pursuit of self-interest; on the other, the vision of a voluntary league of nations founded on the common moral interest of free republics in establishing a peaceful international order. Both ideals are tied to an interpretation of the right to travel—as either free trade or hospitality.

In a contemporary political context, both ideals seem to have lost much of their appeal, and are seen as hollow, if not outright undesirable, by the many opponents of the liberal international order.[5] One reason for this is, I believe, that it was always an illusion to believe that free trade and a cosmopolitan world order could be separated from empire and coercive state power. In particular, the modern regulatory state makes it impossible to divide trade from political power, since international trade requires the harmonisation of national regulatory regimes. And the idea of a voluntary league of nations, whether on the European or global level, is today challenged by what may perhaps be termed the globalisation of poverty, straining the laws of hospitality that Kant hoped would support a cosmopolitan order. Moreover, international politics is not (or no longer, if it ever was) dominated by the autonomous republics that Kant had hoped all nations would one day become. If this diagnosis is

[5]It is perhaps worth noting that the critique of the first form of cosmopolitan empire is particularly prevalent on the political left, while criticism of the second type is particularly prevalent on the nationalist right.

correct, we may face a choice of either abandoning cosmopolitanism and its universalistic values or reconnecting cosmopolitanism and political power, becoming, as it were, Romans once again.

Bibliography

Boucher, D. (1998). *Political theories of international relations: From thucydides to the present.* Oxford: Oxford University Press.

Cicero. (1991). *On duties.* In M. T. Griffin & E. M. Atkins (Eds.) Cambridge: Cambridge University Press.

Cicero. (1999). *On the commonwealth and on the laws.* In J. E. G. Zetzel (Ed.) Cambridge: Cambridge University Press.

de Chauveton, U. (1579). *Histoire nouvelle du nouveau monde, contenant en somme ce que les hespagnols ont fait jusqu'à présent aux Indes occidentales, et le rude traitement qu'ils font à ces povres peuples-là. Extraite de l'italien de M. Hierosme Benzoni Milanois, qui ha voyagé xiiii. Ans en ces pays-là: et enrichie de plusieurs discours et choses dignes de memoire. Par M. Urbain Chauveton. Ensemble, une petite histoire d'un massacre commis par les Hespagnols sur quelques François en la Floride. Avec un indice des choses les plus remarquables.* Genève: Eustache Vignon.

de las Casas, B. (1598). *Narratio regionum Indicarum per hispanos quosdam devastatarum verissima, priùs quidem per episcopum Bartholemaeum Casaum, natione Hispanum Hispanicè conscripta, and anno 1551. Hispali, Hispanicè, anno verò hoc 1598. Latinè excusa.* Francofurti, sumptibus T. de Bry, et J. Saurii typis.

de Montaigne, M. (1962). "Of coaches", *Essays* III. VI, quoted after Montaigne, *Œuvres complètes,* Bibliothèque de la Pléade. Paris: Gallimard.

de Montesquieu, C. (1989). *The spirit of the laws* (A. M. Cohler, B. C. Miller, & H. S. Stone, Ed. and Trans). Cambridge: Cambridge University Press.

de Vitoria, F. (Ed.) (1997). *De indis.* in *Vorlesungen I: Völkerrecht, Politik, Kirche.* Ulrich Horst, Heinz-Gerhard Justenhoven, Joachim Stüben. Stuttgart: Kohlhammer.

Diogenes Laertius. (2005 [1925]). *The lives of eminent philosophers. Loeb Classical Library 185* (Vol. II, R. D. Hicks, Ed. and Trans). Cambridge (Mass.), London: Harvard University Press.

Gliozzi, G. (2000). *Adam et le nouveau monde. La naissance de l'anthropologie comme idéologie coloniale: des généalogies bibliques aux théories raciales (1500–1700).* (A. Estève, & P. Gabellone, French Trans:). Lecques: Théétète.

Grotius, H. (2004). *The free sea.* Indianapolis: Liberty Fund.

Hardt, M., & Negri, A. (2000). *Empire.* Cambridge (Mass.), London: Harvard University Press.

Kant, I. (1996a). *On the common saying: That may be correct in theory, but it is of no use in practice.* In I. Kant, *Practical philosophy* (M. J. Gregor, & A. Wood, Ed. and Trans). Cambridge: Cambridge University Press.

Kant, I. (1996b). *Toward perpetual peace.* In I. Kant, *Practical philosophy* (M. J. Gregor, & A. Wood, Ed. and Trans). Cambridge: Cambridge University Press.

Kleingeld, P. (2012). *Kant and cosmopolitanism.* The Philosophical Ideal of World Citizenship, Cambridge: Cambridge University Press.

Larrère, C. (2014). Montesquieu et le « doux commerce »: Un paradigme du libéralisme. *Cahiers d'histoire. Revue d'histoire critique, 123,* 21–38.

Lestringant, F. (2004). *Le huguenot et le sauvage: l'Amérique et la controverse coloniale, en France, au temps des guerres de religion (1555–1589), troisième édition revue et augmentée.* Genève: Droz.

May, T. (2016). *Conference speech.* https://blogs.spectator.co.uk/2016/10/full-text-theresa-mays-conference-speech/. Accessed 6 April 2019.

Pagden, A. (1990). *Spanish imperialism and the political imagination.* New Haven and London: Yale University Press.
Pagden, A. (2015). *The burdens of empire. 1539 to the present.* Cambridge: Cambridge University Press.
Plutarch. (1989 [1936]). *On the fortune or the virtue of alexander* in *Moralia.* Loeb Classical Library 305 (Vol. IV, F. C. Babbitt, Ed. and Trans). Cambridge (Mass.). London: Harvard University Press.
Valla, L. (2008), *On the donation of constantine.* The I tatti renaissance Library (G. W Bowersock, Ed. and Trans). Cambridge (Mass.), London: Harvard University Press.
von Pufendorf, S. F. (1998). *Of the laws of nature and nations*, quoted after Pufendorf, *De jure naturae et gentium*, In F. Böhling & W. Schmidt-Biggemann (Eds.), *Gesammelte Werke* (Vol. 4/1–2). Berlin: Akademie Verlag.

Adam Diderichsen Ph.D. is Assistant Professor of Emergency and Risk Management at the University College Copenhagen. His research interests include the Enlightenment and the history of political thought. His latest book is a monograph on Montesquieu.

Chapter 4
The Stronger the Patriots—The Weaker the Migrants: Cosmopolitan Perspectives

Rebecka Lettevall

Abstract This chapter offers a discussion of the relation between patriotism and cosmopolitanism in a Swedish context. It takes its starting point in the refugee situation of 2015, where Sweden together with Germany hosted Europe's largest number of refugees in relation to its population. The cosmopolitan right of hospitality as defined by Kant used to have a relation to patriotism, while today the two concepts no longer seem to have that relation. Swedish intellectual Ellen Key shows a way to discuss this relation that opens for an alternative way to consider patriotism.

Keywords Cosmopolitanism · Patriotism · Human rights · Sweden · Kant · Ellen Key

4.1 Introduction

In recent years, processes of migration and mobility, including refugee migration, have challenged the cosmopolitan ideals that gained new actuality after the end of the Cold War. Human rights have a universal character, while citizen rights are connected to specific citizenships. Human rights are closely associated with cosmopolitanism. Historically, patriotism has been an important and integrated aspect of cosmopolitanism. Today, the former mutual dependence between cosmopolitanism and patriotism has changed in a sense that differs substantially from the Enlightenment patriotism that was the foundation for a cosmopolitan attitude, in a Kantian sense. In Europe, patriotism seems to develop towards an increasing political force while cosmopolitanism has a weaker position. This tendency was quite clear around 2015, with large groups of migrants arriving in Europe.

This chapter discusses the preconditions for migration and mobility with the point of departure in the relation between patriotism, human rights and cosmopolitan ideals as discussed by Immanuel Kant and Ellen Key, as well as the historicity of our own concepts. The main example is the recent change of meaning of patriotism in Sweden,

R. Lettevall (✉)
Malmö University, Malmö, Sweden
e-mail: rebecka.lettevall@mau.se

M. C. Jacobsen et al. (eds.), *Cosmopolitanism, Migration and Universal Human Rights*, https://doi.org/10.1007/978-3-030-50645-2_4

a country with a tradition of supporting weaker groups internationally. We will show how the Kantian notion of cosmopolitan right embedded in an Enlightenment context where patriotism and cosmopolitanism are corresponding is far from the twenty-first-century patriotism which is often associated with European populism. We will discuss how Swedish encyclopedias treat the concept of patriotism in different periods and discuss it with Swedish intellectual Ellen Key; we will bring in the attempts and problems in formulating universal human rights, and discuss how an awareness of the relation between patriotism, cosmopolitanism and human rights may open up for new ways forward.

4.2 Human Rights and the Enlightenment Ideal

Mobility and migration are some of the core conditions of human life and have probably always existed. However, the question of who has the right to live where and when is topical every now and then and has been answered in different ways. By the end of the eighteenth century, cosmopolitanism was an important concept culturally as well as politically, and it was connected with universal human rights. Immanuel Kant (1724–1804) was one of the first to develop the topic in a theoretical direction by stating the cosmopolitan right and thus representing something more than just the *cosmopolite* (Kant 2006 [1795], 67–109). Enlightenment cosmopolitanism had several different expressions, but Kant offered the foundation for a coherent meaning, which is still meaningful today (Kleingeld 1999). In *Perpetual Peace* (1795) Kant defines the three definitive articles for a sustainable peace, and in one of them he introduces what he calls cosmopolitan right, which is clearly stated as not philanthropy but a universal right. According to Kant, hospitality means the right of a stranger not to be treated with hostility because of her origin in another territory. She can, however, be turned away, if this can be done without causing her death, but as long as she does behave peacefully, she cannot be treated in a hostile manner (Kant 2006 [1795], 82). Kant's argument for this right goes as follows:

> It is not the right of a guest that the stranger has a claim to (which would require a special, charitable contract stipulating that he be made a member of the household for a certain period of time), but rather a right to visit, to which all human beings have a claim, to present oneself to society by virtue of the right of common possession of the surface of the earth. Since it is the surface of a sphere, they cannot scatter themselves on it without limit, but they must rather ultimately tolerate one another as neighbours, and originally no one has more of a right to be at a given place on earth than anyone else. (Kant 2006 [1795] 82)

Because of the spheric shape of the earth, persons originally have a universal right to live anywhere on the globe. Over history, however, this right has been quite restricted and today it is more or less covered by the right of hospitality. Hospitality, as Kant discusses it, turns out to be quite restrictive as it is limited to a right to visit at the most. But it is also the beginning of a theory of cosmopolitanism.

Concepts come and go out of fashion, not just depending on time but also on space. Changing historical-political situations seem to contribute to making certain concepts visible and other concepts invisible. Many contemporary central concepts have first emerged in their modern form through the Enlightenment thinkers and their critics. They carry with them older meanings that can be activated in the present. For example, the modern concept of citizen emerged with the French Revolution of 1789 and became central to ideologies and political languages about a century later (Koselleck 1972, 1979).

Similar to cosmopolitanism, patriotism was another important concept of the Enlightenment. In the Enlightenment context, patriotism was often associated with freedom, modernity and a movement towards a brighter future, and could be moral as well as political. Sometimes patriotism was also closely connected to citizenship and revolutionary ideas (Viroli 1995). Cosmopolitanism is in this context often closely related to universal human rights, and Enlightenment cosmopolitanism also has a close relation to patriotism—it was not uncommon that defenders of cosmopolitanism also defended patriotism, and this was the case with Kant (Kleingeld 2003). The main argument was that in order to care for humanity as a whole or the universal, you also had to care for the particular, such as your closest neighbour. The relationship between cosmopolitanism and patriotism could thus be symbolically represented as two sides of the same coin—as was the case with the commemorative coin of the city of Hamburg in 1726 (Kleingeld 2003, 299).

In Germany, Romantics and Idealists were influential in forming the patriotic ideal. Johann Gottlieb Fichte (1762–1814) developed a theory where he combined patriotism with cosmopolitanism. According to him, the link between the two concepts is very close, as he argues that in order to contribute to the development of humanity as a whole, you have to believe in your own culture. In every citizen there is also implicitly a world citizen, or a cosmopolitan. These ideas are developed in Fichte's well-known lectures *Addresses to the German nation* (1807–1808). Fichte has been comprehended in several different ways, including being understood as proposing nationalism as an ideology, but it has been suggested by philosopher Peter Kemp that Fichte could also be understood as a cosmopolitan patriot as he stresses that no one can contribute to the world citizenship unless they acknowledge the value of their own culture and know it well enough to be willing to contribute to others (Kemp 2013, 62). His patriotism is permeated by the educational ideal coupled with a strong influence from the humanist tradition, which implies a cosmopolitan perspective. Kemp suggests that when Fichte states that Germans are particularly well suited to become world citizens, this should be understood in its temporal and spatial context: Fichte addressed his audience at the time when Prussia had recently been defeated in battles by Napoleon and soon after he marched towards Berlin. Instead of encouraging his audience to raise in arms, Fichte turned to education and culture as means to defeat the loss (Kemp 2013, 53–54). Kemp points out that Fichte's famous thesis that 'the I sets itself' is to be understood as saying that 'a human being can only be human among humans', that she has to be with others in order to be human, a cosmopolitan. This is a theory of communication and nothing else. Kemp's suggestion is interesting and solid, not least because it is supported by other sources concerning the relationship between cosmopolitanism and patriotism. Fichte was not alone, even if his theory seems to be more radical than those of many of his contemporaries. For Immanuel Kant (1724–1804), the connection was also self-evident (Kleingeld 2012, 13–39).

4.3 Patriotism in Sweden

As in several other modern languages, the word ‘patriot’ enters Swedish in the seventeenth century, in the 1620 s, and seems to be used—quite frequently—in the same way as in the reigning European mercantilistic and physiocratic policy of the seventeenth and eighteenth centuries (Svenska Akademiens Ordbok 1952. col. P488). In expressions, the patriot as a person is often combined with ‘good, virtuous, righteous, benevolent, faithful’ (Svenska Akademiens Ordbok 1952. col. P488. [god, redlig, rättsinnig, välmenande, trogen], my transl.). Being a patriot has, furthermore, the meaning of loving one’s country, sometimes with a suggested implication of being nationalistic. The examples from the early twentieth century are all taken from historical works and it is also mentioned that it can refer to the local place where someone was born, as in German *Heimat* or Swedish *hembygd*.

In the classical Swedish encyclopedia from around 1900, *Nordisk familjebok*, patriotism has a description similar to the Fichtean standpoint. Patriotism is beautifully described as a feeling or an emotion, and it is said that an individual ‘almost by natural necessity’ gets attached to her nation with a commitment similar to the feelings between a father and a son. The individual is proud of the country’s historical past and cares about its power and honour, its future, its nature and language (Nordisk familjebok 1915, vol. 21, 243–244). It is a feeling of belonging founded on the consciousness of its own spiritual and material cultivation of common cultural interests. In its higher forms, patriotism also embraces the awareness of responsibility and duties towards society. The article further refers to the classic tradition, where patriotism was described more or less as a religion. What might be understood as a resemblance with the Fichtean theory is a reference to a ‘modern perspective’ where the polarisation between different countries has diminished as the common belonging to other ‘cultural nations’ becomes clear to the individual who works for the progress of mankind as a whole, and as long as patriotism is developed in a cultivating feeling of love of justice and freedom, it is also united with cosmopolitanism and a spirit of world citizenship.

The article has a reference to the key word ‘Kosmopolit’ [cosmopolitan (as a noun)], where the definition takes its starting point in the affirmation that a cosmopolitan is a human being who does not just have interest in her own country, but in all people on the earth, as she engages in and acts for larger and wider cultural aims (Nordisk familjebok 1911, col. 1133). Further, cosmopolitanism is defined as the belief in mankind as a whole and the ability to consider the world as a society of equal citizens, without any difference concerning race, nationality or religion (gender or class is not mentioned). In the article, it is also explicitly stated that rather than being impossible to unite with a sound patriotism, cosmopolitanism is a complement to it, and even more so the further culture progresses.

The Swedish writer and pedagogue Ellen Key (1849–1926) made a clear distinction between patriotism and nationalism that deserves to be discussed (Key 1914; Lettevall 2011). She, as well as some of her contemporaries, described patriotism in a considerably more nuanced fashion than is normally the case today. Key regarded patriotism as a significant and important part of life that was necessary for peace (Key 1914, 5). Several of her critics argued that she was unpatriotic herself, as she did not want to set arms for war. Key was interpreting patriotism in a new way, and it could be argued that she develops a nuanced theory of patriotism. For her, the 'fosterlandskänsla', the feeling of belonging, being a part of a particular country, was 'a wonderful feeling', often born of a person's earliest impressions in childhood (Key 1914, 29). She believes that this stage has existed since the dawn of culture, and also that it has been of decisive importance for humanity and true cultural development. It strives to create co-operation between different people. For her, the feeling of belonging to a nation (*nationalitetskänsla*) is of a different character, a form of self-assertion with the risk of transformation into political violence (Key 1914, 15). Nationalism implies indifference to those that do not belong to the nation, and this indifference can turn into contempt and hostility which might lead to struggles of power as well as for war.

Ellen Key discusses patriotism and nationalism as emotional entities. Patriotism and nationalism are feelings or emotions. They are not political concepts. Further, she means that the emotional relation to a place is crucial for a person to be able to develop profound feelings for herself as well as for humanity as a whole. She argues that this patriotic emotion will develop the love between people and in the end contribute to increasing internationalism. The counter force for this development is the growth of nationalism, and this aggressive force should be stopped before it gets too strong and turns into a real threat.

The common understanding of patriotism seems to have changed in Sweden in the period between the edition of the earlier mentioned encyclopedia *Nordisk familjebok* and the later *Nationalencyklopedin* of the 1990s. This supports the impression that patriot and patriotism were quite invisible in the Swedish language and that there has been a change again over the last few years, which we will come back to later. In the large project of creating a new national encyclopedia in Sweden in the 1990s, there is no key word or entry such as 'patriot' or 'patriotism' (Nationalencyklopedin 1994). The only entry word is 'Patriot', referring to the English word '*Patriot*', or rather to the name of the US high technological air missile robot system, operative since 1985. Also, the old Swedish *Patriotiska sällskapet* (the patriotic society), founded in 1766, is mentioned in a very short article (Nationalencyklopedin 1994. Vol. 15, 14). In the 2019 electronic edition, 'patriot' has a short definition as 'a person who loves her country and is prepared to unselfishly work for its wealth' (*Nationalencyklopedin*, 2016-04-01. [patriot [patriu:′t], person som älskar sitt land och är beredd att osjälviskt arbeta för dess välgång. My transl.]). Unfortunately the article is unsigned, but the definition relates to the ideas of Ellen Key mentioned above.

One may wonder what happens between 1915 and 1990 to no longer motivate the inclusion of the word 'patriot' in the Swedish encyclopedia *Nationalencyklopedin* (NE). One assumption is that the exclusion of 'patriot' or 'patriotism' is related to the fact that Sweden remained (officially) neutral in the two World Wars, and actually has not officially been at war for more than 200 years (even though Sweden has participated in military operations in Afghanistan and Libya, and Swedish weapons have been used in several conflicts). The long period of peace contributed to an economic, social and cultural transformation that Sweden went through in the twentieth century. From having been a small backward country on the periphery of Europe where a large part of the population had migrated to America in the nineteenth century, it suddenly developed into one of the wealthiest and more socially egalitarian countries in the world. As large areas of Europe and other parts of the world were struggling to rebuild their societies, Sweden was more or less ready to develop the modern industrial state. Sweden considered itself international, not patriotic. Swedish patriotism was, so to speak, *not* to be patriotic, but to express patriotism as internationalism, peace-building, etc.—and perhaps also with the self-image that Swedish solutions are a bit less selfish and more international than those of others. One may perhaps call them a bit cosmopolitan—taking responsibility for making the world a bit better for those who did not have all these rights and opportunities (Lettevall et al. 2012). Politically, Sweden protested against the US during the Vietnam war, supported the ANC in the struggle against apartheid in South Africa and actively received many refugees from the Latin American military dictatorships in the 1970s.

4.4 Formulating Human Rights

Ellen Key does not discuss patriotism in relation to citizenship, even though she seems to assume some universal rights and implicitly the love of humanity with its origins in patriotism. A citizen has rights and duties, where some of them are founded on universal human rights, just as cosmopolitanism is. The idea of universal human rights in the Western tradition is often described as having earlier formulations in the Virginia declaration of 1776, the American Declaration of Independence from 1776 and the French declaration of 1789. The Rights of Man from 1689 is also considered to be a predecessor.

In his work, Danish intellectual historian Mogens Chrom Jacobsen examines the foundation of the idea of human rights and argues that its paradigmatic conception—what he calls the classic monistic expression—can be found in the documents just mentioned. Furthermore, he traces its origin to the encounter between Greco-Roman philosophy and Judeo-Christian thought (Jacobsen 2011, 13–15). Jacobsen also believes that there are two other conceptions of human rights and underlines that it is crucial to keep the three conceptions apart, as well as to realise that they are of different historical origin. Further, he holds that the idea of human rights is an idea of the eighteenth century, but also that it is not cumulative. It was not a guiding star for either Marx or the early working-class movement, as the idea of human rights for them was considered a bourgeois idea. The reformist working-class movement did, however, claim the human rights perspective.

As Jacobsen has shown, citizenship can be considered as the task of the state, founded on the view of the state as a historical created community based on duties and free choices or as the task beyond the state, when the state is considered to be a historical accident with possible instrumental value. The first view is founded on the eighteenth-century declarations, while the 1948 declaration expresses the second view (cf. Chap. 20).

In the Western tradition, universal human rights have often been in focus after periods of conflict, such as the French and American revolutions or the First and Second World Wars. After the First World War, some attempts were made in order to offer persons who had lost their citizenship through the war and the dissolution of several empires, and the most ambitious measure was the Nansen Passports (Lettevall 2013). Even though it contributed to improving some individuals' lives, they also caused several other problems, and they disappeared by the end of the 1930s. However, this was a serious attempt to practise the idea of cosmopolitan citizenship for persons who had lost their citizen's rights. The dissolution of three empires and the formation of new nation states after the First World War had the consequence that hundreds of thousands of persons lost their home, their citizenship, and also their right to have rights.

One of the reasons behind the formulation of the United Nations Declaration of Human Rights was the handling of the refugee situation after the Second World War. But how do human rights handle the question of citizenship and migration? After crises and conflicts, whether they be violent, environmental, economic, social or cultural, homes disappear, identity papers and citizenship are lost, and many persons need new homes. This is a cosmopolitan situation, where the question of universal human rights becomes central. As the United Nations was founded after the Second World War, a commission of human rights was established with the mission to formulate a blueprint for an International Bill of Rights. With Eleanor Roosevelt as chairperson and 18 participants from different parts of the world, the ambition was to find some kind of common ground. Among the participant were the lawyers René Cassin from France and John Humphrey from Canada, and the philosophers and diplomats Peng Chung Chang from China and Charles Malik from Lebanon. The Universal Declaration of Human Rights was adopted on 10 December 1948 by the United Nations General Assembly. The declaration can be referred to as a—in a philosophical meaning—cosmopolitan document, in the way Kant understands the concept. It is related to the cosmopolitan idea that every human belongs to the same world.

A difficult question in relation to the idea of universal human rights is that the universalism does not give any guarantees to any particular case. The hopes and challenges were quite demanding. On the one hand, there was the hope to guarantee every human being her human rights, but, on the other hand, this could only be guaranteed by a state that guaranteed citizenship.

One of the well-known harsh critics of the insufficiency of universal human rights is Hannah Arendt (1906–1975). According to her, pure and abstract human rights cannot possibly also secure these rights, as rights can only be given in a political space where persons are citizens. When a person is described without context, she does not have rights. The idea of rights as rooted in human nature has no content in a time where nature was far away, according to Arendt. The problem of refugees, migrants and *sans-papiers* was definitely not solved, as Hannah Arendt famously put it:

> … migrations of groups, who, unlike their happier predecessors in the religious wars, were welcomed nowhere and could be assimilated nowhere. Once they had left their homeland they remained homeless, once they had left their state they became stateless and once they had been deprived of their human rights they were rightless, the scum of the earth. (Arendt 1976: 267)

Arendt's criticism of human rights is also a criticism of cosmopolitanism, in the Kantian sense. One of the problems with the UN Declaration of Human Rights is that there was no awareness of the meaning of time and place, of the particular situation, and that the supporters of human rights had too little knowledge of the political reality (and perhaps there was too much idealistic work). There is a long step from theory to action. The tension emerged when the UN Declaration of Human Rights was accepted. The document did not solve the relation between the universal rights realm and the condition of the particular person and her citizenship. The tension was a result of the fact that there was not always a state that could guarantee the universal rights for non-citizens. If you are homeless and stateless, you are also rightless, as Arendt puts it.

4.5 Refugees and Patriotism in the Twenty-first Century

Recently, the influence and visibility of patriotism have increased notably in some parts of the world, not the least in Europe. Historically, the two concepts of cosmopolitanism and patriotism have been tied closely together, though they do not always seem to have such a close connection today—indeed, they do not seem to have much in common at all. The cosmopolitan hospitality and openness are threatened in times with more intense migration and mobility. Since the end of the Cold War, with the renaissance of the theoretical debate on cosmopolitanism, cosmopolitanism has often been supposed to be acquainted with human rights. It has, as mentioned above, been criticised for its universalism, as its attempts to include everybody in a similar way might even be oppressive. Individuals or groups with wishes and needs other than those that universalism presupposes might not be recognised and are therefore made invisible (Mouffe 2005). In a situation with much migration and mobility, often caused by conflicts and climate change, the weaknesses of universal rights such as the UN Declaration of Human Rights prove the strength in Arendt's argument about how homelessness and statelessness also imply rightlessness.

In the early twenty-first century, patriotism in Sweden tends to be understood as nationalism, or perhaps even as more nationalistic than nationalism. We have seen how patriotism has been understood differently in the older Swedish encyclopedias, and how it seems to have been invisible around 1990 outside nationalist circles. We have also remarked that there is an attempt to 'reclaim' patriotism to define it in a more neutral way, as love of country without hating what is not your country.

Until recently, it was not common for a Swede to proclaim herself a patriot. The word 'patriot' was associated with right-wing ideologies during large parts of the last century. A search on the Swedish Internet indicates that today 'patriot' is a word that has been picked up by the right-wing nationalists in Sweden. It has been associated with 'white power' and negative attitudes towards persons that are considered as having no Swedish background as well as towards immigrants. The word 'patriot' has thus been more or less monopolised by the far right—for example, through the name of their website, Patriot. Patriotism has been awakened through the fear of threats from the outside. The Swedish non-profit Foundation Expo, founded in 1995, which aims to prevent right-wing extremism and racism, not least through collaboration with schools, have a definition of patriotism on their website where they underline that a patriot is not the same as a nationalist. They can thus be said to try to reclaim the older and international definition of patriotism.

Patriotism in the twenty-first century is often associated with European populism rather than with Enlightenment cosmopolitanism. A quick browse on the Internet shows the patriot to be a Eurosceptic who is against immigration and international co-operation. It does not seem to have much to do with cosmopolitanism or globalisation. Rather than being international, it refers to right-wing populists, Euroscepticism and hostility towards strangers. However, does patriotism have to be placed to the right on a right–left scale, even if it has been put on such a scale throughout history? Patriotism could just as well be used by the left, as it could imply a reference to a belonging to something bigger than yourself—for example, your country—since the left at the same time has the idea of belonging to groups as an important part of its ideological foundation, be it a group defined by class, gender or ethnicity. British MP Lisa Nandy argues that identity is set by the things we have in common and that this is also the basis of patriotism. She suggests that patriotism could be a force for good or bad, which seems to be a fair statement, as long as we know what patriotism is. Twentieth-century use of the concept of patriotism has certainly contributed to its problematic status in Europe today, a mounting problematic, in which there also seems to be a division between East and West.

4.6 Conclusion

Migration and mobility are important core conditions and probably eternal aspects of human life. Since the turn of the current century, several Western countries, and not only them, have experienced a tougher attitude towards migration and strangers. Holding faithfully to the ideal of being international as well as ethical and humanitarian, Sweden accepted many refugees in 2015. In fact, together with Germany and in relation to its population, it was the most generous country in Europe in this respect. But the generosity and openness suddenly stopped. A radically lower number of refugees was accepted, and in November 2015 temporary border controls were introduced by Sweden on the border to Denmark, the main point of entry for refugees coming to Sweden. This was a drastic solution since the Nordic countries had been in a passport union since the 1950s. Simultaneously, the nationalists, or the Swedish patriots, gained more political influence through right-wing parties and groups. The values that are associated with cosmopolitanism and human rights are threatened in debates and in politics, and the populist platform is becoming stronger.

The aim of this text has been to discuss the relation between patriotism, cosmopolitanism and human rights in relation to contemporary migration and mobility. With the help of Ellen Key and the Swedish encyclopedias, the aim was to show how the meaning of patriotism and nationalism may change over time and how the relation between patriotism and cosmopolitanism also has changed drastically over time, from dependency to opposition. According to Key, and perhaps from her readings of Fichte, patriotism is a strong emotion that seems to be necessary in order to experience deeper engagement, in oneself as well as in others. It is also necessary for peaceful international development. For Kant, as well as for many other Enlightenment thinkers, patriotism and cosmopolitanism are mutually dependent—and an image to illustrate this is the Hamburg commemorative coin, where patriotism and cosmopolitanism literally are two sides of the same coin. However, for Kant, cosmopolitanism is not emotional or philanthropic but belongs to pure right. The difficulty of universal rights was demonstrated by the UN Declaration of Human Rights where there was no guarantee for the rights of the *sans-papiers* or non-citizens. The gap between human rights and citizen rights makes it obvious that those who most of all need protection of their human rights do not always have the position and right as citizens that would guarantee them.

Openness towards strangers is a cosmopolitan ideal that is tied to the idea of universal human rights. According to Kant it is a right and not philanthropy. And cosmopolitan ideals are still alive, such as those founded on the universal Enlightenment ideals of equality, human rights, citizenship and an experience of belonging to the world. The universalist thinking is problematic, but these concepts also have qualities that can be said to be existential, ethical, political and even cultural and social. Even in the eighteenth century in Europe, there were different kinds of cosmopolitanisms—and also contradictory meanings of them: from the arrogant, self-centred individual traveller, who might have seen himself as a man of the world, to the theory that embraces all of mankind in the idea of the cosmopolitan. These are all aspects that Kant put forward in his cosmopolitanism. It is from this foundation that the perspective of human rights gets involved, when he introduces the cosmopolitan right, in an attempt to insert it into a system of rights.

Even if there seems to be quite a distance between patriotism and cosmopolitanism today, we know this has not always been the case. On the contrary, we know that the two concepts have often been related. The contemporary horizon of what is visible from a patriotic perspective seems not to cover cosmopolitanism. But if we consider patriotism from Key's perspective, as a constructive platform that opens up for a world outside oneself and an entity far from the aggressive ideology of nationalism, it could well encourage or be a part of a cosmopolitan perspective. Strong patriotism does not have to weaken migrants. A love of country could rather contribute to the will to strengthen values such as human rights and cosmopolitanism. Perhaps more Swedes in general should call themselves patriots, perhaps such a statement of love of country would contribute to a willingness to develop a cosmopolitan right of foreigners to have a right to hospitality, and perhaps also to develop this into political rights so that they no longer have to be in the limbo situation of the *sans-papiers*.

A critical conceptual history must be prepared to reflect upon its own self-understanding. Problematising concepts which now tend to be considered with scepticism can turn out to enable a new understanding of the past as much as of the present, thereby claiming the ground for new perspectives and courses of action. When situated in a different context, many concepts offer new perspectives on questions that still command our engagement. The historicisation of concepts is not merely of historical value; it must form the basis for any attempt to problematise the contemporary world in which we live (Lettevall and Petrov 2014, 23). Such a reflexive conceptual history might perhaps also be a tool for the making of the future. It is a bold thought, but by placing the conceptual past in new contexts, new horizons for the future might be found, and new ways forward may emerge. The former and mutual dependence between cosmopolitanism and patriotism has changed over time. It might be time to flip the coin of cosmopolitanism and patriotism again and see if it is possible that the one would exist better together with the other.

Bibliography

Arendt, H. (1976). *The origins of totalitarianism*. New York: Harvest.

Chrom Jacobsen, M. (2011). *Three conceptions of human rights*. Malmö: NSU Press.

Kant, I. (2006). Toward Perpetual Peace. In P. Kleingeld, (Ed.), *Toward perpetual peace and other writings on politics, peace, and history* (trans: Colclasure, D. L.) (pp. 67–109). New Haven and London: Yale University Press.

Kemp, P, (2013). *Verdensborgeren som paedagogisk ideal: Paedagogisk filosofi för det 21. Århundrede*. Copenhagen: Hans Reitzel.

Key, E. (1914). *Kriget, freden och framtiden*. Lund: Ph. Lindstedts universitetsbokhandel.

Kleingeld, P. (1999). Six varieties of cosmopolitanism in late eighteenth-century Germany. *Journal of the History of Ideas, 60,* 505–524.

Kleingeld, P. (2003). Kant's cosmopolitan patriotism. *Kant-Studien, 94,* 299–316.

Kleingeld, P. (2012). *Kant and cosmopolitanism: The philosophical ideal of world citizenship*. Cambridge: Cambridge UP.

Koselleck, R. (1972). *Einleitung*. In O. Brunner, W. Conze, & R. Koselleck (Ed.), *Geshichtliche grundbegriffe: Historisches lexikon zur politisch-sozialen sprache in Deutschland* (Vol. 1, pp. xiii–xxvii), Stuttgart: Ernst Klett Verlag.

Koselleck, R. (1979). *Vergangene zukunft: zur semantik geschichtlichen Zeiten*. Frankfurt am Main: Suhrkamp.

Lettevall, R. (2011). 'On the historicity of concepts: The examples of patriotism and cosmopolitanism in Ellen Key'. In H. Ruin, & A. Ers (Ed.), *Rethinking time: Essays on history, memory and representation* (pp. 179–188). Stockholm: Södertörn Philosophical Studies 9.

Lettevall, R., Somsen, G., & Widmalm, S. (2012). *Neutrality in twentieth-century Europe, intersections of science, culture, and politics after the first world war*. New York: Routledge.
Lettevall, R. (2013). Cosmopolitanism in practice: Perspectives on the Nansen passports. In U. Ziemer, *East European diasporas, migration and cosmopolitanism* (pp. 13–24). London, New York: Routledge.
Lettevall, R, & Petrov, K. (2014). *Critique of cosmopolitan reason: Timing and spacing the concept of world citizenship* (pp. 3–34). Oxford: Peter Lang.
Mouffe, C. (2005). *On the political*. London: Routledge.
Nationalencyklopedin. (1994). (Vol. 15, p. 14). Höganäs: Bokförlaget Bra Böcker.
Nationalencyklopedin. (2016–04–01). *Patriot*. https://www.ne.se/uppslagsverk/encyklopedi/lång/patriot. Accessed 29 May 2019.
Nordisk familjebok. (1911). (Vol. 14). Stockholm: Nordisk familjeboks förlag. Col. 1133
Nordisk familjebok. (1915). (Vol. 21) Stockholm: Nordisk familjeboks förlag. Col. 243–244
Svenska Akademiens Ordbok. (1952). Lund: Gleerupska universitetsbokhandeln. Col. P488.
Viroli, M. (1995). *For love of country: An essay on patriotism and nationalism*. Oxford: Clarendon Press.

Rebecka Lettevall, Ph.D. is Associate Professor of Intellectual History and Dean at Malmö University. Her research embraces Immanuel Kant's political philosophy and critical conceptual history. She has published in the areas of German idealism and concepts such as peace, cosmopolitanism and neutrality. Among her publications are *Critique of Cosmopolitan Reason: Timing and Spacing the Concept of World Citizenship* (2014). She is currently working on cosmopolitanism as utopia.

Part II
Religious and Cultural Challenges in the Post-Migratory Phase

Chapter 5
No Future for the Palestinians in Lebanon: Power Sharing, Political Stagnancy and Securitisation of (Palestinian) Migration

Lars Erslev Andersen

Abstract This chapter investigates three questions related to Palestine refugees in Lebanon: (1) What is their current situation, (2) how are they affected by the Syrian refugee crisis in Lebanon, and (3) what is their perspectives for the future? After a brief sketch of the history of Lebanon, the political situation is analysed, where it is concluded that the political elite primarily is occupied by power politics among themselves. This has a consequence that the governance system is almost politically paralysed when it comes to developing necessary social and economic reforms, leaving it to Lebanese society and the international donor community to handle the refugee crisis. Based on field studies in Lebanon, including in Palestine refugee camps, the situation for Palestinians is described and the 'Palestinian protection gap' in terms of human rights is discussed. The chapter concludes that the Syrian crisis has resulted in significant social, economic and political pressure on Palestinians, making their situation concerning protection critical. It further concludes that even if Lebanon on the surface appears to be a cosmopolitan and liberal society, there exists a grim human rights situation concerning migrants in general and Palestinian refugees in particular. As the perspectives for a two-state solution in the Israeli–Palestinian conflict seems further away than ever, the chapter end with a question: What are the prospects for Palestine refugees?

Keywords Migration · Refugees · Lebanon · Securitisation · UNRWA · UNCHR

5.1 Introduction

Since its creation under the French Mandate after the First World War and its independence after the Second World War, the republic of Lebanon has suffered a series of crises and conflicts, including the civil war 1975–1990 and the Israeli invasions. The reasons behind the many crises are manifold: a sectarian power-sharing system

L. Erslev Andersen (✉)
Danish Institute for International Studies, Copenhagen, Denmark
e-mail: lea@diis.dk

M. C. Jacobsen et al. (eds.), *Cosmopolitanism, Migration and Universal Human Rights*, https://doi.org/10.1007/978-3-030-50645-2_5

that is stipulated in the constitution and its amendments where the 18 public recognised religious confessions are guaranteed political representation. The main groups, the Maronites Christians, the Sunni Muslims and the Shia Muslims are guaranteed executive and parliamentarian power divided between the speaker of parliament (Shia), the prime minister (Sunni) and the president (Christian). This political system, termed 'consociational democracy', has always made Lebanon vulnerable for external manipulation and interference (Lijphart 1969). Great powers such as the USA and France, neighbouring states, Israel and Syria, and regional regimes such as Saudi Arabia and Iran have interfered in Lebanese politics: Saudi Arabia has exploited its good relations with the Sunni Muslims, both in government and radical networks, and Iran keeps close ties to Hezbollah. Israel has invaded Lebanon several times and for years has conducted military operations and attacks on a regular basis, targeting Shia Muslim Hezbollah.

For many years, until the international community forced a withdrawal in 2005, Syria exerted executive power. Until the Palestinian Liberation Organisation (PLO) was forced out in 1982, Palestinian groups were involved in Lebanese politics and contributed to the destabilisation that triggered the civil war in 1975. Palestinian refugees who arrived in 1948 after Israel's Declaration of Independence, which established the State of Israel, are still living in Lebanon: the United Nations (UN) registers 455,000 and around 300,000 are today living in Lebanon where the vast majority live in very poor slum-like conditions in 12 UN-managed refugee camps (UNRWA). Following the Syrian war, more than 1 million Syrians were registered by UNHCR, until 2013 where the Lebanese government banned registration by the UN.

This chapter outline the consequences of the Syrian refugee crisis for the Palestinians in Lebanon. After a brief sketch of the history of the republic, it analyses the political system. It concludes that the political system today has two faces: on the one side, it has developed into a security state where all the elites prioritise keeping their share of power and resources; on the other side, this has led to a paralysed political system where the elites prioritise their own security and prosperity.

The study behind this chapter is based on an academic literature review including reports from donors, UN agencies, human rights organisations and NGOs working with refugees. Further, it is based on a field study in Lebanon followed up by several study trips to Beirut. The first field study took place in spring 2016 and the second in spring the year after. Both times, I was affiliated with the Institute for Migration Studies, Lebanese American University. I conducted fieldwork in the Palestinian refugee camp Bourj al-Barajneh in Beirut. During my field study, I conducted interviews with Palestine refugees, including those who arrived from Syria after the war broke out in 2011. I also visited Syrian settlements in the Beqaa Valley and talked frequently with Syrian refugees working in shops, bars, hotels in Beirut, as well as the Lebanese I met during my stays. Further, I interviewed members of the UNRWA staff, spokespersons from different Palestinian factions, academics, diplomats, etc.

In order to keep up to date, I went to Beirut for shorter trips in 2018 and again in April and May 2019.[1]

While the US and Israeli policy ever more self-confidently erodes any possibility of establishing a Palestinian state in the future, it raises the question: what are the prospects for the millions of stateless Palestinian people living in the West Bank, Gaza, Jordan and Lebanon? The USA, Israel and probably other so-called liberal states in the international community would see the solution in consisting of the Arab states integrating and offering the Palestinians citizenship; however, looking at the reality in Lebanon, that solution look like a Fata Morgana (Beilin 2019).

An ever-increasing problem in the Arab countries of the Middle East is that the situation of Palestinian stateless people continues to create tensions, human suffering and social unrest, leaving the Palestinians with no sustainable solution in sight or indeed no future at all. This tragic situation is a result of the impotence of the international community to settle a solution for the Palestinian conflict and the political unwillingness of the Arab regimes to contribute with real support for the Palestinians. It is also a consequence of the incompetence of the Palestinian leadership in Gaza and the West Bank, and especially of the US support of the Israeli annexation policy of the Palestinian territories. Until recently, Israel conducted the so-called Jewish settlement policy, which more accurately means a colonisation policy of the West Bank. After US recognition of full Israeli sovereignty over Jerusalem in December 2017, it has become still clearer that neither the USA nor Israel seeks a two-state solution. The two-state solution has so far meant a divided Jerusalem as the capital for Israel and the Palestinians, and the West Bank and Gaza as Palestinian territory. This solution has been taken off the table by the USA and Israel, but it remains unclear what the alternative solution will look like (Miller and Sokolski 2019).

Still, it seems that the only way the USA and Israel imagine a solution for the Palestinian refugee problem is by seeing them integrated into the Arab states. Analysing migration, security and the situation for the Palestinians in Lebanon and the region, it becomes clear that this is a viable solution (Beilin 2019).

5.2 Cosmopolitanism and Migration in Lebanon

On the surface Beirut gives the visitor an impression of cosmopolitan life.[2] The public discourse in Beirut tells a cosmopolitan story about a multicultural city that

[1]I want to thank the Danish Institute in Damascus for substantial funding of my fieldwork and study trips.

[2]As a city, Beirut was built and developed mostly by migrants: by Armenians arriving after the massacres in Turkey at the ending of the First World War, by the French who mandated Lebanon until its independence in 1946, and by the Palestinians who arrived in 1948 and the Shia Muslims from the South who escaped Israeli occupation of South Lebanon until 2000 (The Guardian 2016). Today an unknown number of migrants from Asia and Africa live in Beirut, and Syrians have been migrating to and from Lebanon since the end of the civil war in 1990. Finally, Syrians have arrived, escaping the civil war in Syria, which broke out in 2011.

gives space to the secular, the modern and the Westernized as well as to the religious, the fundamentalists and all the other groups with different cultural backgrounds that emerge between these two poles. Of course, there is a reality behind this cosmopolitan narrative: women do not need to cover their bodies and hair—but they are welcome to do so. There is no shortage of bars and restaurants serving alcohol. However, digging a little bit deeper under the surface of the cosmopolitan aura of Beirut, another side of the city reveals itself: a side impregnated with sectarianism, clientelism, traditional sexual relations, tribal structures combined with paternalistic power performance, and racism (Seidman 2012; Human Right Watch 2019).

Established 70 years ago, the Palestinian refugee camps have developed into small settlements—rather shanty towns—within the city. Bourj al-Barajneh, for example, covers 1 sq. km and houses approximately 42,000 inhabitants. About half of those are refugees arrived from Syria. Some of these are Syrian Palestinians but most are Syrians nationals who rent small rooms in the camp partly because they are cheaper compared with the prices outside the camps. This is partly because they hide themselves from the Lebanese authorities because they are in Lebanon without being formally registered. Approximately half of the estimated one and a half million Syrian refugees in Lebanon are for different reasons also not registered either by the authorities or by the UN. In Beirut, they live in camps, sometimes in slum-like conditions, often with a whole family in a small room. Social dumping and an explosion in unemployment together with rising housing prices and inflation increasingly challenge life in Lebanon. All these problems were making life in Lebanon hard before the Syrian war but now many Lebanese are blaming the refugees for making things worse (Dionigi 2016; Eldawy 2019; Erslev Andersen 2016; Erslev Andersen 2017).

5.3 Political Paralysis

After the First World War, Lebanon came under the control of the French Mandate of Lebanon and Syria. Following military conflicts, the French carved out what is today the territory of Lebanon. In 1943, a newly elected government abolished the French Mandate, but allied forces kept the new republic occupied during the Second World War, and Lebanon only obtained its independence in 1946 (Fieldhouse 2006). However, from 1943 the establishment of Lebanon as a multi-confessional republic took place based on an unwritten agreement, 'The National Pact', which divided executive power and political institutions on confessional lines. The idea behind establishing the new republic as multi-confessional, by giving different groups and constituencies a predetermined representation in government and parliament (known as consociationalism), was to secure for all groups in the highly divided Lebanese society a share of the power and the ruling of the country, thus avoiding internal conflicts or even civil war. The philosophy was that by giving all publicly recognised confessions access to political power through their leaders who would represent the confessional communities, tensions would ease between the groups.

As conflicts arose first in 1958 and again in 1975, leading to a 15-year long civil war, the system had not really fulfilled its aim. Foreign interventions and interference from Syria, Israel, Iran, the USA and France, as well as the presence of hundreds of thousands of Palestinian refugees, including the leadership of the PLO, contributed also to intensifying the conflicts leading to the civil war. However, negotiations in the Saudi Arabian city Taif in 1989 paved the way for an agreement that ended the war in 1990. With some significant amendments—for example, representation in parliament was changed from the original 6:5 in favour of the Christians to a 1:1 divide between Christians and Muslims, and the executive power of the president was reduced—the consociational system continued to constitute the basis for the post-war political system (Lijphart 1969; Erslev Andersen 2017; Vaughan 2018).

The Taif agreement also stipulated the withdrawal of foreign forces, but Israel occupied South Lebanon until 2000, while Syria had forces on the ground until 2005. The year before France and the USA succeeded in drafting a resolution, the UN Security Council passed that act and demanded a withdrawal of Syrian troops. Following the assassination of Prime Minister Rafiq a-Hariri in a bomb explosion in Beirut in February 2005, large demonstrations filled the streets of Beirut demanding the withdrawal of Syrian forces, which happened later that year.

The Taif agreement further demanded all militias to disarm, but the Shia Muslim party Hezbollah, which Iran established during the civil war, refused and today is militarily stronger than the Lebanese Armed Forces. The outcome of the crisis and large demonstrations that followed the assassination of Rafiq al-Hariri in 2005 was the formation of two main blocs in Lebanese politics named after the days of the demonstrations. The first, the 'March 8 bloc', was comprised of Hezbollah, (Shia Muslim) Amal and the Free Patriotic Movement, a Maronite Christian group headed by the current president Michel Aoun. The second, the 'March 14 bloc', was headed by the Sunni Muslim Saad al-Hariri, son of the murdered prime minister, leader of the Future Movement, and supported by the (Christian) Lebanese Forces (LF) and the Druze Progressive Socialist Party.

Tensions between the Sunni Muslims headed by Saad al-Hariri and Hezbollah culminated in a direct confrontation in 2008, but eased with an agreement in Doha in Qatar. From then on, it was clear that none of the blocs had sufficient strength to totally dominate the other, and thus a kind of national consensus on security was developed. The priority for the power-sharing elite, former warlords from the civil war, was to sustain their own power and secure their share of resources and income in the state. The consequence is that society is left to its own devices and private initiatives in solving many social and economic problems that haunt the ordinary Lebanese people, be it reliable electricity and water supply, access to health and education services, unemployment, or problems related to the presence of Syrian and Palestinian refugees. Add to that widespread corruption and a *wasta* (personal network) system, which is an unavoidable precondition for persons navigating through the bureaucratic labyrinths of the public institutions to obtain necessary public authorised documents. The only legitimacy the elites have in the eyes of the people stems from the fact that nobody in Lebanese society wants to see Lebanon pushed into a new civil war (ICG 2010; Fakhoury 2016).

Governance in Lebanon is trapped in a situation where the elite occupies itself with internal power struggles, while necessary reforms step into the uncertain future. Several postponements of parliamentary elections are another example: in 2013, the reason for postponement was disagreement on a new electoral law, and the reason in 2014 was the complicated negotiations to find a new president as the term of the current president ran out. The leaders spent two years discussing what many right from the beginning had anticipated the result would be, namely that Hezbollah's candidate Michel Aoun would become the new president while Saad al-Hariri became Prime Minister 2016. Then discussion of the electoral law was again put on the agenda with the intent of changing the 'winner takes it all system' with proportional representation. However, this could not happen without setting some limitations on the proportionality in order to secure the representation of the established parties' candidates and avoid too many gains from independent candidates. At last, in June 2017 they agreed on the new election law and scheduled 6 May 2018 as the day for the parliamentary election—9 years after the last one. Clearly, using time on these discussions left little energy to solve the social and economic problems in Lebanon.

The election took place as scheduled, Hezbollah together with Amal got their anticipated victory and in the new parliament were able to bloc all legislation they do not approve of. Saad al-Hariri and his Future Movement lost seats, as expected, and few independents made it to the parliament—and those who did do not have much influence. So politics continue as usual: big quarrels on a daily basis indicating vast political disagreements, postponing necessary reforms into a distant future but sticking together when it comes to serious threats against the power-sharing structure.

This is how the system functions: political, economic and social reforms are postponed because, if implemented, they pose the risk of tilting the balance of power among the political elites. When this system is threatened—e.g. by political opposition, external interference, jihadism or migration—the elite cooperate on countering the threat, transforming the republic into a hard-core security state (Yahya 2017). For the Palestinians, the consequence is that their situation becomes further worsened, pressing them into hopeless spaces of exception.

5.4 The Protection Gap and Palestinians in Lebanon

Following the war after the establishment of Israel (Nakba), the UN General Assembly passed Resolution 194 (III) (AR 194) December 1948. Paragraph 11 states that the UN 'resolves that the refugees wishing to return to their homes and live at peace with their neighbours should be permitted to do so at the earliest practicable date, and that compensation should be paid for the property of those choosing not to return and for loss of or damage to property which, under principles of international law or in equity, should be made good by the Government or authorities responsible'. These words constitute the Palestinian *right-of-return* principle that, after more than 70 years, has still not been realised and with little likelihood of ever being realised. Because the Palestinian refugee problem is seen by the UN and the international community as *temporary*, the UN legal framework on the Palestinian conflict is anachronistic. Following AR 194, the UN established the United Nations Conciliation Commission for Palestine (UNCCP) mandated with the task of realising the 'right of return' or compensation as stipulated in the resolution. This basically would consist of solving the Israeli–Palestinian conflict, establishing a Palestinian state and presenting a choice for those registered as Palestinian refugees to be resettled in Palestine or receive compensation. UNCCP has never succeeded and today no one really believes it could have fulfilled its mandate then or is capable of doing so now or in the future.[3]

As a result, the so-called temporary refugee problem is increasing day by day. According to the UN agency assisting the Palestinian refugees—the United Nation Relief and Work Agency for Palestinians (UNRWA)—Palestine refugees are defined as 'persons whose normal place of residence was Palestine during the period 1 June 1946 to 15 May 1948, and who lost both home and means of livelihood as a result of the 1948 conflict. UNRWA services are available to all those living in its area of operations who meet this definition, who are registered with the Agency and who need assistance. The descendants of Palestine refugee males, including adopted children, are also eligible for registration. When the Agency began operations in 1950, it was responding to the needs of about 750,000 Palestine refugees. Today, some 5 million Palestine refugees are eligible for UNRWA services. UNRWA began maintaining Palestine refugees' registration records in May 1950. By the time the initial registration process closed, in June 1952, we had registered 914,000 out of 1,000,000 Palestine refugees. We reopened the registration process in 1992, and now, Palestine refugees can register with UNRWA irrespective of their current place or country of residence' (UNRWA Registration 2019).

With more than 5 million refugees, the Palestinian refugee problem in terms of numbers is the second largest refugee problem in the world—and in today's media, maybe the most ignored. The number is steadily increasing and will continue to do so until a sustainable solution to the Israeli–Palestinian conflicts is implemented, making it possible for the Palestinians to return to the state of Palestine. Only then will their registration by the UNRWA cease. Add to this number an unknown but high number of non-registered Palestinian refugees and an even higher number of Palestinians registered by host states, but not by UNRWA either because they are living outside UNRWA work areas or for other reasons that possibly do not apply to UNRWA criteria. That is why a special terminology has evolved: 'Palestine refugee' is used for those registered by UNRWA while state-registered and non-registered are called 'Palestinian refugees'.

---

[3]The UNCCP still exists as the only UN agency with the task of solving the Palestinian refugee problem by finding a sustainable solution to the Israeli–Palestinian conflict even though it has not produced anything for decades. As Michael Kagan notes in his article on the so called 'protection gap' debate: 'Every year, the General Assembly goes through the ritual of noting "with regret that the UNCCP has been unable to find means of achieving progress" in implementing Resolution 194's provisions for refugee return and compensation, and then asks the UNCCP "to continue exerting efforts" and "to report" the following year' (Kagan, 2009, 517; cf. Goddard, 2009).

Yet the Palestinian refugee problem is treated by the international community as a special and temporary problem. While all other refugees are handled by the UN Refugee Agency (UNHCR) under the provisions of the 1951 UN *Convention Relating to the Status of Refugees* and its 1967 *Protocol*, the Palestinian refugees are exclusively handled by the 'paper tiger' UNCCP and by the UNRWA mandate. While UNHCR thus works on basis of the legal definitions of the Convention, 'UNRWA lacks a legally ratified definition of its mandate. The General Assembly has never established a uniform definition of "Palestine refugee". UNRWA's "working definition" of a Palestine refugee was developed by the Agency for the purposes of determining eligibility for services. This is why it contains an economic element (loss of livelihood), but as a result it is not a comprehensive set of criteria defining the status of a Palestinian refugee. The working definition is also inherently ill-suited for identifying people with current international protection needs because it is based on past events rather than current threats', as pointed by Kagan (2009, 525).

This constitutes what has been labeled *the protection gap* concerning Palestine refugees. Obviously, the UNHCR is on more solid ground when it seeks to confront host governments that might violate or are unwilling to carry out responsibilities towards refugees than UNRWA is—even if UNCHR, for good reason, tries avoiding conflicts with host governments. 'In that regard Palestinian refugees are granted revocable privileges but no rights. As a result, they are less protected under international law than any of their counterparts in the world. This is why in UNRWA zones Palestinian refugees can be forced to live in camp, prohibited from working or cannot benefit from family reunification' (van Engeland 2011).

Thus, the reality is that no UN agency is mandated and working on solving the Palestinian problem; there is also a protection gap because of the Palestinian exemption from 1951 Convention regime. In his analysis of this problem, Michael Kagan, Senior Fellow at the Center for Migration and Refugee Studies at the American University in Cairo, differentiates the protection need into three areas:

"1. Promoting durable solutions
2. Promoting the general welfare of Palestine refugees
3. Individual rights protection." (Kagan 2009, 520).

He concludes that the most acute problem is the lack of protection of individual rights. We can add here that this lack has increased significantly during the crisis following the uprising and war in Syria. Of course, he notes the overall and overwhelming problem of the lack of attempts by the international community to press for a sustainable solution of the Israeli–Palestinian problem. Let us consider the three areas of gaps in protection.

Since the breakdown in 2000 of the so-called Oslo process, attempts to restart a peace process under the auspices of a quartet consisting of the United States, Russia, the EU and the UN began in Madrid in 2002. The idea was that negotiations should lead to a two-state solution establishing a Palestinian state and a negotiated solution to the Palestinian refugee problem. As late as September 2016 a statement from the Quartet concluded that no progress has been made in that respect and that development on the ground was making a two-state solution still more difficult to reach (Quartet 2016). A security barrier built by Israel separating the West Bank and Israel and so-called security roads, enabling Jewish settlers to move from the settlements to Israel. These 'developments' has reduced the Palestinian territory on the West Bank by 60% and Israel continues on daily basis to annex more territory. The Quartet coordinates a range of projects supporting economic and other kinds of development programmes in the Palestinian Authority in the West Bank and Gaza, but these efforts take place at the same time as a still worsening situation in the Palestinian territories due to the de facto Israeli occupation and military campaigns. Since the disastrous war in Gaza in 2014—which resulted in more than 2200 Palestinians killed; over 270,000 displaced persons; 138 schools, 26 health facilities and almost 900 private homes destroyed, and 90,000 homes damaged; infrastructure, water supply and power stations bombed; and an estimated $4–6 billion needed in rebuilding costs—no progress in establishing a Palestinian state that could implement the provisions of AR 194 has been seen (OCHA 2015). The war ended with a ceasefire agreement stating that the Israeli blockage of Gaza should be lifted, but this has not happened yet and the living conditions in Gaza have steadily worsened since the signing of the agreement.

5.5 The No Future Perspectives Has Sparked a Crisis in the Palestinian Identity

Palestinian identity is intimately connected to Palestine as the homeland for Palestinians, and thus the Palestinian problem will not be solved until a Palestinian state is established in the Palestinian territories. That is the reason why Palestinians insist on the definition of the refugee problem as being temporary. Not until all Palestinians will have the free choice of staying where they live, e.g. as citizens in Denmark, in Lebanon, or elsewhere, or returning to a state of Palestine comprising at least the territory of Gaza and the West Bank, which as defined by the June borders of 1967 would fulfil the rights of the Palestinians.

This situation has created a polarised duality in the narrative on Palestinian identity between 'right of return' and settlement (*tawtin*) in host countries, especially in the Middle East. The Arab host countries have exploited this dual narrative by arguing that giving Palestinians full social rights or even citizenship would de facto support Israel policy and thereby undermine the principle of the right of return. Thus, the Arab host countries have developed very different approaches to the dilemma of upholding the right-of-return principle and integrating the Palestinians into their societies with social rights including access to the job market and public services (Bitter Lemons 2011).

Lebanon in particular has exploited the right-of-return dogma to reject integration of Palestinians into Lebanese society using a rather unpleasant rhetoric. Many in Lebanon still accuse the Palestinians of causing the civil war in Lebanon and perceive them as an alien element in Lebanese society. This very unpleasant Lebanese narrative of the Palestinians in Lebanon also shapes the understanding, political rhetoric and policy concerning Syrian refugees. Even if the Arab states differ on the dilemma between right of return versus settlement, they agree that any new interpretation concerning settlement should reject all forms of settlement that conflict with the special circumstances of the Arab host countries as stated in the Arab Peace Initiative (the Saudi Arabia plan) ratified by the Arab League in 2002 and again in 2007. In reality, this gives the Arab host countries a free hand to handle the Palestine refugee problem the way that suits them the best.

5.6 The Right of Return Living on in the Hearts—not in the Real World

The right-of-return principle has also played an important role in Palestinian negotiations with Israel. Thus, the Declaration of Principles signed by the PLO and Israel in Washington in 1993, followed by the so-called Oslo process, excluded the 1948 Palestine refugees in the establishment of the Palestinian Authority, which created a large Palestinian opposition against the peace negotiations both from secular and nationalistic Palestinian factions in especially Lebanon and Syria. The PLO approach, represented by Yasser Arafat's Fatah was pragmatic. Other PLO factions as well as the Islamic groups considered the Declaration of Principles and the Oslo process as treason against the Palestinian course and an undermining of AR 194.

Among the Palestinians, the interpretation of the right-of-return principle has undergone historical changes. Based on fieldwork in refugee camps in West Bank, Lebanon and Jordan, Sophie Richter-Devroe, lecturer at the Institute of Arab and Islamic Studies, University of Exeter, has analysed the changes in discourse. She describes the development from the Nakba generation who tend to long for a permanent return to their homes and villages of origin, thus having a radical claim on the right-of-return principle that excludes *tawtin*, to a middle generation, stressing human and social rights and international law as a platform for gaining better conditions in host countries, to, finally, younger generations who—as Richter-Devroe notes—formulate the most 'innovative political imaginaries on return' (Richter-Devroe 2013, 92). According to my own fieldwork in the camps in Lebanon, I found among the young Palestinians even more incitement to an innovative approach, which sometimes created loud quarrels between the generations and different political communities, which I witnessed both in the camps and seminars (e.g. at the Palestine Institute in Beirut). The arrival of Syrian refugees further influenced the narratives of identity of the Palestinians in Lebanon. From being aliens, they became the 'old refugees' (compared with the 'new' Syrian refugees) that the Lebanese have been used to and almost thought of as part of Lebanese society, in contrast to the Syrians who were considered 'the temporaries'. This gave Palestinians some hope of being more accepted, but this has not happened.

The Syrian Palestinians arriving at the camps in Lebanon were shocked by the living conditions and by the severe restrictions on Palestinians in Lebanon. They did not want to live under such conditions and were motivated to move to other places with better conditions, which they imagined they would find in Europe, in particular in Germany and Scandinavia. This attitude also had influence on the young Lebanese Palestinians who, on the one hand, lost hope for a return to Palestine and, on the other hand, did not believe that conditions concerning social, human rights and living conditions would improve in Lebanon. They keep longing for Palestine in their hearts as an important part of their identity. Even if they lost hope for de facto right of return, they insist on keeping it as an integrated part of their identity in a postmodern narrative that sometimes can be difficult to comprehend by the Nakba generation.

5.7 Conclusion

On the surface, Lebanon appears cosmopolitan and liberal with a vivid modern lifestyle. Looking beneath the surface, another side is disclosed: the apparently free and liberated Lebanese women are often trapped in very traditional roles dominated by a powerful macho culture; migrant workers from Africa and Asia are treated as second-rank people; racism is widespread; LBGT people are often not tolerated and are discriminated against. As such, the liberal cosmopolitan surface hides a rather grim reality when it comes to human rights (Seidman 2012; Human Right Watch 2019).

As society and state are almost entirely constructed and developed by refugees, the present Lebanese state provides an ironic paradox as one of the most migrant-hostile states in the international community. Lebanon has not ratified the 1951 UN *Convention Relating to the Status of Refugees* and *Protocol.* Lebanon has denied Palestine refugees a whole range of basic rights and forced them to live in 'spaces of exception' beyond the rule of law, protection and opportunities to live a decent live, and the only solution to the Syrian refugee problem is to have them sent back as fast as possible. The prevalent discourse in Lebanon on refugees, 'new' and 'old', is securitisation. That has not prevented the Lebanese government from begging the international donor community for aid to assist it in handling the migration crisis even with reference to the Palestinians in Lebanon—an amount the prime minister shamelessly doubles when he speaks at donor conferences. The reality is that the government in Lebanon takes a share of the aid, which ends up in the pockets of the elites, and otherwise leaves it to the international community to handle the challenges for refugees with projects financed by international donors.

The Syrian migration crisis in Lebanon has worsened the situation for the Palestinians, and Lebanese society and state show no signs of willingness to ease the restrictions put on the Palestine refugees—on the contrary. This tragic situation develops at the same time as Israel and the USA openly undermines all conditions for a sustainable solution to the so-called Israeli–Palestinian conflict. The fact is that today there is no hope for the realisation of a Palestinian state. The question is then raised once again: with no Palestinian state, no integration of Palestinians into Lebanon, and surely no chance that the rich states in the international community would offer citizenship to the Palestinians in Lebanon, what are the prospects for these stateless peoples of Palestinian origin who live in tragic conditions that worsen day by day?

Bibliography

Beilin, Y. (2019). *"Why is netanyahu reviving palestinians' 'willing relocation'?* al-Monitor August 26, 2019. https://www.al-monitor.com/pulse/originals/2019/08/israel-palestinians-plo-yasser-arafat-mahmoud-abbas-gaza.html. Accessed 24 Sep 2019.

Bitter Lemons API. (2011). *Refugees: Return or "tawtin"* (Vol. 2, 4 Ed.), February 17, 2011. Accessed 24 Sep 2019.

CNN. (2017). *Oren liebermann: "What you need to know about the israeli settlements"*, 2019/02/03. https://edition.cnn.com/2017/02/01/middleeast/settlements-explainer/index.html. Accessed 24 Sep 2019.

Dionigi, F. (2016). *The syrian refugee crisis in Lebanon: State fragility and social resilience.* London School of Economics and Social Science: Middle East Center.

Economist. (2019). *"Politicians are stoking anti-refugee sentiment in Lebanon", The economist,* 2019/08/22. https://www.economist.com/middle-east-and-africa/2019/08/22/politicians-are-stoking-anti-refugee-sentiment-in-lebanon. Accessed 24 Sep 2019.

Eldawy, D. (2019). *A fragile situation: Will the syrian refugee swell push Lebanon over the edge?* Migration Information Source, February 21, 2019.

Erslev Andersen, L. (2016). *The neglected. Palestinian refugees in Lebanon and the syrian refugee crisis, DIIS Report 2016:12.* Copenhagen and Beirut: DIIS—LAU.

Erslev Andersen, L. (2017). Arrested development in Beirut: Migration, security and dilemmas of consociational democracy. *International Relations and Diplomacy, 5*(December 2017), 594–606.

Fakhoury, T. (2016). Lebanon's consociational politics in post-2011 Middle East. In M. Felsch & M. Wählish (Eds.), *Lebanon and the Arab uprisings. In the eye of the hurricane.* London: Routledge.

Fawaz, M. (2007). Beirut: The city as body politic, *ISIM Review 20* (pp. 22–23). (Autumn 2007).

Fawaz, M. (2014). The politics of property: Hezbollah's reconstruction of haret hreik (Beirut, Lebanon) as case study. *International Journal of Urban and Regional Research, 38*(3), May 2014.

Fieldhouse, D. K. (2006). *Western imperialism in the Middle East 1914–1958.* London: Oxford University Press.

Goddard, B. (2009). UNHCR and the international protection of Palestinian refugees. *Refugee Survey Quarterly, 28*(2–3), 475–510.

Hanafi, S., Chaaban, J., & Seyfert, K. (2012). Social exclusion of palestinian refugees in Lebanon: Reflections on the mechanisms that cement their persistent poverty. *Refugee Survey Quarterly, 31*(1), 34–53.

Human Right Watch. (2019). *Lebanon: No justification for LGBT crackdown,* News HRW 2019/02/11. https://www.hrw.org/news/2019/02/11/lebanon-no-justification-lgbt-crackdown. Accessed 12 Aug 2019.

ICG. (2010). *Lebanon's politics: The sunni community and hariri's future current.* International crisis group, Middle East report no. 96. May 26, 2010.

Janmyr, M. (2018). UNHCR and the syrian refugee response: negotiating status and registration in Lebanon. *The International Journal of Human Rights, 22*(3), 393–419.

Kagan, M. (2009). Is there really a protection gap? UNRWA's role vis-à-vis palestinian refugees. *Refugee Survey Quarterly, 28*(2–3), 511–530.
Lijphart, A. (1969). Consociational democracy. *World Politics, 21*(2), 207–225.
Miller, A. D. & Richard S. (2019). Trump isn't just reversing obama's foreign policies. He's making it impossible for his successor to go back to them. How the administration will fundamentally damage U.S. national interests for years to come. *Politico Magazine*, April 23, 2019. https://www.politico.com/magazine/story/2019/04/23/trump-obama-foreign-policy-226708. Accessed 12 Aug 2019.
OCHA. (2015). "Gaza one year on: Humanitarian concerns in the aftermath of the 2014 hostilities", OCHA, June 2015. https://gaza.ochaopt.org/2015/06/key-figures-on-the-2014-hostilities/. Accessed 12 Aug 2019.
Quartet. (2016). "Mideast quartet warns that Israeli settlements eroding two-state solution", Reuters 23 Sep 2016. https://www.reuters.com/article/us-israel-palestinians-quartet/mideast-quartet-warns-that-israeli-settlements-eroding-two-state-solution-idUSKCN11T207. Accessed 15 Oct 2019.
Richter-Devroe, S. (2013). Like something sacred: Palestinian refugees narratives on the right of return. *Refugee Survey Quarterly, 32*(2), 92–115.
Seidman, S. (2012). The politics of cosmopolitan beirut. from stranger to the other. *Theory, Culture and Society, 29*(2), 3–36.
The Guardian. (2016). Gustafson, jenny: "To beirut with hope: How the city shaped by refugees makes room for new arrivals". *The Guardian,* February 4 2016. https://www.theguardian.com/cities/2016/feb/04/beirut-lebanon-city-shaped-by-refugees-syria-migration-new-arrivals. Accessed 12 Aug 2019.
The Guardian. (2019). Bethan McKernan: "Syrian refugees forced to destroy their own homes in Lebanon. Demolition ordered by military leaves 5000 families homeless again, says Charity", 30 Jun 2019. https://www.theguardian.com/world/2019/jun/30/syrian-refugees-forced-destroy-own-homes-lebanon. Accessed 12 Aug 2019.
United Nations High Commissioner for Refugees (UNHCR), United Nations Children's Fund (UNICEF) and the United Nations World Food Programme (WFP). (2018). VASyR 2018—Vulnerability assessment of syrian refugees in Lebanon. December 2018. https://data2.unhcr.org/en/documents/download/67380. Accessed 15 Oct 2019.
UNRWA Registration. Eligibility and registration. https://www.unrwa.org/what-we-do/eligibility-registration. Accessed 15 Oct 2019.
Van Engeland, A. (2011). "1st ED: International refugees law and the palestinian issues". *Palestine return centre.* https://prc.org.uk/en/post/1301/1st-ed-international-refugees-law-and-the-palestinian-issues. Accessed 15 Sep 2019.
Vaughan, K. (2018). Who benefits from consociationalism? Religious disparities in lebanon's political system. *Religions, 9*(2), 51–66.
Vohra, A. (2019). "Lebanon is sick and tired of syrian refugees", *Foreign policy*, 31 July 2019. https://foreignpolicy.com/2019/07/31/lebanon-is-sick-and-tired-of-syrian-refugees/. Accessed 15 Oct 2019.
Yahya, M. (2017). *The summer of our discontent: Sects and citizens in Lebanon and Iraq*, Brief Paper June 30, 2017, Carnegie Middle East Center, Beirut. https://carnegieendowment.org/files/Maha_Discontent_Final_Web.pdf. Accessed 15 Oct 2019.

Lars Erslev Andersen is Senior Researcher at the Danish Institute for International Studies, Global Transformations. His research areas are Intellectual History of Terrorism, U.S. Security Policy, Middle East in International Politics, China and the Middle East, and theories of World Order. He has published several books and articles on these subjects as well as on philosophy. His most recent publication concerns Lebanon and migration, China in the Middle East, and a forthcoming book on theories of the World Order. During his researches he stays in Washington, Lebanon and China.

Chapter 6
The Aesthetic Dimension of Human Rights: Sensibility as Fundamental Virtue in Relation to Migration

Carsten Friberg

Abstract This chapter concerns how human rights as a universal principle appear in multiple cultural and political contexts. I consider the question whether there corresponds a universal principle to the idea of a universal audience within a cosmopolitan society or whether we should rather acknowledge that we are confronted with expressions relative to different cultural forms. The focus is notably on the built environment which illustrates the problem and forms a study field of concrete actions. How do political principles, like human rights, emerge in the built environment formed by local traditions of construction, human interaction, climate and materials? The built environment plays a role in forming citizens' relations to each other including the practices of political principles within a community. The built environment is also what every migrant will be confronted with and due to the differences in forms of expression conflicts of misunderstandings are likely to arise unless attention is paid to how the environment communicates. A keyword here is sensibility, a keyword in both communication and aesthetics, and this contribution proposes aesthetics as a discipline for enhancing the awareness of how to apply and implement universal principles, such as human rights, in a complex context.

Keywords Globalisation · Aesthetics · Architecture · Communication · Atmosphere

6.1 Introduction

The problem to be discussed in this chapter is how human rights considered as a principle agreed to across various cultures is identified when it may appear differently in different cultures. The problem is one of interpretation and my focus will be on this difficulty of interpretation in relation to the built environment, that is, when one is confronted with an environment different from one's own and experience difficulties in 'reading' correctly the cultural expressions. Furthermore, I will focus

C. Friberg (✉)
Independent Scholar, Copenhagen, Denmark
e-mail: carsten.friberg@gmail.com

M. C. Jacobsen et al. (eds.), *Cosmopolitanism, Migration and Universal Human Rights*, https://doi.org/10.1007/978-3-030-50645-2_6

on the experiences of migrants who might misinterpret the environment in the host country.

This situation of interpretation should also be seen as a situation of communication and as such it implies both the interpreter and the communicator. We will usually say it is essential for the one addressing an audience to show sensitivity towards it; however, a communicative situation comprises power relations and they concern the extent of the efforts made to meet the audience. One could sometimes insist that it is the audience who must make an effort to understand. We can experience this as a political controversy with regard to migrants. Should an effort be made to meet them or will they have to learn how to interpret the new place? Without addressing the practical or the political implication, my assumption is that successful communication is based on paying attention to the audience addressed, not the least if there is an asymmetry between them as may be the case with migrants placed in a difficult and stressful situation. I will discuss this in relation to aesthetics in Sect. 6.4.

Another issue concerns ideals of communication, namely the belief in a universal audience. This ideal permeates much of the Western philosophical tradition and can explain a lack of sensibility in cross-cultural discourses. This ideal will be discussed below in Sect. 6.2.

My overall focus is on the built environment which illustrates how several appearances of the same idea complicate interpretation and cause misunderstanding. The built environment embodies practices that are familiar to us and we may be aware of them while others are difficult to detect and they may even go unnoticed. Difficulties of interpreting the built environment are a matter of sensorial and perceptual skills which belongs to aesthetics and I will return to this particular understanding of aesthetics in Sect. 6.4.

I will discuss the question within the context of human rights. I take them to be universal intended to acquire general consent within the world community. To what extent this is really the case in practice is an empirical question which lies beyond my interest in philosophical questions about perception and interpretation of human rights as they are embedded in the design of the environment. This embeddedness relates to ideas of globalisation and cosmopolitanism, addressed in Sect. 6.2. How cultural products are expected to be universally received and recognised will be viewed in relation to architecture and design produced for the global market supposedly meeting needs and uses that are globally recognised. In a global economy where business is performed according to an idea of globalisation, physical expressions may become similar everywhere and the design asked to follow functions instead of local differences. We find this explicitly expressed in the International Style in architecture that emerged around 1930. Global consumption, with products available anywhere, easily leads to a practice of global standards believed to be expressed in forms universally interpreted in the same way.

This belief in a universal interpretation conceals a conflict between the universal idea and its different forms of appearance. It is a conflict which constitutes a fundamental experience for Western philosophy: the discrepancy of appearance and being—that the form in which something appears does not fully reflect what it is. A particular problem is whether human rights, despite their universality, may appear differently in different places and whether neglecting these differences makes us falsely believe that something is different from what it really is—for example, when we take a friendly-meant gesture to be hostile because it differs from what we are used to; or when we believe that anyone can identify the idea despite its different appearances, thus expecting that our friendly approach will also be perceived as friendly by others.

In this chapter I suggest linking human rights, migration and architecture together through aesthetics. I build on cosmopolitanism as a universal political idea necessary for a global 'polis' and question at the same time the idea of a universal audience through examples of architectural elements that indicate how something universally agreed can be differently interpreted in different contexts. My use of aesthetics understood as sensorial cognition or perception offers awareness of a sensibility for the particular appearances and such awareness rejects a type of cultural relativism which one could take to be the consequence of the different appearances and interpretations. Instead, the awareness paves the way for a hermeneutic universalism that bridges the particular appearance and the common agreement.

6.2 Making a Virtue Out of Necessity: The Cosmopolitan Citizen

Asked about his origin, the first cosmopolite, Diogenes of Sinope in fourth century BC, answered that he was a citizen of the world, a *kosmopolites*, rather than, as expected, naming the city, *polis*, where he was from—the city Sinope, which we now, paradoxically, use to identify him among the other ancient philosophers named Diogenes.

Perhaps the cosmopolitanism of Diogenes was related to his banishment from his hometown after he adulterated the coinage—the circumstances are not entirely clear from the standard account given by another Diogenes, Diogenes Laertius, written in the third century (1995, 22 ff.). The cosmopolite Diogenes was no longer a citizen of Sinope and he was not granted citizen rights in Athens whereto he moved. Our idea about being a citizen of the world rather than a citizen of a specific city or community may not fit with Diogenes who perhaps made a virtue out of necessity, insisting that if he did not belong to any specific city, he belonged anywhere or he protested against the idea of citizenship as such. Apparently, he and his followers, the Cynics, understood self-sufficiency as something fundamental and that implied a rejection of any political community which is based on mutual dependence on other people (Geuss 2003, 26 ff.).

Despite all the ambiguities about what Diogenes might have thought about cosmopolitanism, we can say that cosmopolitanism is about how belonging to a *polis* is no mere geographical characterisation but has to do with an idea. To know Diogenes as someone coming from Sinope is not to place him on the map on the

Turkish north coast. The Greeks of his age would know he came from a Greek settlement, hence from a *polis* implying a specific political idea. The *polis* is a space for free citizens. It is not enough to talk of a city state only as people gathered together in a city, considered as a population; we will have to understand what it means to be a free citizen since a community of slaves is no *polis*.

The *polis* is a political idea, though this definition is not entirely unambiguous. In his *Politics,* Aristotle does speak about *polis* as both a political idea and any community including those we can find among some animals. It serves no purpose to debate these two understandings of *polis* here; it is enough to note that understanding what it means to be a citizen of the world is not without complications. To say that *polis* is an idea of the political form that must be present in any city of the Greek world implies that moving from Sinope to Athens makes no difference in principle for Diogenes as a Greek. Had he moved to Persepolis, it would have been different; it would not have been the Greek world—or we can say it would have been a different world.

Western philosophy has largely assumed that the world is identical to how the Western mindset conceives it. Greek philosophy is about the Greek world and not applicable to the barbarians, a way of thinking we meet again in the Roman period when it is said that all the world (*universus orbis*) should be taxed in Luke 2:1 as the King James version has it—other translations will choose the more precise 'Roman world', though that is not how the Romans would conceive it.

This pattern of thought follows Western thinking and we would not consider this problematic in the scientific culture of modernity where we expect propositions about nature to be universally applicable. We consider nature a field of necessity necessarily implying an unambiguous and universal language of nature (Toulmin 1992, 105 ff.). The difficulty arises when we apply this ideal to culture, humans and values, assuming that statements are universally valid in political discourses because an enlightened community should, in principle at least, be able to reach an agreement when the discussion is open and rational (see Toulmin 1992, 128). This type of discourses is premised upon assuming the existence of a universal audience, and in these discourses we expect everyone to agree about the argumentation, because they all partake in the given experiences and reasons (Perelman and Olbrecht-Tyteca 1971, §7).

Even an idea of universality may have its history. Obviously, this plays a role for a church considered to be Catholic, i.e. universal, something which the pope has expressed in his Easter blessings *Urbi et Orbi* since the thirteenth century. It is also reflected in European cartography which displays the conquest of the world through maps where white spots are gradually turned into coloured ones to indicate which European power controls the area. The European order is imposed everywhere and conceived as universally valid (see Sloterdijk 2005, 47 ff.). Modern Western philosophy is clearly universal in its ambitions, believing that what is said about man characterises everyone everywhere. Two famous references can serve as examples for this. One example is when Descartes opens his *Discourse de la Méthode* (*Discourse on the Method*) from 1637 by stating that good sense is evenly distributed to all; another example is when Hegel in § 209 of his *Grundlinien der Philosophie des*

Rechts (*Elements of the Philosophy of Right*) from 1821 states that man is man not by being Jew, Catholic, Protestant, German or Italian but simply by being man.

Leaving aside that these statements do not necessarily demonstrate an ability also to apply this universality to everyone as there has not been agreement about who is considered as human (e.g. indigenous people who until recently could be considered 'natural folks' and hence closer to nature than culture and humanity), the references to Descartes and Hegel belong to ideas lying behind the declaration of human rights. I will not engage in discussions about the conceptual complexity of human rights (see Jacobsen 2011, 13 ff. and 270 ff.) and I also bypass the complications involved in formulating the UN declaration of 1948 which is supposed to include all humans despite cultural and political differences, thus implying that it 'is not rooted in any particular region of the globe and appeals across cultures, but is sensitive to difference' (McCrudden 2008, 677; see also Carozza 2003). I will grant Diogenes the point of making a virtue out of necessity which in this case concerns the necessity emerging from a world of contacts and exchanges across all borders where a set of norms for everyone to agree about becomes essential. One can then ask if the idea of applying a universal ideal requires the idea of a universal audience or whether such an assumption of a universal audience is an illusion that leaves one blinded by the ideal of universality such that one cannot see the multiple appearances of the ideal. Perhaps the audience is universal when it comes to the ideal, but it expresses itself in different ways and appears differently; therefore we should consider how the execution and implementation of an idea taken to be universal and unconditionally applicable may appear in different forms. Although we are dealing with the same notion of human rights, it may not imply uniformity in its concrete manifestations—we may agree to something but speak of it in different ways.

How does this relate to architecture and migration and why does this not lead to relativism thus undermining the idea of universality?

6.3 The Plurality of Appearances in the Built Environment

Consider the following description:

> Anyone wanting to enter the building must be announced over the intercom (*interphone*) which can come fitted with a camera for additional security. This intercom has buttons, with a name beside each button indicating each particular flat (i.e. 'this' button is for 'that' flat), so that all the visitor has to do is to press the button of the flat he wants, introduce himself and the door is opened for him from above by the pressing of yet another button. The visitor then enters the building, the door closes behind him automatically, he crosses the entrance hall and uses the lift to reach the landing in front of the desired flat (an area which may be shared with one or two other flats). He then rings the bell and is admitted to the reception area, for each flat is clearly divided into areas that are public (the lounge and dining room) and private (the bedroom, living room and kitchen). (Chakar 2002, 46 f.)

This description will probably not raise the reader's eyebrow; it is easily recognised. This trivial description comes from the presentation of an architectural project made in Rouwaysset, a suburb of Beirut, by five students from the Lebanese Academy of Fine Arts in Beirut. What they expected to encounter was such a familiar and trivial experience as the one above of entering a building, but in this neighbourhood it did not work like that. Instead of walking around on their own observing the area as they would do in any other neighbourhood, they were approached by a man asking them for their reasons for being there and after accepting them he offered to help them. 'The man approached them when the students overstepped the unseen, but very real boundaries. Or perhaps those boundaries had in fact been visible, in the sense that the students had seen them but they had not understood the meaning of what they saw' (Chakar 2002, 49). Although the students are visiting a neighbourhood of their own city, they fail to interpret the place correctly from the start. If difficulties in understanding may appear even in one's own city, one may wonder how it is in strange places as when migrants arrive to our—for them strange—place, where they are confronted with boundaries visible to us but invisible to them.

Furthermore the students' system of values is challenged as the neighbourhood even negates some common rules of approaching and entering buildings. They could now, with the man's help, 'go into any house in the quarter without ringing the bell or announcing his arrival. This certainly surprised them, because entering a house without first asking permission is not part of their system of values' (Chakar 2002, 49). The students' expectations are probably those of most readers. A border defining public and private probably seems fundamental to many of us. When Jane Jacobs evaluates the problems of the post-WWII North American cities, she notices that for a street to be a safe one, among its three qualities you find that 'there must be a clear demarcation between what is public space and what is private space' (Jacobs 1992, 35).

But perhaps the drawing of a line between these two spheres of public and private is negated in some places where there even is a third space created for the same intention of making the street safe, as Jacobs mentions—the third space of *al-fina'*. This term is Arabic and relates to defining space in old Islamic cities, a space which is 'bordered by the street and the buildings' and having 'various functions, private, public, or both' (Nooraddin 1998, 67). It has a century-old history including juridical regulation. A question is what happens to this tradition when confronted with modern urban planning taking the European city of the nineteenth century as a model. Hoshiar Nooraddin has conducted a study in Cairo which shows this old tradition is also reflected in modern design due to people's own interventions (Nooraddin 1998, 73 ff.). The intention of organising public spaces to the best use including safety (see Nooraddin 1998, 76) is thus answered in different ways in the American and the Middle Eastern cities. How do we understand this space in Cairo, and how does the migrant from the Middle East understand the Western space when particular features such as the third space are missing?

These examples are about how we encounter conflicts between ideals and interests considered as universal such as designing buildings and environment focussed on safety and protection of privacy, and how there are difficulties in their interpretation. Design and architecture have for decades appeared globally as if formed for a universal audience—most design is for a global market, hence designed for a global user but a global user can only be a fictive figure. An example of how this universality proves problematic and far from as neutral as it pretends to be is the creation of a universal language in pictograms known as Isotypes. The ideal here is explicitly drawn from the natural sciences and requires the elimination of ambiguities in ordinary language so as to use only quantitative elements and neutral figures. One such is a human shape to represent people. However, it very soon reveals a lack of neutrality. We know it from public bathrooms where the gender neutrality of the figure 'people' is abandoned to show the difference between male and female, which in this case turns female into a deviation from the standard figure of a human being (Hartmann 2008, 288 f.).

The interpretations of user needs in design engage our relations to and interaction with the environment. Architecture is a 'space of representation' that 'represents something other than itself: the social structure, the power of the King, the idea of God, and so on' (Tschumi 1996, 36). Space 'is also a means of control, and hence of domination, of power' (Lefebvre 1991, 26). However tempting it may be to perceive space as a neutral physical frame of some given proportions, even this neutrality is itself to be considered as ideological (Lefebvre 1991, 94; cf. 210). Space is both a field of action and a basis of action enabling actions as well as forming them (Lefebvre 1991, 191). The idea of the neutral space is an idea of erasing distinctions (Lefebvre 1991, 49), hence to provide standards—and now one has to ask standards for what and made by whom—for everyone to comply with.

Here we should make a distinction between globalisation inherent in design and architecture as in products designed for a global market and the universal order of cosmopolitanism. According to Peter Sloterdijk, globalisation relates to a universal standard by which we measure the values of activities worldwide: capital (Sloterdijk 2005, 14 ff., cf. 306). He characterises it as the third form of globalisation in Western history whereof the first was the cosmological idea of the sphere also reflected as an ideal figure in thought and the second was the terrestrial making the rest of the world known to the Europeans through expeditions and travels reflected in the physical measurement of the world—for example, the cartographical mapping the world according to Western political ideas.

All three forms imply an interpretation subject to a particular idea, whether it is the spherical cosmology or the becoming a subject of a Western king holding the sphere, the *globus crucier* or *globus imperialis*, symbolising his power over the world (see Sloterdijk 1999, 47 ff.). Disputes about power can be eliminated when the global view is formed by a metric and a monetary system that makes us accustomed to quantitative standards of a universal character. Instead of disputing these standards of powers, we conform by turning ourselves into a universal audience as figures in an excel sheet. One can think of the influence of such standards when they appear in many aspects of the practical life, like our way of measuring time and space and the extent to which ordinary life is affected by, for example, bookkeeping that 'has had a massive and pervasive influence on the way we think' for 'the past seven centuries' where it 'has done more to shape the perception of more bright minds than any single innovation in philosophy or science' (Crosby 1997, 220 f.).

The universal ideal of cosmopolitanism in contrast to globalisation is about a necessary general rule enabling a global community, and this requires sensibility towards how it is interpreted and appears to be different from what is the norm regarding the standards of globalisation. In the idea of globalisation a universal audience is assumed, one for which commodities are produced, design marketed and architecture built disregarding local differences. Globalisation ignores how the built environment could be perceived differently, like the example with *al-fina'*. A cosmopolitan world does require universals such as human rights to ensure the world community, but the universality is of a hermeneutic kind—i.e. of a kind where the starting point is that we do understand each other across differences and where we expect the other to say and act in a meaningful way. Only when confusion appears do we engage in an interpretative effort to reach understanding. We want to meet the other displaying our peaceful and respectful intentions, but sometimes confusion arises: Do we shake hands—and if so, which hand, and if not, what then? How long should I hold the hand and how firmly? How close should we stand? Should I stretch out an open hand or should I keep my hands together? Or is it not even about the hand? When the other acts differently, my preconception is challenged and I have to interpret the other's intention from the situation.

What may sound like a trivial example of differences we learn to handle is in fact something essential for social intercourse and something very complex when it comes to communication across cultures. A sensibility for the situation becomes essential here. An example of such a communication is the reception of migrants in which case the built environment becomes essential. It must correspond to how they perceive things. A sensibility on the side of the receiver of migrants becomes crucial for establishing communication, including perhaps forming facilities for the migrants. This is a central problem for aesthetics which is concerned with forming our sensibility and perception, and in this meeting point between architecture as the embodiment of ideas and sensibility in a context of migration and common ideals such as human rights, we should turn to aesthetics.

6.4 Aesthetics as an Approach to the Other

The introduction of aesthetics requires an explanation of the particular understanding of aesthetics used here. Aesthetics is related to sensorial cognition, or perception, to use the original characterisation given by A.G. Baumgarten in the opening line of his *Aesthetica* from 1750. It is about how artefacts are considered essential for forming and training our perceptual skills enabling us to sense and perceive situations. Through sensorial elements we learn how we should exercise social skills. Fundamental for this is a forming of our senses and feelings which is enacted through the sensorial influence of the environment. An important element in this educational process is then the physical organisation of the environment such as it is found in architecture.

For an example hereof, we can refer to the classical text from 1908: "Ornament and Crime" by Adolf Loos, for whom 'Ornament does not heighten my joy in life or the joy in life of any cultivated person' and is 'a crime […] committed through the fact that ornament inflicts serious injury on people's health, on the national budget and hence on cultural evolution' (Loos 1975, 21). Later, in 1991, the network of design groups Team Zoo writes that architects 'design buildings to inspire an emotional response from the inhabitants. Upon entering our structures, people should experience some slight shock or stimulation of their five senses in order to alert them to the character of the space and its connection with the outside world' (Jencks and Kropf 1997, 155); and the above-mentioned Tschumi can for the 'intensity of a relationship between individuals and their surrounding spaces' use the metaphor violence (Tschumi 1996, 122). 'Architecture, then, is only an organism engaged in constant intercourse with users, whose bodies rush against the carefully established rules of architectural thought' (Tschumi 1996, 123).

This corresponds well to more recent approaches in aesthetics such as the introduction of atmosphere as a fundamental concept in aesthetics by Gernot Böhme (1993). For Böhme, atmosphere is about a change of focus within perception from the object orientation where we perceive something as something to identify in order to get a hold on our environment to a presence as a fundamental feature of our perception. Atmosphere has become a topic of independent studies especially within architecture and urban studies, and often we also come across the notion of ambience used in the same discussions seemingly more or less interchangeably (see Thibaud 2015). I use atmosphere as a technical term in aesthetics and wish to emphasise how important presence is for atmosphere as a concept of perception; one finds it perhaps most explicit in Böhme's lectures on aesthetics as a general doctrine of perception, which is the subtitle of his book *Aisthetik* (Böhme 2001).

Böhme's work on perception is situated within a phenomenological tradition and bears similarities to how Maurice Merleau-Ponty investigates what constitutes the legitimacy of our description of perception. He is thus pursuing the phenomenological strategy of *epoché* by questioning the assumptions made in the context of how we usually characterise perception. Phenomenology is about learning how our characterisation comes about and how learning to see something in a particular way makes us overlook what is also present (see e.g. Merleau-Ponty 1968, 156 ff.). While this is not necessarily what dominates most literature on aesthetics, it remains within a Baumgartian understanding of aesthetics as sensorial cognition.

Discourses on aesthetics take many different directions and this is not the place to dissociate myself from them. I will only name one widespread understanding, the idea that aesthetics is about art and that art is characterised by disinterestedness. However widespread an idea of art it is, there are many different approaches that instead emphasise 'the purpose it may serve in the life of man and of humanity' (Tolstoy 1898/2007, 56). Disinterestedness is often related to the enjoyment of art to which another comment is: 'Whoever concretely enjoy artworks is a philistine' (Adorno 2002, 13). When something may appear as appealing to a disinterested enjoyment, it is never free of cultural elements. The disinterestedness is, despite what it is believed to be, not free of any interests. Any perception 'is itself inherently cultural. Cultural influences pervade our sensory perceptions' (Berleant 2010, 45), and because of this fundamental character giving us 'faith in the world', we ignore its cultural origin and instead believe it to 'incorporate all things into itself, even the perception that has initiated us into it' (Merleau-Ponty 1968, 27).

With this perspective on aesthetics, the focus is on the formation of our concrete sensorial skills and how they can be met with general consent. Aesthetics addresses our sharing of feelings which we express in judgements of taste. Aesthetics is about characterising these judgements through which we learn to act with other people as sentient and sensitive beings endowed with social skills. We may also learn something about ourselves and not least when our sensorial education is confronted with something that conflicts with our expectations, calling out reactions we must learn to deal with. Art may be important for this self-reflection and awareness, but we are also confronted with challenges to our expectations during encounters comprising cultural differences due to social distances as well as distances in time and culture, which could be of the kind the Lebanese students encountered when they were visiting a neighbourhood in their city.

Böhme writes about atmosphere in relation to architecture, which can be seen as the art of creating affective spaces, and architecture is of particular interest as we are most of our time subject to its influence (Böhme 2006). While affecting us anytime and anywhere, we may also notice that not all architects have paid attention to it as much as they have been concerned with what could be described as the intellectual side of architecture rather than the affective. For Böhme, this is the case with functionalist architecture which has often had an exaggerated interest in functional elements at the cost of the sensorial. Perhaps we do not all see the same functions or see them in the same way. This we could see in the example above about organising public and safe spaces in the Western and the south Mediterranean city.

My suggestion of aesthetics as the meeting point between architecture, migration and human rights relates here to how architecture engages in a communicative situation. Either it can appear in the globalised form such as the International Style built for the universal audience with the expectation that user interests are identical everywhere. In a modern globalised capitalism it explains why corporate high-rise buildings look similar everywhere. Or we should ask for an architecture displaying a different form of sensibility to the people using it. This is again a matter of interests and decisions reflected in the design. Perhaps we want the users to learn to use something in a particular way. Perhaps we sometimes find that identical elements may prove to be useful anywhere because they belong to a site-indifferent function as in airports, thus displaying a form of travelling which is more or less identical worldwide and saves travellers problems with orientation in large airports. When the decision, on the other hand, is to acknowledge a communicative challenge in respecting and approaching an audience with different perceptions from one's own and with the intention of forming a common ground for exchange, the keyword then becomes sensibility, and aesthetics has something to offer.

6.5 Conclusion: Aesthetics at Work

I wish to conclude by briefly emphasising what it is that aesthetics can offer as well as how it relates to the hermeneutic universalism mentioned at the beginning.

The meaningful combination of human rights, migration, architecture and aesthetics concerns how aesthetics as sensorial cognition or perception asks for awareness of particular appearances of something paving the way for a common agreement. The awareness is a matter of becoming aware of what is already there within practices we are subject to and actively participating in without paying attention to them. Cultural artefacts have always been essential for educating citizens such that they know about appropriate feelings and attitudes in relation to different situations. The responses we have to what happens to the protagonist in literature, drama and film are, apart from possible enjoyment, also a process of learning how we should respond to these events within a community. Similarly with knowing how to appear and be present among other people; different bodily exercises are not simply for training of one's physique but also of bodily postures in a social environment where it becomes apparent in the performance of the appropriate manners in the specific context. While this has perhaps been scaled down in many aesthetic discourses, it has never disappeared, which my examples from architecture and design above should demonstrate.

While we do engage in these practices and consequently are formed by them, the focus on them and the consequences thereof are often set aside for other interests such as the visual appearance of architecture and urban design whether for pleasure or critique. Aesthetics should help us to become aware of how the organisation of the environment forms us—i.e. help us to improve our critical sense and skills in analysing and characterising the built environment. Aesthetics should help us with the training of our sensorial awareness, just as this was the point of using of aesthetics in education traditionally—to learn to be a sensitive citizen with a developed sense of situations demonstrated in the moral constitution of that person. Aesthetics should help us to become aware of what we easily ignore in perception, because we learn to direct our attention within our perception in specific directions such as to identify what something is rather than how it affects us. Aesthetics is about becoming aware of what affects us and of the formation of perception itself.

As the sharing of rules within a world community is a necessity for forming a community, so is the education for cross-cultural meetings as it enables an exchange and prevents confusion and misunderstanding due to clashes between different perceptual skills while interpreting the cultural artefacts. Hence the danger of relativism does not lie in the acknowledgement of differences but is lurking in the insistence on a communication based on a universal audience that should eventually reach an agreement as to what the argumentation makes explicit. Apart from the practical impossibility of this universalistic position—we simply have no time for reaching the final conclusion and will, in the meantime, have to act out of necessity based on the perception and interpretation we have—this assumption of universalism may prove to be an illusion, leaving the different partners in disagreement and with a set of conflicting beliefs in the truth value of their own positions where none of them may actually be true. The sensibility will instead prove to be stronger in establishing consent between the partners. The objective is not to reach a final truth, but to reach agreement. The differences in communication are no relativistic example of different 'systems of communication' disabling communication as the premise was that we do share a set of necessary values and we also share the necessity of relating to and communicating these values within a global community.

Apart from asking for an educational programme developing our aesthetic sense, what more should then be done?

As the focus here is on architecture, one should pay attention to the organisation of specific places such as educational facilities and specific institutions dealing with migrants meeting the host society. It is then about making institutions easier accessible in terms of understanding how they display a common understanding of human dignity and also as a means to educating new citizens, since the influence of the environment is a key element in forming our perception. Hence it is not only about making something understandable through clear information and argumentation.

Within architecture and design more studies point towards this, in particular in the field of atmosphere/ambience. These studies point towards a change from the understanding of perception as object-oriented to how we are embedded in situations that form our perception through the sensorial and bodily engagement that also affect us (Thibaud 2011). The ambience then becomes a field of study in the organisation of elements that affect us and how these effects are also embedded together with different understandings requiring an interpretative readiness for acknowledging the significance of what appears to us (Friberg 2012). In order to learn how it is possible through architecture and design to meet migrants and enable them to read and react to the environment with respect to specific values, studies should be conducted 'to identify, characterize, and classify various basic sensory phenomena that structure our ways of perceiving'. It is, furthermore, important 'to harness the notion of ambiance as a tool to analyse and specify the sensory ecology of specific urban territories' and explore 'the ways in which social practices and daily activities help generate an ambiance' (Thibaud 2011, 213).

Bibliography

Adorno, T. W. (2002). *Aesthetic theory*. (Hullot-Kentor, Trans.) London/New York, Continuum. (First German edition 1970).

Berleant, A. (2010). *Sensibility and the sense. The aesthetic transformation of the human world*. Exter, Imprint Academic.

Böhme, G. (1993). Atmosphere as the fundamental concept of a new aesthetics. *Thesis Eleven, 36*, 113–126.

Böhme, G. (2001). *Aisthetik. Vorlesungen über Ästhetik als allgemeine Wahrnehmungslehre*. München, Wilhelm Fink Verlag.

Böhme, G. (2006). *Architektur und Atmosphäre*. München, Wilhelm Fink Verlag.

Carozza, P. G. (2003). Subsidiarity as a structural principle of international human rights law. *97 American Journal of International Law, 38*, 38–79. https://scholarship.law.nd.edu/law_faculty_scholarship/564.
Chakar, T. (2002). The suburbs and the vocabulary of urbanisation: Violence as an architectural language. In: *Tamáss. Contemporary Arab Representations* (pp. 40–56). Barcelona, Fundació Antoni Tàpies.
Crosby, A. W. (1997). *The measue of reality. Quantification and western society 1250–1600*. Cambridge, Cambridge University Press.
Laertius, D. (1995). *Lives of eminent philosophers* (Vol. II, Hicks, Trans.). Cambridge, Mass./London, Harvard University Press. (First edition 1925).
Friberg, C. (2012). Hermeneutics of ambiance. In J-P. Thibaud, & D. Siret, (Eds.), *Ambiances in action/ambiances en acte(s)—International congress on ambiances, Montreal 2012* (pp. 671–676). International Ambiances Network.
Geuss, R. (2003). *Public goods. Private Goods*. Princeton/Oxford, Princeton University Press.
Hartman, F. (2008). Visualizing social facts: Otto neurath's ISOTYPE project. In W. B. Rayward (Ed.), *European modernism and the information society* (pp. 279–293). Aldershot, Ashgate.
Jacobs, J. (1992). *The death and life of great American cities*. New York, Vintage Books. (First edition 1961).
Jacobsen, M. C. (2011). *Three conceptions of human rights*. Malmö, NSU Press.
Jencks, Ch., & Kropf, K. (Eds.). (1997). *Theories and manifestoes of contemporary architecture*. Chichester, Willey-Academy.
Lefebvre, H. (1991). *The production of space* (Nicholson-Smith, Trans.). Malden, Blackwell. (First French edition 1974).
Loos, A. (1975). Ornament and crime. In U. Conrads (Ed.), *Programs and manifestoes on twentieth century architecture* (pp. 19–24). The MIT Press.
Merleau-Ponty, M. (1968). *Invisible and the invisible* (Lingis, Trans). Evanston, Northwestern University Press. (French original 1964).
Nooraddin, H. (1998). *Al-fina'*, in-between spaces as an urban design concept: Making public and private places along streets in Islamic cities of the Middle East. *Urban Design Inernational, 3*(1), 65–77. https://www.tandfonline.com/doi/abs/10.1080/135753198350532.
Perelman, Ch., & Olbrecht-Tyteca, L. (1971). *The new rhetoric* (Wilkinson & Weaver, Trans.). Notre Dame, University of Notre Dame Press. (First French edition 1958).
Sloterdijk, P. (1999). *Sphären II. Globen*. Frankfurt a.M., Suhrkamp.
Sloterdijk, P. (2005). *Im weltinnenraum des kapitals. Für eine philosophische theorie der globalisierung*. Suhrkamp, Frankfurt a.M.
Thibaud, J.-P. (2011). The sensory fabric of urban ambiances. *The Senses and Society, 6*(2), 203–215.
Thibaud, J.-P. (2015). The backstage of urban ambiances: When atmospheres pervade everyday experience. *Emotion, Space and Society, 15*, 39–46.
Tolstoy, L. (1898/2007). *What is art?* (Maude, Trans.). London, Bristol Classical Press.
Toulmin, S. (1992). *Cosmopolis. The Hidden Agenda of Modernity*. Chicago, The University of Chicago Press.
Tschumi, B. (1996). *Architecture and disjunction*. Cambridge, Mass./London, MIT Press.

Carsten Friberg independent scholar, Ph.D. (philosophy), has previously held positions at Aarhus School of Architecture and Aalborg University in Denmark. His interests are in aesthetics and atmosphere/ambiance, in particular with focus on education and democracy in relation to design, and in philosophy of culture.

Chapter 7
Reshaped Roles of Faith-Based Actors Towards Refugees in the Balkan Corridor Phase and its Aftermath

Drago Župarić-Iljić

Abstract Increased numbers of refugees transiting through the Balkan corridor triggered not only crisis and emergency management measures but also ethical considerations of enabling hospitality and a welcoming culture. While volunteers together with religious actors were part of a regional humanitarian regime providing aid to migrants within the corridor managerial sites (borders, camps, and local communities), local authorities together with international agencies assisted in the organised and securitised hasty transit of people. Some faith-based organisations who were actively engaged during the corridor phase are now re-orienting their scope of activities to facilitate inclusion into society for a relatively small number of refugees who obtained protection statuses. We analyse the roles and activities of religious actors in Croatia during the corridor phase, based on data gathered in 2016 and 2018, through content analysis of transcribed interviews with actors involved in humanitarian assistance. This humanitarian work has reshaped their usual charity role and to some extent has fostered their political stances on advocating human and refugees' rights, especially in the current situation where many 'irregularised migrants' are stranded on the external borders of the Schengen area. Therefore, complex situation in regard to migration and border management within Balkan societies still represents a challenge for different actors in fostering solidarity towards 'newcomers'.

Keywords Refugees · Religious organisations · Humanitarianism · Integration · Balkan corridor

7.1 Introduction

From September 2015 to April 2016, Croatia faced many challenges in terms of accepting, providing temporary accommodation, care and assistance, as well as organising and facilitating the further transit of numerous refugees and migrants passing through the Balkan corridor (Šelo Šabić 2017). During the period of the

D. Župarić-Iljić (✉)
University of Zagreb, Zagreb, Croatia
e-mail: dzuparic@ffzg.hr

M. C. Jacobsen et al. (eds.), *Cosmopolitanism, Migration and Universal Human Rights*, https://doi.org/10.1007/978-3-030-50645-2_7

corridor, state authorities together with different humanitarian actors, including international agencies, civil society organisations, activists and volunteers, played a pivotal role in assisting refugees and migrants. Local and national religious communities, charitable and faith-based organisations also helped. Their scope of responsibility and assistance included first and foremost engagement on multi-sited locations near the border points of entering or leaving the state territory, and within two transit reception centres temporarily established deeper within Croatian territory, for the purpose of short-term stay and further swift transit of migrants through the corridor.

The gradual closure of the corridor has had detrimental consequences on the safety and human rights of refugees and migrants stranded along the East Mediterranean and Balkan route, as posited in different reports (HRW 2017; Mlinarević and Ahmetašević 2019). After the EU–Turkey agreement in March 2016, the corridor formally ceased to exist, even though migrants have continued trying to enter the Schengen area. Some organisations continued their care for refugees and migrants, through direct humanitarian assistance and charitable work, often in combination with advocating for their human rights, especially in the area of reception and quality of protection. Thus, helping asylum seekers and recognised refugees to integrate into society has now become (or has remained) one of their main missions. For some of them, a more politically engaged role has emerged in the process of reflecting and criticising the dominant state securitisation policies, including the criminalisation of solidarity and irregularisation of mobility. A general hardening of migrants' access to Croatian territory and to asylum procedure is happening daily on borders with Bosnia and Herzegovina, and with Serbia.

Therefore, by acknowledging recent and present-day challenges, we analyse how the Balkan corridor episode in its Croatian section motivated religious, charitable and faith-based organisations to assist refugees, and/or (re)defined the scope of their activities, their organisational aspects, and current objectives in helping refugees and migrants. Some religious organisations that were actively engaged during transit are today facing new challenges related to 'post-crisis' assistance for refugees in order to facilitate their inclusion into society. First, we analyse the 'crisis activities' of these actors in order to understand their present activities and practices in assisting migrants, asylum seekers and refugees. Later, we discuss faith-based actors' understanding of humanitarian work and the socio-political stance they take today, alongside other humanitarian actors, assessing their role in articulating, advocating and defending human and refugees' rights.

7.2 Theoretical and Contextual Standpoints, Research Questions, and Methodology

We are reminded by Ager and Ager (2016, 285) that '[h]umanitarian responses to those displaced by conflict, persecution, and disaster are often rooted within religious tradition and thought'. Nonetheless, authors posit that the modern international humanitarian regime could be suspicious of religion 'as a potential threat to humanitarian principles such as impartiality and neutrality' (ibid., 286). Moreover, due to mere sociodemographic facts that many forced migrants frequently belong to some religious or faith communities, exercising religious practices and sharing religious experiences in host communities, the authors stress that we witness renewed interest of forced migration studies in topics concerning the role of religion in assisting 'people on the move' as 'population in need'. On the premise that many religiously affiliated and faith-based organisations are involved in humanitarian work today, Riera and Poirier (2014) concluded that local faith leaders and communities play an important role in the local reception of aliens, also through their cooperation with UNHCR.

That assistance is often a part of the humanitarian regime in the countries of origin, transit or destination countries, within reception camps, on border crossing points or within reception or detention facilities. Miller (2015) points out that faith-based organisations could have a somewhat different scope than secular humanitarian organisations, and their religious affiliation could at times limit their potential to help; on other occasions, however, it could enable them to reach areas of confined spaces with 'humanitarian exemptions' which other actors cannot enter. The moral convictions and authority of faith-based organisations could influence the framing or reframing of discourses and responses for emergency relief and humanitarian assistance. The inclination to help migrants and refugees, to foster solidarity and to enable hospitality, has usually been conveyed and partly legitimised through official and media discourses framed by different actors, including religious ones.

In a comparative study on human rights issues and discursive positions in public debates of the Catholic Church in Italy and Croatia during 'the refugee crisis', Giordan and Zrinščak (2018, 62) concluded that 'the Catholic Church in Croatia remained a silent public actor in the refugee crisis', using human rights discourses in a selective and ambiguous rhetorical manner when framing its practical responses to refugees. The authors contend that rhetoric and discourses on migration and refugee issues have shifted towards more nuanced messages emphasising their human rights and prospects for necessary integration in receiving societies. In Italy, this response meant more of a solidary and politically engaged mobilisation among Church officials in order to assist and to protect refugees and their human rights. On the other hand, no substantial public involvement of the Catholic Church in Croatia with regard to refugees and migrants was noticed in 2015, besides some minor actions of bishops' visits to refugee camps and expressing gratitude to volunteers and Caritas personnel for their engagement (ibid., 68). The authors posit that staying mostly silent and 'not using this discourse is a way to avoid public debates and (maybe) expressing concerns about the possible threats posed by migrants to particular religious and cultural identities ([in] Croatia)' (ibid., 76).

It is known that migrants and refugees might be perceived as threatening in different ways, including symbolic threats to identity and culture, values and norms, customs and way of life for members of the domestic population (cf. Gornik; Župarić-Iljić and Gregurović, in this volume). Sometimes the negative sentiments could slip into more hostile actions and sabotage efforts for creating a 'welcoming culture' for ‘newcomers’. Deslandes and Anderson (2019), in their meta-analytic review, posited that often religion (understood as affiliation and as religiosity) could play an ambiguous role of facilitating either tolerance or intolerance towards immigrants or refugees. Sometimes, this could become intensified and result in contradicting discourses and actions by religious actors. For example, Andrejč (2018) described a case of Slovenian Catholic Church’s response to the ‘migrant crisis’ where the Church has had self-understanding of being ‘the keeper of Slovenian traditions’ along with anti-migrant and populist sentiments expressed, although rare civic voices also advocated a more humanitarian approach in public.[1]

Acknowledging previous researches, we analyse how local, national and international religious, charitable and faith-based organisations participated in assisting refugees and migrants who transited through Croatia in the period from September 2015 to April 2016, as well as activities and roles they fulfil today for the benefit of human and refugee rights. Our research included 11 respondents, representatives of religious communities and faith-based humanitarian and charitable organisations, from three localities in Croatia that experienced refugees’ transit, including the capital as a place where most of the recognised refugees are living today. Respondents were chosen as key persons, leaders or representatives of those organisations or religious communities who took an active role in conducting humanitarian activities during ‘the crisis’, which unravelled on the border with Serbia as entry point, or with Slovenia as leaving point, and especially within two transit reception camps during the existence of the corridor. Some respondents were chosen by a snowball method (one theologian and one Christian friar/monk), as those who were recognised by other respondents as publicly visible figures commenting on ‘the crisis’ in the media. Few of the respondents are members of Islamic communities in Croatia who occasionally participated in the everyday life of camps. Some of the respondents belong to prominent humanitarian organisations helping those who work within two official reception and accommodation centres for asylum seekers, or they started their activities inside them after the corridor’s closure.[2]

Additionally, after two years (i.e. in 2018) we re-checked our respondents’ opinions, by acknowledging some new challenges stemming from the closure of the corridor, such as the opening of the new route in Bosnia and Herzegovina, securitisation of mobility, criminalisation of solidarity, forced returns, relocation and resettlement quotas, and new solidarity initiatives. Therefore, our discussion is based on an explorative and analytical approach that includes desk research of previous

---

[1] The author concludes that ‘[t]he migrant crisis in Slovenia has shown that what is meant by “Christianity” can be radically different and mutually contradicting’, while welcoming the attitude and commitment to assist according to “genuine Christian values” manifested mostly in activities of Adventist Development and Relief Agency (Andrejč 2018, 60).

[2] The following respondents were included in the research, with codes amended: Jesuit Refugee Service (JRS), Croatian Caritas (CARIT), Croatian Baptist Aid (CBA), Adventist Development and Relief Agency (ADRA), Islamic Community of Zagreb – Meshihat (MESH), Islamic Community of Slavonski Brod municipality (ICSB), Islamic Community of Gunja municipality (ICGU), Muslim religious-humanitarian organisation Zirat (ZIRAT), theologian (THEO), Christian friar (MONK), and Catholic nun-volunteer (VOL).

studies (including media and NGO reports). As the main methodological approach, we employ applied thematic content analysis (cf. Guest et al. 2012) of transcribed interviews collected from October and November 2016, and amended from March to June 2018. We use open coding of all transcribed interviews in order to get to concepts that were then grouped into thematic categories (themes). Those were identified among data that relates to the general focus of research and more specific questions posed in the interviews. Here we focus on the following identified themes of our interest: the role in crisis management and cooperation with other actors; recent activities in assisting refugees and migrants who bring new cultural diversity to society; and current challenges regarding humanitarian work aimed at implementing refugee rights.

7.3 Role of Religious Actors in Crisis Management and Cooperation with other Stakeholders

What was the reaction of the public and of religious actors on the mass arrival of refugees in Croatia? On 31 August 2015, two weeks before refugees started to come to Croatian borders, six religious leaders from Croatia, representatives of the Catholic Church, Orthodox Church, Protestant-Evangelical Council, Islamic community and two Jewish communities, in their joint statement, encouraged the acceptance of refugees and 'establishing human relationships with them' (Giordan and Zrinščak 2018, 67). The initial attempts of the Catholic Church's public involvement included multi-confessional and ecumenical public and media statements before and during the crisis (ibid., 70).[3] The local population of the border areas between Serbia and Croatia in the first days of the mass arrival of refugees (mid-September 2015) expressed solidarity and readiness to assist refugees in transit. Authors concluded that in the early months the 'refugee crisis' was framed through human rights discourse and a charitable lens.

However, such an atmosphere of an initial welcome and humanistic and altruistic approach of authorities and other actors did not encourage refugees to seek protection and look for a chance for new and safe life in Croatia. Due to their desire to reach Germany and other Western destinations, only about 200 persons expressed an intention for protection (asylum) in Croatia during the Balkan corridor phase, even though more than 660,000 people entered and tresspassed its territory. Croatia was just a link in a migration chain from Turkey to Western Europe, which started with the suspension of the Dublin Regulation by Germany in August 2015. Therefore, state

[3]For example, on 18 September 2015, when the first refugees entered into the newly established reception and transit camp, a statement presented by the *Justitia et Pax Committee* of the Croatian Bishops' Conference asserted government responsibility and Church readiness to help and assist refugees. In this statement, the Committee invoked other churches and religious communities as well as domestic and international humanitarian organisations to help people in need with temporary reception, moreover adhering to their transit movement through Croatia (see: https://ika.hkm.hr/iustitia-et-pax/izjava-komisije-iustitia-et-pax-hbk-18-rujna-2015).

policies and responses towards the mass arrival of refugees were balance between humanitarian and security approach, entangled in the process of the overtly organised and excessively controlled fast transit of people through Croatia (cf. Župarić-Iljić and Valenta 2019). Two reception transit centres (camps) that were opened while Hungary was tightening and finally closed its borders were substantive parts of that migration regime.

The organisational and logistical management of two camps with a capacity of 5000 each was controlled by the Ministry of Interior and coordinated by the Croatian Red Cross. Numerous civil society organisations, humanitarian, religious, faith-based and charitable organisations, civic initiatives, local and international volunteers and activists worked together in cooperation in the daily activities of the camp (cf. Larsen et al. 2016). In the camps, people were waiting for registration, provided with food, water, hygiene, medical examinations, first aid, humanitarian aid, and care for particularly vulnerable groups (women, pregnant women, children, elderly, disabled, unaccompanied minors). Most of them spent between three and twelve hours in a camp before getting into organised transport to the Slovenian border. Requirements for food, water, medicines, sanitary supplies, warm clothing and footwear were constant, as were a need for general information (due to a lack of translators), cell phone chargers, internet access, and the like (Hameršak and Pleše 2018).

Various religious actors had different roles and responsibilities in their work during 'the crisis'. Some of them utilised the cross-border experiences of their international partners and acquaintances. Branko Sekulić emphasises that in the initial phase of mass arrivals, the Baptist community in Croatia contributed logistical support in the construction of the camps and with overall cooperation and exchanging of know-how with their partners from the Baptist community in Hungary, together with Croatian Caritas and other civil associations and citizens' initiatives. Soon after, support was provided by the Protestant Evangelical Alliance which had organised 170 volunteers from 22 different countries who worked to provide aid and assistance in reception and transit camps in Croatia (Sekulić 2016, 68). Among more than 20 humanitarian agencies and organisations in the camps were faith-based international organisations such as Nazarene Compassionate Ministries, Remar, Samaritan's Purse, and Protestant Evangelical Alliance, which have all had an indispensable role in the daily activities of the camp. Some organisations also recalled their institutional memory of being active in humanitarian aid provisions during the 'Homeland War' in the 1990s (CARIT, ADRA).

For faith-based organisations present in transit reception camps and at border entry points, primary modes of action were humanitarian activities of collecting and distributing food, clothes and blankets, medical and hygienic products. Volunteers additionally assisted refugees in visiting healthcare facilities, helped in the family-tracing process, and organised workshops for children in the final phase of the camp's existence. Our respondents highlighted satisfactory cooperation with state actors, the Croatian Red Cross, national NGOs, and international actors such as the UNHCR, UNICEF and IOM, as well as among other religious and charitable organisations. Despite the perceived goodwill, enthusiasm, empathy and solidarity expressed through their activities in the camps, one of the major organisational challenges was that barely any organisations had sufficient professional staff that could help in 'crisis situations', such as translators, social workers, psychologists, or paediatricians.

On the other hand, one organisation (JRS) had five professional translators and three more volunteers (the majority of them employed as persons with an immigrant background and/or recognised refugee status) and 'shared' (lent) them with the authorities and other organisations, according to need: 'The principle of our work was fully cooperative with everyone, giving all our capacities, especially translators, to all, to other organizations, to the Ministry of Interior, therefore, for all purposes, to be available for all that is needed. Likewise, with volunteers and employees […] assisting those who assist refugees that was our principle, to serve those who serve refugees' (JRS). One respondent commented that cooperation among humanitarian actors was never in question, but that cooperation with the authorities could had been more 'economical and efficient', meaning that 'more transparent sharing of information and utilisation of available resources' was needed (CARIT).

Some actors from the Islamic community estimated that assistance had mostly come to those in need, not only in terms of material help but also moral and spiritual support (MESH, ZIRAT). However, attempts to systematically approach refugees in transit was diverted due to the very nature of their swift and accelerated transit through the camp (ICSB). Relatively soon, many scholars, practitioners, the general public, as well as refugees and migrants themselves, realised that the '2015 long summer of migration' (Kasparek and Speer 2015) was gradually converting to a 'harsh winter of securitisation', changing humanitarian discourses and practices to securitarian ones. The final days of the camp were marked by detention and deterrence of those who were stuck in it because of the corridor's closure (Hameršak and Peše 2018), and by then even the official Church's discourse was gradually slipping into a more neutral, ambivalent and security-oriented tone (Giordan and Zrinščak 2018).

7.4 Recent Activities of Religious Actors in Assisting Refugees and Migrants

Once the corridor was closed, the emerging trends of border interception and 'pushbacks' of migrants as well as hundreds of forced returns of asylum seekers from European countries back to Croatia continued, following the reinstated Dublin Regulation. Since the closure of the corridor (March 2016), we have witnessed the general deterioration of refugees' human rights in the Balkans, due to 'restrictivisation' of border management policies, securitisation and militarisation of migration issues, and 'irregularisation' and criminalisation of migrants' mobility and of citizens' solidarity (cf. Župarić-Iljić and Valenta 2019). This was especially troublesome in cases of violent incidents involving border police, deaths of migrants on borders and within the territory, and with violent pushbacks of migrants to Serbia and Bosnia and Herzegovina. Reports of humanitarian organisations and media coverage speak of illegal practices of the state, which represent breaching of international protection standards stemming from the *1951 Convention*. This refers to impediments to access the territory and the refugee status determination procedure. According to reports, this has already resulted in the deaths of dozens of migrants at land or river borders with Bosnia, Serbia and Slovenia (cf. AYS et al. 2019).

All this has added to the complexity of the reception and procedural challenges within the semi-functional Croatian asylum system, also burdened with readmissions and returns (ECRE and AIDA 2016). In this context, some of the religious humanitarian organisations present in the camps continued or started new activities in two regular long-standing accommodation centres for asylum seekers located in the city of Zagreb and Kutina (JRS, CBA, MESH, ZIRAT). For some, there has been a shift in their activities from emergency crisis management activities to more long-lasting ones oriented to integration of refugees into Croatian society.[4] For example, after 'the crisis', CBA started to work in the asylum seekers' reception centre in Zagreb, teaching the Croatian language by volunteers and enabling assistance for asylum seekers in need of medical and dental care. JRS continued to work on integration programmes within accommodation centres, on general assistance to asylum seekers and refugees, helping refugee children to enrol in school, intercultural workshops for children and for women, and psychosocial support and counselling. Language learning has been conducted as a non-licensed course with the help of volunteers and translators, as well as more specific workshops aimed at women and children.

In the last couple of years, the Islamic community has also been present in the asylum seekers' reception centre in Zagreb, where in coordination and cooperation with the Croatian Red Cross and the Ministry of the Interior has continued with charitable programmes of collecting and distributing humanitarian aid. Nevertheless, they also care for religious needs, pastoral counselling and psychosocial support for refugees (ZIRAT). In Zagreb's mosque, Croatian language courses for refugees, together with a course of Islamic religious education and intercultural workshops, are organised for women, children and youth. Charitable work has its extension through the idea of establishing 'brotherhood' (*bratimljenje*) of the local population with refugee families and individuals. Through this model, local Muslims can help refugees with material and/or financial donations, and on occasions spend time with them—for example, socialising during the humanitarian (donation) dinners on religious festivities, such as *Bajram* (MESH).

Somewhat similarly, in the last couple of years, JRS has been organising so-called 'Christmas lunch with refugees', where Croatian families of all religious backgrounds, or none, invite a refugee or refugees (usually a family) to their homes, where they meet, have a meal and get to know each other better.

[4]For others, it meant just a continuation of their previous activities and spreading their impact and assistance to new local communities where refugees were settled with their accommodation provided through the relocation and resettlement schemes (Ajduković et al. 2019). In accordance with agreed quotas (around 1500 people), the Ministry of the Interior is running selection missions in order to resettle Syrian families from refugee camps in Turkey. However, only about 250 persons have so far been resettled to Croatia.

Both of these practices have the potential to inform and sensitise the broader public by opening a space where refugees and local cultures meet and interact, making connections between residents and newcomers, cherishing similarities and acknowledging differences. In the words of VOL: '[…] so what we could do, definitely to call a Muslim [*refugee*] family for lunch […], and then call your neighbours […] if they know English, they will expand their horizons. They will see that there is another culture, some other language, some other people … I have become enriched enough to see that potential enemy can become a friend.' If cultural diversity is gradually becoming a state of affairs, we can presume that these kinds of practices could boost the level of social cohesion in local communities where refugees are settled.

Being a relatively small country, with currently strong economic-driven emigration of its own citizens after accession to the EU, and with a relatively insignificant number of foreigners (including refugees) on its territory, Croatia is still struggling to find more cohesive and systematic solutions for the reception and integration of newcomers. While reflecting on the experience of the Balkan corridor and lessons learnt, some respondents estimate that in the event of a possible repetition of mass arrival of migrants and refugees, Croatia probably would not have sufficient legislative nor institutional capacities for longer-term reception (CARIT, CBA, MONK). Whether this would mean an inevitable humanitarian crisis on a larger scale is hard to tell, but not too difficult to imagine. Known gaps and insufficiencies in the Croatian asylum system, especially regarding reception and integration system, are still influencing roles, capacities and orientations of humanitarian actors who work *for, among* and *with* refugees. Thus, old/new challenges for faith-based actors in their humanitarian work are discussed further.

7.5 Current Challenges of Humanitarian Work in Implementing Refugee Rights

Tackling current integration activities and humanitarian work, JRS stresses that the main challenge of integration in the last three years in Croatia stemmed from the fact that the number of those with recognised status tripled from 300 to 900 persons (although, due to JRS assessment, half of them left the country already). Nonetheless, this represents a serious challenge in the context of insufficient integration services, including problems with mismanagement of state-run certified language courses, lack of employment opportunities and lack of information and awareness-raising campaigns, despite the perceived pivotal role of the Government and media. The Croatian Red Cross has remained the main actor in providing integration activities within reception centres; however, other actors are also using the opportunity to continue their humanitarian work. JRS opened its 'Centre for Integration' in one local community in Zagreb, and that example is to be followed by CBA which plans to open an 'Accommodation and Integration House' in the near future. Continuing their work in providing certified language courses, workshops for children and women, and general assistance, JRS and, to some extent, CBA have also started programmes of vocational training and professional orientation that are organised in coordination with the Croatian Employment Bureau.

CBA recognises that one of the most urgent matters is to develop a model of housing and accommodation for refugees in which the state would not be solely responsible. Thus, other organisations, including those in private sector, would be allowed to envisage alternative and decentralised options for enabling adequate living conditions for beneficiaries. Some respondents (JRS, ADRA, CARIT) acknowledge the need for more engaged, accessible and systematic provisions of psychosocial care for traumatised refugees and vulnerable groups. Many respondents recognise the challenge of long-term and durable organisational and logistical aspects for continuing their work on integration. They would use finances for employing translators and intercultural mediators who will work for and with refugees in order to facilitate their communication with authorities during initial reception into local communities and later inclusion into society. An example of good practice by JRS is their policy of employing recognised refugees as translators and intercultural facilitators, a practice that started even prior to 'the crisis', and has continued all along.

Most of the actors agreed that cooperation between religious organisations and secular NGOs, as well as with international humanitarian organisations, should intensify in the future. One of the reasons is to become more connected and united in contesting practices of criminalising solidarity through which the Government tends to penalise humanitarian assistance to 'irregularised migrants'. As pointed by CARIT: 'We have to ensure that all who need help receive one and that care providers do not get into a situation in which these acts are criminalised ... Assistance with moral or humanitarian motives should not be criminalised.' Faith-based actors who stayed involved in working with asylum seekers, refugees and migrants expressed more or less consent to resist against criminalisation of solidarity, even though they, in general, indicated fewer levels of possible engagement in advocating pro-solidary political attitudes, unlike some other secular NGOs and citizens' initiatives. One of the more politically engaged religious actors, a JRS respondent, sums it up: '[…] we ought to think of some kind of stronger actions, projects of civil disobedience. And institutional disobedience. I talk from the position of the Catholic Church […], but I hope and believe that […] those who will help them [*migrants*] will not be legally punished, prosecuted.'

Further on, it seems that respondents, although recognising the necessity for exchanging experiences on good practices, planning mutual and complementary integration activities, networking and collaboration, expressed their doubt about how much ecumenical, interreligious dialogue has been initiated by the experience in 'crisis management' within the camps and fostered ever since the closure of the corridor. Most of them allude to theological and dogmatic foundations of their religions and belief systems in order to call for hospitality and to legitimise their own actions: 'In a society which declares to be of believers, we need to teach the real truths of the gospel, and the doctrine that Jesus taught. He fought against the Pharisees and the hypocrites and stood with the needy and those marginalised in society' (CBA respondent).[5]

An Islamic community respondent pointed out that, today, the Islamic community in Croatia, in accordance with its capabilities, may play 'a bypass/bridging role' by assisting refugees in integration through partnership established with state institutions and other stakeholders. Therefore, he stresses that the Islamic community could act affirmatively, by informing, raising awareness and educating local communities and wider society about the needs and rights of refugees, and about Islam as a religion and a way of life (MESH; cf. Glazer and Brezovec 2018). All of these practices could facilitate conditions for the integration of Muslim refugees into Croatian society, and become a good foundation for building trust and coexistence, as well as a model of helping refugees to approach their religious community. Being aware of new challenges regarding forced returns and relocation and resettlements quotas, the *Meshihat* respondent points out that Islamic community should 'continue to develop a successful model of integration of its members that the Islamic community in Croatia has been developing for more than a century, from the recognition of Islam in Croatia in 1916, as one of the official religions' (MESH). The same respondent assumes that more transparent media appearance and advocating intercultural dialogue may lead to decreased levels of xenophobia, racism and Islamophobia in society, especially in the lights of the new 'crisis' unfolding in bordering areas with Bosnia and Herzegovina.

7.6 Discussion and Concluding Remarks

The religious communities and organisations we interviewed were actively participating in the daily operation of the two temporary reception and transit camps, as well as at international border crossings. As presented, this assistance was largely in the form of charitable work, most notably the distribution of humanitarian aid. Only later, with the longer stay of refugees in the camp due to the gradual closure of the Balkan corridor, need for spiritual and religious practices became more pronounced. However, it seems that transitory character of short-term refugee staying and swift movement towards the West had spared numerous actors from the responsibility of advocating for a more just system of long-term solutions and solidarity. The humanitarian orientation and initial response to refugees expressed by all stakeholders, including authorities, NGOs, volunteers and the general population, recalled Croatians' own experiences of displacement during the Homeland War in the 1990s (cf. Župarić-Iljić and Valenta 2019).

[5]To some extent this corresponds to what Wilson and Mavelli see as one of the possible objectives for religious actors engaging into providing services for newcomers: '[…] religious actors are not only translating their values of sanctuary and hospitality to strangers and foreigners into action, they are also providing an alternative mode of responding to both forced and voluntary migration, accepting some responsibility for the migrants' well-being and thereby challenging the attempts of the state to confer responsibility solely onto the migrants themselves' (2016, 270–271).

However, the other side of the coin clearly pointed to 'uneasiness' and 'securitisation discomfort' among some of the humanitarian organisations operating within the camps and following, at least indirectly, this 'so-called *closed transit system*'. Short-term staying within overtly controlled and organised transit camps, without the possibility for refugees to leave this sort of 'mobile detention structure' (Hameršak and Pleše 2018) precluded any interaction between local citizens and refugees. In this specific sort of humanitarianism, the Catholic Church has not taken any sensible public role in commenting, debating or alternating this system. There were some singular voices of NGOs of religious provenance, some individual theologians, volunteers from clergy and bishops who contested this approach and advocated, or at least questioned, more long-term durable solutions of accepting and providing protection and integration solutions for numerous refugees in transit. But the official Church's attitude and engagement remained mostly silent (silenced), invisible to broader public and strictly in a form of charity for humanitarian emergencies (Giordan and Zrinščak 2018).[6] Also, we saw in case of Poland how the silence of the Catholic Church influenced negative sentiments of politicians and the media towards refugees (cf. Wilczyńska and Wilczyński, this volume).

After the corridor closure, some organisations such as Caritas remained available if needed for collecting and distributing humanitarian aid and other charitable services. According to our respondents, we see that the crisis management approach was framed and conveyed dominantly through a discourse of humanitarianism and charitable actions, within the system of controlled transfer of people in closed camps and at sealed borders. Most of the religious organisations continued their work for refugees because a need to assist newcomers is still an issue. Today, what seems more needed is less project-based and/or charitable humanitarianism and more people-oriented 'rights-based humanitarianism' (Harrell-Bond 2002)—the hospitality, solidarity and welcoming culture, utilised by these actors.

We contend that through the corridor episode, humanitarian role of faith-based actors has been redefined and reinforced in regard to integration issues, which partly include their endeavours to fix all inconsistencies of the integration system, by providing assistance and services on mostly voluntary or project-based bases. Still, this approach lacks more substantive and publicly visible political engagement in their advocacy for solidarity with refugees in Croatian society, except for some organisations (first and foremost, JRS) whose activists and volunteers raised their voices with other secular civil initiatives and prominent advocacy actors such as 'Are You Syrious?' and 'Refugee Welcome Initiative'. This is in line with what Wilson and Mavelli (2016, 272) pointed to, stating that '[a]longside practices of solidarity [...] religious actors also engage in advocacy and activism, endeavoring to reposition immigration as a moral and humanitarian issue, shifting it away from the logic of securitization.'

---

[6]Giordan and Zrinščak (2018) also concluded that in the case of Balkan corridor, religious authorities, communities and organizations adopted and expressed paternalistic, pietistic and charitable deeds to migrants. They found this pattern applied evenly to responses of Catholic, Muslim and Baptist communities during 'the crisis'.

Today's challenges pertain primarily to approaches in which state, civilian, religious, humanitarian and charitable actors address the human rights of refugees that are being admitted to Croatia through resettlement quotas. Integration activities in the post-crisis phase returned to their usual businesses within standard accommodation centres for asylum seekers. Main organisational challenges for humanitarian actors remain sustaining networks of personnel and volunteers who engage with refugees, in order to provide direct assistance, integration services, or to socialise with people. For faith-based actors, it is important to have quality cooperation with main institutional actors in the accommodation centres—the Ministry of Interior and Croatian Red Cross—in order to conduct their daily businesses over there. With their network of translators, faith-based actors sometimes facilitate communication of asylum seekers with officials. They also struggle to secure the minimum financial means to allow them to continue with planned, yet scarce, integration activities. Finances are especially scarce among smaller religious organisations with devotion to humanitarian issues but few professional personnel (ZIRAT) and volunteers (ADRA). The CARIT respondent criticised possible competitiveness among humanitarian actors and very formal, yet inefficient, ways of cooperation.

Every day, the current humanitarian situation in Bosnia and Herzegovina gets more and more complicated with hundreds of people waiting in inhumane conditions with no proper reception capacities, and with a vague hope they will succeed in collecting money for smugglers in order to cross into Croatian territory and enter the Schengen area without being intercepted by Croatian police and returned to Bosnia. CBA and JRS continue to work in the field of emergency response given the situation of high humanitarian needs in worsened reception conditions in Bosnia. Both organisations posit that their help is mostly charitable, trying to network with other actors and to establish more sustainable means of assistance. A respondent from the Islamic community in Croatia asserts they have been observing the situation in Bosnia, yet have not had any significant activities due to the lack of personnel and finances that would allow them more proactive engagement.

Designing an overall systematic institutional integration policy at the state level and its more consistent implementation in local communities could eventually raise public awareness and concerns about refugees' issues (Giljević and Lalić Novak 2018). In this context, the respondents positively refer to the present and future roles of Catholic, Protestant and Islamic congregations in Croatia and their cooperation with state and other civilians, humanitarian and faith-based actors to act in synergy on preventing hostility and discrimination. Today, decentralised models of housing and inclusion in the community has been pioneered by some faith-based organisations (JRS and CBA). A model of inclusion and exercising human rights and specific rights of national minorities, such as for a Croatian Muslim minority, could probably help for integration of tomorrow's 'new minorities' of Islamic background.

Therefore, a role of religious communities and faith-based actors in the process of cherishing diversity and fostering social cohesion among the domestic population and the population of newcomers could be a crucial one.

Bibliography

Ager, A., & Ager, J. (2016). Religion, forced migration, and humanitarian response. In J. Saunders, E. Fiddian-Qasmiyeh, & S. Snyder (Eds.), *Intersections of religion and migration: Issues at the global crossroads* (pp. 285–310). Pallgrave Macmillan.

Ajduković, D., Čorkalo Biruški, D., Gregurović, M., Matić Bojić, J., & Župarić-Iljić, D. (2019) *Challenges of integrating refugees into Croatian society: Attitudes of citizens and the readiness of local communities.* Zagreb: Government of the Republic of Croatia Office for Human Rights and Rights of National Minorities.

Andrejč, G. (2018). Infiltrators, imposters, or human beings? The Slovenian socio-political imaginary, christianity, and the responses to the 2015–2016 migrant crisis. In: U. Schmiedel & G. Smith (Eds.), *Religion in the European refugee crisis* (pp. 39–60). Palgrave Macmillan.

AYS et al., Are You Syrious, Centre for Peace Studies, & Refugee Welcome Initiative. (2019). *5th report on pushbacks and violence from the Republic of Croatia: Illegal practices and systemic human rights violations at EU borders*, Zagreb, April 3, 2018. https://www.cms.hr/system/article_document/doc/597/5_5TH_REPORT_ON_PUSHBACKS_AND_VIOLENCE_20052019.pdf. Accessed June 22, 2019.

Deslandes, C., & Anderson, J. (2019). Religion and prejudice toward immigrants and refugees: A meta-analytic review. *The International Journal for the Psychology of Religion.* https://doi.org/10.1080/10508619.2019.1570814

ECRE and AIDA—The European Council on Refugees and Exiles and the Asylum Information Database (2016). *Balkan route reversed: The return of asylum seekers to Croatia under the Dublin system.* https://www.asylumineurope.org/sites/default/files/resources/balkan_route_reversed.pdf. Accessed May 14, 2019.

Giljević, T., & Lalić Novak, G. (2018). Coordination instruments in Croatian integration policy: Classification, evaluation, and proposals for improvements. *Hrvatska i komparativna javna uprava, 18*(3), 373–396.

Giordan, G., & Zrinščak, S. (2018). One pope, two churches: Refugees, human rights and religion in Croatia and Italy. *Social Compass, 65*(1), 62–78.

Glazer, E. K., & Brezovec, E. (2018). Religious identity as a contributing factor of the integration of Middle Eastern immigrants into the Croatian society. *Multidisc. J. Sch. Educ., 14*(2), 11–29.

Guest, G., MacQueen, K. M., & Namey, E. E. (2012). *Applied thematic analysis.* Thousand Oaks: Sage Publications. https://doi.org/10.4135/9781483384436.

Hameršak, M., & Pleše, I. (2018). Confined in movement: The Croatian section of the Balkan Corridor. In: E. Bužinkić & M. Hameršak (Eds.), *Formation and disintegration of the Balkan refugee corridor: Camps, routes and borders in Croatian context.* Zagreb—München: Institute of Ethnology and Folklore Research—Centre for Peace Studies—Faculty of Political Science—Bordermonitoring.eu e.V., 9–41.

Harrell-Bond, B. (2002). Can humanitarian work with refugees be humane? *Human Rights Quarterly, 24*(1), 51–85.

HRW—Human Rights Watch. (2017). *Croatia: Asylum seekers forced back to Serbia. Asylum seekers denied access to protection; Subject to Violence.* January 20, 2017. www.hrw.org/news/2017/01/20/croatia-asylum-seekers-forced-back-serbia. Accessed July 20, 2019.

Kasparek, B., & Speer, M. (2015). *Of hope. Hungary and the long summer of migration.* Boredrmonitoring.eu, February 9, 2015. https://bordermonitoring.eu/ungarn/2015/09/of-hope-en/. Accessed February 15, 2019.

Larsen, M., Demir, E., & Horvat, M. (2016). *Humanitarian responses by local actors: Lessons learned from managing the transit of migrants and refugees through Croatia*. IIED Working Paper. August 2016. London: International Institute for Environment and Development. https://pubs.iied.org/pdfs/10795IIED.pdf. Accessed June 22, 2018.

Miller, S. (2015). Faith based organizations and international responses to forced migration. In S. D. Brunn (Ed.), *The changing world religion map: Sacred places, identities, practices and politics* (pp. 3115–3133). London: Springer.

Mlinarević, G., & Ahmetašević, N. (2019). People on the move in Bosnia and Herzegovina in 2018: Stuck in the corridors to the EU. Heinrich Böll Stiftung Bosnia and Herzegovina. https://ba.boell.org/sites/default/files/people_on_the_move_in_bosnia_and_herzegovina_-_21-02-2019_-_web.pdf.

Riera, J., & Poirier, M.-C. (2014). 'Welcoming the stranger' and UNHCR's cooperation with faith-based organisations. *Forced Migration Review, 48*, 64–67.

Sekulić, B. (2016). No Country for foreigners: Christian praxis in Croatian migration crisis. *Occasional Papers on Religion in Eastern Europe, 36*(4), 53–73. https://digitalcommons.georgefox.edu/ree/vol36/iss4/5. Accessed June 22, 2019.

Šelo Šabić, S. (2017) Humanitarianism and its limits: The refugee crisis response in Croatia. In M. Barlai, B. Fähnrich, C. Griessler, & M. Rhomberg (Eds.), *The migrant crisis: European perspectives and national discourses* (pp. 93–106). LIT Verlag Münster.

Wilson, E. K., & Mavelli, L. (2016). Taking responsibility: Sociodicy, solidarity, and religious-sensitive policymaking in the global politics of migration. In: J. Saunders, E. Fiddian-Qasmiyeh, & S. Snyder (Eds.), *Intersections of religion and migration: Issues at the global crossroads* (pp. 261–284). Pallgrave Macmillan.

Župarić-Iljić, D., & Valenta, M. (2019). Opportunistic humanitarianism and securitization discomfort along the Balkan Corridor: The Croatian experience. In M. Feischmidt, L. Pries, & C. Cantat (Eds.), *Refugee protection and civil society in Europe* (pp. 129–160). Palgrave Macmillan.

Drago Župarić-Iljić Ph.D., is a sociologist, working as an Assistant Professor at the Department of Sociology, Faculty of Humanities and Social Sciences, University of Zagreb. He has published articles and chapters within the interdisciplinary fields of forced migration, asylum, ethnicity, population and environmental studies, focusing on various structural causes and drivers of migration, mobility and post-migration phenomena, with a special interest in the Central East European region.

Chapter 8
In Poland the Stranger Threatens Christianity: Polish Catholics and Their Attitude Towards Refugees

Anna Wilczyńska and Karol Wilczyński

Abstract This chapter aims to analyse the official statements of members of the Catholic hierarchy in Poland concerning the issue of welcoming refugees. After presenting data concerning the number of refugees and followers of Islam as well as the status of the Catholic Church in Poland, this chapter explains why—despite the low numbers of Muslims and refugees and a dominant position of the Church in the country—many Polish Catholics are against accepting newcomers on their land. Different statements of Church officials—from Pope Francis to regular parish priests—are quoted and examined. Additionally, the reactions of the Catholic media to the so-called refugee crisis are presented. The last part of this chapter presents the reaction of the Polish society—the results of nationwide surveys are presented and statements of politicians as well as media responses are analysed. The main thesis of this chapter is that the silence of the Catholic Church in Poland was one of the main reasons why Islamophobic and anti-refugee sentiments were easily developed and used by politicians and media in Poland. Strong support from the Church in Poland to Pope Francis, supporting pro-refugee policy, might have made it much harder.

Keywords Catholic Church · Polish catholicism · Refugees · Migration crisis · Islamophobia · Muslims in Poland

8.1 Introduction

In Polish society, migration and exile are two phenomena that have had a significant impact on the shaping of the country's history, culture and national mythologies. Beginning in the nineteenth century, Poland's many prominent figures in the field of literature and art were refugees in the countries of Western Europe. During the Second World War, Poles seeking shelter settled not only in the countries of Western Europe, USA or South America but also in the Middle East. Also, today, the migration of

A. Wilczyńska · K. Wilczyński (✉)
al. Ignacego Daszyńskiego 16/5, 31-534 Krakow, Poland
URL: https://www.islamistablog.pl

M. C. Jacobsen et al. (eds.), *Cosmopolitanism, Migration and Universal Human Rights*, https://doi.org/10.1007/978-3-030-50645-2_8

Poles abroad, especially to the UK and Germany, is an important element of Poland's social landscape.

Despite the vivid memory of Polish refugees in history and the still present strong emigration trend from Poland to the Western countries since 2015, the attitude of Poles towards migrants and refugees has changed completely. In May 2015, a survey conducted by Public Opinion Research Centre CBOS (2015a, 2) gave proof of the openness of the majority of the Polish people towards international migration and the presence of foreigners in the country. The percentage of people opposed to accepting refugees in Poland at that time was 21%. But in September 2015, the percentage suddenly reached 40%. In December, the number of opponents who accepted refugees exceeded the number of people who were ready to provide shelter for refugees [53% against accepting refugees and 42% for accepting refugees (CBOS 2015b, 2)]. Catholics in Poland, who account for 86% of the population in Polish society (GUS 2018, 196), were largely responsible for this shift in attitudes.

Apart from the increased influx of migrants to Europe and the fact that the refugee figure started to be identified with a Middle Eastern Muslim, it seems that one of the major factors contributing to this shift in social attitudes towards refugees in Poland was the role played by the Catholic Church in shaping the public debate in the country. We argue that despite the fact that public statements of the members of Church hierarchy and other authorities associated with the Catholic Church disseminated in the media were in favour of welcoming refugees, its overall impact was of a great importance in spreading the atmosphere of fear of newcomers as well as in reproducing Islamophobic rhetoric in public debate. We claim that generally the voice of the Church in Poland was silent and its leaders did not oppose the anti-refugee rhetoric of the state media and governing politicians. Moreover, the voice of priests and bishops openly opposing traditional Catholic doctrine and Pope Francis was much louder than the few Church leaders who tried to promote the idea of welcoming refugees.

In the first part of this chapter, we present the attitudes of Polish Catholics—both the Church leaders and ordinary believers—towards refugees in the context of the Church's influence on social trends in the country. First, the paper presents information on the presence and official status of the Catholic Church in Poland. Second, the actual numbers of refugees and Muslims, as well as their status in Poland, are analysed. Third, we demonstrate statements of Polish episcopate members, articles from major Catholic media sources, as well as Pope Francis's instructions and official documents regarding the response of the Catholic Church to the challenges of the so-called migration crisis. Next, we introduce and analyse reasons for changing the discourse on refugees among Catholics who make up officially the majority of Polish society.

8.1.1 *Status of Catholic Church in Poland*

Poland is a religiously homogeneous country. The Catholic Church is the most prominent religious institution in Poland and has one of the most developed Catholic parish networks in the world (ISKK 2017, 2). According to the recent census, Catholics in Poland account for 32.9 million, representing 86.7% of the Polish population (GUS 2018, 196). The parishes, as well as structural organisations and Church offices, are served by 25,000 priests (ISKK 2018, 11). Although the total number of Catholics in the country seems to be very high, the statistics concerning attendance at obligatory Sunday masses are a lot lower. On average, only 36.7% of Polish Catholics attend regular Sunday mass (ISKK 2018, 36) and only 16% participate fully in the service by receiving Communion during mass (ISKK 2018, 38). The majority of Poles seem to declare their affiliation to the Church but do not participate in its rituals.

Despite the statistics, the Catholic Church and Christian tradition shape the core identity for the vast majority of Polish people. During the communist period, when the functioning of religious institutions was significantly impeded, the Church managed to maintain its structures. Due to the political involvement of the Church in Poland during this period in time, the number of its faithful gradually increased. At that time, identifying with the Catholic Church was a sign of opposition to the communist regime. Taking part in religious gatherings was viewed as a way to participate in active resistance to oppressive authority. Today's statistics on the Church's members in Poland, the Church's position and its influence on public life are largely based on the status of this institution in society at this moment in history.

The leaders of the Church who are considered to be public authorities have an influencing power on modelling public opinion. The Episcopal Conference of Poland takes part in the social debate concerning issues usually considered as belonging to the private life sphere, such as shaping legislation on tightening the ban on abortion, the use of in vitro fertilisation, limiting trade on Sundays and displaying religious symbols in the public space (Pędziwiatr 2015, 163–178). Although, according to the Polish Constitution (Poland's Constitution 1997, 6), all religious institutions are considered to be of equal status, Catholics in Poland are the only religious group whose religious holidays are automatically recognised as days off from work for all persons residing in Poland. The Catholic Church is the only religious institution that established close relations with the state on the basis of an international agreement with the Holy See (concordat). Also, the Catholic catechism is a default school subject for students aged 6–18. The Catholic Church enjoys tax refunds and gets the majority of public funds designated for the Church Fund—a government-controlled trust for religious organisations' support. What is important to see here is that the Catholic Church in Poland developed its own media platforms including radio stations (best known is Radio Maryja, which in 2011 was listened to by 15% of the Polish population—CBOS 2011) as well as TV stations (TV Trwam) and internet portals administered by various entities, e.g. religious orders.

8.1.2 *Presence of Refugees and Muslims in Poland*

Although, in Europe, the year 2015 was marked by a significant increase in the number of incoming migrants and, consequently, an increased number of asylum seekers, the changes noticed in the number of migrants coming to Poland in 2015 were not so drastic.

Between 2012 and 2014, 34,199 citizens of different countries applied for international protection in Poland (UdsC 2012–2014). During this period, citizens of the Russian Federation were the most represented national group among those applying for refugee status. Their applications constituted 67.3% of all applications for international protection submitted in Poland. During those three years, refugee status was granted to 557 people (87 in 2012, 208 in 2013 and 262 in 2014). In addition, during the same period, subsidiary protection was granted to 456 people and a tolerated stay was granted to 997 people. The national composition of persons who have been granted refugee status by 2014 mainly consisted of citizens from Russian Federation, Ukraine, Georgia and Armenia (UdsC 2012–2014).

In 2015—the year which marked the beginning of the so-called migration crisis in Europe—the number of applications for international protection in Poland doubled in comparison with the previous year (6625 people submitted their applications for refugee status in 2014, and 12,325 persons did so in 2015—UdsC 2015, 8). However, looking at the absolute numbers, it can be noticed that the number of people covered by the applications submitted in 2015 did not exceed the number of people covered by applications submitted in 2013.[1] Still, the number of applicants was not overwhelming compared with the neighbouring countries of Western Europe.[2]

In addition, in 2015, a large number of applications for refugee status in Poland did not translate into a rapid increase in positive decisions granting international protection to applying foreigners. Although there was a 33% increase in the number of positive decisions compared with the number of positive decisions given in 2014,[3] in 2015 persons granted asylum accounted for 3% of all applications considered. Only 348 people received refugee status in Poland (UdsC 2015, 8).

Based on the data provided by the Polish Office for Foreigners, it can also be noted that the breakdown by country of people applying for international protection in Poland has not undergone drastic change. In 2015, as well as in the previous years, the largest number of applications for asylum was submitted mainly by citizens of Russia, Ukraine and Georgia. But when it comes to 2015, Syria was the first country of origin of the applicants who were granted asylum.[4]

In 2016, the trend of an increased number of asylum applications prevailed (12,321 persons were covered by the applications submitted that year, 73% of whom were

---

[1] In 2013 there were 15,253 persons covered by applications (UdsC 2012–2014).

[2] In 2015 there were 33,226 applications for asylum registered in Germany (AIDA 2015a: 15), 50,840 people applied for refugee status in France (AIDA 2015b: 8), 59,165 people applied for asylum in Italy (AIDA 2015c: 6) and 149,028 in Sweden (AIDA 2015d: 5).

[3] In 2014, 262 persons were granted asylum in Poland (UdsC 2012–2014).

[4] 203 persons from Syria were granted asylum in Poland in 2015 (UdsC 2015: 8).

citizens of the Russian Federation), but the percentage of people who have been granted refugee status has dropped. The refugee status was received by 108 people that year, accounting for 1% of the applicants (UsdC 2016, 5). In turn, in both 2017 and 2018, a twofold decrease in the number of incoming applications was noted and the breakdown by country of the applicants was the same as in previous years. The number of asylum applications granted both in 2017 and 2018 did not exceed 200 individuals (UdsC 2017, 5–6; UdsC, 2018). Accordingly, in the whole European Union, the number of asylum applications submitted came down to how it presented itself in 2014.

Since the end of 2015 and the increased influx of migrants to Europe, the figure of the refugee started to be identified with a Middle Eastern Muslim. That trend persisted not only in Western countries but also in Poland. It dwells in Polish society despite the fact that Poland has a Muslim minority that settled in the north-eastern regions of the country in the fourteenth century (Górak-Sosnowska 2011, 13). As a result of this identification of refugees with Middle Eastern Muslims in the public debate in Poland, statements about refugees and Muslims are intertwined despite the fact that Muslims in Poland represent less than 1% of Polish society (Narkowicz 2018, 4).

Since the settlement of Muslims on Polish lands in the fourteenth century (Chazbijewicz 1997), no mass negative reactions towards this minority have been registered in history (Dziekan 2011). Muslim settlers in the seventeenth century not only received noble privileges but also enjoyed religious freedom. Members of the Muslim religious minority took an active part in creating Polish culture through their involvement in the political life of the country. In the minds of the Poles professionally active in the 1970s and 1980s, Middle Eastern states were perceived as the countries where Polish engineers and construction workers were sent within the framework of agreements signed by the government of the Polish People's Republic. At present, the view of Muslims in Poland is shaped by reports of terrorist attacks starting from the events of 11 September 2001 (Nalborczyk 2003) and Islam is being seen as a religion of invasion and oppression.

As the *Perils of Perception* study shows, Poles overestimate the number of Muslims living in their country, stating that there are five times more followers of Islam in Poland than there actually are. The same applies to migrants. In the survey, Poles estimated that there are eight times more migrants in the country than in reality (Ipsos 2018, 28).

8.1.3 Reactions to Refugees and Muslims Among Polish Clergy

From the year 2015 and the rapid development of the so-called migration crisis in Europe, Pope Francis, the supreme authority of the Catholic Church in the world, regularly called on local churches and Catholic initiatives to support and welcome refugees in their countries irrespective of their religious affiliation. The most significant appeal of the institutional Church given to the faithful were the words of the Pope in which he encouraged every Catholic parish to accept a refugee family in 2015: 'I appeal to the parishes, the religious communities, the monasteries and sanctuaries of all Europe to … take in one family of refugees' (Reuters 2015).

As a basis of the explanation for this attitude of acceptance towards refugees, the Pope used a theological reason recalling the teaching of Jesus expressed in these words: 'For I was hungry and you gave me food, I was thirsty and you gave me drink, I was a stranger and you welcomed me' (Matthew 25, 35). In other statements of the Pope, his explanation referred to a certain vision of global social justice.

While the research shows that, before 2015, Pope Francis was highly regarded by Polish Catholic (CBOS 2014), his instructions did not prevent the deterioration of the attitude towards refugees among Catholics in Poland; and that even though the Pope visited the country in 2016 for World Youth Day to recall his message, attitudes towards receiving refugees from conflict countries have not changed since the attacks in Paris in November 2015 (CBOS 2016b). Short-term deterioration of attitudes towards refugees was reported after the March 2016 attacks in Brussels and after the July 2016 attacks in Nice and Munich.

What was crucial, however, was the fact that the views of some Polish Church leaders who repeated the Pope's words from 2015[5] were drowned out by numerous anti-refugee and anti-Muslim statements of Polish priests and bishops. Starting from the terrorist attacks in Paris in 2015, the figure of a Muslim terrorist posing as a refugee has become a central trope through which xenophobic politics have been employed. Church leaders, as well as ordinary members of the Catholic Church in Poland, began using the figure of a Muslim pretending to be a refugee as a synonym of a threat to the Catholic identity of the country. The influx of refugees was portrayed as an 'Islamisation' and a threat to Church institutions (Pędziwiatr 2017, 411–443). In the public debate, the Polish Conference of Bishops, the central organ of the Catholic Church in Poland, tried to take the middle ground between the Pope and dominating attitudes in the Polish society and struggled to pass the responsibility of accepting refugees to the state. In its statement on the so-called refugee crisis on 8 September 2015, the Polish Episcopacy stated: 'The assistance is necessary for those who suffer as a result of wars in their countries … in Poland the main initiative and responsibility lies on the shoulders of the secular authorities. It is they who are the inviting side' (KEP 2015).

Although the manifestation of the anti-refugee attitude of the higher representatives of the Church in Poland was visible, the statements of the Polish Church hierarchy appeared in the Church media as well as in those media related to the Church.

[5]Bishop Krzysztof Zadarko, delegate of the Polish Episcopate Conference for Immigrants, said: 'A wave of hate, or hatred, is poured over the internet. The Pope is accused of betrayal of the Church; instead of giving his hand to Christians, he gives it to the Muslims. The discussion begins. I trust in the Pope' (Deon 2016).

Possibly the most popular critic of accepting refugees (especially from Muslim countries) within the Catholic Church was a former priest and ex-member of Congregation of Missionary Fathers of St. Vincent de Paul, Jacek Międlar. Międlar. Until his resignation from the priesthood in 2016, he delivered anti-refugee and Islamophobic homilies in churches as well as speeches during rallies of the nationalist group ONR, attracting a large group of followers. In 2015 during his speech on anti-migration demonstration in Wrocław, Międlar was quoted saying: 'They will say about you that you are fascists! I often hear that I am a fascist priest. Nonsense! Let them talk […]. We need bravery and courage, but not from Allah and leftists […]. We do not attack, we defend ourselves against the invasion, against the attack from the East, which is perfectly programmed' (Deon 2015).

While still a member of a religious order, Jacek Międlar organised a mass in the city of Białystok to celebrate the anniversary of the birth of the radical nationalist group ONR. After the sermon, the group held a march in the city during which its attendants shouted: 'We don't want Islam, terrorists or Muslims […] and Zionists will hang from trees' (SNW 2016). The anti-refugee and anti-Semitic speeches of Jacek Międlar were popularised by the Catholic website PCh24.pl (PCh24 2016). Similar statements expressing opposition to the admission of refugees, especially to Muslims, were also expressed by Polish bishops. Abp Marek Jędraszewski (2015), vice-president of the Commission of Polish Episcopacy (number two among Polish Church leaders) expressed his stance on refugees by connecting them to those who 'want to create the caliphate in Europe': 'Media say that many refugees openly claim that they want to create the caliphate in Europe. We cannot disregard this and say that there is no problem' (Jędraszewski and Łoziński 2015).

In a homily during a religious celebration of the Day of Atonement in Gietrzwałd in July 2018 bishop Józef Zawitkowski was recorded saying: 'There will be no German spit in our face, now we ourselves spit on ourselves. There will be no refugee in my house because I swore that: "Every threshold will be our stronghold, let us help God!" So, I will not change my oaths. And if someone in my house would take off the cross and tried to bring us children, he is not from my country. Let him come back to himself' (PCh24 2018). The sermon was published in the Catholic media and was quoted as 'important' in PCh24.pl and 'beautiful' in another Catholic media outlet Fronda.pl (Fronda 2018). The celebration was also transmitted by the Church media: Radio Maryja and TV Trwam. The Day of Atonement was attended by representatives of state and local government authorities. Also, Bishop Edward Frankowski was recorded saying during a homily in 2015: 'Radical Islamists close their ranks, assume an increased attack on Christians. Many of them are heading for Europe, among the mass immigration of refugees. Masked jihadists are among them' (Fronda 2015). Other public figures representing Catholic media and identifying with right-wing Catholicism have commented on Pope Francis's pro-refugee standpoint and qualified his speeches as having a destructive effect on the institution of the Church and Polish national identity. Most controversial was the homily of a famous Catholic professor and priest, Father Edward Staniek, who prayed for a quick death of the Pope if he does not change the politics of openness towards Muslims (PCh24 2018a).

It is also worth mentioning that many of the major Catholic media were not in favour of welcoming refugees. For example, the biggest Catholic newspaper—*Gość Niedzielny*—presented the so-called migration crisis in September 2015 with the cover photo of young men crossing the bridge, calling it the 'new migration period'. A smaller newspaper—*Idziemy*—called it, in the same manner, a 'storm on Europe' (using a similar photo of young men). On the opposite side of the spectrum, there are instances of a more pro-refugee narrative among Polish Catholic media (such as *Więź* quarterly or Deon.pl website), but they were unsuccessful in shaping the public debate. Similarly, in the case of Pope Francis, followers of these media platforms preferred to ignore the articles on refugees or even change the source of information about migration to one that would not question their opinions.

8.1.4 Reactions to Refugees Among Polish Catholics

The influence of the anti-refugee rhetoric of the Catholic media and the effect of statements of the members of the Polish Church hierarchy on believers can be seen in the surveys conducted in Poland in 2016. This is best illustrated by statistics presenting the correlation between religious practices of Polish Catholics and their attitude towards refugees. Among the Poles who in 2016 attended sermons in the Church several times a week, 81% were anti-refugee. Also, 75% of Catholics who attended religious gatherings in Church once a month stated they were opposed to accepting refugees and 69% of persons who go to Church once a year were against hosting refugees in Poland (CBOS 2016a).

On a similar note, negative attitudes towards refugees were also expressed by candidates for the priesthood in the four senior seminaries in Poland. Pope Francis's address on the migration crisis in 2015, which urged Catholic parishes to provide assistance and shelter to refugees, was supported by 34% of the future clergy, whereas the majority of respondents (41%) were moderately or strongly opposed to this idea. Only 10% of the future priests surveyed in the research also claimed that bilateral understanding between Islam and the West could be accomplished; 58% of surveyed seminarians expressed a belief that violent clash with Muslims was unavoidable and 22% stated that smaller conflicts with Islam would keep emerging in the future (Pędziwiatr 2018). The same research confirmed that the majority of future priests who took part in this research were learning about Islam as well as migration from Catholic media and predominantly from social media.

It is difficult to predict what would happen if the Catholic Church in Poland became more decisive in defending the pro-refugee option. We argue, however, that the silence of most of the bishops and the clear opposition to the papal stance was the major reason why the Church and the idea of 'Catholic Poland' were easily used by politicians, anti-refugee media and activists. It is also the reason why the number of people who are against welcoming refugees is rising in the Catholic community in Poland.

First of all, the Polish government welcomed the stance of the Polish Episcopacy that the main initiative and responsibility lies on the shoulders of the secular authorities. It helped to develop the main anti-EU policy of 'supporting refugees on-site', which was presented by the head of the Law and Justice (PiS) party, Jarosław Kaczyński, before the parliamentary elections in October 2015. Its essence is to depict refugees as a threat to the Polish economy and culture, which makes supporting on-site a necessity. Representatives of the government used the support of Catholic organisations—especially Pomoc Kościołowi w Potrzebie,[6] which provide humanitarian aid in Syria and Iraq—to promote its policy of not helping refugees in Poland.[7] In January 2018 the head of the Polish Episcopacy, archbishop Stanisław Gądecki, claimed that 'support on-site' is not enough (Gość Niedzielny 2018). It had no effect on the policy of the Polish government, though.

However, the Catholic Church also had an indirect influence on the anti-refugee sentiments in Polish society. We may connect it to the idea of defending 'Christian civilisation' against Western liberalism as well as Islamic or Jewish (i.e., non-Christian) values. It started in 2015 when Miriam Shaded, a politician and the president of the Estera Foundation, tried to lobby to welcome only Christian refugees from Syria in Poland and recommended acceptance of the ban on Islam in the country (Dziennik.pl 2016). She was one of the first public figures to use quite old Islamophobic narratives present in Polish culture since the sixteenth century (Bobako 2017). According to research conducted in 2016, more future priests in the Catholic seminaries agree with Shaded's idea and supported it entirely (23%) or partially (21%) than opposed it partially (27%) or completely (13%) (Pędziwiatr 2018, 474–475). Anti-Islamic sentiments connected to defending 'Catholic Poland' were also used by pro-government media, which openly said that 'they are invaders, not refugees',[8] presenting very often, for instance, the topic of crusaders or wars of Rzeczpospolita against the Ottoman Empire. Most controversial were covers of *wSieci* weekly, which linked welcoming refugees to 'Islamic rape on Europe' and an EU conspiracy against independent Poland,[9] which will create 'hell in Poland' because of 'clear orders from Berlin',[10] as well as covers of *Gazeta Polska*, which spread fear against refugees not only by referring to the threat of 'traditional Catholic values',[11] but also by saying that they 'brought deadly diseases'.[12] This type of narrative was never undermined by documents or official statements of the Polish Episcopacy. Its silence or sometimes sympathy expressed more or less indirectly was fundamental, though, in maintaining (and developing) anti-refugee narrative by politicians and pro-government media.

---

[6]PKWP is the Polish branch of the German NGO Kirche in Not.

[7]See Radio Maryja (2018).

[8]Cf. *Do Rzeczy* weekly, 13 Sep 2015.

[9]Cf. *wSieci* weekly, 14 Feb 2016.

[10]Cf. *wSieci* weekly, 21 Sep 2015.

[11]Cf. *Gazeta Polska* weekly, 30 Aug 2017.

[12]Cf. *Gazeta Polska* weekly, 30 Jul 2017.

8.2 Conclusion

I was a stranger and you did not welcome me—these words of Jesus Christ from the Gospel of Matthew are the basis of the Christian and Catholic stance on welcoming refugees. Since 1914, the Catholic Church has organised the initiative of the World Day of Migrant and Refugee, which aims to motivate Christian communities to take responsibility for migrants and to cooperate in solving their diverse problems. One may not find an answer to why the Catholic Church in Poland did not take up this responsibility, although this chapter has aimed to answer questions on the effects of this decision. As demonstrated, the overall influence of the Church on anti-refugee sentiments presents widely in Polish society was positive though indirect. As an important factor in Polish politics and public debate, the so-called refugee crisis was generally either silenced or presented as a threat by representatives of the Polish Church. As we tried to show in the first part of this chapter, this happened despite the very low number of Muslims and refugees living in Poland and the very privileged status of the Catholic Church. Reactions of the Polish clergy, episcopacy, as well as regular Polish Catholics, show that religion is an important factor in shaping opinions on the issue of migration.

It seems, though, that refugees are no longer an issue in Polish public debate. Recent surveys show that people are no longer interested in this topic and, more importantly, they no longer believe the statements of the ruling party in stories related to the so-called refugee crisis.[13] It seems that this change in position of the Polish society is not religiously motivated. Still, there is a lack of in-depth study of current opinions on refugees and Islam among Catholics in Poland. Religion, though, seems to play a lesser role nowadays and the Church has lost its authority quite steadily in recent years.

Bibliography

Asylum Information Database AIDA. (2015a). Country Report: Germany. https://bit.ly/2TeO01s. Accessed January 18, 2019.

Asylum Information Database AIDA. (2015b). Country Report: France. https://bit.ly/1RQR39q. Accessed January 18, 2019.

Asylum Information Database AIDA. (2015c). Country Report: Italy. https://bit.ly/2832r83. Accessed January 18, 2019.

Asylum Information Database AIDA. (2015d). Country Report: Sweden. https://bit.ly/2GLWh72. Accessed January 19, 2019.

Bobako, M. (2017). Islamofobia jako technologia władzy. Studium z antropologii politycznej, Universitas.

Chazbijewicz, S., & Bohdanowicz, L. (1997). Tatarzy Muzułmanie w Polsce. Gdańsk: Niezależne Wydawnictwo.

[13] There was a study conducted by a small Polish NGO—uchodźcy.info—in Warsaw concerning the 'anti-immigrant' election spot of PiS, which was one of few reasons why the ruling party lost the last election in autumn 2018.

Deon.pl. (2015). Ks. Jacek Międlar: bronimy się przed inwazją. https://bit.ly/2Y0BaDu. Accessed January 30, 2019.

Deon.pl. (2016). Bp Zadarko: Papież wyciąga rękę do imigrantów. https://bit.ly/2XY4VES. Accessed January 30, 2019.

Dziekan, M. (2011). History and culture of polish tatars. In Górak-Sosnowska (Ed.), *Muslims in Poland and Eastern Europe*. Warsaw: Faculty of Oriental Studies University of Warsaw.

Dziennik.pl. (2016). Miriam Shaded kontra islam. "Powinien być w Polsce zakazany, jest sprzeczny z konstytucją". https://bit.ly/2W0mUIQ. Accessed February 12, 2019.

Fronda.pl. (2015). Mocne słowa bp. Frankowskiego: "Radykalni islamiści zwierają szyki, przypuszczają wzmożony atak na chrześcijan". https://bit.ly/2FbcJL3. Accessed February 12, 2019.

Fronda.pl. (2018). Niepokalana u źródełka Gietrzwałdu, zdepcz głowę węża, moc szatana! Mocne i piękne kazanie bp. Zawitkowskiego. https://bit.ly/2HCRGUw. Accessed February 12, 2019.

Główny Urząd Statystyczny GUS. (2018). Statistical yearbook of the Republic of Poland. https://bit.ly/2udlHSE. Accessed January 18, 2019.

Gość Niedzielny. (2018). Abp Gądecki: Bezpieczeństwo uchodźcy, który potrzebuje pomocy, jest ważniejsze niż bezpieczeństwo narodowe. https://bit.ly/2HC9BKN. Accessed March 12, 2019.

Górak-Sosnowska. Katarzyna. (2011). Muslims in Europe: Different communities, one discourse? Adding the Central and Eastern European perspective. In K. Górak-Sosnowska, (Eds.), *Muslims in Poland and Eastern Europe. Widening the European Discourse on Islam* (pp. 12–26). Warsaw.

Instytut Statystyki Kościoła Katolickiego SAC ISKK. (2017). Annuarium Statisticum Ecclesiae in Polonia. https://bit.ly/2hQnoBI. Accessed January 18, 2019.

Instytut Statystyki Kościoła Katolickiego SAC ISKK. (2018). Annuarium Statisticum Ecclesiae in Polonia. https://bit.ly/2Cr7sy6. Accessed January 18, 2019.

Ipsos. 2018. Perils of Perception. https://bit.ly/2Qu9GpM. Accessed January 30, 2019.

Jędraszewski, M., & Łoziński, B. (2015). Uchodźcy muszą nas szanować. In *Gość Niedzielny*. https://www.gosc.pl/doc/2731491.Uchodzcy-musza-nas-szanowac/2. Accessed March 12, 2019.

Komisja Episkopatu Polski. (2015). Komunikat Prezydium Konferencji Episkopatu Polski ws. Uchodźców. https://bit.ly/2CoD5bD. Accessed February 12, 2019.

Nalborczyk, A. (2003). The Image of Islam and Muslims in the polish mass media before and after 11 September 2001. In *TRANS. Internet-Zeitschrift für Kulturwissenschaften*. 15/2003. https://www.inst.at/trans/15Nr/01_4/nalborczyk15.htm. Accessed January 30, 2019.

Narkowicz, K. (2018). 'Refugees not welcome here': State, church and civil society responses to the refugee crisis in Poland. *International Journal of Politics, Culture, and Society*, 357–373.

PCh24.pl. (2016). Ksiądz Jacek Międlar: wyzwolenie z więzów strachu musi poprzedzać intronizacja Chrystusa w naszym sercu. https://bit.ly/2Wa5ry3. Accessed February 12, 2019.

PCh24.pl. (2018a). W Gietrzwałdzie odbył się Dzień Pokuty. Podczas homilii bp Zawitkowskiego padły ważne słowa. https://bit.ly/2O5tkDO. Accessed February 12, 2019.

PCh24.pl. (2018b). Ksiądz Staniek: „Jeśli papież nie słucha Jezusa to nie uczestniczy w Jego autorytecie". https://bit.ly/2TKSIVI. Accessed March 12, 2019.

Pędziwiatr, K. (2015). Church and state relations in Poland with special focus on the radio station mary. In F. Simons & D. Westerlund (Eds.), *Religion, politics and nation-building in post-communist countries* (pp. 163–178). London: Ashgate.

Pędziwiatr, Konrad. (2017). Islamophobia in Poland: National Report 2016, In E. Bayralki & F. Hafez (Eds.), *European Islamophobia report 2016* (pp. 411–443), Istanbul.

Pędziwiatr, K. (2018). The Catholic Church in Poland on Muslims and Islam. *Patterns of Prejudice, 52*(5), 472–475.

Poland's Constitution. (1997). Article 25. Constitute. https://www.constituteproject.org. Accessed January 18, 2019.

Public Opinion Research Center CBOS. (2011). Dwadzieścia Lat Radia Maryja. Komunikat z badań 168. https://www.cbos.pl/SPISKOM.POL/2011/K_168_11.PDF. Accessed January 18, 2019.

Public Opinion Research Center CBOS. (2014). *Pontyfikat Papieża Franciszka w opiniach Polaków*. https://www.cbos.pl/SPISKOM.POL/2014/K_057_14.PDF. Accessed January 30, 2019.

Public Opinion Research Center CBOS. (2015a). O uchodźcach w przededniu unijnego szczytu poświęconego kryzysowi imigracyjnemu. Komunikat z badań 133. https://www.cbos.pl/SPISKOM.POL/2015/K_133_15.PDF. Accessed January 18, 2019.
Public Opinion Research Center CBOS. (2015b). Stosunek do uchodźców po atakach terrorystycznych w Paryżu. Komunikat z badań 172. https://www.cbos.pl/SPISKOM.POL/2015/K_172_15.PDF. Accessed January 18, 2019.
Public Opinion Research Center CBOS. (2016a). Stosunek do przyjmowania uchodźców. Komunikat z badań 169. https://www.cbos.pl/SPISKOM.POL/2016/K_169_16.PDF. Access January 30, 2019.
Public Opinion Research Center CBOS. (2016b). Stosunek do przyjmowania uchodźców. Komunikat z badań 24. https://www.cbos.pl/SPISKOM.POL/2016/K_024_16.PDF. Accessed January 30, 2019.
Radio Maryja. (2018). Ks. W. Cisło: Ponad 13 tys. Syryjczyków skorzystało z leczenia, dzięki pomocy z Polski. https://bit.ly/2HABSkY. Accessed March 12, 2019.
Reuters. (2015). Pope calls on every European Parish to Host One Migrant Family Each. https://bit.ly/2W3hjS6. Accessed January 30, 2019.
Stowarzyszenie Nigdy Więcej. (2016). *Katalog Wypadków - Brunatna Księga* [Catalogue of Incidents—The Brown Book]. No. 22.
Urząd do spraw Cudzoziemców. 2012–2014. Biuletyn Statystyczny. https://bit.ly/2UgOHUU. Accessed January 18, 2019.
Urząd do spraw Cudzoziemców. (2015). Sprawozdanie z wykonywania ustawy o ochronie międzynarodowej za 2015 rok. https://bit.ly/2rtwuIL. Accessed January 18, 2019.
Urząd do spraw Cudzoziemców. (2016). Sprawozdanie z wykonywania ustawy o ochronie międzynarodowej za 2016 rok. https://bit.ly/2tDmf3U. Accessed January 18, 2019.
Urząd do spraw Cudzoziemców. (2017). Informacja Szefa Urzędu do Spraw Cudzoziemców o stosowaniu w roku 2017 ustawy z dnia 13 czerwca 2003 r. o udzielaniu cudzoziemcom ochrony na terytorium Rzeczypospolitej Polskiej. https://bit.ly/2J6iiON. Accessed January 30, 2019.
Urząd do spraw Cudzoziemców. (2018). Podsumowanie: ochrona międzynarodowa w 2018 r. https://bit.ly/2H4JfAQ. Accessed January 30, 2019.

Anna Wilczyńska is a journalist, specialist in Arabic Culture and Islam, author of Islamista Blog, covering topics of migration and integration of migrants in the EU, interreligious dialogue, war and conflict resolution, education for peace, Islamophobia and social exclusion. She visited Aleppo and Damascus in February 2017 and refugee camps and migration centers in Poland, Turkey, Lebanon, Germany, Denmark, Sweden and Morocco.

Karol Wilczyński is a journalist and author of islamistablog.pl, covering news on social issues, religion, the so-called migration crisis and the war in Syria. He visited Aleppo and Damascus in February 2017 and refugee camps in Turkey, Lebanon, Morocco as well as several European countries. He did his Ph.D. on early Arabic philosophy at Artes Liberales Academy, Warsaw.

Part III
Disentangling Migration, Gender and Human Rights: The Jurisprudence of the European Court of Human Rights

Part III
Disentangling Migration, Gender and Human Rights: The Jurisprudence of the European Court of Human Rights

Chapter 9
Legal Cosmopolitanism and Political Sovereigntism: European Asylum Law and Illiberal Policies in Central Europe

Joseph Krulic

Abstract Since 2010, the EUCJ in Luxembourg and the Commission in Brussels have developed a kind of 'European legal cosmopolitanism' in the area of the right of asylum, which has been violently opposed by the 'political Sovereigntism' of the Visegrád Group (notably Hungary), thus challenging the legal order of the EU.

Keywords Right of asylum · Rule of law · Effectiveness · International protection · Jurisprudence · Directive · Dublin regulation · Systemic failure · Visegrád group

9.1 Introduction

Since Viktor Orban came to power in Hungary in 2010, we have seen in a series of litigation a confrontation regarding the law and around the law between, on the one side, the jurisprudence of the European Union Court of Justice (EUCJ) in Luxembourg with regard to the right of asylum, and also that of the European Court of Human Rights (ECtHR) in Strasbourg, together with several jurisdictions and governments in the EU member states, all this being made in the name of an emerging Europe expressing a form of cosmopolitanism, and, on the other side, countries like the 'Visegrád Group' (Hungary, Poland and Slovakia), members of the European Union (EU), which express a conscious rejection of any form of cosmopolitanism.

Certain decisions are emblematic such as the EUCJ's decision of 6 September 2017, which goes against the Visegrád Group regarding the 'distribution' of asylum applicants among the EU member states. The complaint was launched by Hungary and Slovakia, challenging the competence in this matter of the EU Council and the states represented in the Parliament of the EU.

In parallel, other European jurisdictions (ECtHR in Strasbourg) and national jurisdictions have examined the systemic failures of Hungary within the framework of

J. Krulic (✉)
The National Court of Asylum, Montreuil, France
e-mail: joseph.krulic@cnda.juradm.fr

M. C. Jacobsen et al. (eds.), *Cosmopolitanism, Migration and Universal Human Rights*, https://doi.org/10.1007/978-3-030-50645-2_9

the Dublin Regulation, which distributes the responsibilities among the countries in the processing of asylum applications.[1]

The European Parliament and the Commission launched in 2017 and 2018 legal procedures against Budapest, Warsaw and Bratislava because of their refusal to receive asylum applicants or because of a systemic failure in the rule of law. How far can these countries go in their distrust? How has this difference come about between EU law and the Visegrád Group notably regarding migration?

9.2 Appraisal of EU Law Regarding the Right of Asylum for Central European Countries

9.2.1 Cosmopolitical Countries' Favourable Past Towards the Right of Asylum

Numerous factors seemed to predispose these countries to make human rights-based cosmopolitanism their political ideal. Among these factors, we can note the following:

- The role of the 'Helsinki Group' in Budapest in furthering human rights and their expertise regarding the geopolitical analysis of asylum applications: the important role of Gyulai Gabor is recognised by specialists in the area.
- The IARLJ (International Association of Refugees Law Judges) Foundation in Warsaw in 1997 is a symbol.
- The 'Tocquevillian' liberalism of Fidesz during the years 1987–1991, a new Hungarian party of which Viktor Orban was a co-founder. The party adhered to a Hungarian liberal tradition for which Jozsef Eötvös, Minister of Education in 1848 and 1867, was a prominent figure. However, when Fidesz came to power for the first time from 1998 to 2002, it became conservative and nationalistic.[2]
- The prestige that human rights enjoyed from 1975 to 2005 and the multiplication of 'Helsinki committees' in these countries, which Orban's first term in power (1998–2002) had not destroyed (Kende 2004; cf. Thibaud 2011).
- The historical role in the development of international criminal law of theoreticians of Polish origin born before 1914 near Lwow or Lwiw. Hersch Lauterpacht and Raphael Lemkin invented the legal qualifications of 'crime against humanity' and 'genocide' respectively (Sands 2017).

[1] The Dublin Convention of 15 June 1990, the regulation 'Dublin 2' of 18 November 2002, as well as the regulation 'Dublin 3' of 26 June 2013 have established the principle that the country responsible for handling an application for asylum is the applicant's first country of arrival, though with some nuances regarding the reunion of families in Dublin 3.

[2] According to Kende (2012), the narrow defeat of Viktor Orban in 2002 (he had the majority of votes but not of seats in Parliament) traumatised him and constitutes one of the reasons for his radicalisation.

9.2.2 The Shift After 2010

The 'illiberal' aspects of the politics of Central Europe have multiplied at the very moment the jurisprudence of the EUCJ has asserted itself in asylum matters. In fact, the coming into force of the Lisbon TFEU[3] on 1 December 2009 integrated asylum matters into EU law. The 'European' sources of asylum law have multiplied since 1997, where the Treaty of Amsterdam was aiming to 'communitarise' within a five-year period. The so-called 'Qualification' directives (Council Directive 2004/83/EC) in their first edition from 29 April 2004, and the 'Procedures" directive from 1 December 2005, which have seen a second edition from 13 December 2011[4] and 26 June 2013 (Directive 2011/95/EU) constitute truly a second charter of asylum, which prolongs the Geneva Convention of 28 July 1951.

From the decision *El Gafaji* of 17 February 2009 and onwards, the EUCJ continues to make decisions regarding asylum matters that will profoundly modify the legal asylum regime in the European Union. Certain decisions provide answers to claims or preliminary rulings from the Visegrad Group.

Some of these decisions are very technical and concern the relationship between various United Nations conventions (UNWRA and the 1951 Geneva Convention, EUCJ, 19 December 2011, *El Kott v Hungary*), but others have effects on the 'Euro-compatibility' of the system. In this way, the case C-/10NS *Secretary of State for the Home Secretary* of 20 December 2011, which duplicates the reasoning of the ECtHR decision *MMS against Greece and Belgium* (20 January 2011), resulted in declaring Greece to be 'systematically' failing in the field of asylum rights.

In fact, as legislation and decisions are made at an accelerated pace following the 2015 refugee crisis, the suspicion of systematic failure in matters of asylum rights will constantly reappear and develop with regard to Hungary and also Poland, within the 'European' jurisdictions both at the national and European level.

The EU has launched procedures against Budapest, Warsaw and Prague because of their refusal to receive asylum applicants, but also because of their refusal to accept the rule of law model, born in the heart of Central Europe. It originated first in the southern part of Germany and Austria before 1918, including, at the very limits of the empire, Lemberg (Lwiw, Lwow), where two qualifications from international criminal law (i.e. crime against humanity and genocide) were added.

---

[3]TFEU (Treaty on the Functioning of the European Union) succeeds the Treaty of Nice on 1 December 2009.

[4]Directive 2011/95/EU of the European Parliament and of the Council of 13 December 2001 on Standards for the qualification of third-country nationals or stateless persons as beneficiaries of international protection, for a uniform status for refugees or for persons eligible for subsidiary protection, and for the content of the protection granted.

9.2.3 *The Climate of Distrust in the Visegrad Group of Countries After 2015*

A general climate of resistance developed during and after the 2015 Refugee Crisis. However, one must distinguish between:

- The various procedures of the European institutions (Commission, Parliament) against the countries in the Visegrád Group (Hungary, Poland) because of their refusal to receive migrants and respect the minimal requirement of the rule of law and
- The mistrust of jurisdictions in many EU countries as well as the ECtHR regarding the 'systemic' failures in these countries (Hungary and for other reasons Poland) in the effective protection of refugees or regarding international protection generally.

9.3 The Legal Proceedings Between EU Institutions and the Visegrád Group

9.3.1 *The Proceedings Under Article 7 of the TFEU*

One should note the following:

- A Parliamentary resolution of 12 September 2018 inviting the Council to note the existence of a clear risk of a serious breach by Hungary of the values of the Union because of its legislation notably with regard to the right of asylum.
- The European Commission procedure of 20 December 2018 triggering the article 7 procedure after having noted a clear risk of serious violation by Poland of the rule of law because of the forced retirement of the Supreme Court's judges and a new system of appointment of judges endangering their independence. An emergency interim ruling of 19 October 2018[5] allowed the suspension of this law and a decision on the content from the EUCJ from 24 June 2019 declared the law contrary to EU law (Judgment of the Court (Grand Chamber) of 24 June 2019–C-619/18).

9.3.2 *Conflicts Regarding the Right of Asylum*

On 10 December 2015, the European Commission published a press release announcing the opening of an infringement procedure against Hungary. The Commission stated that it has noted that the Hungarian legislation in matters of asylum was

[5]Court of Justice of the European Union, Order of the Vice-president of ECJ in Case C-619/18 R, Commission v Poland, 19 October 2018. CJEU delivered its judgment on the merits, recognising the incompatibility of the measures of the law of 3 April 2018 with EU law.

incompatible on several counts with the European Union Law. The letter of formal notice to the Hungarian government outlines several points of concern:

- The impossibility of presenting new facts and circumstances during an appeal.
- The fact that asylum applicants are obliged to leave Hungarian territory before the period for lodging an appeal has expired or even before a decision has been made concerning their application.
- The absence from Hungarian legislation of any accelerated procedure applicable to cases of unauthorised border crossing, and of any right to interpretation and translation provided for in the provisions of the 'Procedure' directive (Directive 2013/32/EU).

On 17 May 2017, the Commission published a press release about the infringement procedure. It indicated that it would not only continue the proceedings engaged in December 2015 but extend them to new incompatibilities in the Hungarian legislation on matters of asylum resulting from legislative amendments, such as the adoption of a law on 7 March 2017, providing for the systematic detention of all asylum applicants. It expressly stated that Hungarian asylum law does not respect, in this matter, EU law, notably the three Procedure, Qualification (Directive 2011/95/UE) and Reception (Directive 2013/33/EU) directives as well as several provisions in the Fundamental Charter.

As far as asylum procedures are concerned, the Commission considers that, by not allowing the applications for asylum to be made outside the special transit zones at the border and by restricting access to these areas, Hungarian legislation infringes the obligation to guarantee effective access to asylum procedures in Hungary. The procedures at the border do not comply with the conditions laid down by Union law.

Finally, the Commission criticises the systematic and indefinite confinement of asylum seekers in closed centres in the transit area in breach of the required procedural safeguards such as the right of recourse. It condemns the use of systematic detentions, contrary to EU law, in particular the Reception Directive[6] and the Charter of Fundamental Rights. The Hungarian legislation does not provide for the material conditions of reception, which is contrary to the Reception Conditions Directive.

The Council of Europe's Commissioner for Human Rights made similar remarks in a report of 13 January 2016, on the restrictive detention regime without access to effective remedies against such measure. In addition, he noted a very peculiar interpretation of the European concept of 'safe countries of origin'. Since Serbia is deemed 'safe', asylum seekers from Serbia are returned as the merits of their claim are not considered in Hungary. But if Serbia is a 'safe country of origin' in the sense that Serbian nationals are unlikely to obtain international protection in the EU, this does not mean that migrants passing through Serbia come from safe countries of origin. This is a real abuse of not only the due process of asylum law and EU law, but also Article 33 paragraph 1 of the Geneva Convention prohibiting refoulement to the country of origin which is obviously overlooked.

---

[6]Directive 2013/33/UE of the European Parliament and of the Council of 26 June 2013 laying down standards for the reception of applicants for international protection (recast of a 2004 directive).

A decision of the CJEU of 6 September 2017, rejecting a claim from Hungary and Slovakia requesting the Court to revoke a decision of the European Council of September 2015 on the 'relocation' of refugees allocating them a modest quota (1700 for Slovakia and 2040 for Hungary) inaugurates the series. The CJEU considers that, in case of emergency, the Lisbon TFEU, like the Charter of Fundamental Rights of the EU, allows the Council to decide on this matter without a vote by the European Parliament and without consultation of the national parliaments.

The relevance of this decision lies in the mitigation of the Dublin 3 Regulation governing the reception of asylum seekers. Paragraph 23 of that decision states that the relocation of an applicant to a state other than that considered to be responsible for the application by the Dublin 3 Regulation is a 'temporary derogation' from the regulation.

Is it possible to derogate from a legislative text of the EU Parliament by a non-legislative act of the EU? Does the EU Council's decision to 'relocate' asylum seekers constitute a 'provisional' derogation, considering that Article 78 TFEU only allows provisional measures?

With regard to the first question, the Court considers that the derogations provided for in the decision do not call into question legislative acts. They are strictly limited to responding quickly and effectively to a specific crisis situation through a temporary arrangement. Thus, considering this set of precautions, the derogations fulfil the requirement of ensuring the control of their material and temporal scope. It is neither the purpose nor the effect of the derogations to replace or modify the provisions of legislative acts permanently (paragraph 79).

With regard to the second question, the Court notes first that Article 78 TFEU remains silent on the nature of 'provisional measures' without being able to reduce them in a restrictive manner. On the contrary, they must be 'sufficiently broad in scope to enable the EU institutions to adopt all the provisional measures necessary to respond effectively and swiftly to an emergency situation characterised by a sudden inflow of nationals of third countries' (point 77). It also emphasises that unlike Article 64 of the previous Treaty of Nice, the Treaty no longer mentions temporal limitations concerning them and that the margin of appreciation recognised by the Council during this two-year period is justified by the 'unprecedented and complex' nature of the operation.

The Court technically answered both questions at stake, but many lawyers and specialists of EU Law expected a general and directive answer, recognising or not the very existence of a principle of solidarity between the member states of the EU in the field of asylum.

Is there or is there not a principle of solidarity within the Union? The question went beyond the mere fact of knowing whether a relocation mechanism was proportionate or not to the situation. Despite the allusion to solidarity, the fact that the 'temporary protection' directive[7] could have served as an alternative depends on the goodwill

[7]Council Directive 2001/55/EC of 20 July 2001 on minimum standards for giving temporary protection in the event of a mass influx of displaced persons and on measures promoting a balance of efforts between Member States in receiving such persons and bearing the consequences thereof.

or unanimity of the member states. An exhortation of a political nature or a legal obligation, the scope of the principle of solidarity, which Article 80 TFEU provides that it 'governs' asylum policy, needed to be finally specified.

The Court recognizes the importance of solidarity in the EU, even if it does not deem it necessary to devote to it a paragraph of principle related to a 'European cosmopolitanism' to asylum. Advocate General, Yves Bot, stressed the importance of solidarity as the founding and existential value of the Union, convinced that 'we are referring to the quintessence of what is both the raison d'être and objective of the European project' (Advocate General's Opinion, points 17 and 18).

The CJEU confirms the ongoing priority of ensuring that the EU's common asylum system functions effectively. The interpretation made by the Court logically gives precedence to an objective approach.

It also notes that the lack of an opportunity for applicants to choose the member state responsible for examining their application expresses the same rule as the Dublin system: there is no possibility for applicants to choose their favoured destination. They must, therefore, have an effective right of appeal against the decision to relocate for the purposes of respect for their fundamental rights. The reason is objectively expressed by the Court: 'the objective of the decision [...] is to take pressure off the Greek and Italian asylum systems by actually relocating, within a short time frame, a significant number of applicants to other Member States, in compliance with EU law and, in particular, with the fundamental rights guaranteed by the Charter' (point 337). The mandatory review of the application is 'a particular expression of the principle of non-refoulement, which prohibits the expulsion of an applicant for international protection to a third country as long as a decision has not been taken on his application' (point 341).

The transfer of an applicant from one member state to another, in the context of a relocation operation, for the purpose of examining his application 'cannot be regarded as refoulement to a third State', i.e. a country outside the EU. We are dealing here with 'a crisis-management measure, taken at EU level, whose purpose is to ensure that the fundamental right to asylum, laid down in Article 18 of the Charter, can be exercised properly, in accordance with the Geneva Convention' (point 343).

The Court pursues a cautious jurisprudence of the right to asylum. At a time of a tense European political context, the Court's 'European cosmopolitanism' remains legal and pragmatic. In a Hungarian case, a judgment of the Luxembourg Court of 25 January 2018 prohibits, in the investigation proceedings concerning asylum applications of homosexuals, psychological tests to assess the credibility of an asylum application based on alleged membership of the 'social group' of homosexuals. However, the Advocate General, in favour of the Hungarian arguments, reached a different conclusion, advising that these tests be allowed, with various precautions related to the respect of individual rights.

9.4 The Issue of 'Systemic Failures' of Hungary and Poland with Regard to Asylum

9.4.1 The Split Between the Hungarian Asylum System and the European Common Asylum System

In his conclusions, Mr Errera,[8] the public rapporteur, in the decision of 28 June 2017 (published in the AJDA journal) of the Administrative Court of Appeal of Versailles stresses the failure of the Hungarian system to comply with its European obligations in the case of an asylum seeker that France is likely to return to Hungary under the Dublin 3 Regulation.

It recalls a judgment of 17 March 2017 in which the Strasbourg Court analyses the numerous irregularities and systemic misconceptions of Hungary since 2014 with regard to a fair application of the Geneva Convention and the relevant European directives. As highlighted in the Commission's criticism, the plaintiffs are, among other things, held in detention during the review of their application. The systematic nature of this detention is clearly contrary to EU law.

The applicable European legislation—the Procedure Directive 2013/32 and the Reception Conditions Directive 2013/33 of 26 June 2013—strictly prohibits the detention of a third-country national solely on the basis of his status as an asylum seeker. Such detention is possible only if it is necessary, proportionate and decided on a case-by-case basis on grounds interpreted restrictively (national security, public order, risk of flight, identity or nationality checks, etc.) and shall be applied in the absence of a less coercive measure which can be more appropriate. These European laws must be applied in compliance with the obligations deriving from international law, and in particular from Article 33 of the Geneva Convention on refugees, guaranteeing criminal immunity to asylum seekers in the event of an irregular crossing of a border. The right of asylum enshrined in the 1951 Geneva Convention has also been derived, since 2009, from Article 18 of the EU Charter of Fundamental Rights. The Procedures Directive 2013/32 (Article 43) clearly provides for the possibility for member states to set up an asylum procedure at the border with detention in the transit zone. However, while the Procedures Directive 2013/32 introduces a number of safeguards, the Hungarian legislation clearly misuses this possibility by considering that any asylum seeker arrested in its territory is subject to this procedure. Assuming that Serbia can be considered a safe country (CJEU 17 March 2016, Shiraz Mirza, C-695/15 PPU), Hungary may declare applications for asylum from people from that country inadmissible and proceed to their readmission to Serbia.

In plenary session, the Administrative Court of Appeal of Versailles preferred to consider, in a reasoned explanation, and contrary to the Administrative Court of

---

[8]This magistrate is the son of Roger Errera, member of the Council of State, specialist in civil liberties and Hungary.

Appeal of Nancy and Bordeaux and contrary to the conclusions of its own 'public rapporteur', Mr Errera, who is recognised as a specialist in human rights law and Hungarian legislation, that the Hungarian system was not in systemic failure. How can this be explained or understood? This decision surprised many specialists of Hungary and asylum law if we compare it with the EU Jurisprudence[9] concerning the Greek asylum system, which is supposed to be, since 2011, in systemic failure.

On the one hand, Hungary does not have material difficulties as extensive as Greece to materially manage asylum seekers since 2010. On the other hand, Hungary still has experienced officers and highly qualified judges. Some thousands of asylum seekers have been granted status from 2010 to 2019.

Sometimes, they manage to get this status. Admittedly, the legal pathways to get there are complex. In principle, the EU countries offer, from the mere fact of being in the EU, common guarantees to asylum seekers to obtain the status and to benefit from effective protection where appropriate. The Treaty of Amsterdam in 1997 established the principle of a common asylum system in the EU.

9.4.2 The Effective Protection of Recognised Refugees in Poland

There is an exception to the presumption of effective international protection in all EU states provided for by the 'Aznar Protocol',[10] if the presumption of protection of a status holder is refuted by an applicant demonstrating the absence of effective protection in the EU country where he obtained the status.

This is what the National Asylum Court (CNDA)[11] and the Council of State decided in France, respectively, in 2011 and 2012 in the Umarov decisions. The French act of 29 July 2015 stated that these requests were 'inadmissible' to the French Office for the Protection of Refugees and Stateless Persons (OFPRA), but that the CNDA could reverse these decisions of inadmissibility if the protection was found to be ineffective in another EU country and if the presumption of protection was rebutted by the refugee who obtained international protection in that country, without actually being protected by that EU country where he obtained the status. This is often the case with Chechens in Poland, who claim to be harassed by Russian services in this country, especially those of Chechen President Kadyrov. Therefore,

[9]See Judgment in Joined Cases: N. S. (C-411/10) v Secretary of State for the Home Department and M. E. and Others (C-493/10) v Refugee Applications Commissioner and Minister for Justice, Equality and Law Reform (about Greece), 21 December 2011. And recently, see Rectification order of 29 July 2019, European Commission v Republic of Poland, C-619/18 R which shows that administrative authorities in Hungary do not implement, in asylum law, the decisions of their own courts.

[10]Protocol on Asylum for Nationals of Member States of the European Union, also known as the 'Aznar Protocol', is an Annex of the 1997 Amsterdam Treaty.

[11]CNDA—Cour nationale du droit d'asile.

they ask for a second status in France, or in another EU country. In these cases, it is not the legal failure of Poland that is being discussed, but the effectiveness of the state in Poland and its engagement for the protection of refugees who have obtained a status.

9.5 Conclusion

These conflicts between EU law, whose project is 'cosmopolitan' in a legal sense of effective protection of certain rights such as the right to asylum, also defined by the Geneva Convention of 28 July 1951, and the will of certain states, of which Viktor Orban's Hungary is the most extreme example, to ensure state sovereignty that dreams of being absolute, constitute a true 'ideal type' of all cosmopolitanism. Should a transnational right or the sovereign right of the state be supreme? Should the fundamental rights of the people prevail over the limitation of individual rights by means of exceptional state legislation or a state of exception? The schism between Hans Kelsen and Carl Schmitt, between Grotius and the reason of state, is still pertinent.

Bibliography

Administrative Court of Appeal of Versailles Case n°16VE02239, 28 June 2017.

Directive 2011/95/EU of the European Parliament and of the Council of 13 December 2011 on standards for the qualification of third-country nationals or stateless persons as beneficiaries of international protection, for a uniform status for refugees or for persons eligible for subsidiary protection, and for the content of the protection granted. https://eur-lex.europa.eu/legal-content/EN/TXT/?uri=CELEX:32011L0095&qid=1565947614462. Accessed August 16, 2019.

Directive 2013/32/EU of the European Parliament and of the Council of 26 June 2013 on common procedures for granting and withdrawing international protection.

Directive 2013/33/EU of the European Parliament and of the Council of 26 June 2013 laying down standards for the reception of applicants for international protection.

El Kott v Hungary Case C-364/11 (CJEU, 19 December 2011).

European Commission v Republic of Poland Case C-619/18 (CJEU, 24 June 2019).

European Commission v Republic of Poland Case C-619/18 R Rectification order (CJEU, 29 July 2019).

Kende, P. (2004). *Le défi hongrois. De Trianon à Bruxelles*. Paris: Buchet-Chastel.

Kende, P. (2012). "Viktor Orban, portrait historique d'un populiste.", *L'Histoire*. https://www.lhistoire.fr/portrait-historique-dun-populiste. Accessed August 16, 2019.

Lendvai, P. (2017). *Orban, Europe's new strongman*. C Hurst & Co Publishers.

N. S. v Secretary of State for the Home Department Case C-411/10 and M. E. and Others v Refugee Applications Commissioner and Minister for Justice, Equality and Law Reform Case C-493/10 (Joined cases CJEU, December 21, 2011).

Order of the Vice-president of ECJ in Commission v Poland Case C-619/18 R (CJEU, October 19, 2018).

Sands, P. (2017). *Retour à Lemberg*. Paris: Albin Michel.

Shiraz Baig Mirza v Bevándorlási és Állampolgársági Hivatal Case C-695/15 PPU (CJEU, March 17, 2016).
Thibaud, P. (2011). "La Hongrie, de l'Empire à l'Europe. Pierre Kende, Istvan Bibo.", *Esprit*, June 2011.

Joseph Krulic studied History at the Ecole Normale Supérieure de Saint Cloud (1976–1981) and became Agrégé d'histoire in 1979. He has done extensive research about Titoist Yugoslavia, theory of nationalism and different types of populism, and he has published numerous books and articles on these subjects. From 1985 to 1987, he studied at the ENA (Ecole Nationale d'Administration) and became an administrative judge with the administrative courts of Versailles and Paris. In 2009, he was admitted as an asylum law and refugee law judge at the CNDA (Cour Nationale du Droit D'asile). He has been Président de section since 2017, one of the few senior Presidents of this French National Asylum Court. In 2003 he successfully defended his HDR (Habilitation à diriger les recherches) in Political Science at the IEP (Institut d'études politiques) in Paris, an academic habilitation to supervise Ph.D. research in political science.

Chapter 10
Human Rights Facing Terrorism: A Lose-Lose Situation? A Problematic Trend for the Observance of the Non-Refoulement Principle

Emnet Berhanu Gebre

Abstract Human rights are without doubt tested by terrorism. But the equivocal relationship mainly stands on the fact that the fight against terrorism threatens the free exercise of human rights. Despite their absolute character, the principle of non-refoulement and the prohibition of ill-treatment were mangled by the recent practice of states, which, in the name of the fight against terrorism, adopt legislation and practices that have an adverse impact on the effective enjoyment of human rights.

Keywords Terrorism · Human rights · Counterterrorism · Ill-treatment · Non-refoulement

10.1 Introduction

Alongside several significant issues tormenting the international community such as environmental, developmental, migratory, or security issues, terrorism can be scrutinised as one of the considerable challenges of the twenty-first century. Terrorist attacks became less and less isolated, affecting not only developing countries, which remain under-equipped to face the phenomenon, but also developed countries. Despite their high logistical, economic and military capacities to counter terrorism, Western countries quickly realised that they are not immune to the crisis as their enemies are more and more determined to shake the whole democratic foundation of their societies including the free exercise of human rights.

The concept of terrorism can be considered as a 'ghost' concept notably because of the difficulties in defining it. In the absence of consensus among states, there is indeed no universal definition unanimously approved by the international community (Tercinet 2007, 581–600). Attempts to define the term can be traced in international and regional conventions but also in the General Assembly and the Security Council resolutions. In 1994, the United Nations General Assembly (GA) defined terrorism as 'criminal acts intended or calculated to provoke a state of terror in the general public, a

E. B. Gebre (✉)
University of Toulouse 1 Capitole, Toulouse, France
e-mail: emnet.berhanu@yahoo.com

M. C. Jacobsen et al. (eds.), *Cosmopolitanism, Migration and Universal Human Rights*, https://doi.org/10.1007/978-3-030-50645-2_10

group of persons or particular persons for political purposes' (GA, Resolution 49/60, 1995, § 3). The Security Council for its part defined it in a more detailed manner as 'criminal acts, including against civilians, committed with the intent to cause death or serious bodily injury, or taking of hostages, with the purpose to provoke a state of terror in the general public or in a group of persons or particular persons, intimidate a population or compel a government or an international organization to do or to abstain from doing any act', whether motivated by a political, ideological, philosophical, racial or religious considerations (Security Council, Resolution 1566 [2004], 2004, § 3).

Historically, if religious or political motivations were behind terrorist acts, a mix of both of these grounds marks the twenty-first century. One can say, in a more precise way, that religious rhetoric has been used for political claims. From this perspective, the attack of 11 September 2001 is an emblematic example, which has marked the beginning of a new era in international relations. Since then, other devastating terrorist attacks have happened from Kenya to Pakistan and from Spain to Mali, placing terrorism at the core of the international community's concern. Recently, Western countries have also experienced horrifying attacks, which led their governments to respond in various ways.

After the Manichean vision introduced by President Georges W. Bush with the rhetoric of 'axis of evil', the expressions 'internal enemy' and 'war on terror' were also used by government officials and the media. This new rhetoric around the phenomenon can, however, conceal difficulties in its legal qualifications and consequently in the identification of appropriate responses to it. States facing terrorism usually try to address the problem in two different ways. A military intervention that mostly occurs outside the territory of a given country is one of them. For instance, since 2001, the United States, along with an international coalition, has been engaged in an armed conflict in Afghanistan. Even developing countries have been engaged in this path. The second way usually reflects the fight against an internal threat that has mostly materialised as a result of the adoption of a preventive and repressive legislative arsenal.

However, the lack of a universally accepted definition undoubtedly has repercussions for the shaping of a legal regime and policies under which counterterrorism should be pursued. While the need to enforce international law and not to rule out international human rights law is stronger than ever, some states choose to take unilateral exceptions to international law. From military interventions to the establishment of legal tools, the repercussions that followed for the protection of human rights should not be overlooked. It is, therefore, necessary to examine how human rights are affected not only by the scourge of terrorism itself but also by the countermeasures framed to fight it. Human rights and terrorism keep an equivocal relationship mainly for two reasons that we will try to discuss throughout this chapter. For this purpose, the European Court of Human Rights (ECHR) case law enjoys a prominent place in our demonstration.

First, human rights are indeed without doubt tested by terrorism because of all the pernicious effects the latter has on the enjoyment of a variety of rights. But the equivocal relationship mainly stands on the second line of our study dedicated to the challenge posed by the fight against terrorism. In the light of the laws related to national security, the fight against terrorism represents an adverse impact on the effective enjoyment of human rights including the principle of non-refoulement.

10.2 Human Rights Tested by Terrorism: The Obvious

The specific feature of terrorism is the intent to cause death, severe injury or the deprivation of freedom with the purpose of creating fear, chaos and a state of terror in the general public. In this respect, human rights are profoundly threatened and violated in the context of terrorism. Its effects on the enjoyment of human rights and the very existence of the rule of law are indisputable.

10.2.1 The Repercussions on the Enjoyment of Human Rights

From the right to life to the right of physical integrity and the principle of human dignity, terrorism affects a wide range of human rights. It has a pernicious effect on the exercise of various fundamental freedoms such as the freedom of thought, conscience and religion. The right to liberty of movement is also affected since people are often constrained to limit their actions out of fear of potential attacks. Terrorism has also direct and indirect effects on the enjoyment of economic, social and cultural rights. Attacks perpetrated on educational, work, social and health facilities directly threatened the enjoyment of the right to health, the right to education or the right to work. As far as cultural rights are concerned, general destruction of historical sites in Mali, in Syria or Iraq directly violated cultural rights guaranteed by international norms. For instance, in the case of the wreckage of Palmyra's ancient temple in Syria, war crimes were committed and entailed the application of humanitarian law which forbids the destruction of cultural objects and places of worship whether in internal or international armed conflicts.

Regarding the indirect effect of terrorism, its negative impacts on the economy cannot be ignored. Countries such as Egypt or Tunisia have suffered a great deal of economic loss due to the drop in tourism activities. Since tourism represents the primary source of foreign currency and employment opportunities, their developmental process is harshly undermined, thus threatening the socio-economic well-being of entire communities (Liu and Pratt 2017).

Terrorism is characterised by violence perpetrated in defiance of the established order. It represents the rejection of the rule of law and democratic values such as pluralism. When committed against religious and ethnic minorities, terrorism threatens the peaceful coexistence of communities. In 1993, the condemnation of terrorism by the General Assembly of the United Nations listed many of its detrimental effects. It described terrorism as 'activities aimed at the destruction of human rights, fundamental freedoms and democracy, threatening the territorial integrity and security of States, destabilizing legitimately constituted Governments, undermining pluralistic civil society and having adverse consequences on the economic and social development of States' (GA, Resolution 48/122, 1994, § 1). Above all, it rejects the idea of peaceful resolution of conflicts that is at the heart of the international legal system. It can threaten peace by destabilising a specific country, but its effects can also spread at the regional and international level, endangering international peace and security. Considering all these adverse effects of terrorism on the rights of citizens and the danger for states' institutions, states have a legal obligation to react by providing timely and appropriate responses to terrorist attacks and threats by virtue of their international human rights commitments.

10.2.2 The Ensuing Obligations for States

The due diligence obligation is a general obligation which imposes on states the duty to behave in such a way as to ensure that no damage will occur to other states as a result of their activities under their jurisdiction and control (Flemme 2004). The due diligence obligation, traditionally known in environmental law, has been imposed upon states in the context of the fight against terrorism. States must refrain from helping or tolerating terrorist activities inside and outside their territory. They also need to take preventive and repressive measures to tackle terrorism, first of all by prosecuting or extraditing persons suspected of terrorist activities by virtue of the principle of *aut dedere aut judicare*. They must refuse to allocate refugee status to persons related to terrorist activities. All states must cooperate in the exchange of information regarding international terrorism (Security Council, Resolution 1373 [2001], 2001, preamble).

The obligation of due diligence in the context of counterterrorism takes its foundation in other fields of international law such as human rights law. There is a general due diligence obligation incumbent upon states, which are required to take preventive measures to protect their population. International human rights law imposes on states a duty to respect, to protect and to fulfil human rights. If states must refrain from interfering with the enjoyment of human rights, they also have a positive obligation to protect individuals from private interference and to take action in the legislative, judicial and administrative fields to fulfil their international commitments. By extension, states must protect every person under their jurisdiction from the detrimental effects of terrorism on the enjoyment of human rights (GA, Resolution 52/133, 1997, preamble and § 4).

Until 1989, the resolutions of the General Assembly related to the fight against terrorism had an explicit and larger purpose. Resolution 42/159 urges states 'to contribute to the progressive elimination of the causes underlying international terrorism and to pay special attention to all situations, including colonialism, racism and situations involving mass and flagrant violations of human rights and fundamental freedoms […] that may give rise to international terrorism' (GA, Resolution 42/159, 1987, § 8). However, the reference to the need to address the root causes of terrorism disappeared after 1990, mostly because of Western countries which saw in it a way to justify terrorism (Dubuisson 2002, 157; see also GA, Resolution 46/51, 1991; Resolution 49/60, 1995 and Resolution 68/119, 2013). Recently, the debate around the causes emerged with the recent terrorist attacks and the involvement of European youngsters in the ISIS army. One can say that, without necessarily justifying their acts, their decisions to be engaged in such deadly activities have their source in social injustice, misery or frustration. Therefore, states must consider means of addressing the causes of terrorism by strengthening their social and democratic institutions. It should be acknowledged that the achievement of social justice and the reduction of social and economic disparities is also an important vector of peace.

While the need to eliminate the root causes of terrorism by strengthening the exercise of human rights law and by guaranteeing social and economic justice must be encouraged, the response against terrorism both on the preventive and reactive level must be in accordance with the standards of human rights. The General Assembly itself admitted early in 1995 in its resolution 49/60 that while states must fulfil their obligations with respect to combating international terrorism, their measures in this regard must also be taken in 'accordance with the relevant provisions of international law and international standards of human rights' (GA, Resolution 49/60, 1995, Part II, § 5). It is of paramount importance that the fight against terrorism is not carried out in an abusive and critical manner for the protection of fundamental rights. Leading the fight against terrorism outside the scope of human rights law and fundamental legal principles can be counterproductive.

10.3 Human Rights Tested by Counterterrorism Measures: The Perverse Effect

In reaction to violent attacks and the subsequent crisis, governments must respond in a quick, efficient and steady manner in order to sanction those responsible for the attacks and prevent others from undergoing the same actions. The military responses expected in the context of an armed conflict must comply with international humanitarian law (IHL). Denying the applicability of IHL to suspected terrorists by considering these persons as 'unlawful combatants', and thus outside the scope of categories of protected persons under IHL, is not based on a valid legal ground (Scheinin and Vermeulen 2011, 43–44). In this context of war, it is also important to note that even though IHL is applicable, international human rights law (IHRL) does not cease to apply 'as both spheres of law are complementary and not mutually exclusive' (Human Rights Committee, 2004, General comment 31, § 11). By virtue of the principle of *lex specialis* (ICJ, Advisory opinion, Threat or Use of Nuclear Weapons, 1996, § 25;

Legal consequences of the construction of a wall in the occupied Palestine territory, 2004, § 106), some norms of IHL could nevertheless serve as a reference to interpret IHRL.

As far as the preventive and repressive legislative arsenal is concerned, unfortunately states do not often learn the lessons either of their past experiences or of each other's mistakes. This is why the laws and the actions encountering terrorism are not always in conformity with the international and regional obligations of states in the field of human rights (Almqvist 2005, 4). If exceptional measures are needed to tackle terrorism effectively, these actions must be not only relevant but also consistent with the international legal commitments of the state.

10.3.1 The Impact of Counterterrorism on Human Rights: A Double-Edged Sword

Recently, the American Senate admitted that torture was used as a method of interrogation during the investigation after the September 11 attacks (Senate Selected Committee on Intelligence, 2013). Sadly, this unlawful method is not always categorically condemned and banned by all governments, while there is no doubt it would not conform to international human rights standards (art. 5, *Universal Declaration of Human Rights*, 1948 and art. 2 § 2, *Convention against Torture and Other Cruel, Inhuman or Degrading Treatment or Punishment*, 1984). Other international instruments at the regional level contain the same prohibition (art. 3, *European Convention of Human Rights*, 1950; art. 5, *African Charter on Human and Peoples' Rights*, 1981; *Inter-American Convention to Prevent and Punish Torture*, 1985). One may think that torture can be legitimately used to fight terrorism considering the deadly effects of the latter on human rights, the stability of states, international peace and security, etc. However, this justification is a legally invalid argument, knowing that the end cannot justify the means. The prohibition of torture is a norm of *jus cogens*. Thus, a peremptory norm of general international law which is 'accepted and recognized by the international community of states as a whole as a norm from which no derogation is permitted and which can be modified only by a subsequent norm of general international law having the same character' (art. 53, *Vienna Convention on the Law of Treaty*, 1969). The Convention against Torture and Other Cruel, Inhuman or Degrading Treatment or Punishment (CAT) confirms the non-derogable nature of the prohibition. As such, 'no exceptional circumstances whatsoever, whether a state of war or a threat of war, internal political instability or any other public emergency, may be invoked as a justification of torture' (art. 2 § 2, *CAT*, 1984). Human rights courts like the ECHR have noted that some measures such as harsh interrogation techniques and conditions of detention are prohibited whatever the emergency the state is facing. Causing intense physical and mental suffering through the practice of psychological interrogation methods or encroachment on one's dignity through degrading physical searches have also been held to be in violation of article 3 of the European Convention of Human Rights (ECHR, *Ireland v. the United Kingdom*, 1978; *Aksov v. Turkey*, 1996; *Frérot v. France*, 2007; *Öcalan v. Turkey*, 2014).

If the direct use of torture in the context of counterterrorism is a strict violation of international human rights law, the outsourcing of torture or inhuman or degrading treatments is also prohibited. Some states practice what is known as an 'extraordinary rendition' which is 'an extraordinary judicial transfer of persons from one jurisdiction or State to another, for the purposes of detention and interrogation outside the normal legal system, where there was a real risk of torture or cruel, inhuman or degrading treatment' (ECHR, *El-Masri v. The Former Yugoslav Republic of Macedonia*, 2012, § 221). As a former CIA agent recognised, 'if you want a serious interrogation, you send a prisoner to Jordan; if you want them to be tortured, you send them to Syria; if you want someone to disappear—never to see them again—you send them to Egypt' (American Civil Liberties Union 2011). In the *El-Masri v. The Former Yugoslav Republic of Macedonia* case, the plaintiff, a German national, was transferred to the American authorities that brought him to Afghanistan where he was tortured for over four months (ECHR, El-*Masri v. The Former Yugoslav Republic of Macedonia*, § 120–122). The court held that there had been a breach of article 3 of the CAT not only because of the ill-treatment the applicant had been subjected to before and after his transfer to the CIA but also because of 'the failure of the authorities of "the former Yugoslav Republic of Macedonia" to carry out an effective investigation into the applicant's allegations of ill-treatment' (European Court of Human Rights 2016, 9). In 2014, the ECHR had condemned Poland in two similar cases related to secret rendition operations (ECHR, *Al Nashiri v. Poland and Husayn* [*Abu Zubaydah v. Poland*] 2014). The claimants endured ill-treatment and secret detention by the CIA in the Stare Kiejkuty for six and nine months respectively. They were subsequently transferred from the Polish territory to Guantanamo Bay. The court concluded a violation of article 3 on account of the cooperation of Poland 'in the preparation and execution of the CIA rendition, secret detention and interrogation operations on its own territory' and on account of the fact that 'by enabling the CIA to transfer the applicant[s] to its other secret detention facilities, the Polish authorities exposed him to a foreseeable serious risk of further ill-treatment and conditions of detention' (ECHR, *Al Nashiri v. Poland* 2014, § 518 and 519). Other cases on secret 'rendition operations' concerning Romania and Lithuania have also been rendered in which the court recognised the violation of multiple provisions including of article 3 of the Convention as a result of their cooperation with the CIA that led to ill-treatment suffered by the applicants.

Besides the context of extraordinary rendition, human rights bodies have condemned the practice of states in cases of deportation and extradition in which persons suspected of terrorist activities were sent back to countries in which they were at risk of being subjected to torture or inhuman treatment. One could concede that by virtue of the Convention Relating to the Status of Refugees, 'the benefit of [the principle of non-refoulement] may not […] be claimed by a refugee whom there are reasonable grounds for regarding as a danger to the security of the country in which he is, or who, have been convicted by a final judgment of a particular serious crime, constitutes a danger to the community of that country' (Art. 33 § 2, Convention

Relating to the Status of Refugees, 1951). In the field of international refugee law, the principle of non-refoulement does not have an absolute nature.[1] However, this observation cannot be reiterated when it comes to international human rights law as the latter offers a much greater protection than international refugee law. In two cases against Sweden, the Committee against Torture and the Human Rights Commitee condemned the transfer of two Egyptian nationals to their home country where their lives were at risk. These two individuals were transferred to Egypt after the refusal of their asylum claims due to suspicion of terrorist activities (Committee against Torture, Decision *Agiza v. Sweden* 2004; Human Rights Committee, Decision *Alzery v. Sweden* 2012; see also ECHR, *Shamayev and others v. Georgia and Russia* 2005). There is indeed an obligation for states not to send persons in another state where he/she can face a real risk of ill-treatment. This obligation has an absolute character since public interest considerations cannot balance the risk of ill-treatment, whatever the offence or conduct.

The threat of terrorism and the necessity for states to protect their populations cannot call into question the absolute nature of the prohibition of torture and inhuman treatment. For the ECHR, 'the prospect that [the person] may pose a serious threat to the community if not returned does not reduce in any way the degree of risk of ill-treatment that the person may be subject to on return' (ECHR, *Saadi v. Italy*, 2016, § 139; see other cases: ECHR, *Chahal v. the United Kingdom* 1996; *Aswat v. the United Kingdom* 2013). The position of the ECHR on the absolute nature of article 3 has so irritated some states such as the United Kingdom that the former Prime Minister Tony Blair was in 2003 considering denouncing the Convention after the *Chahal* case (Scheinin and Vermeulen 2011, 55). As a growing number of states parties criticised the case law of the court, now the question is: how long will the court withstand the pressure coming from the states (Brown 2015)?

Indeed, some scholars expressed their concern about the future of the prohibition of ill-treatment in counterterrorism matters. They do not seem very optimistic about the perseverance of the ECHR in the face of pressure around growing security stakes. The protection from ill-treatment is a judge-made protection. Even though human rights bodies manage to enlarge this protection, it 'suffers from a weak construction which can, in the long run, make it permeable to the sovereign concern of States' (Delas 2015, 33). In its case law, the trend of the ECHR, for instance, is to always start its reasoning by restating the discretionary sovereign rights of the states in matters related to the access to the territory, the establishment and the forced return of foreigners. The court concedes that this sovereign right can only be limited in exceptional cases.

Lately, the reaffirmation of the sovereign right of states in immigration matters has, however, become automatic. And it is the automaticity that alerts scholars because it tends to reverse the paradigm in human rights law (Delas 2015, 35). States have,

[1] Art. 33§2: The benefit of the principle of non-refoulement may not be claimed by a refugee 'whom there are reasonable grounds for regarding as a danger to the security of the country or who, having been convicted by a final judgement of a particular serious crime, constitutes a danger to the community of that country'.

in principle, the obligation to guarantee the full exercise of human rights of persons under their jurisdiction. Exceptionally, whenever the conditions are fulfilled, they can allow restriction of their enjoyment. The position of the ECHR in cases related to the return of foreigners makes it seem that the guarantee of the exercise of human rights falls within the reserved domain of states. From the moment a state has ratified and accepted the obligation enshrined in human rights treaties, it cannot pretend that any matter related to the enjoyment of human rights belongs to its reserved domain. The deportation of foreigners engaged in terrorist activities cannot be considered as an exception. Despite the absolute character of the prohibition of ill-treatment even in cases related to terrorism, there is a legitimate concern that with the growing security issues, the ECHR might bow to a state's pressure and therefore challenge the absolute character of the prohibition. One has to concede that the court has so far refused to put in balance the risk of ill-treatment and the potential security risks as the prohibition of torture and inhuman treatment is 'one of the most fundamental values of democratic societies'. For the ECHR, 'even in the most difficult circumstances, such as the fight against terrorism […], the Convention prohibits in absolute terms torture and inhuman or degrading treatment or punishment.[…] Article 3 makes no provision for exceptions and no derogation from it is permissible under Article 15 § 2 even in the event of a public emergency threatening the life of the nation' (ECHR, *Lapita v. Italy* 2000, § 119).

According to Professor Olivier Delas, the concern about an eventual questioning of the absolute character of article 3 may be raised after the case of *N. v. the United Kingdom* in which the court seemed to have yielded to the needs of the respondent state. The court deemed lawful the deportation of the applicant by the British authorities despite the fact that he claimed the need to stay in the country to continue to receive antiretroviral medication for AIDS-related illness. Even though this case does not deal with the risk of torture in the context of terrorism, it can potentially give us a preview of the evolution of the ECHR case law. In this case, the court only refers to paragraph 89 of the Soering case in which it stated that 'the search of a fair balance between the demands of the general interest of the community and the requirements of the protection of the individual's fundamental rights [is] inherent in the whole of the Convention' (ECHR, *Soering v. the United Kingdom* 1989, § 89). It seems that the court did not entirely exclude a possible balancing test between the risk of ill-treatment related to the lack of access of medication in the country of destination and the resulting financial burden for the host state (ECHR, *N v. the United Kingdom* 2008, § 44: cited by Delas 2015, 37). In this regard, Professor Delas projects that if the court introduced some softening of the principle of non-refoulement for budgetary reasons, how can it explain to states the impossibility of transposing this same reasoning in cases related to national security (Delas 2015, 38)? Needless to say, this kind of trend casts uncertainty over the sustainability of such norms and the respect of the rule of law in general. Now more than ever the need for a tailored 'under the law' approach has to be underlined.

10.3.2 *The Need for a Tailored 'Under the Law' Approach to Counterterrorism*

When specific bills, enacted mostly proactively, do not prevent an attack from happening, emergency solutions devised to tackle urgently a grave and endangering situation can be contemplated. One can say whenever the rule of law is highly endangered, the declaration of a state of emergency can be considered as an option. Nevertheless, does this imply that the emergency state could be viewed as a regime that is outside the rule of law, an exception to the rule of law? For instance, after the September 11 attacks, the United States did not use the derogation provisions allowed by the International Covenant on Civil and Political Rights. Considering the exceptional nature of the situation, which amounted to 'a public emergency threatening the life of the nation' as provided for in the covenant, the US could have lawfully derogated from their international human rights obligations. They chose nevertheless not to pursue this path. According to Professor Klein, for the US, considering the exceptional nature of the situation, their counter-response cannot seemingly be confined in existing legal frames. The latter are deemed ill-suited to respond effectively to the attack and the threat they were facing. In holding international human rights law inapplicable due to its inadequacy, there is in some ways a will to go 'beyond the derogation' (Klein 2006, 427) foreseen by international law. Whether states need to declare a state of war or a state of emergency, minimum standards for the protection of human rights are applicable. If humanitarian law is considered to be applicable to armed conflicts, human rights law is not suspended for that matter. In the absence of 'lex specialis related to anti-terrorism law', there seems to be a willingness to engage in the fight against terrorism outside the conventional frameworks provided by international law. Why do states accept dealing with an enemy or internal belligerent in the course of an armed conflict or with other public emergencies within the limits set by international norms, while refusing to play by the rules when dealing with terrorism?

Whenever a terrorist attack strikes, government, police officials and even journalists usually speak about 'a state of war' while evoking the state in which the country and the population are found after a terrorist attack. The use of this expression cannot be considered accurate from a purely legal perspective but still creates discrepancy among jurists. For Professor Sorel, we are indeed facing a situation of war. Based on the definition given by Clausewitz that defines war as 'an act of force to compel our enemy to do our will' (Clausewitz 2014, 37), Professor Sorel considers that terrorism fits into the definition even though he admits that the legal accuracy of this characterisation can be questioned. Professor Alain Pellet, on the other hand, writing in the aftermath of September 11 refused to approve the legal accuracy of the phrase. He reckons that it is politically legitimate but legally wrong and fraught with dangers (Pellet 2001). Beyond the semantic debate, the effective existence of a state of war has legal implications, as it requires the application of humanitarian law norms rather than those of human rights, which may not be fully applied in certain circumstances. However, this rhetoric can also be interpreted in the collective subconsciousness as a drive to place counterterrorism in middle tiers between a situation of war and a situation of peace. The risk of this schizophrenic position arose from the fact that, on the one hand, humanitarian law will not be applicable because the elements characterising armed conflict are not considered to be fulfilled. And on the other hand, the full application of human rights law is also limited as they tend to limit the enjoyment and exercise of some rights, claiming they face an exceptional situation. Therefore, it is more relevant and cautious to evoke the existence of an internal crisis or to qualify terrorism as a 'serious form of crime [that should be] fought within a law-enforcement paradigm' (Scheinin and Vermeulen 2011, 40).

For that matter, international human rights law recognised the existence of exceptional situations that can require the suspension of freedoms for a limited period. It provides for strict conditions (the principle of exceptional threat, the principle of proportionality, the principle of non-discrimination and the principle of non-derogability of fundamental rights), which, if they are respected, will determine the lawfulness of the derogation of human rights (Oraa 1999, 429–433). On the internal level, states have applied state of emergency laws to face challenges posed post-attacks. However, even though these laws were intended to be applicable in the case of 'exceptional situations threatening the life of the nation', the question remaining is whether they are well suited to deal specifically with the aftermath of terrorist attacks.

In situations of chaos created by terrorist attacks, there is a need for more democracy and not an absence or a suspension of democracy, which cannot be considered as an option. There is a substantially fundamental necessity to put all counterterrorism measures under parliamentary and judicial control. Judicial control should not be considered a hindrance to counterterrorism but should be put at the heart of its credibility and effectiveness. The 'judiciarisation' of counterterrorism is of paramount importance because it is a viable solution for the fight against terrorism while limiting its drifts. It is not because the enemy does not play by the international legal and moral rules that we set that we should also give up playing by those rules: '[w]e should not respond to terrorism with terror. It would be disastrous that in the name of our values we use the hideous means of the opponent' (Pellet 2001). The reciprocity argument cannot be used to derogate from core elements instituted by international law. The violations of fundamental rights in the context of counterterrorism tend to fuel the acts of violence because these loopholes are used as an argument to demonise democracy and its deriving values. The repressive actions engaged by governments in breach of fundamental rights and principles are a real goldmine for terrorist groups because it allows them to acquire more legitimacy in the face of their supporters. The serious breach of human rights and the abuses perpetrated by police forces have a snowball effect and reinforce their determination. This tends to create a vicious circle fed by a spiral of violence.

10.4 Conclusion

Terrorist attacks have become frequent occurrences, destroying many innocent lives around the world, creating regional and international instability and blurring the traditional conception of peace and war. The worldwide nature of the problem and the frequency at which these criminal acts occur can potentially reveal the inefficiency of the political and legal strategies set to address it. Even though our enemies use war methods, the expression 'war against terrorism' used by states is not a concept legally accepted by all. The characterisation of the situation can be quite controversial, but it should not prevent us from focusing on the essential elements: the respect of international law, especially international human rights law. The strength to address the phenomenon aptly must be drawn from the spirit and the philosophy of human rights. One can concede that counterterrorism can also use forceful methods and that states have the monopoly of legitimate violence, which allows them to respond to threats of any kind. Even though states must protect their citizens from threats arising from third parties, their actions should not, however, be arbitrary and disproportional. The principles of necessity and proportionality both in legislative and operational activities should not be flouted 'because it addresses whether deviations from human rights will increase security and whether less drastic measures can be used to prevent terrorism' (Scheinin and Vermeulen 2011, 63).

Exceptional measures justified by the seriousness of the circumstances should be conducted in accordance with the law and under judicial scrutiny despite the temptation to take shortcuts. The law is the reflection of one's society since it is shaped by the latter's political and socio-economic concerns. However, these matters can be influenced, even manipulated, by the discourse of politicians. Hence, the importance of the right to access information must be underlined. As for governments, they must govern wisely with shrewdness, devoid of all passion, while always having in mind the protection of citizens' rights and the effectiveness of their policies to achieve this goal. There is a need for states to legislate by keeping in mind these two goals that are far from being contradictory.

The problematic of the relationship of human rights and terrorism launches the long-standing philosophical dilemma of freedom and security. It is needless to say that freedom and security enjoy a negative correlation as the former is indubitably restrained in the name of national security. One would concede that security is the first of all freedoms because it is a vital condition for the free exercise of all fundamental freedoms. However, fundamental freedoms should not be sacrificed in the name of security: 'the point is not to guarantee security for itself but for the community's needs' (Granger 2009, 296), more specifically for the safeguarding and the free exercise of fundamental rights. The arbitration between the guarantee of freedom and security is not easy to settle, but much attention should be given to making sure that neither the disease nor the therapy measures set up to encounter the syndrome affect the foundation of our being. To avoid such a situation, security needs to be understood and construed not from the point of view of states but rather from the community's perspective. Terrorism affects people's lives, destroys entire communities and their freedoms. Therefore, it should be all the more evident that counterterrorism measures need to be devised to restore the loss induced by such violations and not provoke further damage. Thus, such measures need to be geared towards protecting human security[2] rather than national security, which has quiet "undefined aims" (Galani 2017, 7) and justifies the use of a wide range of actions regardless of their compatibility with human rights law standards.

Bibliography

Abu Zubaydah v. Lithuania App no 46454/11 (ECHR, May 31, 2018).
African Charter on Human and Peoples' Rights (1981).
Aksov v. Turkey App no 21987/93 (ECHR, December 18, 1996).
Almqvist, J. (2005). Rethinking security and human rights in the struggle against terrorism. Paper Presented at the ESIL Forum in the Workshop on 'Human Rights under Threat' on May 27, 2005 (pp. 1–21).
Al Nashiri v. Romania App no 33234/12 (ECHR, May 31, 2018).
Al Nashiri v. Poland App no 28761/11 (ECHR, July 24, 2014).
American civil liberties Union. (2011). *Fact sheet: Extraordinary rendition.* https://www.aclu.org/fact-sheet-extraordinary-rendition. Accessed February 16, 2018.
Aswat v. the United Kingdom App no 17299/12 (ECHR, April 16, 2013).
Chahal v. the United Kingdom App no 22414/93 (ECHR, November 15, 1996).
Clausewitz, C. v. (2014). *De la guerre.* Paris: Perrin.
Delas, O. (2015). L'articulation complexe entre enjeux sécuritaires et le principe de non-refoulement. In A.-M. Tournepiche (Ed.), *La coopération: enjeu essentiel du droit des réfugiés* (pp. 13–38). Paris: Pedone.
Dubuisson, F. (2002). Vers un renforcement des obligations de diligence en matière de lutte contre le terrorisme? In K. Bannelier (Ed.), *Le droit international face au terrorisme, Cahiers internationaux, no 17* (pp. 141–157). Paris: Pedone.
El-Masri v. The Former Yugoslav Republic of Macedonia App no 39630/09 (ECHR, December 13, 2012).
European Convention on Human Rights (1950).
European Court of Human rights. (2016). Fact sheet on Terrorism and the European Convention of Human Rights June. https://www.echr.coe.int/Documents/FS_Terrorism_ENG.pdf. Accessed August 3, 2018.
Flemme, M. (2004). Due Diligence in International Law. Master thesis. University of Lund. https://lup.lub.lu.se/luur/download?func=downloadFile&recordOId=1557482&fileOId=1564336 Accessed on July 25, 2019.
Frérot v. France App no 70204/01 (ECHR, June 12, 2007).
Galani S. (2017). Human security versus national security in anti-terrorist operations: Whose security interests does the ECtHR's margin of appreciation serve? *Report: Human Dignity and Human Security in Times of Terrorism.* https://www.asser.nl/media/4206/report-14-dec-final.pdf. Accessed on June 30, 2019.

[2]"Human security means protecting fundamental freedoms—freedoms that are at the essence of life. It means protecting people from critical (severe) and pervasive (widespread) threats and situations. It means using processes that build on people's strengths and aspirations. It means creating political, social, environmental, economic, military and cultural systems that together give people the building blocks of survival, livelihood and dignity" (Human Security Now 2003, 4).

General Assembly, Resolution 46/51 (1991).
General Assembly, Resolution 48/122 (1994).
General Assembly, Resolution 49/60 (1995).
General Assembly, Resolution 52/133 (1997).
General Assembly, Resolution 68/119 (2013).
General Assembly, Resolution 42/159 (1987).
Granger, M.-A. (2009). Existe-t-il un droit fondamental à la sécurité? *Revue de science criminelle et droit pénal comparé*, (2009-04/06) n°2, 273–296.
Human Security Now. (2003). Report of the Independent Commission on Human Security. https://reliefweb.int/sites/reliefweb.int/files/resources/91BAEEDBA50C6907C1256D19006A9353-chs-security-may03.pdf. Accessed June 30, 2019.
Husayn (Abu Zubaydah) v. Poland App no 7511/13 (ECHR, July 24, 2014).
Inter-American Convention to Prevent and Punish Torture (1985).
Ireland v. The United Kingdom App no 5310/71 (ECHR, January 18, 1978).
Klein, P. (2006). Le droit international à l'épreuve du terrorisme. *Recueil des cours de l'Académie de La Haye* (pp. 203–484).
Lapita v. Italy App no 26772/95 (ECHR, April 6, 2000).
Legal consequences of the construction of a wall in the occupied Palestine territory, Advisory Opinion, I.C.J Reports 2004.
Legality of the threat or use of nuclear weapons, Advisory Opinion, I.C.J Reports 1996.
Liu, A., & Pratt, S. (2017). Tourism's vulnerability and resilience to terrorism. *Tourism management, 60*(C), 404–417.
Martyn, B. (2015, August 19). Fury at European court as terrorists with human rights. *Daily Express*.
Nasr and Ghali v. Italy App no 44883/09 (pending case).
N v. the United Kingdom App no 28341/95 (ECHR, May 27, 2008).
Öcalan v. Turkey App no 10464/07 (ECHR, March 18, 2014).
Oraa, J. (1999). The protection of human rights in emergency situations under customary international law. In G. S. Goodwin-Gill & S. Talmon (Eds.), *The reality of international law: Essays in honour of Ian Brownlie* (pp. 413–437). Oxford: New York, Clarendon Press.
Pellet, A. (2001, September 21). Non, ce n'est pas la guerre. *Le Monde*.
Petropoulou, A. (2014). *Liberté et sécurité: les mesures antiterroristes et la Cour européenne des droits de l'homme*. Paris: Pedone.
RTL. (2016, February 4). Amnesty International dénonce que l'état d'urgence a bouleversé des centaines de vies. https://www.rtl.fr/actu/societe-faits-divers/amnesty-international-l-etat-d-urgence-a-bouleverse-des-centaines-de-vies-7781693269. Accessed February 24, 2019.
Saadi v. Italy App 37201/06 (ECHR, February 28, 2008).
Scheinin, M., & Vermeulen, M. (2011). Unilateral exceptions to international law: Systematic legal analysis and critique of doctrines that seek to deny or reduce the applicability of human rights norms in the fight against terrorism. *Essex Human Rights Review, 8*(2011), 20–56.
Security Council, Resolution 1373 [2001], 2001.
Security Council, Resolution 1566 [2004], 2004.
Senate. (2014). Report of the Senate selected committee on intelligence, committee study of the central intelligence agency's detention and interrogation program, Foreword by Senate Select Committee on Intelligence Chairman Dianne Feinstein: Findings and conclusion, Executive summary, Approved December 2012, updated for release April 2013, Declassification Revisions December 3, 2014. https://download.repubblica.it/pdf/2014/esteri/nothing1.pdf. Accessed February 16, 2018.
Shamayev and others v. Georgia and Russia App no 36378/02 (ECHR, April 12, 2005).
Soering v. The United Kingdom App no 14038/88 (ECHR, July 7, 1989).
Sorel, J.-M. (2002). Existe-t-il une définition universelle du terrorisme? *Le droit international face au terrorisme: après les attentats du 11 septembre, Cahiers internationaux, no 17* (pp. 35–68). Paris: Pedone.

Tercinet, J. (2007). Brèves remarques sur une arlésienne: la définition du terrorisme au niveau universel. In J. Tercinet (Ed.), *La sécurité internationale entre rupture et continuité: mélanges en l'honneur du professeur J-F. Guilhaudis* (pp. 559–579). Bruxelles: Bruylant.
Trabelsi v. Belgium App no 140/10 (ECHR, September 4, 2014).
Universal Declaration of Human Rights (1948).
UN Committee against torture, *Decision Agiza v. Sweden*, May 20, 2004, CAT/C/34/D/233/2003.
UN Convention against Torture and Other Cruel, Inhuman and Degrading Treatment or Punishment (1984).
UN Convention Relating to the Status of Refugees (1951).
UN Human Rights Committee, *Decision Alzery v. Sweden*, November 10, 2012, CCPR/C/88/D/1416/2005.
UN Human Rights Committee, *General comment no. 31, The Nature of the General Legal Obligation Imposed on States Parties to the Covenant*, March 29, 2004, CCPR/C/21/Rev.1/Add.13.
Vienna Convention on the Law of the Treaty (1969).

Emnet Berhanu Gebre is a researcher affiliated to the Maurice Hauriou Institute and an international consultant specialised in human rights protection in the context of migration. Her Ph.D. thesis focused on the international protection of persons displaced by climate change. Her research publications notably pertain to protection issues raised by environmental displacement and climate change litigation at the international and national levels. Her Ph.D. thesis in Public Law at the University of Toulouse 1 Capitole focused on the International Protection of Displaced Persons by Climate Change (2016). After working as a research and teaching fellow at the University of Toulouse 1 Capitole and the Catholic Institute of Toulouse (2010–2018), she is currently working as an international consultant in the field of migration, focusing notably on migrant protection and assistance issues.

Chapter 11
From a Right-Based Approach to a Humanitarian Approach: In What Way Does Migration Impact Human Rights?

Camille de Vulpillières

Abstract This chapter aims to assess the impact of migration on human rights. My hypothesis is that migration tends to draw human rights closer to humanitarian law. What I want to analyse is why and how terms from international humanitarian law are transferred into human rights law when dealing with migration in contemporary French and European law. I will, therefore, underline the way human rights are undermined by European states in order to lessen their obligations towards migrants, and how this strategy changes the very definition of the subject of human rights, by shifting from freedom and universality to vulnerability and exception as well as by focusing on the migrant's passive body instead of allowing him or her to act as a political being.

Keywords Human rights · Migration · Humanitarian rights · Vulnerability · Exception

11.1 Introduction

The current so-called 'migrant crisis' is often referred to as a humanitarian crisis. Hotspot centres in Greece and Italy to accommodate passengers of boats that have crossed the Mediterranean Sea are very similar to humanitarian camps, with a strong emphasis placed on identifying the most vulnerable migrants. This chapter aims to draw the consequences of this observation and, more specifically, to assess the impact of migration on human rights. My hypothesis is that migration tends to bring human rights closer to humanitarian law. What I want to analyse is why and how terms from international humanitarian law are transferred into human rights law when migrations are concerned. To analyse this, I will stick to the contemporary European context.

C. de Vulpillières (✉)
Paris-Nanterre University, Sophiapol - Paris 1 Panthéon-Sorbonne, Iredies, ICM Migration Fellow, Paris, France
e-mail: camille.de.vulpillieres@outlook.fr

M. C. Jacobsen et al. (eds.), *Cosmopolitanism, Migration and Universal Human Rights*, https://doi.org/10.1007/978-3-030-50645-2_11

Having discussed the differences between human rights law and humanitarian law, I will provide some examples from positive law to illustrate their coming closer, and I will finally reflect upon its theoretical consequences.

11.2 Human Rights Law and Humanitarian Law

Stating that international humanitarian law (IHL) and human rights law (IHRL) become closer may be surprising since they are two very different areas of law. In all their three fundamental levels, they indeed differ: their origin, their legal sources, their purposes, and scopes are all very different. I will explain these differences in order to define what 'humanitarian' means in its legal sense. This will enlighten the change at stake when migration law uses it.

First, in terms of origin, IHL is far older than IHRL; rules restricting violence in times of war can be found in every moral, religious and philosophical tradition. On the legal level, IHL starts to take shape in the middle of the nineteenth century. Thanks to Henri Dunant's commitment, 12 countries signed the first Geneva convention in 1864.[1] In contrast, even though human rights were proclaimed in the American and French Declarations at the end of the eighteenth century, it is only since 1948 that they have endorsed an effective legal scope, through the Universal Declaration of Human Rights[2] and the following regional charters.[3]

Second, in terms of sources, IHL and IHRL are two different areas of international law. The former is based upon the Geneva and the Hague Conventions,[4] the latter upon the Universal Declaration of Human Rights and regional conventions. Furthermore, their application is supervised by different monitoring bodies: the International Committee of the Red Cross and the international criminal tribunals[5] on the one side, regional courts[6] and United Nations Committees[7] on the other side.

---

[1] Convention for the Amelioration of the Condition of the Wounded in Armies in the Field, Geneva, adopted on 22 August 1864.

[2] Universal Declaration of Human Rights, proclaimed on 10 December 1948. See also the two 1966 Covenants (International Covenant on Civil and Political Rights and International Covenant on Economic, Social and Cultural Rights).

[3] Such as the European Convention of Human Rights, the American Convention on Human Rights, the African Charter on Human and Peoples' Rights, the Asian Human Rights Charter, and the Arab Charter on Human rights, although their content, scope and legal coercive force are different.

[4] See especially the four 1949 Geneva Conventions: The Geneva Convention (I) on Wounded and Sick in Armed Forces in the Field; the Geneva Convention (II) on Wounded, Sick and Shipwrecked of Armed Forces at Sea; the Geneva Convention (III) on Prisoners of War; and the Geneva Convention (IV) on Civilians.

[5] Such as the different *ad hoc* Tribunals and the International Criminal Court.

[6] The European Court of Human Rights, the Inter-American Court of Human Rights and the African Court of Justice and Human Rights.

[7] Nine committees monitoring the implementation of different conventions related to human rights, including the UN Human Rights Committee.

Finally, in terms of purposes and application scope, IHL intends to alleviate as much as possible the sufferings of civilians in times of conflict and to limit the use of violence between armed forces. Therefore, it applies mainly in times of war (whether it is an international conflict or not) and its fundamental principles are the following: the distinction between combatants and civilians, proportionality when using force, the protection of civilians and wounded and captured combatants. In other words, it aims at promoting 'humanity', meaning respect of human beings, generosity and compassion. IHL is indeed supposed to give reality to compassion and to express this moral approach in legal terms, in order to limit the suffering of civilians in times of war and to prohibit degrading treatment. Finally, IHL mainly deals with the question of how a state and its army should treat the population of another state with which it is at war.

IHRL, however, aims at promoting the human rights that have been proclaimed; it thus asserts the existence of subjective rights, which individuals can claim against the state. Human rights are universally valid; they are involved not only in the relationship between a state and its national members but also in that between a state and non-national members living on its territory or under its jurisdiction. IHRL also deals with 'humanity', but understood in a different sense than the respect of humanity and therefore the definition of strict rules for the exercise of violence: it means promoting and guaranteeing the essential features of human beings that are freedom and dignity.

11.3 The Paradigm Shift in Migrants' Human Rights

These differences that I have underlined will help me demonstrate that a paradigm shift is at stake when migrants' human rights are concerned, which explains why the difference between IHL and IHRL becomes blurry.

But before developing that point, it is useful to recall another case in which they come closer, namely in times of war. Indeed, even if humanitarian law is only valid in times of war and aims at alleviating the sufferings of combatants, protecting civilians and regulating the relationships between combatants from opposite sides, whereas human rights law claims to be valid everywhere, at all times and for all human beings, some of the latter's provisions may be restricted in times of war. But some of them, referred to as the 'hard core', are considered as non-derogable, such as the right to life, the prohibition of slavery and of inhuman or degrading treatments, and the legality of criminal offences and penalties. This list provided by the UN International Covenant on Civil and Political Rights in article 4§2[8] is the counterpart of the common article

[8] 'No derogation from articles 6 [right to life], 7 [prohibition of torture and degrading treatments], 8 (paragraphs 1 and 2) [prohibition of slavery and servitude], 11 [prohibition of imprisonment "merely on the ground of inability to fulfil a contractual obligation"], 15 [principle of the legality of criminal offences and penalties], 16 [right to legal personality] and 18 [right to freedom of thought, conscience and religion] may be made under this provision'.

3 of the four 1949 Geneva Conventions.[9] Hence the junction between the two set of laws on that precise list, although their scopes of application remain different: humanitarian law aims at protecting potential victims (both civil or military victims) from inhuman war violence, namely from excessive, disproportionate violence, while human rights law intends to protect human life and freedom under all circumstances.

Identifying the hard core of human rights also implies that states may be allowed to derogate to the other human rights, mainly in times of war.[10] In times of war, human rights are restricted to their hard core, namely to the rights listed in the Geneva Conventions: in such cases, humanitarian law takes precedence over human rights law, according to the legal maxim *lex specialis derogat legi generali.*[11]

We can therefore identify at least some points of convergence between human rights law and humanitarian law, although they are different areas of law. But my hypothesis goes beyond the idea of points of convergence, even if it means that priority is given to humanitarian law. I will demonstrate that human rights law borrows the terminology of humanitarian law; this refers to two different cases. Sometimes, IHRL directly borrows this terminology in its legal provisions. But in some cases, it is the state that borrows this terminology when referring to migrants'

[9] 'In the case of armed conflict not of an international character occurring in the territory of one of the High Contracting Parties, each Party to the conflict shall be bound to apply, as a minimum, the following provisions:

(1) Persons taking no active part in the hostilities, including members of armed forces who have laid down their arms and those placed "hors de combat" by sickness, wounds, detention, or any other cause, shall in all circumstances be treated humanely, without any adverse distinction founded on race, colour, religion or faith, sex, birth or wealth, or any other similar criteria.

To this end, the following acts are and shall remain prohibited at any time and in any place whatsoever with respect to the above-mentioned persons:

(a) violence to life and person, in particular, murder of all kinds, mutilation, cruel treatment and torture;

(b) taking of hostages;

(c) outrages upon personal dignity, in particular humiliating and degrading treatment;

(d) the passing of sentences and the carrying out of executions without previous judgment pronounced by a regularly constituted court, affording all the judicial guarantees which are recognized as indispensable by civilized peoples.

(2) The wounded and sick shall be collected and cared for.

An impartial humanitarian body, such as the International Committee of the Red Cross, may offer its services to the Parties to the conflict.

The Parties to the conflict should further endeavour to bring into force, by means of special agreements, all or part of the other provisions of the present Convention.

The application of the preceding provisions shall not affect the legal status of the Parties to the conflict'.

[10] UN International Covenant on Civil and Political Rights, article 4, 3: 'Any State Party to the present Covenant availing itself of the right of derogation shall immediately inform the other States Parties to the present Covenant, through the intermediary of the Secretary-General of the United Nations, of the provisions from which it has derogated and of the reasons by which it was actuated. A further communication shall be made, through the same intermediary, on the date on which it terminates such derogation'.

[11] See ICJ, Advisory opinion, Threat or Use of Nuclear Weapons, 1996, § 25; Legal consequences of the construction of a wall in the occupied Palestine territory, 2004, § 106; ICJ, Congo v. Uganda, 2004. For a thorough analysis of this matter, see Qureshi (2018) and Sassoli (2007).

human rights. In either case, I think this is worth highlighting since it reveals a strategy to restrict the scope of human rights as far as migrants are concerned. My hypothesis is that, by translating migrants' human rights into terms borrowed from humanitarian law, states reduce their content and their legal obligations towards non-national members living on their territory.

In my view, this heralds a paradigm shift as far as the conceptual structure of human rights is concerned.

The key elements of this paradigm shift are the shift from terms such as equality and freedom to vulnerability and dignity, from acknowledgement to protection, from unconditional validity and universality to emergency-based selection and from inalienability to temporary enforcement.

This means we shift from subjective rights with legal remedy to protection, which lowers the legal guarantee ensuring their effectiveness. While human rights prevail against states and therefore involve a right to legal remedy, the logic at stake in humanitarian provisions[12] is very different. It no longer deals with acknowledged and guaranteed subjective rights, but with the possible protection the administration freely gives to some selected persons. In terms of who is concerned, we shift from universality to selection. In other words, the main difference between 'authentic' human rights and their paradigm shift is that the former binds the state, whereas the latter depends on its goodwill. The kind of individual protection thereby granted is very different and borrowing terms from humanitarian law appears to be a way to weaken it, so as to preserve the state's freedom to make its own decision.

Finally, and I think this is the most important point, this protection is no longer based upon human freedom, a freedom to be preserved for all human beings, as human rights aim at, but it is based upon some selected persons' vulnerability. By targeting ill foreigners or vulnerable asylum seekers, as we will see, the law dealing with foreigners thus borrows humanitarian terms and loses a part of its scope; it only aims at alleviating specific persons' suffering, at reacting and adapting to an emergency, and no longer at acknowledging universal and non-derogable rights. I will provide some case studies in the next part in order to explain this.

[12]This does not mean that humanitarian law involves no path for appeal (the existence of the *ad hoc* Tribunals and the International Criminal Courts tends to prove the contrary); what I mean here is that qualifying migrants' rights in humanitarian terms is a way to weaken their legal coercive force by presenting them as freely granted by the administration. What I comment upon in the following examples is thus the use of the term 'humanitarian', not of some characteristics of humanitarian law, as I did in the first part.

11.4 References to Humanitarian Grounds in Human Rights Law and Refugee Law

I will try to illustrate this through four legal examples: first, the 'exceptional humanitarian circumstances' criterion that is found in several provisions of the French law dealing with foreigners; second and third, the humanitarian clause introduced in the Common European Asylum System and the Schengen Visa Code. Finally, I will deal with a recent evolution of this common European asylum system, which entails an increasing focus on vulnerable asylum seekers. All these provisions borrow IHL terminology and apply it to a completely different context: in the legal system, 'humanitarian' only refers to IHL and times of war, but in the examples I comment, it is imported into IHRL.

My first example is that of the 'exceptional humanitarian circumstances' criterion, which appears several times in French law. It can, in particular, justify the granting of an exceptional permission to reside [Article L313-14 of the Code of Entry and Residence of Aliens and the Right to Asylum (CESEDA[13])]. This means that, on humanitarian grounds, the French administration can decide to regularise the stay of an illegal alien. It can justify the granting of free state medical aid even if the foreigner does not meet all legal requirements (article L251-1 of the social work and family code[14]). It can also protect some aliens against the obligation to leave the territory or against expulsion. In most of these examples, the foreigners concerned are seriously ill; the mention of 'exceptional humanitarian circumstances' impedes the automatic enforcement of ordinary law. The aim is twofold: on the one hand, to avoid the spread of diseases within the French population and, on the other hand, to avoid severe adverse health consequences for the foreigner. In such circumstances, the 'humanitarian' criterion implies that the foreigner is exceptionally treated as a national member, and therefore allowed to stay and benefit from health care. However, even if it is in varying degrees, such regularisation is always discretionary, namely at the discretion of the administration and thus depending on its goodwill and its interpretation of the foreigner's situation.

'Discretionary' means here, as opposed to the mandatory exercise of a power ('compétence liée'), that the exercise of its competence by the administration is not tied in all its elements (so that there remains a margin of discretion). It is nevertheless still subject to review by the administrative judge. This discretionary power is therefore opposed to a situation in which the administration has no margin of discretion

[13] 'La carte de séjour temporaire mentionnée à l'article L. 313-11 ou la carte de séjour temporaire mentionnée au 1° de l'article L. 313-10 sur le fondement du troisième alinéa de cet article peut être délivrée, sauf si sa présence constitue une menace pour l'ordre public, à l'étranger ne vivant pas en état de polygamie dont l'admission au séjour répond à des considérations humanitaires ou se justifie au regard des motifs exceptionnels qu'il fait valoir, sans que soit opposable la condition prévue à l'article L. 311-7'.

[14] 'En outre, toute personne qui, ne résidant pas en France, est présente sur le territoire français, et dont l'état de santé le justifie, peut, par décision individuelle prise par le ministre chargé de l'action sociale, bénéficier de l'aide médicale de l'État dans les conditions prévues par l'article L. 252-1. Dans ce cas, la prise en charge des dépenses mentionnées à l'article L. 251-2 peut être partielle'.

and in which its decision results necessarily from a rule that applies without a doubt to a specific case. In most cases, the discretionary power can be identified because the judge only exercises minimal supervision and not a normal one, which means that he only examines whether the decision was legal, without examining the legal characterisation of the facts. Indeed, the judge only looks for a manifest error of assessment ('erreur manifeste d'appréciation').

That is why we may say that such a legal provision is no more than a valve, a way of exceptionally making the rules dealing with the stay of foreigners in France more flexible. The term 'humanitarian' seems to justify these flexible rules, by pointing out that because someone's situation is very specific, it is necessary to act with 'humanity', namely to respect a threatened human life and to take into account exceptional and urgent circumstances. However, from a formal and legal point of view, this protection, based upon a discretionary power, is uncertain and weak, all the more so because its application depends on a subjective medical evaluation. From one region to another, from one doctor to another, the rate of granting residence permits, for example, varies widely. We can thus see that this kind of provision leads to legal uncertainty: after the 2016 reform,[15] the number of residence permits granted for this purpose has fallen from almost 7000 to 4187, although the number of applications remained the same (more or less 40,000) (Fraysse et al. 2019).

What is also noticeable in this type of legal provision is the increasing role the immigrant's body plays in the examination of the migrant's administrative situation. As Sayad (1999, 300) puts it, 'the immigrant is only a body'. What he meant was that to be allowed to stay in France, the foreigner is supposed to be in good health so that he can work, referring to the young and active body of the foreign worker. Nowadays, however, labour immigration is almost a distant memory, and the body taken into consideration is the suffering and passive body of the sick foreigner. Fassin (2001, 13) refers to a 'legal compassionate protocol' on that matter to emphasise that the legislator has switched to the level of empathy. What I want to underline is that this empathy is a quality the French administration *can* decide to embody, instead of being *obliged* to: it is very different from granting the ill foreigner a subjective right to reside.

My second example, the humanitarian clause in the Common European Asylum System, involves the same meaning of the term 'humanitarian'. At the European level, a 'humanitarian clause' allows that the rules establishing the state responsible for the asylum application are more flexible. According to the Dublin III Regulation,[16] this derogation from the responsibility criteria can occur 'on humanitarian and compassionate grounds, in order to bring together family members, relatives or

[15]The key point is that the doctors responsible for examining the applications have been transferred from the Ministry of Health to the Ministry of the Interior.

[16]On that matter, the May 2016 'Proposal for a regulation of the European Parliament and of the Council establishing the criteria and mechanisms for determining the Member State responsible for examining an application for international protection lodged in one of the Member States by a third-country national or a stateless person (recast)' makes no fundamental change (although the discretionary clause is narrowed, the use of humanitarian grounds remains possible).

any other family relations'.[17] Therefore, member states are allowed to derogate from the Regulation upon humanitarian grounds. Although it is not an obligation but only a possibility, the decision of the Court of Justice of the European Union in *K. versus Bundesasylamt*[18] made it mandatory when a family member depends on the asylum seeker. All the elements of the paradigm shift I mentioned earlier can be identified here: the decision does not aim at acknowledging an asylum seeker's freedom to be reunited with his or her family, but at protecting vulnerable persons. Not all asylum seekers could claim for family reunification: the ordinary rules were more restrictive.[19] The humanitarian clause was used to compensate for this restrictive approach. And this paradigm shift was made possible and justified by diffusing expressions reflecting humanitarian considerations such as 'humanitarian circumstances'.

Therefore, by using terms of humanitarian inspiration or connotation, member states are allowed to disregard ordinary rules, given the particular situation of an individual. As in the previous examples, such a possibility can appear to be protective for aliens, since it is based upon an individual examination of their situation. But this also results in the loss of a central characteristic of human rights law, namely the fact that it legally binds states and provides the individuals with a legal path for an appeal if their rights are not respected. Humanitarian clauses are very different: they proclaim no individual right that prevails over the state and that binds the administration; on the contrary, they give the administration an important freedom of decision.

My third example deals with another humanitarian clause mentioned in the Schengen Visa Code,[20] the code governing the issuance of short-stay visas (less than three months). Its article 25 states that 'a visa with limited territorial validity shall be issued exceptionally, in the following cases: (a) when the Member State concerned considers it necessary on humanitarian grounds, for reasons of national interest or because of international obligations'. The international obligations mentioned mainly refer to recital 29 of the same code, according to which 'this Regulation respects fundamental rights and observes the principles recognised in particular by the Council of Europe's Convention for the Protection of Human Rights and Fundamental Freedoms and by the Charter of Fundamental Rights of the European Union'. Such a recital implies that issuing a humanitarian visa may sometimes be mandatory when someone's fundamental rights would otherwise be threatened. However, article 25 clearly states a discretionary provision, identifiable by the use of the verb 'shall' and the adverb 'exceptionally'.

This choice of words may seem anecdotal, but it has very concrete consequences. To illustrate these consequences, I will refer to a recent ECJ judgement, *X and X*

---

[17] https://eur-lex.europa.eu/legal-content/en/ALL/?uri=celex%3A32013R0604, §17. For an analysis of the Dublin III system, see in particular Chetail et al. (2016: 151) as far as this humanitarian clause is concerned.

[18] CJEU, Grand Chamber, 6 November 2012, K. v. Bundesasylamt, case C-245/11.

[19] The current regulation is more protective on that matter (partly thanks to the K. versus Bundesasylamt case): see the articles 8–11 of the Dublin III Regulation.

[20] Regulation (EC) No 810/2009 of the European Parliament and of the Council of 13 July 2009 establishing a Community Code on Visas (Visa Code).

versus Belgium (7 March 2017).[21] In this case, a Syrian family went to the Belgian embassy in Lebanon in order to ask for humanitarian visas allowing them to file an asylum application in Belgium. The Belgian authorities refused the visa, and the ECJ agreed with them, arguing that since they intended to apply for asylum, their stay on Belgian territory would last much longer than three months and that they in fact had to apply for a long-stay visa, the issue of which was discretionary. What is relevant to me here is that in order to justify their refusal, the Belgian authorities argued that if they had to grant a humanitarian visa to every individual whose life was threatened, it would no longer be a discretionary provision… We can measure here the extent to which the formulation of humanitarian measures leads to weak protection compared with human rights protection. The Belgian authorities' reasoning is all the more questionable because the very reason why humanitarian visas exist is to protect human rights even in cases where common legal conditions cannot be fulfilled; in other words, its purpose is to save lives. But what governments retain from this provision is that they may or may not deliver this visa, according to their own opinion, and therefore that they may refuse it even to this obviously threatened Christian Syrian family. Thus, by adopting a non-mandatory formulation, this humanitarian clause, which at first seemed rather protective, appears to be in fact nothing but empty words since states are reluctant to apply as much as they ought to.

In my last example, the borrowing of humanitarian law terms is less overt: it deals with the identification of 'vulnerable' asylum seekers. In the Common European Asylum System, member states are indeed asked to focus on vulnerable asylum seekers. According to article 21 of the Reception Conditions Directive, vulnerable persons are those 'such as minors, unaccompanied minors, disabled people, elderly people, pregnant women, single parents with minor children, victims of human trafficking, persons with serious illnesses, persons with mental disorders and persons who have been subjected to torture, rape or other serious forms of psychological, physical or sexual violence, such as victims of female genital mutilation'.[22] Member states have to conduct a vulnerability assessment in order to adapt the material reception (or detention) conditions and guarantee access to health care. This provision was implemented in French law through a questionnaire with two sets of questions: accommodation and special needs (such as pregnancy or disability). At first sight, once again, this might appear as more protective, since there might indeed be very vulnerable persons among asylum seekers (even if asylum seekers as such are already legally regarded as a vulnerable group); however, since there is a notorious lack of places in accommodation centres[23] and since non-accommodated asylum seekers are only given 11 euros a day to live, this leads to the selection of some asylum

---

[21] X and X versus Belgium, ECJ, 7 March 2017, ECLI:EU:C:2017:173.

[22] Directive 2013/33/EU of the European Parliament and of the Council of 26 June 2013 laying down standards for the reception of applicants for international protection, chapter IV, article 21.

[23] According to the French institution (OFII) responsible for the accommodation of asylum seekers, there are currently 22,493 accommodation places, to be compared to the 61,903 asylum applications in 2015.

seekers whose human rights will be respected. As for the others, they are left roofless, although providing accommodation for all asylum seekers is an obligation for the state,[24] since they are not allowed to work and make a living.

More generally, a change has occurred in the past decades as far as the examination of asylum applications is concerned: more and more often, asylum seekers provide medical certificates in order to 'prove' that they have been tortured or that they suffer from post-traumatic stress syndrome, which would acknowledge their past sufferings. This change is noteworthy since asylum judges are used to receiving such documents as part of the applicant's file. I think it is closely connected to the influence of humanitarian considerations on migrants' human rights law, and it has deep implications as far as asylum is concerned.

First, this implies that the status of victim is becoming more and more important in order to be granted asylum, whereas asylum was originally designed to protect those who fight for their freedom, whether they can be recognised as victims or not. Therefore, a progressive shift of the reasons why asylum is granted occurs. Indeed, it is supposedly granted to every person who 'owing to well-founded fear of being persecuted for reasons of race, religion, nationality, membership of a particular social group or political opinion, is outside the country of his nationality and is unable or, owing to such fear, is unwilling to avail himself of the protection of that country'.[25] To be granted the status of refugee, one does not have to prove that he or she has actually been tortured or mistreated, but that he or she has good reason to fear persecution. In contrast, the increasing importance of medical certificates implies that those who can prove past mistreatment will be more easily granted asylum than those who only fear it, since there is almost no way to prove a good reason to fear an event that has not yet occurred. Therefore, the growing focus on the applicant's mind and body through the medical certificate may weaken asylum law or at least reduce the scope of its application.

Second, since it is supposed to be granted to any person who has reason to fear mistreatment from its state, the key element of an asylum application used to be the asylum seeker's account of his or her reasons to flee—that is, the applicant's speech. But the increasing role of doctors and medical experts has weakened the persuasive power of this speech in favour of medical certificates. Therefore, the humanitarian and laudable care for torture victims finally leads to a new necessity for them to prove what they have suffered: '[t]he psychotraumatology of exile, whose gradual emergence around the asylum seeker and the victim of torture we have described, takes on a new

---

[24]According to the reception conditions directive (2013/33/EU), article 18, 'Where housing is provided in kind, it should take one or a combination of the following forms:

(a) premises used for the purpose of housing applicants during the examination of an application for international protection made at the border or in transit zones.

(b) accommodation centres which guarantee an adequate standard of living;

(a) private houses, flats, hotels or other premises adapted for housing applicants.'.

So, housing may be provided through financial allowances, but, according to article 17, they 'shall be determined on the basis of the level(s) established by the Member State concerned either by law or by the practice to ensure adequate standards of living for nationals'.

[25]1951 Geneva Convention relating to the status of refugees.

social significance here. It was born out of a recognition of the uniqueness of this experience of persecution and a need for specific trauma management. It becomes an instrument for assessing the truth of stories in the service of refugee decision-making bodies. For the doctors and psychologists who had been involved in this humanitarian cause, it was about healing. They are now required to certify' (Fassin & Rechtman 2007, 219). Furthermore, they are not required to certify the reasons asylum seekers have to fear mistreatment, as asylum law puts it, but to certify that they have already suffered it… This illustrates the growing suspicion that weighs on the asylum seekers' testimony. As Fassin and Rechtman (2007, 223–224) puts it, '[m]ore emphasis is placed on medical and psychological expertise because less and less is given to political asylum.[…] The remarkable fact we want to highlight is that today trauma, as certified by mental health specialists, has become a regular and expected part of the claimant's case.' In other words, the body becomes proof because speech is devalued. Through this example, we can see that a humanitarian provision can express an intention very different from a generous concern to protect and to take care: in this particular case, it is much more synonymous with suspicion and a way to deeply transform the asylum procedure.

Henceforth, according to these examples, we can assert than interpreting human rights law and refugee law through a humanitarian lens leads to a less strict application of human rights: human rights as such will only fully apply to national citizens, but, in many respects, the rights migrants are granted are what we could call humanitarian rights. All the legal 'humanitarian' provisions I commented upon aim to ensure the guarantee of certain human rights, such as the right to life and the prohibition of inhuman or degrading treatments, or the right to family life; these human rights are respected for some foreigners and asylum seekers. However, they are also undermined and stripped of most of their content, since they are awarded at the discretion of the administration or only granted to a limited category of individuals, namely the most vulnerable. The supposed universality of human rights is thereby contradicted by its application as far as migrants are concerned.

I think this deserves attention since the very definition of the holder of human rights is altered.

11.5 Which Human Being Really Holds Human Rights?

Indeed, the beneficiaries of all these provisions are ill, vulnerable or dependent foreigners. The aim is to avoid or delay one's death, to alleviate one's sufferings. This points out the gap between these humanitarian provisions and the original *raison d'être* of human rights, since the latter aimed to protect not only human life but also human freedom, not only to proscribe degrading treatments but also to give individuals the means of developing their potential and having control of their life, by protecting them from discrimination, oppression and arbitrariness, and by granting them the right to get married, to travel, to express one's opinion… Laying emphasis upon illness or vulnerability, namely on 'humanitarian' grounds points out that those who benefit from these legal provisions are passive, dependent, in distress, whereas human rights aim at enabling human beings to exercise their freedom; this underlines the gap between these humanitarian provisions and a true implementation of migrants' human rights.

In other words, the only human rights migrants are granted and acknowledged are the rights of the biological human being, not those of the active members of society, with its projects and initiatives. That is why I think that speaking of human rights in terms referring to humanitarian considerations betrays the meaning the first promotors of human rights gave to the term 'human being'. By regularising foreigners upon humanitarian grounds and targeting vulnerable asylum seekers, the administration reduces these men and women to the status of suffering or dependent bodies. Foreigners passively receive protection granted on a discretionary basis, for which they are not allowed to claim, instead of acknowledgement being given to the central characteristic of human being according to human rights law, namely freedom. There is a clear shift from reason, action and empowerment to empathy and emotion. I think this deeply betrays the very logic of human rights that is being replaced by a 'humanitarian reason' (Fassin & Rechtman 2007, 13) in which vertical compassion for one's sufferings replaces the horizontal dialogue of reasonable and political actors. Whereas the original intention of human rights was to allow people to gain power in respect of their own lives, humanitarian reason only 'claims a right to keep alive the one who has only his existence in his hands' (ibid.). In other words, such a shift from horizontality to verticality is synonymous with a shift from equality to domination, and from universality to a more or less arbitrary selection of dramatic cases.

11.6 Conclusion

In this chapter, by examining humanitarian-grounded legal provisions, I have tried to show how a migrant's body tends to be more and more at the very centre of his or her administrative and legal situation; even if this goes beyond the scope of this chapter, we can notice that this is also true as far as border management is concerned: 'smart borders' and the techniques they depend on, such as facial or fingerprint recognition, exemplify this assertion. But what seems most relevant is the paradox according to which, while claiming to protect a *human* being, the humanitarian approach tends to *reify* him or her by focusing on the body and reducing him or her to a passive being.

Bibliography

Chetail, V. (Ed.). (2016). *Reforming the Common European Asylum System: The New European Refugee Law*. Leiden/Boston: Brill.

Fassin, D. (2001). Quand le corps fait loi. La raison humanitaire dans les procédures de régularisation des étrangers. *Sciences sociales et santé, 19*, 5–34.

Fassin, D., & Rechtman, R. (2007). *L'Empire du traumatisme, Enquête sur la condition de victime.* Paris: Flammarion.

Fraysse, A., Laneelle, E., Hammadi, Y., Lagorsse, C., & Mben, R. (2019). Le parcours des étrangers malades en France. *La Revue des droits de l'homme, Actualités Droits-Libertés*. https://journals.openedition.org/revdh/5977. DOI : https://doi.org/10.4000/revdh.5977

Qureshi, W. A. (2018). Untangling the complicated relationship between international humanitarian law and human rights law in armed conflict. *Penn State Journal of Law & International Affairs, 6*, 204–235.

Sassoli, M. (2007). Le droit international humanitaire, une lex specialis par rapport aux droits Humains? In A. Auer, A. Flückiger, & M. Hottelier (Eds.), *Les droits de l'homme et la constitution: études en l'honneur du Professeur Giorgio Malinverni* (pp. 375–395), Genève: Schulthess.

Sayad, A. (1999). *La double absence. Des illusions de l'émigré aux souffrances de l'immigré*. Paris: Le Seuil.

Camille de Vulpillières obtained her Ph.D. in Philosophy from the University of Paris-Nanterre, with her thesis entitled "The Gates of the Law. Sovereignty, human rights, hospitality: which rights for foreigners?" She lectures on political philosophy and philosophy of law at the University of Poitiers, and she is a qualified lecturer in philosophy having passed her 'agrégation' in 2013.

Chapter 12
Gender, Migration and Human Rights in the Case Law of the European Court of Human Rights

Athanasia Petropoulou

Abstract Recent case law of the ECtHR points to the increasing relevance of the gender perspective in migration and asylum cases. Human rights violations claims emanating from women or sexual minorities raise a fundamental gender dimension, which is not usually addressed as such by the Court. The failure to effectively respond to gender-oriented arguments, coupled with the limits inherent in the vulnerable status of the applicants, continues to restrict access of this category of claimants to international asylum protection and hinder the consolidation of their human rights claims. The chapter calls for more sociologically informed decision-making practices and a more contextualised and relational approach in the assessment of the risk of ill-treatment. Such an approach is essential for unearthing the gendered patterns of persecution and addressing effectively related claims.

Keywords Gender · Human rights · Sexual minorities · Migrants · Asylum law · European court of human rights

12.1 Introduction

The present analysis aims to critically assess some important aspects of the case law of the European Court of Human Rights (ECtHR) on matters concerning gender-related claims of migrants and asylum seekers, including those based on sexual orientation and gender identity. While there is a common understanding that a person's sex, gender, gender identity and sexual orientation shape every stage of the migration experience (IOM, UN 2004 world survey), theories of international migration had until recently not been focused on exploring and incorporating a gender perspective in their analysis. In a similar vein, refugee law has long been the object of criticism

A. Petropoulou (✉)
University of Paris I, Panthéon-Sorbonne, Paris, France
e-mail: petropoulou.athanasia@yahoo.com

M. C. Jacobsen et al. (eds.), *Cosmopolitanism, Migration and Universal Human Rights*, https://doi.org/10.1007/978-3-030-50645-2_12

for failing to recognise and respond appropriately to women's and sexual minorities' experiences of persecution (Arbelet al. 2014).[1]

Addressing these criticisms, the UNHCR has, during the last decades, published a series of guidelines on the protection of Refugee Women (1991), on refugee status determination (Gender Guidelines 2002) and on sexual orientation and/or gender identity (2012), in an attempt to promote the mainstreaming of gender- and sexual-orientated considerations in the examination of asylum claims. Moreover, these developments were part of similar advancements in the area of human rights concerning women's rights (CEDAW, Istanbul Convention). At the regional level, both the European Union (EU) and the Council of Europe (CoE) have taken important initiatives aiming to promote a gender- and sex-orientated perspective in migration and asylum laws and policies. The basic normative instruments of the Common European Asylum System (CEAS) provide that EU member states should take gender issues into consideration both in the refugee status determination process and in the reception conditions for asylum seekers and refugees (Directives 2011/96/EU, 2013/32/EU and 2013/33/EU). However, it has been pointed out that despite the aim of harmonisation of asylum legislation at the EU level, disparities in the way the different EU states handle gender- and sexual-orientated related claims subsist (European Parliament, Study 2012; UN Women report 2017). These disparities have the result that the claims of women and sexual minorities are not properly addressed and that policies incorporating a gender perspective and considerations related to sexual orientation are not implemented in practice.

The CoE has developed a significant role in the field of asylum, most notably through the case of law of the ECtHR and its interpretation of the European Convention on Human Rights (ECHR) and Protocols. In this respect, the parliamentary assembly has also, during recent years, constantly been encouraging states to protect the rights of women and sexual minorities, and the European Committee for the Prevention of Torture and Inhuman or Degrading Treatment or Punishment (CPT) has produced guidelines on the treatment of migrants and asylum seekers (Danisi 2009).

The case law of the ECtHR reflects the predicaments faced by members of the LGBTI community and women asylum seekers in advocating their cases before national and international adjudication bodies. In this chapter, it is argued that while the Strasbourg Court has developed a strong jurisprudential line in addressing the human rights claims of women and members of the LGBTI community, particularly in asylum cases, it needs to take more into account the structural, institutional and social dimension of the risk of ill-treatment under Article 3 of the Convention when adjudicating in similar cases. As it will be shown, the Court pays too much consideration to the individual conditions and capabilities of the particular applicant and downplays the social and institutional factors underlying the risk of violation of Article 3.

[1] According to the Guidelines of the UNHCR 2002, § 1: "Gender-related persecution … is used to encompass the range of different claims in which gender is a relevant consideration in the determination of refugee status".

12.2 De-gendering the Claims of Women Asylum Seekers Under Article 3 of the ECHR

Refugee law has been evolving during the last decades under the growing influence of the international human rights regime. Asylum seekers are increasingly articulating their plight in human rights law terms and administrative and judicial bodies have been interpreting the criteria established for the refugee definition through the lens of human rights. It has been stated that the development of 'gender[2] asylum law' has relied to a great extent on the influence of the human rights regime (Anker 2002). Indeed, the human rights paradigm has been a source for evaluating the claims related to violence against women as serious harm in the context of persecution. In this regard, many forms of gender-related persecution and violence against women, such as rape and sexual violence, or female genital mutilation (FGM) which can qualify as persecution under the Refugee Convention, constitute serious human rights violations. On the other hand, it has been shown that refugee law can contribute to the elaboration of human rights norms, deepen understandings and produce substantive changes if it is embraced as part of human rights law (Anker 2002, 143). Cross-fertilisation between the two regimes has been critical for the development and strengthening of women's rights both in the field of human rights and in the field of refugee law.

In the context of the ECHR, women asylum seekers' claims of gendered ill-treatment are examined not in view of implementing the criteria of the refugee definition and granting protection, but under the non-refoulement principle, enshrined in Article 3 of the Convention. The protection offered under Article 3 involves an assessment of the actual risk faced by the applicant in the country of destination. While this risk was traditionally considered as emanating from state agents and perpetrated by state agents in the public sphere, it has been recognised under the human rights and refugee law that a state can be held responsible for ill-treatment perpetrated by private actors and that violence committed in the private sphere can amount to a human rights violation or to persecution. Refugee law acknowledges that serious acts by non-state agents can be considered persecution 'if such acts are knowingly tolerated by the authorities, or if the authorities refuse, or are unable, to offer effective protection' (UNHCR 2002, para. 19).

It is not disputed that several harms, such as rape and FGM, inflicted on women by private actors are contrary to Article 3 of the Convention and can be invoked in order to prevent an expulsion even in cases where these harms would be inflicted by persons 'who are not public officials'(ECHR, Salah Sheekh v. the Netherlands 2007, § 137), when the state is 'not able to obviate the risk by providing appropriate protection'(ECHR, H.L.R. v. France 1997, § 40; Sow v. Belgium 2016). In this section, it will be shown that the ECtHR, while recognising that private violence can

[2]'Gender' refers to 'the relationship between women and men based on socially and culturally constructed and defined identities, status, roles and responsibilities that are assigned to one sex or another, while sex is a biological determination. Gender is not static or innate but acquires socially and culturally constructed meaning over time' (UNHCR Guidelines 2002, § 3).

result in state accountability and can amount to ill-treatment prohibited by Article 3, has been reluctant until now to address the gender dimension of the applicants' claims, namely to recognise the social and institutional structures from which the harm originates, and give them the appropriate weight in the evaluation of the risk.[3] As it has also been argued by Peroni, downplaying the role of gendered structures, as well as focusing on the private capacity for protection from the harm, may result in undermining the applicant's access to the protection of the Convention (Peroni 2018, 362).

In some of the most relevant decisions in this regard, the Court has either cursorily examined the general conditions in the receiving country or failed to examine them altogether, or vaguely assessed the real possibility of relocation. The Court lays particular emphasis on the legislative steps in some countries criminalising the practice of FGM, while overlooking the enforcement of the rules in practice. For example, the Court rejected the application (ECHR, Izevbekhai and others v. Ireland 2011) of a Nigerian woman fearing circumcision if returning to her country, by underlining that Nigeria had ratified the Maputo Protocol, prohibited inhuman treatment in the Constitution and passed legislation against FGM. While admitting that there was an 'absence or low level of legal action' to enforce existing laws, the Court still insisted on the federal government's public opposition to FGM in order to declare the application manifestly ill-founded. This line of reasoning concerning the situation in Nigeria, specifically in the Delta State (ECHR, Collins and Akaziebie v. Sweden 2007) and Sudan (ECHR, R.B.A.B and others v. the Netherlands 2016), was adopted in other similar cases. A cursory evaluation of the actual willingness and ability of the authorities in Kenya to protect the applicant from FGM has led the Court to dismiss the applicant's complaint, despite reports indicating that action from the authorities was not generalised and that existing laws concerned only women under 18 years old (ECHR, R.W. and others v. Sweden 2012, § 9).[4]

The case law referred seems to suggest that the criminalisation of particular forms of violence against women can alone demonstrate that the state of destination offers the level of protection required. However, the enforcement practice of the legal framework by state authorities has to be carefully examined, as well as the social structures that might still condone abusive practices despite institutional advancements. In this regard, UNHCR states: 'Even though a particular State may have prohibited a persecutory practice, it may nevertheless continue to condone or tolerate the practice, or may not be able to stop the practice effectively' (UNHCR 2002, § 11). On the other hand, systematic failure of the authorities to provide protection to women against acts of persecution can explain the reticence or fear of women to seek protection from the police or the public authorities in general. Consequently, this fact cannot

---

[3] In this regard UNHCR urges states to recognise gender-related asylum claims as such: 'These guidelines specifically focus on the interpretation of the refugee definition … from a gender perspective, as well as propose some procedural practices in order to ensure that proper consideration is given to women claimants in refugee status determination procedures and that the range of gender-related claims are recognised as such' (Guidelines 2002, § 1).

[4] The Court states: '… there is no indication that the domestic authorities would be unwilling or unable to protect the applicant'.

be taken into consideration in order to invalidate the credibility of the claims of an applicant.[5] However, the ECtHR seems to reproach an applicant for the fact that she 'hadn't attempted to report any issue concerning their daughters and FGM to the police' (Izevbekhai and others, § 80).

Assessment of gendered social and institutional structures is also diminished in the context of the possibility of relocation. The Court has thus summarily admitted that women escaping violence in Nigeria have the option of internal relocation in view of the protection provided by the government (Izevbekhai and others, § 75). While the reports on internal relocation cited by the Court indicated that the government's support of the concerned women was progressing but remained weak, the Court accepted that the applicants could relocate, as they could benefit from considerable family and financial resources in the place of relocation. In a more recent case (ECHR, A.L. v. UK 2018), the Court concluded that the applicant wouldn't be facing a risk of being subjected to FGM if relocated in Abuja, despite the threats of her relatives in this regard, because, among others, it would be difficult for them to find her and her educated parents would protect her. The Court also relied on evidence showing that the practice of FGM is lower in this region than in other parts of the country. In this regard, the CEDAW committee (CEDAW 2014, § 28[6]) has drawn particular attention to the strict requirements that states should apply while evaluating the relocation perspective, which can also entail gender-related aspects and risks (ECHR, M. Y. H. and others v. Sweden 2013, § 62).

12.3 Relying on Gender Stereotyping

Low-intensity scrutiny of the gendered social and institutional structures in the country of origin of a woman asylum seeker can be combined with the particular attention paid by the Court to her personal capacities to cope with the risk or to the protection afforded to her by private agents. It can be argued that in some cases overemphasising the strength, independence and education of an applicant woman results in undermining her access to protection. In a case concerning the return of the applicant to Yemen, the Court, while relying also on credibility issues and the presence of a male protective network, noted: 'The first applicant has shown proof of independence by going to court in Yemen on several occasions to file for divorce

[5]See CEDAW 2014, § 29: '... the Committee notes that the fact that a woman asylum seeker has not sought the protection of the State or made a complaint to the authorities before her departure from her country of origin should not prejudice her asylum claim, especially where violence against women is tolerated or there is a pattern of failure in responding to women's complaints of abuse…'

[6]'States should also take into account gender-related aspects and risks in the assessment as to whether internal relocation is permissible. Difficulties faced by women in relocating to other parts of their countries of origin can include legal, cultural and/or social restrictions or prohibitions on women travelling or living alone, practical realities such as problems of securing accommodation, childcare and economic survival without family or community support, and risk of harassment and exploitation, including sexual exploitation and violence'.

… and shown strength by managing to obtain the necessary practical and financial means to leave Yemen' (ECHR, A. A. and others v. Sweden 2012, § 83). Using similar reasoning in a case discussed earlier concerning deportation to Nigeria (Collins and Akaziebe v. Sweden), the Court dismissed the application as manifestly ill-founded. The Court referred to the strength and independence shown by the applicant in order to conclude that she could protect her daughter, the second applicant, from being subjected to FGM. It is as if the Court was implying, as Brems argues, that 'if a woman is strong enough to stand against cultural oppression, she is too strong for outsider protection' (Brems 2010).

In other cases already discussed, after downplaying the gendered social structures, the Court moves on to focusing on the resourcefulness of the applicants based namely on education, work experience and financial resources (Izevbekhai and others v. Ireland). The Court thus concluded that even though the applicant was an unmarried woman without support of her family, 'owing to her education and working experience as a seamstress', she would not need such support to relocate in another part of the country (ECHR, Omeredo v. Austria 2011, § 5). In another case, the applicant, fleeing a second circumcision in Guinea, was dismissed by the Court because, among others, she was a 28-year-old woman who has a progressive education and opposed the practice of circumcision. It was concluded that she cannot be considered as a 'particular vulnerable young woman' (Sow v. Belgium, § 68).

The reasoning adopted by the Court might be said to 'depoliticise' and 'privatise' the gender-related claims of women asylum seekers, by refusing to recognise and address the gendered dimension of these claims and by overemphasising the role of personal agency. By showing deference to the stance of state authorities, the Court in reality condones the practice of a stereotyped treatment of claims concerning gendered violence. It has been argued that the 'vulnerable victim' approach underpinning the argumentation of the Court (Peroni, 263) rests on Western-constructed narratives of victimhood of women of non-Western origin. A vulnerable woman that can be considered a victim and worthy of protection should be unassertive, dependent, uneducated, passive and deprived of any financial resources. These gendered stereotypes can result in undermining the credibility of an asylum's seekers arguments regarding risk of persecution in her country of origin. This was the case of an Iraqi woman before the Court allegedly fleeing violence from her male relatives for having dishonoured them because of her relationship with a man. The Court, stressing that she had run her 'own business in Iraq' and led an 'independent life', found it doubtful that 'her family has such a strong honour culture that an illegitimate relationship would lead to a risk of her being killed' (ECHR, I. F. W. v. Sweden 2014, § 1).

On the other hand, depicting women as vulnerable victims legitimises forms of dependence of women on powerful men, who can assure them protection (Otto 2013, 199). This stereotype is also present in the case law of the Court. Strangely, the Court relies on the existence of a male network even in cases where it has recognised that the applicant is strong enough and independent so as to protect herself. In a case concerning the deportation of the applicant in Yemen, the Court took into particular consideration the family support available from the brother and the adult sons of the applicant, whose strength and independence had been also stressed in its reasoning. The applicant's sons can, according to the reasoning, help the applicant and her daughter to be 'able to live away from her husband and father' (A. A and others v. Sweden, § 90). The conclusion of the Court comes despite the fact that the risk of forced marriage had materialised for three of the four female applicants, who had been forced to marry at a young age in Yemen. In another case (ECHR, R.H. v. Sweden 2015, § 73) concerning the return of an applicant to Mogadishu, where her uncles would allegedly force her to marry or kill her if she refused, the Court assumed that she could rely on her brother and uncles for protection. In this regard, the Court, expressing in parallel serious doubts about the applicant's credibility, did not duly pay attention to country reports indicating that family members were among the actors committing violence against women with impunity in Somalia, even in the case of the applicant, whose relatives were allegedly the source of risk, a factor that the dissenting judges highlighted.[7] Inversely, where the applicant is unable to access male support, her removal would be contrary to Article 3 of the Convention (ECHR, N. v. Sweden 2010).

Peroni argues that it is highly problematic to assume that 'the mere presence of male relatives automatically equals women's protection'. On the other hand, this assumption seems to be in opposition to the principle under Article 3 of the Convention, according to which the failure of the authorities to 'obviate the risk by providing appropriate protection' (Salah Sheekh v. the Netherlands, § 137) can substantiate the applicant's allegation as to the reality of the risk. It can be appropriate to take into consideration family support in order to assess the risk of persecution faced by an applicant in her country of origin. However, it must also be taken into consideration that, in some cases, a male relative can be the source of the risk. Similar reasoning resonates with the assumption that state protection is lacking and this deficiency can be compensated by a 'male protection network'. The reliance on the male factor reproduces the stereotype that, in non-Western societies, deficient state protection mechanisms can and should be legitimately substituted by private male networks. In consequence, instead of revealing the gendered structures of the risk faced by women, the Court's reasoning in the examined cases results in reproducing conceptions of male supremacy and female dependence in human rights discourse (Peroni, 365).

[7] The dissenting judges Zupancinc and De Gaetano noted that the applicant's male relatives may be equally or more hostile than society to her status (par. 44). However, the Court had serious doubts about the veracity of her allegations, as she had not convincingly explained why she presented such allegations to the migration authorities.

12.4 "Neutralising" Sexual Orientation and Gender Identity

Gender is also relevant in the refugee claims based on differing sexual orientation (UNHCR 2002, § 16). According to the Yogyakarta Principles, sexual orientation refers to 'each person's capacity for profound emotional, affectional and sexual attraction to, and intimate relations with, individuals of a different gender or more than one gender'. Gender identity refers to 'each person's deeply felt internal and individual experience of gender, which may or may not correspond with the sex assigned at birth, including the personal sense of the body and other expressions of gender, including dress, speech and mannerisms'. It is undisputed that 'a claimant's sexuality or sexual practices may be relevant to a refugee claim where he or she has been subject to persecutory (including discriminatory) action on account of his or her sexuality or sexual practices' (UNHCR 2002, § 16). From a human rights perspective, a claimant's actual or perceived sexual orientation and/or gender identity (SOGI) may be relevant for assessing the risk under Article 3 of the Convention when the claimant risks being subjected to torture or ill-treatment because of his sexual orientation and/or gender identity.

The case law of the ECtHR in this domain is not particularly robust and the related jurisprudential principles have not yet been crystallised. The cases examined by the Court, like those concerning women asylum seekers, reflect the difficulties encountered by LGBTI (Lesbian, Gay, Bisexual, Transgender and Intersex) asylum seekers in defending their case before national authorities and obtaining international protection. As a recent report of the European Union Fundamental Rights Agency shows, the reception and protection needs of LGBTI asylum seekers in the EU are still frequently not met (FRA 2017). The case law of the ECtHR addresses some of the basic issues, often perceived as particularly complex, in the domain of SOGI-related persecution claims, namely under Article 3 of the Convention.

One of the first cases dealt by the Court in 2004 (ECHR, F. v. UK 2004) involved an Iranian homosexual who left Iran after the authorities became aware of his homosexual relationship, following a period in detention and release upon payment of a bribe. The Strasbourg Court dismissed the claims of the applicant under Articles 2 and 3, as it considered that there was no active prosecution by the Iranian authorities of adults involved in consensual and private homosexual relationships. The Court thus overlooked the possibility of prosecution, the under-reporting of such instances, and the reported instances of criminal punishment of homosexual conduct, all mentioned in the evidence adduced by the applicant. In this case, the national authorities had pointed to the lack of credibility of the applicant, a position which had been described as being part of the 'culture of disbelief' of the UK asylum authorities (Milibank 2009). The conclusion of the Court thus resulted in endorsing the assessment of the national authorities and their deficient practice.

On the other hand, the Court seems to introduce two levels of protection under the Convention with regard to the criminalisation of homosexuality. It is well established that the criminalisation of homosexuality in a member state is contrary to Article 8 of the Convention (ECHR, Dudgeon v. UK 1981). However, concerning a homosexual asylum seeker fleeing from the criminalisation of homosexuality in his country of origin and the risk of prosecution, such criminalisation does not necessarily amount to a violation of the same article. In the case involving the return of the applicant in Iran, the Court found that it had not been established that the 'applicant's moral integrity would be substantially affected to a degree falling within the scope of Article 8 of the Convention' (F v. UK).

Similar considerations with regard to the criminalisation of homosexual activity prevailed in another case concerning a gay Iranian asylum seeker (ECHR, I.I.N. v. Netherlands 2004), who had also participated in protests against the local regime. The applicant claimed that he had been raped by a policeman twice. The Dutch authorities had dismissed his claims on the grounds of credibility. While the Strasbourg Court had taken into consideration a wide range of materials, it stated that a situation of active prosecution by the authorities of adults involved in consensual and private homosexual relationships was not established and thus rejected the application as manifestly ill-founded. The Court adopted a similar position regarding the case of a homosexual from Guinea (ECHR, M.B. v. Netherlands 2017), in which, endorsing the conclusions of the national authorities, it stated that 'it cannot be derived that … the Guinean authorities pursued an active prosecution policy … or that this criminalisation had such consequences that the social position of homosexual was untenable' (M.B. v. Netherlands, § 15).

In view of the above, it can be argued that the Court does not exercise particular scrutiny with regard to the actual enforcement of these laws and ignores altogether the social and institutional structures underpinning them, thus creating a context favourable or tolerant to persecutory harms against homosexuals.[8] A similar approach places a disproportionate burden of proof on the applicant. On the other hand, the absence of any possibility for the applicants to seek state protection against violent acts inflicted by private agents in a country which criminalises homosexual relationships[9] has not been given duly consideration by the Court in its assessment.

Both the ECtHR and the Court of Justice of the European Union (CJEU) adopt a strict position regarding the criminalisation of homosexuality and the level of risk required in order for the prohibition of non-refoulement to be applied. In 2013, the CJEU concluded that existence of criminal laws targeting LGBTI individuals supports the finding that those persons form or belong to a particular social group

[8]According to the UNHCR Guidelines, 2012, § 27: 'Even if irregularly, rarely or ever enforced, criminal laws prohibiting same-sex relations could lead to an intolerable predicament for an LGB person rising to the level of persecution. Depending on the country context, the criminalization of same-sex relations can create or contribute to an oppressive atmosphere of intolerance and generate a threat of prosecution for having such relations…'

[9]See UNHCR Guidelines, 2012, § 36: 'Depending on the situation in the country of origin, laws criminalizing same-sex relations are normally a sign that the protection of LGB individuals is not available. Where the country of origin maintains such laws, it would be unreasonable to expect that the applicant first seeks State protection against harm based on what is, in the view of the criminal law act'.

for the purposes of the Refugee Convention, but the criminalisation of homosexual acts does not in itself constitute an act of persecution (CJEU, X, Y and Z 2013).

Another decision of the ECtHR which has been criticised as being particularly 'cruel' (Steendam 2014) towards SOGI asylum seekers concerns a Libyan-asylum-seeker in a same-sex relationship in Sweden who had been required to return to Libya to obtain a family reunification visa (ECHR, M.E. v. Sweden 2014). Although the Swedish Migration Board considered the applicant's account to be non-credible, the homosexuality of the applicant had not been questioned. Yet, for family reunion purposes, the applicant was required to return to Libya and apply for a visa there, despite having been the target of death threats from his family for having married someone of the same sex in Sweden. The Court found that requiring that the claimant to be discreet about his sexuality for a period of time in Libya was not in violation of Article 3. The Court thus disregarded the fact that independently of whether the criminal sanctions against homosexuality were enforced in Libya or not, a 'hostile attitude towards anyone suspected of being homosexual permeated the local culture', instances of massive violence against gay men had been reported and all diplomatic representation in Libya had been closed down.

More significantly, the decision endorsed and legitimised the 'discretion requirement', which seems to be implicitly endorsed by the Court also in previous cases (F. v. U.K, I.I.N. v. the Netherlands). The dissenting judge, Powder-Forde, legitimately criticised the position of the majority on this point.[10] By requiring a homosexual to be discreet in his social relations, the majority denaturises the essence of the applicant's claim, asking him to be visible only in so far his way of life is in conformity with the predominant social and cultural patterns in his country of origin. Such a requirement stems from a superficial understanding of the experiences of LGBTI persons and stereotypical assumptions concerning their relations to their cultural and social environment. It also disregards the psychological and other personal harms that a 'concealing attitude' may entail for the individual, as well as the objective harms which he may endure if he is discovered.[11]

---

[10] 'Such a requirement of forced reserve and restraint in order to conceal who one is, is corrosive of personal integrity and human dignity'.

[11] UNHCR, Guidelines, §§ 31–33: 'It is also important to recognise that even if LGBTI individuals conceal their sexual orientation or gender identity they may still be at risk of exposure and related harm for not following expected social norms ... The absence of certain expected activities and behaviour identifies a difference between them and other people and may place them at risk of harm. Being compelled to conceal one's sexual orientation and/or gender identity may also result in significant psychological and other harms. Discriminatory and disapproving attitudes, norms and values may have a serious effect on the mental and physical health of LGBTI individuals and could, in particular cases, lead to an intolerable predicament amounting to persecution. Feelings of self-denial, anguish, shame, isolation and even self-hatred, which may accrue in response an inability to be open about one's sexuality or gender identity, are factors to consider, including over the long-term'.

12.5 Embracing a Holistic Approach of Risk Assessment

In this section, it is argued that the assessment of risk needs to be approached most globally or holistically by the Court of Strasbourg.[12] Examination of both the institutional and social context in the country of origin as well as the personal background and experiences of an applicant in assessing the reality of the risk that he/she might face upon return helps to avoid stereotypical reasoning and inappropriate generalisations. A balanced approach overcomes the dangers of foregrounding one factor to the detriment of the other. In a similar vein, Perroni argues that the Court needs to pay more attention to the gendered context in which the vulnerability of an asylum seeker is constructed. In her view, it is important to examine the structural and individual relationally (see also Crawley 2000). She proposes that the risk of ill-treatment be assessed structurally and relationally. This kind of assessment implies an examination of the gendered structures and social patterns in which a woman or a person of a sexual minority shape their personal autonomy.

The Strasbourg Court has already deployed this kind of holistic and balanced assessment in two cases concerning women asylum seekers. In a case (ECHR, R. D. v. France 2016, § 40) involving a Guinean Muslim woman fearing violence by her father and brothers for having married a Christian, the Court concluded that her deportation would violate Article 3, because of police failure to protect women in a similar situation. It thus gave particular attention to country reports highlighting widespread violence against women and police ineffectiveness. In another case (ECHR, N. v. Sweden 2010, §§ 57–58) concerning an Afghan woman who had been disowned by her family and was escaping reprisals from her ex-husband, her family and local society, the Court found a violation of Article 3 by relying on the absence of prosecution of violence against women and on the fact that women do not seek help from the authorities for fear of police abuse and retaliation by perpetrators.

The Court of Luxembourg has also paid due attention to the relational shaping of an individual's identity and sexual orientation as a fundamental part of the latter when it recognised that the discretion requirement should not have a place in assessing the risk of persecution for granting refugee status (CJEU, X, Y and Z 2013). The Court considered in this regard that requiring a person to conceal his sexual orientation is incompatible with the fundamentality of this characteristic of a person's identity and in consequence the asylum seeker cannot be reasonably expected to 'conceal his homosexuality in his country of origin or to exercise reserve in the expression of his sexual orientation'.

---

[12]This approach is inspired by the UNHCR Guidelines 2002, loc.cit.: § 7: 'It is important to approach the assessment holistically and have regard to all relevant circumstances of the case. It is essential to have both a full picture of the asylum-seeker's personality, background and personal experiences, as well as an analysis and up-to-date knowledge of historically, geographically and culturally specific circumstances in the country of origin…'

12.6 Conclusion

The present analysis attempted to depict the challenges faced by an international judicial institution when adjudicating in cases involving asylum claims with a gendered perspective. The ECtHR plays a fundamental role in safeguarding human rights protection in Europe, not only for European citizens but also for people fleeing violence, war and dire living conditions. However, this role becomes more difficult to fulfil not only because of the obvious institutional constraints but also because cases related to claims of asylum seekers concern a domain closely linked to state sovereignty. Amid the current 'refugee crisis', risk assessment performed by national authorities, as in the process of asylum determination, is shaped by wider geopolitical and economic considerations. The failure to recognise and duly address the gendered dimension of non-refoulement claims, one of the many shortcomings of these processes, is reflected in the decisions of the ECtHR. This chapter calls for more sociologically informed decision-making practices and a more contextualised and relational approach in the assessment of the risk of ill-treatment. Such an approach is essential for unearthing the gendered patterns of persecution and addressing effectively related claims.

Bibliography

A.A. and others v. Sweden App no 14499/09 (ECHR, 28 June 2012)

Anker, D. E. (2002). Refugee law, gender, and the human rights paradigm. *Harvard Human Rights Law Journal, 15*, 133–157.

A.L. v. UK (dec.) (committee) App no 32207/16 (ECHR, 13 March 2018).

Arbel, E., Dauvergne, C., & Millbank, J (Eds.), 2014 Introduction Gender in Refugee Law: From the Margins to the Center Routledge London (pp. 1–16).

Brems, E. (2010). Strong women don't need asylum (The European Court on FGM). Strasbourg Observers Blog. https://www.Strasbourgobservers.com. Accessed 6 March 2019.

Collins and Akaziebie v. Sweden (dec.) App no 23944/05 (ECHR, 8 March 2007).

Convention on the Elimination of All Forms of Discrimination against Women (CEDAW) (1979).

CEDAW. (2014). General Recommendation No 32 on the Gender-related Dimensions of Refugee Status, Asylum, Nationality and Statelessness of Women, 17 November 2014.

Convention on Preventing and Combating Violence against Women and Domestic Violence, The "Istanbul Convention". (2011).

Crawley, H. (2000). Engendering the state in refugee women's claims for asylum. In S. Jacobs, R. Jacobson, & J. Marchbank (Eds.), *States of conflict: Gender, violence, resistance* (pp. 87–104). London: Zed books.

Danisi, C. (2009). Preventing torture and controlling irregular immigration: The role of the European committee for the prevention of torture and its activity in Italy. *Essex Human Rights Law Review, 6*, 151–176.

Declaration on the Elimination of Violence against Women (1993).

Directive 2011/96/EU on Standards for the qualification of third-country nationals or stateless persons as beneficiaries of international protection for a uniform status for refugees or for persons eligible for subsidiary protection, and for the content of the protection granted (recast) ("the qualification directive").

Directive 2013/32/EU on common procedures for granting and withdrawing international protection (recast) (the "Asylum Procedures Directive").
Directive 2013/33/EU laying down standards for the reception of applicants for international protection (recast) (the "Reception Conditions Directive").
Dudgeon v. UK App no 7525/76 (ECHR, 22 October 1981).
European Parliament, Directorate General for Internal Policies, Citizens Rights and Constitutional Affairs (2012). Gender Related Asylum Claims in Europe. Study. https://www.europarl.europa.eu/meetdocs/2009_2014/documents/femm/dv/asylum_claims_/asylum_claims_en.pdf. Accessed 6 March 2019.
European Union Agency for Fundamental Rights (FRA) (March 2017). Current migration situation in the EU: Lesbian, gay, bisexual, transgender and intersex asylum seekers. https://fra.europa.eu/en/publication/2017/march-monthly-migration-focus-lgbti. Accessed 6 March 2019.
F. v. UK App no 17341/03 (ECHR, 22 June 2004).
H.L.R v. France, [GC] App no 24573/94 (ECHR, 29 April 1997).
I.F.W. v. Sweden (dec.) (committee) App no 68992/10 (ECHR, 9 October 2012).
I.I.N. v. Netherlands App no 2035/04 (ECHR, 9 December 2004).
International Organization for Migration (IOM). (2019). UN Migration, Gender and Migration, https://www.iom.int/gender-and-migration. Accessed 17 February 2019.
Izevbekhai and others v. Ireland (dec.) App no 43408/08 (ECHR, 17 May 2011).
Joint cases C-199/12, C-200/12, and C-201/12, X, Y and Z v. Minister voor Immigratie, Integratie en Asiel (CJEU, 7 November 2013).
Maputo Protocol to the African Charter on Human and People's Rights on the Rights of Women in Africa, 11 July 2003.
M. B.v. Netherlands (dec.) (committee) App no 63890/16 (ECHR, 28 November 2017).
M.E. v. SwedenApp no 71398/12 (ECHR, 26 June 2014).
Milibank, J. (2009). From discretion to disbelief: Recent trends in refugee determinations on the basis of sexual orientation in Australia and the United Kingdom. *International Journal on Human Rights, 13,* 391–414.
M.Y.H. and others v. Sweden App no 50859/10 (ECHR, 27 June 2013).
N. v. Sweden App no 23505/09 (ECHR, 20 July 2010).
Omeredo v. Austria App no 8969/10 (ECHR, 20 September 2011).
Otto, D. (2013). International human rights law: Towards rethinking sex/gender dualism. In Davies & Munro (Eds.), *The ashgate research companion to feminist legal theory, ashgate.* https://ssrn.com/abstract=2178769.
Peroni, L. (2018). The protection of women asylum seekers under the European convention on human rights: Unearthing the gendered roots of harm. *Human Rights Law Review, 18*(2), 347 370.
R.B.A.B and others v. the Netherlands App no 7211/06 (ECHR, 7 June 2016).
R. D. v. France App no 34648/14 (ECHR, 16 June 2016).
R.H. v. Sweden App no 4601/14 (ECHR, 10 September 2015).
R.W. and others v. Sweden (dec.) App no 35745/11 (ECHR, 10 April 2012).
Salah Sheekh v. the Netherlands App no 1948/04 (ECHR, 11 January 2007).
Sow v. Belgium App no 27081/13 (ECHR, 19 January 2016).
Steendam S. (2014). *M.E. v. Sweden: Back to the closet.* https://strasbourgobservers.com. Accessed 6 March 2019.
UN Women. (2017). *Report on the legal rights of women and girl asylum seekers in the European Union*, Istanbul.
UN. (2006). 2004 World Survey on the role of women in development, Women and international migration.
UNHCR. (2002).*Guidelines on International Protection: Gender-Related Persecution within the context of Article 1A (2) of the 1951 Convention and/or its 1967 Protocol relating to the Status of Refugees.*

UNHCR. (2012).*Guidelines on International Protection No 9: Claims to Refugee Status based on Sexual Orientation and/or Gender Identity within the context of Article 1 A(2) of the Convention and/or its 1967 Protocol relating to the Status of Refugees.*
Yogyakarta Principles. (2007). Principles on the Application of International Human Rights Law in relation to Sexual Orientation and Gender Identity.

Athanasia Petropoulou was born in Athens, Greece. She studied law in Athens and Paris. She has taught law in the University of Lille, France, and in the Idef College of Athens, Greece. In 2013, she obtained a Ph.D. in international law from the University of Paris I in co-direction with the University of Athens. In 2015, she was awarded the prize Rene Cassin of the Academy of Moral and Political Sciences of Paris for the publicaton of her PhD. She has worked as a lawyer in Athens and as a jurist in the European Court of Human Rights, in Strasbourg. She has participated in many conferences on human rights issues. Her publications encompass different areas including international law, the European Convention on Human Rights, human rights and philosophy of law.

Part IV
Migration in the Eyes of the Public: Surveying National Sentiment

Chapter 13
Democratic Values of Young Belarusians and Attitudes Towards Refugee Rights

Olga Breskaya

Abstract This chapter examines the preferences of young Belarusians towards the values of political culture and their perception of civil and political rights with a particular focus on refugee rights. We explored if and how the attitudes of young people in Belarus (N = 677) towards authoritarianism, governing institutions, and political powers predicted their perception of refugee and citizens' rights relying on the results of the *Religion and Human Rights Project 2.0*. We analysed the migration context of our respondents and the role of pluralist views, interreligious contacts, and positive attitudes towards diversity vis-à-vis perception of refugee rights. This research suggests that the migration context matters for citizens' right to vote and freedom of speech. Critical attitudes towards governing institutions together with positive attitudes towards multiculturalism and pluralism serve as strong predictors of refugee rights.

Keywords Refugee rights · Citizens' rights · Democratic citizenship · Migration · Belarus

13.1 Introduction

Human rights are crucial for understanding the relationship between the concepts of migration, democracy, and citizenship. In understanding the dichotomy of cosmopolitan and national citizenship, human rights serve as a normative and empirical category for identifying exclusion, inequality, or injustice. Human rights have 'certain ontological and epistemological characteristics that make [them] ideal for extending coverage to new social subjects such as migrants' (Estèvez 2012, 134), since they respond to the problem of deprivation of fundamental freedoms. At the same time, the challenges of granting rights to migrants or expanding some rights of citizens to migrants cannot be understood without problematising the link between the concept of cosmopolitan citizenship and forms of participating in a democratic

O. Breskaya (✉)
University of Padua, Padua, Italy
e-mail: olga.breskaya@phd.unipd.it

M. C. Jacobsen et al. (eds.), *Cosmopolitanism, Migration and Universal Human Rights*, https://doi.org/10.1007/978-3-030-50645-2_13

society (Calder et al. 2009). The process of gaining special rights by migrants and their struggle for that ‘can be seen as an often neglected part of the process of democratization’ (Piper and Rother 2015, 5).

The challenges of the refugee crisis and lasting migration in Western Europe renewed this debate, while the post-Soviet period brought ‘dramatically shifting migration trends’ (Makaryan 2012) in Eastern Europe. The necessity of recognition of inviolable rights of citizens and the importance of membership in a political community, which were highlighted by Hanna Arendt in 1950s, encourage modern human rights scholars to reread these ideas in the context of current migration processes. The novelty of the socio-political condition put Arendt’s ‘right to have rights’ (1951) in a situation when it ‘offers a key resource for thinking and acting politically in our own moment, especially in an age where an ever-increasing number of people across the globe are unable to secure meaningful membership in any political community’ (DeGooyer et al. 2018, 2).

Along with the questioning of the nexus between human rights and citizenship rights by political scientists and philosophers, the understanding of values of public life, conditions of participation, and awareness of the meaning of political community emerged as a call for sociologists of human rights. As Somers noted, various condition including ‘institutional, associational, cultural, normative, economic, etc.—that can account for varying genealogies of citizenship and rights over time and space’ (2008, xiv) have to be studied by sociologists to explain the current relationship between human rights, membership in a political community, and citizenship.

In this research, we are interested to test several theoretical hypotheses about the relationship between migration and human rights. Relying on the primary data from the *Religion and Human Rights Project 2.0*[1] collected on a convenience sample (N = 677), we will examine the preferences among young people in Belarus towards the values of political culture and civil and political rights, with particular focus on refugee rights. This chapter explores if and how the democratic and authoritarian values of young people in Belarus predicted their perception of citizens’ and refugee rights. In doing that, we first analyse the migration context of our respondents and their parents, and provide a broader information on migration in Belarus. Second, we present descriptive and inferential statistics about the perception of citizens’ and refugee rights. Finally, we examine the predictive power of respondents’ views towards authoritarianism and governance, pluralist views, interreligious contacts, and positive attitudes towards diversity vis-à-vis perception of the refugee rights.

13.2 Between Citizens’ and Refugee Rights

Following the arguments of Somers (2008), we suppose that normative, institutional, political, and cultural conditions as well as rules of organisational and associational practices have to be taken into account for the analysis of human rights, including

[1] For more information see the website of the project “Religion and Human Rights”: https://www.theologie.uni-wuerzburg.de/rp/research/religion-and-human-rights-2012-2019/.

citizens' rights and the rights of refugees. In this regard, the international human right regime serves as a source of transnational membership (Yasemin 1994) and does 'ascribe universal rights to persons regardless of their membership status in a nation-state' (ibid. 1994, 145). However, citizenship is not merely 'a bundle of rights, nor even just a status possessed by individuals—although it is both of those' (Somers 2008, 70), but it is 'inexorably attached to that relational and public body [political, civil, and social community]' (ibid.). Considering citizenship as a foundational public good, Somers emphasised that the condition of membership in a community is an important characteristic of citizenship. However, the relationship between citizenship and non-citizenship status concerning human rights has an internal challenge. Alison Brysk and Gershon Shafir described this challenge through the conflicting aims of 'anchoring rights in membership versus disconnecting them from membership and thus universalizing them' (Brysk and Shafir 2004, 11). They noted that the citizenship gap is supported by the growing number of non-citizens in the countries with a developed system of democratic participation. They wrote:

> Migrants, refugees, and undocumented residents all lack basic membership in the state; certain ethnic groups, rural residents, and laborers are often granted a lesser, conditional, or ambiguous status. This means that they may be ineligible for rights of political participation, social services, and sometimes even international recognition of their status. (Brysk and Shafir 2004, 6)

The pitfalls of the citizenship gap thus regard the impossibility of participating in a political community without citizenship status at the conditions of lacking recognition and absence of rights. It raises the successive question: 'who constitutes the demos in a democracy and how the migrants can get access' (Piper and Rother 2015, 5). The integration into political community in a liberal democratic society, according to Benhabib (2004), means the understanding of human rights, citizen's rights, constitutional traditions, and practices of elections and representation (Benhabib 2004, 121). In our research, we test this theoretical argument on the sample of young people who grew up in Belarus and neighbouring countries. We were interested to understand whether there is a correlation between migration status and perception of citizens' rights. The measuring instrument allowed us to consider the migration context (see operationalisation below) and specify this difference. Following this theoretical framework, we test if and how the migration context is correlated with the perception of human rights in our empirical research, hypothesising that:

> **Hypothesis 1 (H1)**: The migration context of the respondents, i.e. the fact of being born outside of the country or the fact that the respondents' parents were born outside of the national community, creates a difference in perceiving the citizens' and refugee rights in comparison with those respondents who were born in the country. We suppose that respondents with the migration origin are more in favour of some citizens' rights in comparison with those who were born in Belarus.

Along with the conditions of migration and participation, we are interested in analysing how the pluralist views, interreligious contacts, and positive attitudes towards multiculturalism produce the modes of perception of citizens' and refugee rights. In this regard, the concepts of multiculturalism, intercultural dialogue, or pluralism are linked with the promotion of democratic values and implementation of human rights in different cultural, religious, and minority group contexts (Bekemans 2013). The link between democratic citizenship and the values of diversity and pluralism are implemented in policy papers of the Council of Europe showing conceptual, instrumental, and practical ties. In the introduction of the White Paper on Intercultural Dialogue,[2] we could find the idea that 'If there is a European identity to be realised, it will be based on shared fundamental values, respect for common heritage and cultural diversity as well as respect for the equal dignity of every individual' (Council of Europe 2008, 3). For Belarus, a neighbouring country to European Union, the same set of values was claimed by the Council of Europe Action Plan for Belarus (2016–2018), highlighting the necessity of the further involvement of Belarus in European intercultural dialogue and support of the policies of diversity and multiculturalism.

The sociological analysis of interrelationship of pluralism, diversity, and human rights (Giordan and Pace 2014; Beaman 2017; Giordan and Lynch 2019) provided us with the ideas of how socio-cultural and legal-political aspects of diversity and pluralism could be understood through the application of concepts of equality, human rights, and increasing interreligious contacts. Richardson (2014) focused his research on the relationship between religious diversity, legal pluralism, and religious freedom, while considering the modes of inclusion or exclusion of minority groups in a society. Richardson stated in that regard:

> If there is openness and flexibility, with religious diversity actually being promoted by a society, then minority groups may be more prone to come into that society, and indigenous religious groups may also be encouraged to develop. If there is a perception that the society is closed and unwelcoming of religious diversity, this may discourage attempts to develop different religious traditions within the society, which also would mean less legal pluralism. (Richardson 2014, 33)

According to this argument, the societal values supporting openness and flexibility towards religious minorities and welcoming religious diversity, on the one hand, and legal pluralism, on the other hand, have to be taken into consideration together, in order to understand how particular civil and political rights, such as religious freedom, function in a society. Thus we are interested to test the second theoretical hypothesis:

Hypothesis 2 (H2). Pluralist views, interreligious contacts, and positive attitudes towards multiculturalism have strong predictive power for citizens' and refugee rights.

Understanding of human rights through the prism of 'overlapping consensus universality' (Donnelly 2007, 289), grounded in political and moral doctrines, cannot ignore the conceptualisation of human rights within the theory of human rights as social representations (Doise et al. 1999; Devos et al. 2002; Staerklé et al. 2011). The

[2]Launched by the Council of Europe Ministers of Foreign Affairs at their 118th Ministerial Session (in Strasbourg, 7 May 2008).

latter approach encourages us to study human rights at various levels of national societies as well as cross-nationally, in order to understand how normative principles inform political and social actions. Staerklé, Clémence, and Spini stated that 'individuals elaborate common understandings of social reality which then enables them to communicate in order to take action on the basis of this shared knowledge' (Staerklé et al. 2011, 760). The international human rights regime, routinised in the practices of domestic and international legal norms, produced the conditions for conceptualising citizens' and refugee rights through the social representation framework. One specific hypothesis of Devos et al. (2002) is considered in our study of the perception of citizens' and refugee rights. The trust in governmental institutions tends to have different predictive power for human rights in democratic and non-democratic countries (Staerklé et al. 1998), since the institutions often 'contribute to the preservation and transmission of traditions and ensure the stability and continuity of society' (Morselli et al. 2012, 49). Considering the previous research and results about the impact of trust in governmental institutions on the right to freedom of religion in Belarus (Breskaya and Botvar 2019), in this study we will test the following hypothesis:

Hypothesis 3 (H3). Authoritarianism and trust in governing institutions have a negative significant statistical effect on citizens' and refugee rights.

In the following section, we describe the research population and the design of the study. We start with a description of migration context in Belarus and explain the sampling procedure and research model which was developed for the study of the relationship between the migration context, trust in governmental institutions, diversity, and citizens' and refugee rights in which the latter two concepts were considered as dependent variables.

13.3 Migration Context and Human Rights: Conceptual Model

Despite the economic hardship and non-democratic political conditions, Belarus has been considered to be 'one of the primary migration-receiving countries in the post-Soviet region' (Makaryan 2012) along with Russia. In Belarus, net migration is continuously positive with significant peaks in 2014 and 2015. The Belarusian state explained that peak as a result of the improving investment climate and not of the war in neighbouring Ukraine (Dzesiatava 2016); however, the data of 2019 showed that from 2016 the migration inflow was decreasing with CIS countries (Table 13.1).

As we can see from Table 13.1, migration dynamics had a positive character both for the immigrants from the Commonwealth of Independent States (CIS) and non-CIS countries. Belarus is an ethnically homogenous country, where 84% of the population are ethnic Belarusians, and the minority groups are Russians, Poles, Ukrainians, Jews, Armenians, Tatars, and Roma (Ulasiuk 2013). As the 2018 Pew Research Center (2018) report showed, Eastern and Western Europeans differ on

Table 13.1 Net migration in Belarus (2012–2018)

	2012	2013	2014	2015	2016	2017	2018
Total	9328	11,643	15,722	18,494	7940	3874	9362
With CIS countries	6946	9315	13,943	15,826	6618	3747	7179
With non-CIS countries	2382	2328	1779	2668	1322	127	2183

Demographic Yearbook of the Republic of Belarus (On 30 August 2019, the National Statistical Committee of the Republic of Belarus released the Demographic Yearbook of the Republic of Belarus)

the importance of religion, views of minorities, and key social issues. In general, populations in the countries of Eastern Europe are less supportive of the ideas of religious diversity in comparison with Western Europeans. Young Belarusians from 18 to 34 years old who say 'they would be willing to accept Muslim or Jews as members of their family' were 19% and 43% respectively. Thus Belarus occupied the fourth and the fifth places in the ranking of 34 European countries showing unwillingness to accept people from other religions.

In our empirical study, the migration context was operationalised to measure the individual level of respondents' migration background. For the question 'Where were you and your parents born?' the following answering scheme was suggested: 'In Belarus', 'In a neighbouring country', 'In another European country', 'In another continent'. This list was suggested to analyse the places of birth of the respondents and their mothers and fathers.

The concept of citizens' rights was operationalised with the variables measuring civil, political, and socioeconomic rights. Even though Somers and Roberts noted that 'citizenship split can also be found the longstanding hierarchical privileging of civil rights over socioeconomic rights' (Somers and Roberts 2008, 385), we kept the right to vote, the right to protest, freedom of speech and freedom of religion, and the right to social security and equal payment for equal work as important dimensions of citizens' rights (Fig. 13.1). The questionnaire applied in the *Religion and Human Rights Project 2.0* was developed to measure various rights including civil rights, right to life, judicial rights, political rights, and socioeconomic rights. For the purposes of current research, we selected the list of civil-political and socioeconomic rights, as basic citizens' freedoms.

As mentioned above, we are interested in analysing the values of pluralism, diversity, and intercultural contacts and exploring their effects on citizens' and refugee rights. In other words, we are interested in understanding whether the perception of human rights has any resemblance to attitudes towards pluralism, multiculturalism, and interreligious contacts (Fig. 13.2). For the concepts of 'pluralism'[3] and 'multiculturalism', 5-point Likert-type response scales were used (from total disagreement to full agreement). For the concept of 'interreligious contacts', the following response scheme was applied: 1 = never; 2 = very seldom; 3 = occasionally; 4 = often; 5 = very often; 6 = don't know. The concept of

[3]See Astley and Francis (2016) for the discussion about the operationalisation of pluralism concept.

Refugee rights
The government should guarantee political refugees freedom to travel
The government should provide a decent standard of living for political refugees
Active and passive right to vote
Everybody, living here for some period prescribed by law, should have the right to vote for political leaders
Everybody, living here for some period prescribed by law, should have the right to run for public office
Right of protest
The police should not use force against political demonstrations that put public order at risk
The government should not forbid public protests, however controversial they might be
Freedom of speech
People should be free to express any opinion whatsoever
People should be free to discuss all moral ideas, no matter what
Freedom of religion
The state should not interfere with missionary activities in both the majority and minority religions
The state should stay out of the public manifestations by the majority and minority religions
State's obligation regarding the right to social security
The government should provide health care for the sick
The government should provide a decent standard of living for the old
State's obligation regarding living wages
Everyone should have the right to equal pay for equal work
Everyone should have the right to just and reasonable pay for work performed

Answer scheme: 1= I totally disagree; 2= I disagree; 3= I am not sure; 4= I agree; 5= I fully agree

Fig. 13.1 Refugee and citizens' rights

Pluralism (openness to religious truth)
Religions are all equal; they are just different paths to a flourishing life
There is no difference between religions, they all long for a flourishing life
Multiculturalism
The variety of customs of people in this country is enriching
The many points of view are good for our society and make it colourful
Interreligious contacts
Do you talk to people of another religion?
Do you spend leisure time with people who belong to another religion?
Do you visit people who belong to another religion in their homes or vice versa?

Fig. 13.2 Dimensions of pluralism, multiculturalism, and interreligious contacts

'interreligious contacts' was originally developed to measure the influence of interreligious attitudes on interreligious learning (Van der Ven and Ziebertz 1995). These three scales were developed for the questionnaire used in the international research *Religion and Human Rights Project 2.0* mentioned above.

The concept of authoritarianism (Fig. 13.3) as an element of political culture and personal characteristic was measured with Altemeyer's right-wing authoritarianism scale (Altemeyer 1996, 1998; Altemeyer and Hunsberger 1992; Manganelli Rattazzi et al. 2007). The values of political culture of young Belarusians were considered together with trust in governmental institutions and respondents' attitudes towards the three powers of political life—legislative, executive, and judicial (Fig. 13.4).

Devos et al. (2002) indicated in their study that trust in institutions tends to go hand in hand with the protection of traditional practices. Trust in institutions implies that trust is placed in public authorities to make the right decisions. Thus, trust in institutions may have different meaning and consequences in democratic versus

Right-wing authoritarianism
The majority of those who criticise proper authorities in government and religion merely create useless doubts in people's minds
What our country really needs instead of more 'civil rights' is much more law and order
Obedience and respect for authority are the most important values children should learn

Answer scheme: 1 = I totally disagree; 2 = I disagree; 3 = I am not sure; 4 = I agree; 5 = I fully agree

Fig. 13.3 Scale of the 'authoritarianism'

Trust in governmental institutions
On the whole how satisfied are you with the present state of the economy in your country?
Now thinking about the government in your country, how satisfied are you with the way it is doing its job?
And on the whole, how satisfied are you with the way democracy works in your country?
Please say what you think overall about the state of education in your country nowadays?
Please say what you think overall about the state of health services in your country nowadays?
Three powers
Legislative Power: Parliament succeeds in making law for political refugees
Administrative Power: The government manages the country's economic crisis well
Judicial Power: The courts act impartially, they decide cases of different ethnic groups equally

Fig. 13.4 Dimensions of the concept of 'trust in governmental institutions' and 'three powers'

authoritarian countries as the level of trust in them varies. Figure 13.4 presents operational variables measuring 'trust in institutions' and 'three powers' of political life. The former was measured with the scheme: 1 = extremely dissatisfied; 2 = dissatisfied; 3 = neither dissatisfied nor satisfied; 4 = satisfied; 5 = extremely satisfied. The latter was developed for the questionnaire used in the international research *Religion and Human Rights Project 2.0* and was measured with the following response scheme: 1 = I totally disagree; 2 = I disagree; 3 = I am not sure; 4 = I agree; 5 = I fully agree.

The sensitivity for tensions and injustice between citizens and non-citizens (Doise et al. 1999) was measured with two items (Fig. 13.5).

While testing the four theoretical hypotheses described above, the conceptual model keeps human rights as the dependent variable and the political and cultural contexts of our respondents as independent variables. Migration context, socio-demographic characteristics, and belonging to religious groups are considered as control variables in our research (Fig. 13.6).

Please indicate to what degree such tensions and cases of injustice present in our society between citizens and non-citizens?
How often have you been personally treated in an unjust manner because of citizen and non-citizen status?

Answer scheme: 1 = never; 2 = very seldom; 3 = occasionally; 4 = often; 5 = very often

Fig. 13.5 Sensitivity for tensions between citizens and non-citizens

Control variables	Independent variables	Dependent variable
Migration context: Place of birth of the respondent Parents' place of birth (mother, father) **Socio-demographic characteristics:** Gender Age	Pluralism (openness to religious truth) Multiculturalism Interreligious contacts Authoritarianism Trust in institutions Three powers Sensitivity for tensions	**Refugee rights** **Citizens' rights**

Fig. 13.6 Conceptual model for the analysis of refugee and citizens' rights

13.4 Migration Context and Refugee Rights

The data presented in this chapter was collected during the period 2014–2015 as a part of *Religion and Human Rights Project 2.0* in the largest cities in Belarus. The questionnaire was filled in online, and participation in the survey was secured with individual passwords.

The convenience sample of 677 respondents (16–19 years old) participated in the survey, most of whom were undergraduate university students from Minsk, Vitebsk, Brest, Hrodna, Gomel, and Mogilev. In the sample, the average age of young people who participated in the survey was 18.2 years (Table 13.2).

Among the research population, about 94% of the young people were born in Belarus and 5% in a neighbouring country, while only 1% had migrated from another

Table 13.2 Sample characteristics (frequencies (%), except age)

	Belarus (N = 677)
Age (mean)	18.2
Female	67.2
Respondents born outside of the country	5.8
Respondent's mother born outside of the country	16.0
Respondent's father born outside of the country	17.9
Religious affiliation	
Christian Orthodox	56.3
Protestant	1.3
Roman Catholic	5.2
Muslim	0.7
Non-religious	24.7
Believe in God or divine power	46.9
Pray at least weekly or more	20.3
Attend religious services at least monthly	11.3

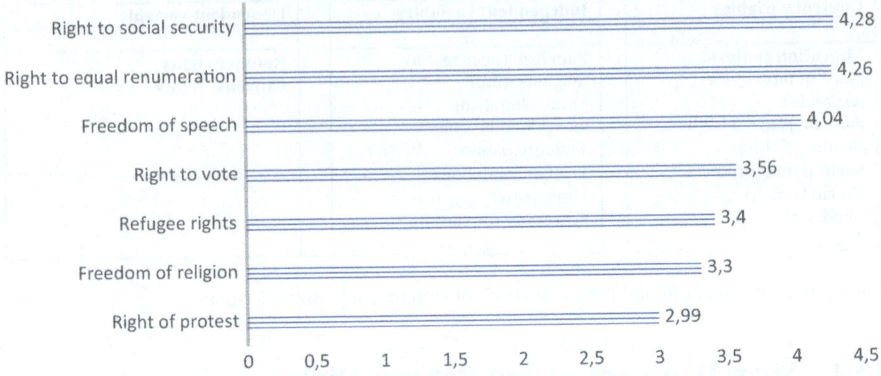

Fig. 13.7 Perception of refugee and citizens' rights (means)

country (non-neighbouring) or another continent. The migration context of the family measured by the percentage of respondents' parents who were born abroad was the following: 16% of respondents' mothers and 18% of fathers were born outside the country (among them 14% were born in neighbouring countries).

The 56.3% of the Belarusian sample was affiliated with the majority religion—Eastern Orthodoxy, 10.6% with religious minorities (including 1.3% of Protestants, 5.2% of Catholics, 0.7% of Muslims), 8.4% identified themselves as 'religious in a general sense' without affiliation, and 24.7% with non-religious group. Nearly half of the respondents have a religious belief and one-fifth express that they practise regular weekly prayer and one-tenth participate in religious services monthly.

Two types of rights were operationalised as dependent variables—refugee and citizens' rights—since we aim to understand the relationship between migration and democracy through the analysis of the perception of human rights. First, we looked at the degree to which young Belarusians supported both types of rights (Fig. 13.7).

We can see from Fig. 13.7 that the perception of refugee and citizens' rights had a particular trend. Socioeconomic rights are on the top of the list and they were supported with 'total agreement'.[4] Right of speech, right to vote, and refugee rights were positively perceived by young people. Freedom of religion and right to protest were evaluated with positive ambivalence, even though the right to protest is on the margin between negative and positive ambivalence ($M = 2.99$). From this data, we can assume that refugee rights were perceived as a constituent part of human rights, positioning them between civil-political and socioeconomic rights and not differentiating them from the set of citizens' rights.

A Pearson product-moment correlation coefficient was computed to assess the relationship between refugee and citizens' rights (Table 13.3). The correlation matrix revealed that refugee rights are more strongly correlated with the right to protest (r

[4]We rely on the following rule in interpreting the means: 1.00–1.79 = disagree totally; 1.80–2.59 = disagree; 2.60–2.99 = negative ambivalence; 3.00–3.39 = positive ambivalence; 3.40–4.19 = agree; 4.20–5.00 = agree totally.

Table 13.3 Pearson correlation for refugee and citizens' rights

	Right to social security	Right to equal remuneration	Freedom of speech	Right to vote	Refugee rights	Freedom of religion	Right to protest
Right to social security	1						
Rights to equal remuneration	.744**	1					
Freedom of speech	.407**	.420**	1				
Right to vote	.325**	.313**	.322**	1			
Refugee rights	.244**	.246**	.256**	.368**	1		
Freedom of religion	.154**	.161**	.331**	.209**	.238**	1	
Right of protest	.097*	.130**	.284**	.327**	.424**	.281**	1

*Correlation is significant at the 0.05 level (2-tailed)
**Correlation is significant at the 0.01 level (2-tailed)

= .424) and right to vote (r = .368) than with the right to social security (r = .244), right to equal remuneration (r = .246), or freedom of speech (r = .256) and freedom of religion (r = .238).

These results could be explained by the specifics of the measuring instrument as it emphasised the status of political refugees in the process of operationalising the concept of 'refugee rights'. At the same time, the findings about the relationship between the right to protest, to vote, freedom of speech, and refugee rights could signify that the absence of political participation by non-citizens (for example, the foreign citizens do not vote) correlate with the challenges of political participation and weakness of political freedoms to protest or of speech in Belarus.

An independent samples t-test was conducted to compare the perception of refugee rights by those respondents who were born in Belarus and whose parents were born in Belarus with those of non-Belarusian origin. The results showed that there was no significant difference in the scores for refugee and citizenship rights in the group of respondents with migration and non-migration origin. This result also reflects the family migration context for our respondents with one exception.

There was a significant statistical difference in the scores for the right to vote in the group of respondents whose mothers had a migration context (M = 3.74, SD = 0.834) and whose mothers were born in Belarus (M = 3.52, SD = 0.854); t(662) = −2.34, p = .019. This result suggested several considerations. First, migrants in Belarus do not experience problems with integration since the immigration inflows are mostly from the neighbouring countries of CIS. Thus, cultural and linguistic integration does not require a long time in most cases. Second, the right to vote, which is the only citizens' right in our list that cannot be exercised in Belarus without the citizenship status, revealed the existing gap in the family migration context. It is not clear why 'fathers' migration context' did not produce the same difference, but it is important to consider that the absence of participation in the political process produces a significant difference in the perception of rights.

Other important concepts seen as independent variables for the study of the perception of refugee and citizens' rights are the contextual variables of pluralism, interreligious contacts, and multiculturalism and the context of political culture which we measured with the scales of authoritarianism, trust in governmental institutions, 'three powers', and sensitivity to tensions between citizens and non-citizens at the societal and personal levels. From Table 13.4, we can conclude that the concepts measuring the context of diversity and pluralism were positively evaluated by respondents, while the right-wing authoritarianism, trust in governmental institutions, and attitudes towards the three democratic powers were evaluated with the negative scores of the means. It is also important to mention that the conflicts between citizens and non-citizens were perceived as low ($M = 2.05$). That finding signified that our respondents did not perceive and experience the gap between citizens and non-citizens in Belarusian society to any great extent (Table 13.4).

The negative attitudes towards the authoritarianism scale allow us to conclude that young people in our sample are looking for more active participation in the discussions about public life and the advancement of the culture of civil rights in Belarus. They also did not accept the value of 'obedience and respect to authority as the most important values of education for children'.

Table 13.4 Means and reliability of scales for pluralism, political culture, and citizens' rights

	Mean	Standard deviation	Cronbach's Alpha
Pluralism (openness to religious truth)	3.31	1.122	.81
Interreligious contacts	3.31	1.030	.89
Multiculturalism (diversity)	3.55	.859	.63
Right-wing authoritarianism	2.44	.771	.62
Trust in governmental institutions	2.59	.765	.80
Democracy (three powers)	2.56	.727	.66
Sensitivity for tensions	2.05	.800	.51
Refugees' rights	3.40	.814	.71
Right to vote	3.56	.850	.57
Right of protest	2.99	.870	.58
Freedom of speech	4.04	.749	.60
Freedom of religion	3.30	.851	.70
Right to social security	4.28	.729	.80
Right to equal remuneration	4.26	.770	.81

13.5 The Predictive Power of Migration Context, Pluralism, and Political Culture for the Refugee Rights

The intersecting relationship between democracy and migration in the era of globalisation and transnationalisation (Piper and Rother 2015) has particular relevance to the process of claiming civil, political, socioeconomic, and cultural rights and the changing nature of citizenship. When we question this relationship within the context of low participation and a non-democratic political regime, we observe that critical attitudes towards governing institutions and diversity appeared to be the strongest predictive factors for the perception of refugee rights (Table 13.5). While the former had a negative significant influence on the dependent variable ($p = -.244$), the latter had a positive significant influence ($p = .202$). Along with these two variables, the evaluation of legislative, administrative, and judicial powers, which keeps the relevance for political refugees and ethnic equality in our study, had a significant positive statistical influence on refugee rights ($p = .103$). We can also conclude that the intensity of interreligious contacts has a predictive power ($p = .078$) for refugee rights.

Table 13.6 shows the results of a series of linear regression analyses of citizens' rights. We examined the main effect of independent variables on the six variables measuring political, civil, and socioeconomic rights of citizens. The first finding concerns the migration context of our respondents and their parents (mothers in this case). Respondents who were born outside Belarus support stronger freedom of speech in comparison with those respondents who were born inside the country. The second finding concerns the right to vote. Respondents whose mothers were born

Table 13.5 The influence of migration context, pluralism and political culture on the refugee rights

	Beta	Sig.
Respondent born outside of Belarus (*ref*. born in Belarus)	−.006	.884
Respondent's father born outside of Belarus (*ref*. born in Belarus)	.023	.568
Respondent's mother born outside of Belarus (*ref*. born in Belarus)	.046	.236
Pluralism (openness to religious truth)	.067	.081
Interreligious contacts	.078	.045
Diversity	.202	.000
Authoritarianism	−.068	.108
Trust in governmental institutions	−.244	.000
Democracy (three powers)	.103	.038
Sensitivity to citizens/non-citizens conflicts	.021	.585
Age	.025	.514
Sex	−.012	.745

Explained variance: 10%

Table 13.6 The influence of migration context, diversity and political culture on the citizens' rights

	Right to vote	Right of protest	Freedom of speech	Freedom of religion	Right to social security	Right to equal remuneration
Respondent born outside of Belarus (*ref.* born in Belarus)	−.018	−.062	.093*	−.042	.032	.056
Respondent's father born outside of Belarus (*ref.* born in Belarus)	.021	−.028	−.063	.038	−.021	−.003
Respondent's mother born outside of Belarus (*ref.* born in Belarus)	.104**	.039	−.021	−.023	−.013	−.062
Pluralism (openness to religious truth)	.051	.077*	.123***	.171***	.086*	.093*
Interreligious contacts	.056	.064	.094**	.011	.041	.047
Diversity	.185***	.142***	.225***	.165***	.136***	.157***
Authoritarianism	−.036	−.120**	−.189***	−.034	.004	−.034
Trust in governmental institutions	−.226***	−.367***	−.325***	−.257***	−.175***	−.128*
Democracy (three powers)	.058	.039	.139**	.014	.080	.045
Sensitivity to conflicts between citizens and non-citizens	−.067	.103**	−.087*	−.043	−.148***	−.123**
Age	.053	−.031	−.003	.014	.060	.074
Sex (*ref.* male)	−.050	−.046	−.029	−.046	−.099*	−.080*
Explained variance (%)	*10*	*19*	*23*	*12*	*7*	*7*

N = 677; *p ≤ 0.05; **p ≤ 0.01; ***p ≤ 0.001; Reference = born in Belarus; Sex = female

outside of Belarus support much stronger right to vote in comparison to those young people whose mothers were born in the country (b = 104, p = .007).

Thus we can conclude that migration context matters for basic citizens' rights, and those who do not vote or do not exercise freedom of speech to a full extent cannot feel themselves fully participating in the public life of the country due to exclusion from certain civil activities. The data prove the reality of the existing gap between citizen and non-citizen and suggest ways of better understanding how the migration policies and civil society could support the migrants with more inclusive integration practices.

The concept of pluralism, which in this research measured individual ways of searching the religious truth (Astley and Francis 2016), showed a positive significant influence on the rights to freedom of religion and freedom of speech. Interreligious contacts had predictive power only for the freedom of speech, while the concept of 'diversity' had predictive power vis-à-vis all citizens' rights analysed in this study.

The scale of 'authoritarianism' had a negative significant statistical influence on the political right to freedom of protest and freedom of speech. The concept of 'trust in governmental institutions' had a negative significant influence on all six citizens' rights with the highest absolute value of beta for the freedom of speech ($b = -.325$). At the same time, the attitudes towards 'three powers' of political life in Belarus had a positive influence on freedom of speech. The concept of 'sensitivity to citizens and non-citizens conflicts' showed that the more young people face them at the level of society and experience them, the more they support the right to protest and the less they support socioeconomic rights. From the regression models, we observed that the age of the respondents had no significant statistical influence on citizens' rights, while for male students socioeconomic rights were more important than for the females in our sample. It is interesting to observe that the balance of political power measured by 'three powers' scale, showed predictive power for refugee rights and right to freedom of speech, by establishing a link between participation in public debates and understanding of refugee rights.

13.6 Conclusion

This research examines how inclusion and membership in a political community create a difference in perception of various human rights. The migration context along with attitudes towards multiculturalism and political culture have to be taken into account if we are to understand the changing nature of modern citizenship. By our research, we have tested three theoretical hypotheses about the relationship between the migrants' context, values of political culture and multiculturalism, and attitudes towards human rights. We can conclude that Hypothesis 1 (H1) was partly confirmed. The migration context of the respondents, i.e. fact of being born outside of the country or the fact that the respondents' parents were born outside of the national community, created a difference in perception of citizens' rights but not of refugee rights in comparison with those respondents who were born in the country. Even though the concept of migration context' did not show its predictive power for refugee rights and most of citizens' rights we had studied, it showed its predictive power for the right to vote and free speech.

Our second hypothesis suggested the centrality of pluralist views, interreligious contacts, and positive attitudes towards multiculturalism for the positive perception of citizens' and refugee rights. We can conclude that views about the equality of various religious truth systems and multiculturalism are good predictors of both refugee and citizens' rights, while interreligious contacts matter only for refugee rights and the right to freedom of speech. Thus, the second hypothesis (H2) was confirmed with some qualifications.

The third hypothesis stated that authoritarianism and attitudes towards governing institutions would have a negative significant statistical effect on refugees' rights. H3 was partly confirmed since negative attitudes of young Belarusians towards authoritarianism did not predict the perception of refugee rights but right of protest and freedom of speech. In both cases, the impact had a negative statistical influence on the dependent variables. However, trust in governing institutions had negative statistical effect in all cases. The balance of political power affects both refugee rights and freedom of speech, while sensitivity to conflicts between citizens and non-citizens has the opposite effect for the right of protest and socioeconomic rights.

This research provides us with the consideration of how migration and citizenship concepts could be understood through the perception of human rights, which from our study highlighted the tight relationship between citizens' participation and democratisation processes. Our research suggests that refugee and citizens' rights are strongly interlinked and that various levels of sociological analysis of these relationship, which have been emphasised by Somers (2008), depict the most problematic gaps between citizens and non-citizens, participation and exclusion, and processes of actively claiming rights and silent presence in a political community.

Bibliography

Altemeyer, B., & Hunsberger, B. (1992). Authoritarianism, religious fundamentalism, quest, and prejudice. *International Journal for the Psychology of Religion, 2*, 113–133.

Altemeyer, B. (1996). *The authoritarian specter*. Cambridge: Harvard University Press.

Altemeyer, B. (1998). The other 'authoritarian personality'. *Advances in Experimental Social Psychology, 30*, 47–92.

Arendt, H. (1951). *The origins of totalitarism*. New York: Harcourt, Brace and Co.

Astley, J., & Francis, L. J. (2016). Introducing the Astley-Francis theology of religions index: construct validity among 13- to 15-year-old students. *Journal of Beliefs & Values, 37*(1), 29–39.

Beaman, L. G. (2017). *Deep equality in an era of religious diversity*. New York: Oxford University Press.

Bekemans, L. (2013). *Globalisation vs Europeanisation. A human-centric interaction*. Brussels, Berlin, Bern, Frankfurt am Main, New York, Oxford, Wien: International Academic Publishers Peter Lang.

Benhabib, S. (2004). *The rights of others: Aliens, residents, and citizens*. Cambridge: Cambridge University Press.

Breskaya, O., & Botvar, P. K. (2019). Views on religious freedom among young people in Belarus and Norway: Similarities and contrasts. *Religions, 10*(6), 361. https://doi.org/10.3390/rel10060361.

Brysk, A., & Shafir, G. (2004). *People out of place: Globalization, human rights and the citizenship gap*. New York and London: Routledge.

Calder, G., Cole, P., & Seglow, J. (2009). *Citizenship acquisition and national belonging: Migration, membership and the liberal democratic state*. New York: Palgrave Macmillan.

Council of Europe. (2008). *White Paper on Intercultural Dialogue "Living Together as Equals in Dignity"*. https://www.coe.int/t/dg4/intercultural/Publication_WhitePaper_ID_en.asp. Accessed 17 Aug 2019.

Devos, T., Spini, D., & Schwartz, Sh H. (2002). Conflicts among human values and trust in institutions. *British Journal of Social Psychology, 41,* 481–494.

DeGooyer, S., Hunt, A., Maxwell, L., & Moyn, S. (2018). *The right to have rights*. London and New York: Verso.

Doise, W., Spini, D., & Clémence, A. (1999). Human rights studied as social representations in a cross-national context. *European Journal of Social Psychology, 29*(1), 1–29.

Donnelly, J. (2007). The relative universality of human rights. *Human Rights Quarterly, 29*(2), 281–306.

Dzesiatava, G. (2016). *Migration and national security in Belarus. BelarusDigest*. https://belarusdigest.com/story/migration-and-national-security-in-belarus.

Estèvez, A. (2012). *Human rights, migration, and social conflict: Towards a decolonized global justice*. New York: Palgrave Macmillan.

Giordan, G., & Lynch, A. P. (2019). *Interreligious dialogue: From religion to geopolitics*. Leiden: Brill.

Giordan, G., & Pace, E. (2014). *Religious pluralism: Framing religious diversity in the contemporary world*. Cham: Springer.

Makaryan, S. (2012). Estimation of international migration in post-Soviet republics. *International Migration, 53*(5), https://doi.org/10.1111/j.1468-2435.2012.00740.x.

Manganelli Rattazzi, A. M., Bobbio, A., & Canova, L. (2007). A short version of the right-wing authoritarianism (RWA) scale. *Personality and Individual Differences, 43*(5), 1223–1234.

Morselli, D., Spini, D., & Devos, T. (2012). Human values and trust in institutions across countries: A multilevel test of Schwartz's hypothesis of structural equivalence. *Survey Research Methods, 6,* 49–60.

Pew Research Center. (2018). *Eastern and Western Europeans differ on importance of religion, views of minorities, and key social issues*. https://www.pewforum.org/2018/10/29/eastern-and-western-europeans-differ-on-importance-of-religion-views-of-minorities-and-key-social-issues. Accessed 17 Aug 2019.

Piper, N., & Rother, S. (2015). Migration and democracy: Citizenship and human rights from a multi-level perspective. *International Migration, 53*(3). https://doi.org/10.1111/imig.12186.

Richardson, J. T. (2014). From religious diversity to religious pluralism: What is at stake. In G. Giordan & E. Pace (Eds.), *Religious pluralism. Framing religious diversity in the contemporary world* (pp. 31–49). Cham: Springer.

Somers, M. (2008). *Genealogies of citizenship: Markets, statelessness, and the right to have rights*. Cambridge: Cambridge University Press.

Somers, M., & Roberts, C. N. J. (2008). Toward a new sociology of rights: A genealogy of "buried bodies" of citizenship and human rights. *Annual Review of Law and Social Science, 4,* 385–425.

Staerklé, C., Clémence, A., & Doise, W. (1998). Representation of human rights across different national contexts: The role of democratic and non-democratic populations and governments. *European Journal of Social Psychology, 28,* 207–226.

Staerklé, C., Clémence, A., & Spini, D. (2011). Social representations: A normative and dynamic intergroup approach. *Political Psychology, 32,* 759–768.

Ulasiuk, I. (2013). What can migration policymakers learn from legal frameworks on national minorities? National minorities and migration in Armenia and Belarus. *International Migration, 52*(5). https://doi.org/10.1111/imig.12129.

Van der Ven, J., & Ziebertz, H.-G. (1995). Jugendliche in multikulturellem und multireligiösem Kontext. Schülerinnen zu Modellen interreligiöser Kommunikation – ein deutsch-niederländischer Vergleich. *RpB, 35,* 151–167.

Yasemin, S. (1994). *Limits of citizenship: Migrants and postnational membership in Europe*. Chicago: University of Chicago.

Olga Breskaya PhD, is a researcher at the Department of Philosophy, Sociology, Education and Applied Psychology, University of Padova. She obtained her doctorate from the International Joint PhD Programme 'Human Rights, Society, and Multi-level Governance' at the University of Padova (Italy). Her research interest is focused on sociology of human rights and quantitative study on religious freedom. She served as Board member of the International Sociological Association (Research Committee 22 Sociology of Religion, representative for Europe) from 2014 to 2022. Among her recent publications is Human Rights and Religion: A Sociological Perspective in the Journal for the Scientific Study of Religion with G. Giordan and J. T. Richardson (2018).

Chapter 14
Dismantling Security Discourses and Threat Perceptions Related to Asylum Seekers and Refugees in Croatia

Drago Županić-Iljić and Margareta Gregurović

Abstract Between mid-September 2015 and mid-April 2016, more than 650,000 refugees and other forced migrants transited through Croatia, moving along the Balkan corridor towards Western countries. During this period a series of risk events, such as terrorist attacks in Paris and Nice or sexual assaults in Germany, have left their mark on the public perceptions of refugees and other migrants coming to Europe. One of (un)intended consequences of these events has been the further securitisation of state rhetoric and practices regarding the 'humanitarian crisis' which resulted in borders closing at the very edge of Schengen. The shift in attitudes has manifested in more negative sentiments towards refugees and migrants expressed among political elites and in public. The main aims of this chapter are to investigate public attitudes and perceptions of refugees and asylum seekers, to analyse the mechanisms of constructing and (re)creating the images of them and to discuss the possible effects of addressing, utilising and/or withdrawing their human rights. With theoretical models of 'integrated threat' and perception of refugees' rights, the central analysis deals with the results of three studies conducted in 2011, 2013 and 2015 in Croatia aimed at exploring specific attitudes towards asylum seekers and/or refugees expressed by selected groups of Croatian citizens.

Keywords Refugees · Asylum seekers · Balkan corridor · Public opinion · Securitisation · Threat perception · Refugee rights

---

D. Županić-Iljić (✉)
University of Zagreb, Zagreb, Croatia
e-mail: dzuparic@ffzg.hr

M. Gregurović
Institute for Migration and Ethnic Studies, Zagreb, Croatia
e-mail: margareta.gregurovic@imin.hr

M. C. Jacobsen et al. (eds.), *Cosmopolitanism, Migration and Universal Human Rights*, https://doi.org/10.1007/978-3-030-50645-2_14

14.1 Introduction

The global mass displacement of Syrian refugees accompanied by Chancellor Angela Merkel's decision in August 2015 to suspend the Dublin Regulation resulted in increased arrival of refugees to Europe during the so-called 'long summer of migration' (Kasparek and Speer 2015). This process triggered many problems related to the admission and reception of numerous people on the move, as well as suspicion on the part of some European politicians and parts of the public about the security issues of these arrivals. Furthermore, while reporting on the mid-November 2015 Paris terrorist attacks, some media emphasised unconfirmed information that one of the attackers was registered in the transit camps for refugees and migrants along the Balkan corridor.[1] This event consequently linked the issues of the mass arrival and transit of refugees to the notion of threat, terrorism, fear and danger among the Croatian public. These contextual changes manifested in negative sentiments and open hostility towards refugees and other forced migrants expressed among politicians, but also to some extent by the public. Observed changes have contributed to a redefinition of the initial 'welcoming culture' and the closing of the Balkan corridor in March 2016, after the signing of the EU–Turkey deal.

Prior to the 2015/16 events, some researchers noted relatively tolerant public attitudes towards 'classic immigrants' and towards 'asylum seekers' in Croatia (Čačić-Kumpes et al. 2012; Gregurović et al. 2016). However, the terrorist attack in Paris has certainly changed the perception of European security and (in)stability. Even though domestic and international politicians have condemned this act, one of the possible (un)intended consequences of this crime was the further securitisation of state rhetoric, discourses and practices as well as the radicalisation of public opinion on the so-called 'Refugee crisis' (cf. Župarić-Iljić and Valenta 2019). As a consequence, erosion of the refugees' rights was first and foremost revealed in deportations and readmissions of rejected asylum seekers, as well as in practices of interception and deflection on the EU maritime and Schengen land borders (Perkowski 2016). Thus, the interest in human rights of migrants and refugees did not seem to remain of primary concern to European governments in comparison with mostly humanitarian politics of those stakeholders who were working directly with refugees.

Political approaches to refugees passing through Croatia from late summer 2015 to spring 2016 shifted from swiftly organised and controlled transit to other modalities of acceptance or rejection. From then on, one of these modalities adheres to the EU relocation and resettlement scheme in which Croatia decided to participate by hosting mostly Syrian refugee families being transferred from Turkish camps, and timidly distributed to different local communities across Croatia. In this process we assume that public opinion is one of the most important prerequisites for the societal dimension of integration. Thus, public perception of newcomers, be they asylum seekers or refugees, unveil the role of citizens' attitudes in adhering to or resisting the official state discourses and perceptions of refugees and other migrants. In order

[1] See: www.theguardian.com/world/2015/nov/17/serbian-police-arrest-man-with-syrian-passport-matching-paris-attackers.

to present and analyse changes in the general discourses about refugee issues in Croatia, we focus on the determination of the interrelation between three agents: the state, the media and the public, with an emphasis on the last one. We contest the security approach while analysing the mechanisms of constructing and (re)creating the images and categories of displaced persons and investigating the possible effects of addressing and guaranteeing or withdrawing the human rights of refugees.

We do so by analysing public attitudes towards asylum seekers and refugees in the periods prior to and at the beginning of the mass arrival, in order to observe and investigate possible changes in the perception of these two categories of migrants among several distinct groups of Croatian citizens. After a short description of the context and the theoretical standpoints, we will analyse the set of questionnaire items used in the three empirical studies from 2011, 2013 and 2015 in order to detect differences in attitudes expressed towards asylum seekers and refugees in subsequent time periods. Finally, we try to put together a complete picture of the actors involved in the change of approach towards refugees in Croatia, providing possible explanations and interpretations of the observed shift in regard to the perception of refugees and their human and other refugee-related rights.

14.2 The Croatian Context of Dealing with Asylum Seekers and Increased Arrivals of Forced Migrants

Public attitudes are context-dependent. They are shaped by and conveyed through the legal framework, socio-political institutions, media portrayals and daily interactions within the national and regional context where they occur. Dempster and Hargrave (2017) posit that the government's asylum and integration policies as well as the migration system and border regime set a context in which those public attitudes form.

Being throughout centuries an emigration country in which the main reasons for leaving were of political or economic nature, emigration from Croatia during the 1990s was connected to forced movements as a consequence of the war. At one point in time Croatia hosted more than half a million internally displaced persons, and several hundred thousand refugees from Bosnia and Herzegovina. This historical legacy together with the contemporary situation unveils a difficult and long transition period from Yugoslav socialism to a burdensome and crony version of capitalism. Recent economic-driven emigration from Croatia coincided with the liberalisation of the job market after accession to the EU in 2013. Over the last couple of years the demographic pool of migrant workers coming from the surrounding countries has diminished, and today is being replaced by immigrant workers from Ukraine, India, Bangladesh, and elsewhere.[2]

Until now, the Croatian asylum and integration systems have largely been conditioned by the EU regulations and the process of harmonisation with the EU acquis. Since 2003 Croatia has been developing a legal and institutional framework for granting asylum statuses. However, out of almost 10,000 who applied for the protection status less than 10% obtained it.[3] Due to low social capital and the non-existence of compatriot networks, as well as difficult economic conditions and poor integration prospects, many of the asylum seekers and half of the population of recognised refugees actually continued their venture, often in an irregular manner, towards the West (cf. Ajduković et al. 2019), even before the Balkan corridor enabled temporary transit for so many of them.

In the period of the Balkan corridor, the securitisation approach took precedence, expressed in control of mobility on borders and in temporary reception and transit centres, over humanitarian practices. From September 2015 to April 2016 more than 660,000 refugees and other forced migrants passed through Croatia, yet only 211 people requested protection/asylum in Croatia. Media attention focused on reporting on the so-called 'migration/refugee crisis', and crisis management mechanisms for accelerated accepting, registering and organising of further transit (cf. Župarić-Iljić, in this volume). Rather than focusing on the long-term perspective of including asylum seekers and refugees into society, today the government is still struggling to find more cohesive and systematic solutions to the reception and integration of newcomers.

Being at the forefront of the Schengen area today, we witness manifestations of the border management regime in dealing with numerous irregular migrants who try to cross Croatian territory, entering from Bosnia and Herzegovina and to a lesser extent from Serbia, on their path to reach Slovenia and move further into Western Europe. Various actors and the latest human rights reports have warned the international community about the possible violation of the human rights of refugees and migrants at the Croatian borders,[4] primarily those rights stemming from the Convention Relating to the Status of Refugees, and the positive standards from the Common

[2]Croatia records a very low share of immigrants, including recognised refugees as third-country nationals, at less than 1% of the total population. Consequently, this affects a possible formation of ethnic communities and migrant networks, and also makes difficult social interaction and intercultural dialogue of Croatian citizens with newly arriving migrants and refugees.

[3]According to the official data, from July 2004 to June 2019, asylum seekers in large numbers have come from the war-affected areas of the Middle East and Africa (MoI 2019). The procedure cancellation rate is very high because applicants were leaving the country. With only around 800 persons being granted some sort of protection (full asylum status or subsidiary protection) during the same period, Croatia is one of the EU countries with the lowest asylum recognition rates.

[4]One of the most important issues is violation of the EU laws and, most notably, the Asylum Procedures Directive when denying migrants access to state territory and access to asylum procedures, through pushbacks, collective expulsions and forced returns (www.hrw.org/news/2018/12/11/croatia-migrants-pushed-back-bosnia-and-herzegovina; www.ecre.org/op-ed-asylum-seekers-in-croatia-in-a-human-rights-vacuum; www.amnesty.org/en/latest/news/2019/03/croatia-eu-complicit-in-violence-and-abuse-by-police-against-refugees-and-migrants/).

European Asylum System, its Directives and regulations. In this context of a combination of humanitarian and securitisation policies we must analyse and understand the ways different determinants shape societal attitudes and public opinion towards our subjects of concern.

14.3 Refugees, Human Rights, Media Portrayals and Public Attitudes—Theoretical Standpoints

There is no doubt that today's attitudes and portrayals of refugees are influenced by securitisation and humanitarian discourses and policies across Europe. It might seem these are not brand-new tendencies, yet they have been accentuated after the Balkan corridor. In her critical discourse analysis of European migration and border regimes Perkowski (2016, 332) contended that:

> What we are seeing in response to the recent movement of people in the Mediterranean region is the coexistence and simultaneous mobilization of security, humanitarianism and human rights discourses. Rather than being opposed to one another, the three discourses share a number of fundamental commonalities. First, it is the figure of the citizen which functions in all three discourses as an implicit 'us', whereas those on the move are 'othered' in various ways. Meanwhile, security discourse produces 'welfare scroungers', 'illegals' or 'terrorists', opposing them to a homogenized notion of EU citizens to be protected. Humanitarianism relies on the juxtaposition of 'victims', who are pitied and debased, and their European 'saviours'. Similarly, human rights discourse relies on the construction of victims, saviours and perpetrators.

The author sees these three discourses as serving a functioning role for techniques of government(ality) and crisis management through 'disciplinary means', 'security discourses', and 'techniques of power' (Perkowski 2016).

Refugees' right to access the territory and to access the asylum recognition procedure of any state signatory party to the Refugee Convention could be hindered by restrictive migration, asylum and border policies. Gündoğdu (2015, 19) posits that the human rights of asylum seekers and of undocumented migrants 'remain dependent on highly arbitrary political and legal decisions as well as unreliable sentiments such as compassion'. Moreover, arbitrary detentions and deportations without right to appeal leave them in a situation of legal and status limbo, without a real chance of exercising any other social, economic, cultural and political rights in European societies. Excluding refugees from society means putting them in a condition of 'rightlessness' (in Arendtian terms), when the guarantee of having an opportunity to exercise their human rights depends on their chance for obtaining protection status.

Nonetheless, a relation of asylum and integration policies with public attitudes is seldom a simple one. Brad Blitz contends that European societies often express general sympathy towards refugees and humanitarian assistance to them; however, governments decide to develop and enact restrictive asylum policies, and to securitise migration issues. What is common to both the public and the government is a somewhat discriminatory attitude, according to which they both prefer and favour skilled and qualified workers who could easily be integrated into the labour market and assimilated into society (Blitz 2017, 381). Thus, negative public attitudes and political discourses could be mutually shaped by aggravating fragmented support to refugees, leaving them in marginal and vulnerable positions at labour markets, education systems and in society in general.[5]

Within different theoretical explanations, a threat perception was found to be the strongest predictor of negative sentiments towards refugees, according to Cowling et al. (2019). In their meta-analysis encompassing 70 studies, the authors conclude that there are at least four factors we need to acknowledge when investigating prejudices towards refugees:

> In the case of demographic factors, being male, religious, nationally identified, politically conservative, and less educated were associated with negative attitudes […]. For ideological factors, increases in right-wing authoritarianism (RWA) and social-dominance orientation (SDO) correlated with negative attitudes, while the endorsement of macro (but not micro) justice principles were associated with positive attitudes […]. Perceptions of refugees as symbolic and realistic threats were the strongest correlates of negative attitudes […]. (Cowling et al. 2019, 1)

Moreover, Anderson and Ferguson (2018) came to a similar conclusion in regard to the demographic and ideological factors within the Australian context, finding that those ideological factors of RWA and SDO were the strongest predictors of negative attitudes.

Further on, according to the Integrated Threat Theory of Stephan et al. (1998, 559), perception of threat comes from 'symbolic threats based on value differences between groups, realistic threats to power, resources, and well-being of the ingroup; anxiety concerning social interaction with outgroup members; and feelings of threat arising from negative stereotypes of the outgroup'. Symbolic threats mean that refugees are being perceived as threatening to national identity, culture, values and customs, while realistic threats mean they are perceived as threatening and competitive to the economy and/or social and welfare system of the reception country. Even though different studies report on the obtained correlations, it is debatable to what extent these threat perceptions could be fuelled and reinforced by personal false beliefs and by media representations of refugees through the prism of security: portraying them as criminals and terrorists, or job takers (Augoustinos and Quinn 2003). Nevertheless, Klocker and Dunn (2003) found negative representations of refugees in Australian newspapers where the terminology used had very problematic connotations of portraying refugees as something less than human, lacking human qualities and stripped of human rights. The final consequence of this 'propaganda model' could mean that negative constructions and categorisations are being formed and conveyed from government to media, and finally to the public.

Public attitudes towards refugee rights and human rights in general are influenced only partly by media coverage, while other contextual and ideological factors and

---

[5] Often these attitudes are shaped and conveyed by media and by attitudes of opinion makers, including humanitarian actors and politicians. They differ according to diverse socio-demographic, contextual, ideological and personal presets and patterns, creating an inclination for positive, negative or ambiguous sentiments towards refugees and migrants.

values might have more a prominent role in co-creating those attitudes (Pritchard 1991, 133). Media coverage on refugee issues could provide the necessary information to the domestic population about the newcomers as members of their local communities, but the media portrayals and framing could also non-intentionally or purposely serve a role in spreading moral panic, fear and outgroup distrust. In their critical discourse analysis of online news releases on the topic of asylum after the closure of the Balkan corridor, Baričević and Koska (2017) noticed desubjectivisation, victimisation and criminalisation of asylum seekers and irregular migrants through the media discursive practices. Media framing was based on a securitised discourse very similar to that of the Ministry of Interior (MoI), with a strong emphasis on the potential threat that newcomers might pose to Croatian society, rather than conveying messages on long-term solutions and integration perspectives for refugees.[6]

Has anything changed after the terrorist attacks and the sexual assaults, and (how) did it affect public attitudes? Czymara and Schmid-Catran (2017) contend that the ways German media covered the sexual harassment in Germany on New Year's Eve of 2015/2016 seemed to have increased negative sentiments towards the immigration of persons of Arab and African origin to the country, rather than having a negative effect on opinions about acceptance and reception of refugees. Research in the Croatian context by Bilić et al. (2018, 59) posit that '[t]here is a noticeable change from a humanitarian rhetoric to a security-orientated rhetoric that mobilizes fear to legitimize stronger control of national borders. […] [T]he majority of digital news media changed reporting style due to widespread moral panic and the economic incentive to commodify audience interest in the topic of the refugee crisis.' All of this has to be taken into account when discussing public attitudes and perception of newcomers in Croatian society.

14.4 Public Perceptions of Asylum Seekers and Refugees

The analysis of the shift in public perceptions of asylum seekers and refugees is based on three research studies conducted in the period 2011–2015 in Croatia. It is important to stress that in the research on perceptions and attitudes towards strangers or all other sorts of 'newcomers', i.e. regular and irregular immigrants, similar dimensions of threat are overlapping. Among the most commonly used attitudinal research paradigms and concepts is the concept of a 'threat perception', according to which different (ethnic/cultural) groups are considered to be the source of potential symbolic

[6]On the other hand, in her content analysis of visual representation of refugees in Croatia during 2015 and 2016 Šarić (2019) concludes that representations and discourses of victimhood were far more prevalent in the national context than those of threat. Consequently, this situation triggered the humane and humanitarian approach to people in transit who did not aspire to stay in Croatia, but rather continued to Slovenia as the next country in the migration chain of the Balkan corridor (cf. Župarić-Iljić and Valenta 2019).

or realistic threat to ingroup members of domestic society (Berg 2009; Rustenbach 2010).

The data presented in this chapter were collected in three separate studies: the 2011 study was conducted on a convenience sample (N = 277) of students from Zagreb University (see Župarić-Iljić and Gregurović 2013); the 2013 study was conducted on a convenience sample (N = 1110) of residents from two Croatian counties in Slavonia (Osijek-Baranja and Vukovar-Srijem county), as the easternmost part of Croatia on the border with the Republic of Serbia (see Gregurović et al. 2016); and the 2015 study was conducted in November 2015, during the peak of the transit migration of refugees along the Balkan corridor, on a systematic random sample (N = 299) of residents from two city quarters in Zagreb (see Gregurović et al. 2019). The samples are diverse in terms of their target population of respondents; however, some consistent characteristics as well as differences could be found between them: although females are more represented in all studies, they are significantly more represented in the students' sample. Among the other two studies, age distributions are congruent, while level of education shifts towards the more highly educated in the Zagreb sample. The ethnic distribution of the Slavonia study implies a similar proportion of respondents of Croatian and Serbian ethnic affiliation, while the other samples are highly ethnically homogeneous.

Even though all three studies employed different research and questionnaire design, there were eight items (addressing attitudes towards asylum seekers and refugees) included in all three studies which allow speculation on possible trends and shifts in perceptions of them. Items used in all three studies are presented in Table 14.1 along with the proportions of those agreeing with them[7] in each of represented studies. Limitations on conclusions based on the selected results are grounded in different sampled populations as well as the use of convenience sampling. Furthermore, the cross-sectional character of the analysed studies reflects the contextual implications of each of the studies, also reflecting the situational factors that might have affected the attitudes. These contextual frameworks prevent us from making any direct comparisons, yet we are able to provide some implications of possible differences and shifts.

Results indicate relatively high agreement with all presented items. Mean values show moderate agreeing except in the case of the statement referring to asylum seekers' skin colour, according to which respondents across all studies do not agree that they should be of similar 'skin colour' to the domestic population. There is somewhat stronger agreement to the statement that asylum seekers do not jeopardise the stability of the Croatian political order (especially in the 2015 sample). More distinct differences between the studies refer to the estimation of the ethnicity of asylum seekers and their culture mixing with Croatian culture, where the 2015 respondents expressed a stronger perception of the cultural threat posed. The dimension consisting in compromised security is also visibly stronger in the latter study, whereas the economic dimension is more accentuated among the 2013 respondents.

[7] A 5-point answer scale from 1 (Strongly disagree) to 5 (Strongly agree) was used in all studies.

Table 14.1 Item descriptives across the selected studies

	2011		2013		2015	
	Agree and strongly agree (%)	M (SD)	Agree and strongly agree (%)	M (SD)	Agree and strongly agree (%)	M (SD)
1. I would like AS[a] in Croatia to be similar to the Croatian residents by their ethnic affiliation	39.0	**3.09** (1.19)	31.8	**2.95** (1.25)	42.4	**3.14** (1.37)
2. I would like AS in Croatia to be similar to the Croatian residents by their skin colour	13.0	**2.12** (1.54)	18.6	**2.43** (1.26)	15.7	**2.13** (1.30)
3. The culture of AS should not be mixed with Croatian culture	29.6	**2.84** (1.23)	29.3	**2.88** (1.26)	38.1	**3.09** (1.45)
4. AS do not jeopardise the stability of Croatian political order	53.4	**3.57** (1.02)	49.1	**3.58** (1.15)	60.5	**3.72** (1.30)
5. AS are not a burden for the economic development of our country	39.4	**3.23** (0.97)	38.4	**3.23** (1.24)	32.8	**2.89** (1.38)
6. AS do not represent a burden for the taxpayers	13.9	**2.65** (0.93)	27.1	**2.92** (1.20)	19.8	**2.45** (1.28)
7. AS do not pose a security threat in the local community where they are present	50.2	**3.39** (1.00)	37.8	**3.18** (1.16)	36.6	**3.04** (1.31)

(continued)

Table 14.1 (continued)

	2011		2013		2015	
	Agree and strongly agree (%)	M (SD)	Agree and strongly agree (%)	M (SD)	Agree and strongly agree (%)	M (SD)
8. Shelter for AS does not cause decline of real estate prices in the immediate vicinity	22.7	**2.95** (0.97)	32.4	**3.19** (1.16)	26.1	**2.66** (1.34)

[a] AS stands for 'asylum seekers'

Conducted factor analyses yielded slightly different latent constructions of these eight items, resulting in a bi-factorial structure in 2011 presenting the separation of cultural and economic dimensions (each also assigned by one of the security items). A uni-factorial solution was obtained on the 2013 sample while, again, two factors were obtained for 2015 sample: the first referring solely to the cultural dimension and the second combining economic and security dimensions. In order to detect possible determinants of these latent constructs, the regression analyses were conducted using the selected socio-demographic characteristics as predictor variables (Table 14.2). Political orientation and religious self-identifications were also included in the models due to their widely proven effect on (anti)immigrant attitudes (cf. Semyonov et al. 2006; Karyotis and Patrikios 2010).

The significant effect of selected predictors varies across the studies. The full model better explains the cultural dimension of asylum seekers' perception than the economic/security dimensions. Age and education are significant among the 2013 sample, indicating that the older and less educated residents of Eastern Croatia perceive asylum seekers as a cultural-economic threat to higher extent. Ethnicity was significant in the 2011 and 2013 studies, according to which Croatian students perceived them to be a cultural or economic threat to a lesser extent in comparison with students of other ethnic affiliations, whereas Croats in the 2013 sample (in comparison with the Serbian respondents) perceived asylum seekers to be a greater threat. Political orientation has a significant effect on almost all dependent variables and could be described as a constant indicator affecting attitudes across all studies, indicating that respondents leaning towards the political right perceive asylum seekers primarily as a cultural but also as an economic and security threat. A similar conclusion could be drawn for religious self-identification in the 2011 and 2015 samples, where more religious respondents perceived them as a cultural threat and in 2015 also as an economic-security threat. Gender proved to be non-significant in all tested models.

Having also hypothesised that possible contact with asylum seekers and refugees and information provided about them by the media might have had significant effect on the expressed attitudes towards asylum seekers and refugees, additional analyses were conducted on the 2011 and 2015 samples. However, no significant correlations were obtained between any of the contextual variables with the expressed attitudes in either of the analysed studies.

14.5 Perception of Refugees' Rights

In two of the analysed studies (2011 and 2015) the questionnaire also included items measuring the importance of refugees (i.e. asylum grantees) exercising specific rights and some obligations in Croatia. Even though there was a slightly different

Table 14.2 Predictors of attitudes towards asylum seekers

	2011		2013	2015	
	F1—Predominantly cultural dimension	F2—Predominantly economic dimension	F1—Cultural-economic dimension	F1 – Cultural dimension	F2 – Economic-security dimension
Gender (female)	0.033	0.091	0.025	0.048	−0.098
Age	−0.008	−0.034	**−0.111*****	−0.078	−0.018
Education	–	–	**0.083***	0.031	0.019
Ethnicity (Croatian)	**0.158***	**0.213****	**−0.090****	0.004	−0.005
Political orientation[a]	**−0.227****	−0.038	**−0.135*****	**−0.322*****	**−0.214****
Religious self-identification[b]	**0.221****	0.081	0.037	**0.183***	**0.168***
	$R^2 = 0.191$ $F = 10.932$ $p = 0.000$	$R^2 = 0.074$ $F = 3.704$ $p = 0.003$	$R^2 = 0.058$ $F = 10.358$ $p = 0.000$	$R^2 = 0.217$ $F = 9.551$ $p = 0.000$	$R^2 = 0.127$ $F = 5.029$ $p = 0.000$

*$p < 0.05$; **$p < 0.01$; ***$p < 0.001$

[a]Left → right

[b]Convinced believer → not religious/against religion

wording in the statements used,[8] the presented results enable us to make some general comparisons. The items used for measuring the perception of rights and obligations are presented in Table 14.3 along with their general descriptives.

The importance of recognising refugees' rights has become more accentuated over the years. There are differences in the average and positive recognition of almost all presented rights. Having in mind different sample populations and different contexts (especially the one referring to the so-called 'refugee crisis' of 2015/16) this shift is somewhat expected. On the other side, the different nature of the posed question items and scales used could also have contributed to a more or less rigid perception of refugee rights. Among the more pronounced differences we should mention the right to work without a permit, which only 6% of Zagreb residents support (generally indicating the rejection of this right) in comparison with 41% of the 2011 students, and the recognition of the same rights to the refugee's family members, which is more favoured among the students. A greater difference could also be noticed with regard to attending courses on the Croatian language, history and culture, which over 80% of Zagreb residents favour in comparison with slightly over half of student respondents.

Due to the different nature of the wording and scales used, we decided not to analyse the latent dimensions of perceptions of the refugees' rights scale. Instead, we calculated the correlation coefficients between selected socio-demographic variables of each subsample with the attitudes relating to every analysed right (Table 14.4). Selected socio-demographic characteristics include gender, age, political orientation and religious self-identification. The 2015 sample also included respondents' highest education level. Ethnic affiliation was omitted from these analyses due to very high homogeneity of both samples (over 90% of each sample was composed of Croats).

Pearson correlations between selected characteristics of respondents and all 14 refugees' rights presented in Table 14.4 are very low and vary in their significance. In general, more statistically significant correlations were obtained in the 2015 sample (in spite of one more variable). The most frequently obtained significant correlation of perception of refugees' rights is with the political orientation of both groups of respondents. This relation indicates that the greater agreement and importance of exercising specific rights are among respondents orientated more towards the political left. Religious self-identification is also often significantly correlated to the perception of refugees' rights: respondents who describe themselves as less religious express greater support for refugees' rights.

Other demographic characteristics are seldom correlated with the analysed rights. Only among the students did females attach greater importance to the right of freedom of religion and stronger support of Croatian Ministry of Interior in providing useful information to refugees. Younger respondents among the Zagreb residents agreed more that refugees should be able to work without a permit and that the family

[8]The first study used the terminology 'The state must ensure' while the second study used 'The state should ensure'. The list of specific rights was the same in both studies; however, the respondents used different scales to assess the importance of these rights: 2011 respondents used the scale from 1 (Not important at all) to 5 (Very important), and 2015 respondents used the scale from 1 (Strongly disagree) to 5 (Strongly agree).

Table 14.3 Perception of refugees' rights item descriptives across the selected studies

	2011		2015	
	Important and very important (%)	M (SD)	Agree and strongly agree (%)	M (SD)
1. Refugees should have the right to work in the Republic of Croatia without work or business permit	40.8	3.07 (1.518)	6.0	1.51 (1.019)
2. The Government should pay the costs of Croatian language learning to refugees	37.3	2.99 (1.358)	45.6	3.05 (1.582)
3. The Government should ensure accommodation to refugees during the first two years following the granting of their status	40.8	3.23 (1.182)	47.4	3.21 (1.486)
4. The Government should ensure the fulfilment of the rights to health insurance for refugees	65.9	3.96 (2.152)	70.3	3.96 (1.315)
5. Refugees should have the right to freedom of religion and religious education of their children	74.9	4.05 (1.202)	77.1	4.17 (1.187)
6. The Government should ensure social welfare for refugees	64.0	3.79 (1.186)	65.0	3.78 (1.356)
7. The Government should ensure the inclusion of refugees in the country's political life	25.7	2.78 (1.238)	32.9	2.8 (1.513)
8. The Government should ensure the right to family reunification and unity for refugees	64.1	3.84 (1.156)	75.0	4.05 (1.178)
9. The Government should ensure the learning of Croatian language, history and culture for refugees, for the purpose of their inclusion in Croatian society	70.0	3.96 (1.041)	77.5	4.17 (1.258)

(continued)

Table 14.3 (continued)

	2011		2015	
	Important and very important (%)	M (SD)	Agree and strongly agree (%)	M (SD)
10. Refugees should have the right to the recognition of their foreign educational qualification	66.9	3.94 (1.099)	70.8	3.99 (1.236)
11. A member of the family of a refugee who is legally residing in the Republic of Croatia should exercise the same rights as a refugee	39.7	3.34 (1.167)	27.4	2.56 (1.444)
12. Refugees should have the right to free legal assistance	31.1	3.00 (1.224)	49.7	3.39 (1.466)
13. The (Croatian) Ministry of the Interior should provide refugees with general information about the rights and obligations relating to asylum status	81.5	4.37 (0.931)	88.2%	4.57 (0.921)
14. Refugees should attend a course of Croatian language, history and culture	54.8	3.62 (1.222)	82.5	4.38 (1.022)

Table 14.4 Sociodemographic correlates of perception of refugees' rights

		Gender	Age	Education	Political orientation	Religious self-identification
1. Refugees should have the right to work in the Republic of Croatia without work or business permit	*2011*	0.051	0.000	–	−0.006	−0.053
	2015	0.027	**−0.138***	−0.066	**−0.133***	0.087
2. The Government should pay the costs of Croatian language learning to refugees	*2011*	−0.021	0.023	–	**−0.142***	0.070
	2015	0.032	0.047	0.012	**−0.148***	**0.208****
3. The Government should ensure accommodation to refugees during the first two years following the granting of their status	*2011*	0.108	−0.054	–	**−0.172****	**0.206****
	2015	0.068	−0.109	−0.037	**−0.279****	**0.147***
4. The Government should ensure the fulfilment of the rights to health insurance for refugees	*2011*	0.087	−0.077	–	**−0.179****	0.082
	2015	−0.024	0.004	0.041	**−0.181****	**0.135***
5. Refugees should have the right to freedom of religion and religious education of their children	*2011*	**0.201****	−0.073	–	**−0.140***	0.023
	2015	−0.014	−0.023	0.072	−0.118	0.073
6. The Government should ensure social welfare for refugees	*2011*	0.101	−0.093	–	**−0.203****	**0.156***
	2015	0.006	−0.033	0.058	**−0.134***	**0.136***
7. The Government should ensure the inclusion of refugees in the country's political life	*2011*	0.001	0.025	–	−0.041	0.055
	2015	−0.023	−0.036	**0.173****	**−0.272****	**0.220****
8. The Government should ensure the right to family reunification and unity for refugees	*2011*	0.111	−0.069	–	**−0.166***	0.061
	2015	0.041	0.032	**0.135***	**−0.246****	**0.189****
9. The Government should ensure the learning of Croatian language, history and culture for refugees, for the purpose of their inclusion in Croatian society	*2011*	0.095	−0.082	–	0.044	−0.032
	2015	0.100	0.018	0.044	−0.032	**0.128***
10. Refugees should have the right to the recognition of their foreign educational qualification	*2011*	0.034	−0.108	–	−0.108	0.100
	2015	0.047	−0.092	0.017	**−0.177****	**0.127***
11. A member of the family of a refugee who is legally residing in the Republic of Croatia should exercise the same rights as a refugee	*2011*	−0.011	−0.101	–	−0.062	**0.135***
	2015	0.081	**−0.119***	**0.161****	**−0.224****	**0.173****
12. Refugees should have the right to free legal assistance	*2011*	−0.053	0.033	–	−0.103	0.071
	2015	0.036	−0.080	−0.016	**−0.228****	**0.180****
13. The (Croatian) Ministry of the Interior should provide refugees with general information about the rights and obligations relating to asylum status	*2011*	**0.167****	**−0.159****	–	**−0.204****	**0.166****
	2015	0.062	−0.056	0.038	−0.013	**0.157***
14. Refugees should attend a course of Croatian language, history and culture	*2011*	−0.006	0.022	–	0.095	−0.099
	2015	0.028	0.018	0.023	0.016	−0.010

*$p < 0.05$; **$p < 0.01$

members of refugees should exercise the same rights as the refugees themselves. Statistically significant correlations of the education level of Zagreb residents indicate that respondents with higher education agreed more that the Croatian Government should ensure the inclusion of refugees into the country's political life, the right to family reunification and the same rights to refugees' family members. Interestingly, the perception of refugee obligation to attend courses on Croatian language, history and culture is not significantly correlated with any of the respondents' characteristic in any of the samples.

14.6 Conclusion, Theoretical and Practical Implications

Our results are in line with previous research (cf. Cowling et al. 2019) explaining that levels of education, religious, national and political affiliation correlate with negative attitudes and perception of threat(s). However, the significant effect of selected predictors varies across our studies due to the methodological constraints on the different samples, slightly different scales and item wording, and is most likely due to the change of context. The dimension of cultural threat is in general more strongly perceived among older and less educated respondents of Eastern Croatia in particular and among those respondents leaning towards the political right. Economic and security threat are present to a lesser degree, although one year of Croatian membership of the EU and the liberalisation of the labour market brought forward more of the economic threat dimension. The security dimension was accentuated in the latest survey conducted within the mass arrival and transit context of 2015, even though 60% of respondents agreed that 'Asylum seekers do not jeopardise the stability of Croatian political order'.

The closing of the Balkan corridor and national borders reinforced by 'politics of fear and exclusion' (Squire 2009) has brought the gradual deterioration of the human and refugee rights, and most likely lowered the levels of trust of the domestic population towards refugees. Ethnicity was significant in the 2011 and 2013 studies: in the 2013 sample, Croats perceived asylum seekers as a greater threat in comparison with Serbs, and the same could apply to more religious respondents in comparison with others in the 2011 and 2015 samples.[9] Nowicka et al. (2017, 11) claim that explicit attitudes towards helping refugees reflect differently accentuated discourses that oscillate between cosmopolitan inclusiveness, on the one hand, and religious and ethnic exclusiveness on the other. Croatia is one of the Central East European countries where ethnonational identities and religious affiliations are overlapping, so some research results suggest that prejudices and religion are strongly connected in the sense that dogmatic believers do have more negative attitudes towards foreigners (cf. Gregurović et al. 2016; Kumpes 2018).[10]

In future research it could be fruitful to focus on the triad of 'conservative values' (tradition, conformity and security) as predictors of public attitudes. Part of the limitation of all three research phases is the fact that they did not ask questions that would include attitudes to the ethnicity of asylum seekers and refugees in the light of the known fact that for many years citizens from Serbia, Kosovo and Albania have usually represented one of the top five nationalities of asylum seekers in the EU28 countries (cf. Zoppi 2019).[11] Yet in our questionnaires three common items

[9] In another context, strong national identification among Australians meant less welcoming attitude towards asylum seekers, while those who had more of a universalistic and cosmopolitan attitude (identified strongly as 'humans') were more welcoming (Nickerson and Louis 2008).

[10] Notwithstanding, Karyotis and Patrikios (2010) conclude that depending on circumstances religion could worsen prejudices, but it could also help to reduce them.

[11] These nationalities together with Bosniaks and Macedonians are traditional immigrants in Croatia sharing many common linguistic and cultural features. However, they are not at all perceived as

measured a perceived closeness in regard to racial, ethnic and cultural proximity. It was interesting that in 2015 respondents did express a stronger perception of the cultural threat posed by asylum seekers and an inclination for cultural separateness. However, the relatively low level of agreement that asylum seekers should be of similar 'skin colour' as the domestic population points to the fact that the perception of cultural threat does not have to have any connotations of racism.

In our studies public perception of exercising refugee rights and respecting obligations has become accentuated over the years, and varies in significance. Refugees' right to work without a permit is highly rejected among Zagreb residents but not among the sample of students. What might contribute partly to explain this is the fact that students were not (yet) in a position of looking for jobs in the labour market, and thus perceived refugees less in terms of competition. The results indicate that support for the exercise of specific refugee rights is greater among politically left-orientated respondents as well as the less religious. In the 2015 sample, Zagreb residents with higher education agree more that the Croatian Government should ensure the inclusion of refugees in the country's political life and the right to family reunification, as well as granting the same rights to all family members.

Whether public attitudes could change through contact between the domestic population and refugees is a rather provocative question. Following the logic of the contact theory, research by Gregurović et al. (2019) indicates that media portrayals have a significant impact on the possible desirability for the local population to live in a neighbourhood with reception and accommodation facilities for asylum seekers. Those respondents who were more open to establishing some sort of social contact with asylum seekers were also open to living in the vicinity of these facilities. Unlike those respondents 'who perceived asylum seekers as a greater economic and health threat, those who preferred ethnocultural similarity of asylum seekers, and those who perceived asylum seekers as less credible and primarily identified them as economic migrants, expressed a weaker desire to live in the same neighbourhood with them and did not support state-organized asylum seeker reception' (Gregurović et al. 2019, 254).

The role of scholars might be in analysing migration and asylum discourses, and in offering empirically grounded and pragmatic alternatives which will contribute to public debates, expert discussion and engagement of policymakers (Pritchard 1991). We are aware that media sources could have a crucial role in informing the public about the human rights situation across the globe, more prominently than any empirical research. However, media reports could also add to fatigue, apathy and lessening of empathy towards refugees as a desubjectivised, silenced mass of dying and missing bodies in the Mediterranean that one may become desensitised to.

The results obtained in the analysed studies did not indicate a direct correlation between the public attitudes and contact with asylum seekers/refugees and media being the primary source of information about asylum issues. However, the change in public discourse, higher frequency of contact with the asylum seekers and

---

asylum seekers since there are only a few of them nowadays seeking asylum in Croatia according to statistics (MoI 2019).

refugees, and public problematisation of human rights and specific refugee rights remain constant sources of research curiosity and, more importantly, an incentive to objectively investigate and describe the social construction of relations between them. Finally, the captured shift in expressing more negative attitudes among some groups of Croatian citizens reflects the importance of the contextual framework, which largely depends on media portrayals of ongoing political discourses.

The irregularisation and criminalisation of migration has led to the radicalisation of state rhetoric, and to a lowering of solidarity among humanitarian actors (cf. Župarić-Iljić and Valenta 2019). Humanitarian moral claims for resettlement programmes that have brought Syrian refugee families from Turkish camps to Croatia have paradoxically reinforced further restrictions and securitisation policies through justification of violent pushbacks and collective expulsions of irregular, 'undeserving' migrants in transit, who every day try to cross Croatian territory on their way further west. It seems that Croatia adhered to the role of an EU policeman, one 'who will do its best' in order to control EU external borders, and not to become 'a hotspot' itself. At the same time, the lack of integration or mis-implementation of integration policies is rendering the country primarily as a transit country and unattractive for either asylum seekers or already recognised refugees, who also leave after their status is obtained.

Lower economic conditions resulting in burdened socioeconomic emancipation of refugees as well as other institutional problems with their adaptation may bring a social divide and a gap at the level of local communities. Citizens who perceive these problems with integration may undermine the process of social cohesion and communal trust towards asylum seekers and refugees as those who are left on the margins. All this sets the conditions for a depoliticised, securitised and 'humanitarianised' public space in which, in Arendt's words, it seems that outsiders are 'dispossessed of legal personhood and denied of political community' (Gündoğdu 2015, 3), which assists in reaffirming the exclusionary nationhood and sense of belonging, leaving outgroup members aside/outside.

Bibliography

Ajduković, D., Čorkalo Biruški, D., Gregurović, M., Matić Bojić, J., & Župarić-Iljić, D. (2019). *Challenges of Integrating Refugees into Croatian Society: Attitudes of Citizens and the Readiness of Local Communities*. Zagreb: Government of the Republic of Croatia Office for Human Rights and Rights of National Minorities.

Anderson, J. R., & Ferguson, R. (2018). Demographic and ideological correlates of negative attitudes toward asylum seekers: A meta-analytic review. *Australian Journal of Psychology, 70*(1), 18–29.

Augoustinos, M., & Quinn, C. (2003). Social categorization and attitudinal evaluations: Illegal immigrants, refugees, or asylum seekers? *New Review of Social Psychology, 2*(2003), 29–37.

Baričević, V., & Koska, V. (2017). *Stavovi i percepcije domaće javnosti o nacionalnim manjinama, izbjeglicama i migrantima*. Zagreb: Centar za mirovne studije.

Berg, J. A. (2009). Core networks and whites' attitudes toward immigrants and immigration policy. *Public Opinion Quarterly, 73*(1), 7–31.

Bilić, P., Furman, I., & Yildirim, S. (2018). The refugee crisis in the Croatian digital news: Towards a computational political economy of communication. *The Political Economy of Communication, 6*(1), 59–82.
Blitz, B. (2017). Another story: What public opinion data tell us about refugee and humanitarian policy. *Journal on Migration and Human Security, 5*(2), 379–400.
Cowling, M. M., Anderson, J. R., & Ferguson, R. (2019). Prejudice-relevant correlates of attitudes towards refugees: A meta-analysis. *Journal of Refugee Studies*, fey062.
Czymara, C. S., & Schmidt-Catran, A. W. (2017). Refugees unwelcome? Changes in the public acceptance of immigrants and refugees in Germany in the course of Europe's 'Immigration Crisis.' *European Sociological Review, 33*(2017), 735–751.
Čačić-Kumpes, J., Gregurović, S., & Kumpes, J. (2012). Migracija, integracija i stavovi prema imigrantima u Hrvatskoj. *Revija za sociologiju, 42*(3), 305–336.
Dempster, H., & Hargrave, K. (2017). *Understanding Public Attitudes Towards Refugees and Migrants*. Chatham House, The Royal Institute of International Affairs: Working paper 512.
Gregurović, M., Kuti, S., & Župarić-Iljić, D. (2016). Attitudes towards immigrant workers and asylum seekers in Eastern Croatia: Dimensions, determinants and differences. *Migracijske i etničke teme, 32*(1), 91–122.
Gregurović, M., Radeljak Kaufmann, P., Župarić-Iljić, D., & Dujmović, M. (2019). Are attitudes determined by location? Differences in perceptions of asylum seekers between residents of two Zagreb neighbourhoods. *Geoforum, 104*(2019), 244–258.
Gündoğdu, A. (2015). *Rightlessness in an Age of Rights: Hannah Arendt and the Contemporary Struggles of Migrants*. Oxford: Oxford University Press.
Karyotis, G., & Patrikios, S. (2010). Religion, securitization and anti-immigration attitudes: The case of Greece. *Journal of Peace Research, 47*(1), 43–57.
Kasparek, B., & Speer, M. (2015). Of hope. Hungary and the long summer of migration. [online]. Boredrmonitoring.eu, February 9, 2015. https://bordermonitoring.eu/ungarn/2015/09/of-hope-en/. Accessed February 15, 2019.
Klocker, N., & Dunn, K. M. (2003). *Who's driving the asylum debate: Newspaper and government representations of asylum seekers*. University of Wollongong, Faculty of Science, Medicine and Health—Papers (pp. 71–92).
Kumpes, J. (2018). Religioznost i stavovi prema imigrantima u Hrvatskoj. *Migracijske i etničke teme, 34*(3), 275–320.
Ministry of Interior (MoI). (2019). *Statistika – Tražitelji međunarodne zaštite* [online]. https://mup.gov.hr/pristup-informacijama-16/statistika-228/statistika-trazitelji-medjunarodne-zastite/283234. Accessed February 15, 2019.
Nickerson, A. M., & Louis, W. R. (2008). Nationality versus humanity? Personality, identity, and norms in relation to attitudes toward asylum seekers. *Journal of Applied Social Psychology, 38*(3), 796–817.
Nowicka, M., Krzyżowski, Ł, & Ohm, D. (2017). Transnational solidarity, the refugees and open societies in Europe. *Current Sociology, 67*(3), 383–400.
Perkowski, N. (2016). Deaths, interventions, humanitarianism and human rights in the Mediterranean 'Migration Crisis.' *Mediterranean Politics, 21*(2), 331–335.
Pritchard, K. (1991). Human rights: A decent respect for public opinion. *Human Rights Quarterly, 13*, 123–142.
Rustenbach, E. (2010). Sources of negative attitudes toward immigrants in Europe: A multi-level analysis. *International Migration Review, 44*(1), 53–77.
Semyonov, M., Raijman, R., & Gorodzeisky, A. (2006). The rise of antiforeigner sentiment in European societies, 1988–2000. *American Sociological Review, 71*(3), 426–449.
Squire, V. (2009). *The Exclusionary Politics of Asylum*. London and New York: Palgrave Macmillan.
Stephan, W. G., Ybarra, O., Martinez, C., Schwarzwald, J., & Tur-Kaspa, M. (1998). Prejudice toward immigrants to Spain and Israel: An integrated threat theory analysis. *Journal of Cross-Cultural Psychology, 29*(4), 559–576.

Šarić, Lj. (2019). Visual presentation of refugees during the "Refugee Crisis" of 2015–2016 on the online portal of the Croatian public broadcaster. *International Journal of Communication, 13*(2019), 991–1015.
Zoppi, M. (2019). A flow within the flow: Dynamics of 2015 and post-2015 migration from the Western Balkans to EU countries. *Southeastern Europe/L'Europe du Sud-Est, 43*(1), 50–74.
Župarić-Iljić, D., & Gregurović, M. (2013). Stavovi studenata prema tražiteljima azila u Republici Hrvatskoj. *Društvena istraživanja, 22*(1), 41–62.
Župarić-Iljić, D., & Valenta, M. (2019). Refugee Crisis' in the Southeastern European countries: The rise and fall of the Balkan Corridor. In C. Menjívar, M. Ruiz, & I. Ness (Eds.), *The Oxford Handbook of Migration* (pp. 367–388). Oxford: Oxford University Press.

Drago Župarić-Iljić, Ph.D. is a sociologist, working as an Assistant Professor at the Department of Sociology, Faculty of Humanities and Social Sciences, University of Zagreb. He has published articles and chapters within the interdisciplinary fields of forced migration, asylum, ethnicity, population and environmental studies, focusing on various structural causes and drivers of migration, mobility and post-migration phenomena, with a special interest in the Central and South-East European region.

Margareta Gregurović, Ph.D. is a Research Associate at the Institute for Migration and Ethnic Studies, Zagreb, Croatia. In 2014 she received her Ph.D. from the Department of Sociology of the Faculty of Humanities and Social Sciences, University of Zagreb, in the field of sociology of ethnic relations. She has participated in several research projects, published more than twenty scientific papers, and presented at over thirty international scientific conferences. Since 2014 she has been the Executive Editor of the scientific journal *Migration and Ethnic Themes*. Her main research areas include sociology of ethnic relations, sociology of migration, sociology of education and sociological methodology.

Chapter 15
Cosmopolitanism, Nationalism, and Refugees: Implications Revealed Through Slovenian Public Opinion

Barbara Gornik

Abstract The chapter discusses the results of a public opinion poll carried out in November 2015, during a period when between 3,000 and 12,000 migrants transited the Republic of Slovenia daily on the so-called Balkan refugee route. The principal aim of the analysis has been to assess the interrelatedness of the ideals of nationalism and cosmopolitanism on the level of commitment to their particular values and in relation to the endorsement of refugees' rights. The multidimensionality of cosmopolitan and nationalistic attitudes and their relationship to the question of refugees have been investigated. The chapter testifies that respect for the ideals of cosmopolitanism, including human rights on the declarative level, scores high in public opinion; however, considerably less support is given to human rights ideals when respondents assess concrete situations related to the respect of refugees' human rights. Moreover, the results show that nationalism and cosmopolitanism as ideologies and concepts at a normative level do not mutually exclude each other. The chapter argues that although nationalism does not necessarily challenge cosmopolitanism, it adapts it to its own criteria, and, most importantly, affects the perception of cosmopolitan universality by imposing its selective character. It concludes that this is no longer cosmopolitanism as envisioned by cosmopolitans, but cosmopolitanism adjusted to the discourse of the nation-state and therefore necessarily exclusive in terms of state membership.

Keywords Cosmopolitanism · Nationalism · Human rights · Refugees · Public opinion

15.1 Introduction

The relationship between cosmopolitanism and nationalism is an intriguing one. Although for some the notions appear to be in conflict with each other, other scholars persuasively maintain their compatibility (Pogge 1992; Beitz 1999; Tan 2004). The

B. Gornik (✉)
Science and Research Centre Koper, Koper, Slovenia
e-mail: barbara.gornik@zrs-kp.si

M. C. Jacobsen et al. (eds.), *Cosmopolitanism, Migration and Universal Human Rights*, https://doi.org/10.1007/978-3-030-50645-2_15

underlying argument of this chapter is that this relationship cannot be examined only by looking at the incorporation of some basic cosmopolitan principles within nation-state institutions (e.g. cultural diversity and human rights). Any examination of cosmopolitanism must necessarily confront also the question of one's political recognition justified in the idea of humanity. To examine the relationship between cosmopolitanism and nationalism in relation to refugees is revealing, because they are unquestionably 'the place' where cosmopolitanism and nationalism intersect. On one hand, the UN Convention Relating to the Status of Refugees endows refugees with rights, which stem not from nationality but humanity. Yet, on the other hand, refugees' legal personality is, as evident in numerous instances of contemporary dealings with refugees, confronted with and bounded by the interests and politics of nation-states (Gibney 2004).

The recent refugee situation in Europe has been accompanied by both nationalist and cosmopolitan responses. Human rights, as one of key principles of cosmopolitanism, were often evoked by politicians, government officials and representatives of international and nongovernmental organisations. In this context, the use of the term 'human rights' turned out to be uncritical and imprecise, and, even more importantly, able to be incorporated into the ethnic and exclusionary ideological premises of political parties. This brings attention to our concern regarding how to understand the innumerable differences between what is said about human rights and what is done about them. How does one explain these incongruities? Can someone expressing cosmopolitan views while acting in an anti-cosmopolitan manner still be understood to be cosmopolitan?

With the aim to contribute to our understanding of the relationship between cosmopolitanism and nationalism, a public opinion poll was conducted in late October 2015.[1] The research had several goals. Most notably, it aimed to grasp the overall atmosphere manifested in relation to refugees as well as at acquiring insights that might provide a descriptive account of how the Slovenian public comprehends cosmopolitan principles in the context of the Balkan refugee route. How well embedded is the 'cosmopolitan culture', if it is present at all? What is the impact of nationalism's values on the interpretation of refugees' rights? How does public understand the responsibility of the states toward refugees? Do they recognise them as rightful political subjects?

This chapter does not provide a complex statistical analysis of public opinion but rather embarks on some of the highlighted questions by devoting itself to empirically embedded discussion situated within wider theoretical frameworks. The results of the public opinion survey are therefore analytically merged with theoretical argument that arises from scholarship dealing with the nationalism and cosmopolitanism debate. A key standpoint of the present chapter is that cosmopolitanism cannot be

[1] At that time Slovenia had become one of the main transit countries with between 3000 and 12,000 refugees per day passing through its territory and continuing northwards to Austria. The Hungarian border closure in autumn 2015 precipitated the redirection of the Balkan route to Slovenia and finally led to 326,956 refugees crossing Slovenia between 20 October and 15 December 2015. The situation resembled a state of emergency for the government, which activated the entire national security system, including humanitarian and civil protection organisations.

examined in a vacuum of intellectual ideas but needs to be set against the tangible context of practices and implementations. Following this view, this chapter offers an interpretation of the public opinion survey and tackles the question of compatibility between nationalism and cosmopolitanism. The chapter contends that nationalism and cosmopolitanism entail multiple dimensions, and that they are differently related to the rights of refugees. Finally, it turns to the irreconcilability of the concepts, and labels cosmopolitan nationalism a 'doublethink', defined as the power of holding two contradictory beliefs in one's mind simultaneously and accepting both of them.

15.2 Cosmopolitanism and Nationalism

Cosmopolitanism is generally conceived as a subjective outlook, attitude or practice characterised by conscious openness to the world and to cultural differences (Vertovec and Cohen 2002), capacity to mediate between different cultures, recognition of increasing interconnectedness of political communities, and approval of political responsibility at the supranational and global levels (Mau et al. 2008; Beck and Sznaider 2010; Hannerz 1990). It is considered a worldview that imagines a global order in which the idea of human rights is an operative principle of justice (Fine 2009, 8), which builds on recognition of moral obligations owed to all human beings based solely on humanity as such and without reference to race, gender, nationality, ethnicity, etc. (Brown and Held 2013, 1).

Nationalism, in contrast to cosmopolitanism, consists of attitudes that the members of a nation have when they care about their national identity, and the actions that the members of a nation take when seeking to achieve (or sustain) some form of political sovereignty (Miscevic 2018). Nationalism as a sociological notion embraces doctrines or ideologies, movements, sentiments, processes of 'nation-building', symbols and discourses (of nationalism), which, *pace* Smith, are based on three main goals: national autonomy, national unity, and national identity (2003, 187). It relates to interconnected concepts of national community (Hobsbawm 2007), nation-state, ethnicity, self-determination (Kedourie 1961, 9), national identity defined by language (Gellner 1983), faith (Hastings 1997), tradition, social practice, myths, memories and historical experiences (Smith 1991), and state institutions (Breuilly 1993).[2] Nationalism has also been described, in the words of Kohn (1965, 9), as 'a state of mind, in which the supreme loyalty of the individual is felt to be due the nation-state'. Consequently, nationalism is frequently alleged to be anti-cosmopolitan by definition.

Nonetheless, numerous authors do not hold this to be true. Nearly two centuries ago, Mazzini (2009 [1832]) argued that genuine democracy within states, together

[2]In social sciences particularly, nationalism has never been considered as a mere sentiment that an individual expresses towards non-nationals, as, for instance, the word 'nationalist' is commonly used in current political discourse. Rather, it has been regarded as a historical sociopolitical movement that accompanied and facilitated the emergence of nations and nation states, an ideology based on the idea of a nation, nation-state, national history, national interest, national security and so on.

with generalised humanitarian education, would set in motion a moral culture in the name of a common humanity that would challenge the existing practices of exclusion. In the same vein, contemporary thinkers maintain that there is no necessary conflict between cosmopolitanism and nationalism. For instance, Pogge (1992, 49), Beitz (1999, 287) and, more recently, Tan (2004, 93–96) have advocated for a distinction between *moral* and *institutional* cosmopolitanism, within which the former is regarded as consistent with the nation-state system; here, cosmopolitanism is explained as a moral basis—a standpoint based on human rights and the position that all persons stand in ultimate units of moral concern—on which the aim, policies and measures of the state institutions should be decided. Moral cosmopolitanism is thus not concerned with the question of establishing world government but represents an ethical line of reasoning regarding the nation-state institutions and their policies, which build on equal human worth, human rights and dignity. In this way, it is not inconsistent with the existence of autonomous territorial states and not at odds with nationalism. On the contrary, argues Tan (2004, 94), moral cosmopolitan can defend national self-determination if one believes that the ideal of equal and impartial concern for individuals is best realised within the framework of national sovereignty.

A similar argument was put forward by authors who have tended to reconcile cosmopolitanism and nationalism through the concept of a *liberal* or *civic* nationalism, which rests on human rights principles and liberal values, such as individual autonomy, cultural neutrality and diversity, social justice and democracy. Liberal nationalism, often also called universalist, inclusive and even cosmopolitan nationalism (Nielsen 1999), is in contrast to ethnic nationalism explained as bounded by common political principles and institutions (human rights principles and liberal values) and allows individuals from various ethnic backgrounds to enter a national community by committing themselves to loyalty to the public institutions and way of life of their residential homeland (Brown 2000; Kohn 1944; Ignatieff 1993; Kymlicka 2001).

15.3 Cosmopolitanism and Nationalism in Public Opinion

The relational complexity identified through the work of Pogge (1992), Beitz (1999) and Tan (2004), among others, clearly indicates that nationalism and cosmopolitanism are not necessarily contradicting concepts. Nevertheless, our study intended to test this assumption at the level of people's attitudes, views and opinions. To allow generalisations with a sufficient degree of precision and certainty, 570 individuals above 18 years of age were involved in the study.[3] The questionnaire used in the

[3]Of the 570 individuals, 279 (48.9%) were male and 291 (51.1%) were female. Among the participants 53.0% had graduated from high-school and 39.1% from university (undergraduate or postgraduate degree). The smallest proportion of respondents had primary school education or less (7.9%). The respondents were divided by age into five classes: between 15 and 29 years (10.0%), 30 and

public opinion survey consisted of items concerning basic principles of cosmopolitanism, nationalism values and refugees' rights. A five-point Likert scale was used to rate the degree to which respondents agree or disagree with each statement. Textual interpretation in the following pages is based on summing up the responses indicating agreement (all 'agree' and 'strongly agree' responses) and disagreement (all 'disagree' and 'strongly disagree' responses), whereas tables retain the original five-point scale and indicate all responses separately. As already explained, the principal aim of the analysis has been to assess the interrelatedness of the ideals of nationalism and cosmopolitanism on the level of commitment to their particular values and in relation to the endorsement of refugees' rights. Additionally, the survey aimed to grasp the overall atmosphere manifesting in relation to refugee situation as well as to acquire insight that might provide a descriptive account of how the Slovenian public comprehends cosmopolitan principles in the context of the Balkan refugee route.

In regard to the question of compatibility, the study clearly reveals that to be both a cosmopolitan and a nationalist is not an impossible pursuit. For instance, the highest support was expressed in relation to the statements 'Human rights should be the fundamental principle of all political action' (agreed by 88.0%) and 'I am proud of my national identity' (80.8%). Respondents also commonly agreed that 'In case of massive human rights violation international institutions should intervene' (agreed by 74.8%), that 'Our children should be raised in the spirit of harmony of cultural diversity regardless of the interests of particular national interests' (agreed by 74.2%) and that 'It is important that every nation have their own state' (agreed by 67.9%). The results revealingly confirmed low levels of disagreement in the case of all statements (Table 15.1).

Clearly, one can at once be proud of one's national identity and endorse human rights as a key principle of all political actions, and simultaneously advocate the system of nation-states and defend cultural diversity, etc. Yet the concern is that these opinions reflect a simplistic endorsement of cosmopolitan and nationalist values, which are affected by social desirability concerns. As noted in several studies (see Chung and Monroe 2003), people have a need to appear more altruistic than they actually are; they tend to deny socially undesirable actions and behaviours and to admit to socially desirable ones. How could one oppose human rights as one of the fundamental moral standards of contemporary societies? How could one criticise cultural diversity, valued as it is in liberal societies?

What could be concluded from this is that political tolerance and general views expressed in the survey are indeed an important aspect of measuring commitment to cosmopolitanism and nationalism, but too narrow in scope. The idea of cosmopolitanism might in this case indeed prove to be, as noted by Kendall et al. (2009, 12), 'in danger of being an almost meaningless and glib catchphrase', which suffers from the problems of indeterminacy and identification (ibid., 14); it appears essential, then, to assess people's commitments at the level of politics and measures taken even at the cost of the nation (see McFarland and Mathews 2005). Such

44 years (21.2%), 45 and 59 years (33.0%) and over 75 years (9.3%). 93.0% of the participants were ethnic Slovenians; 97% had Slovenian citizenship.

Table 15.1 Public opinion on intersections of human rights and nationalism values

	Strongly agree (%)	Agree (%)	Neither agree nor disagree (%)	Disagree (%)	Strongly disagree (%)
Human rights should be the fundamental principle of all political action	63.8	24.2	7.1	2.1	2.8
I am proud of my national identity	51.1	29.7	13.7	4.3	1.3
In case of massive human rights violation international institutions should intervene	46.8	28.0	15.5	4.3	5.4
Our children should be raised in the spirit of harmony of cultural diversity regardless of the interests of particular national interests	51.0	23.2	14.9	3.9	7.1
It is important that every nation have their own state	48.7	19.2	15.2	7.5	9.3

an approach explicitly addresses not only principled ideas, sentiments, empathy, emotional commitment, openness or intellectual domains but also practical effects, outcomes and consequences, which are more accurate indicators of cosmopolitanism and nationalism.

Public opinion therefore needed to be further examined in relation to more contextualised statements. The results in these cases showed that the inclination toward cosmopolitanism is not as strong as previously presented percentages suggest. For example, this could be seen in connection to the statements 'Members of my nation should have precedence over members of other nations' (agreed by 56.1%), 'The distress of people in Syria personally worries me' (agreed by 51.3%), 'If the existence of my country is threatened, the government can limit some basic human rights' (agreed by 47.3%) and 'I could never feel the same affiliation towards humanity that I feel toward my own nation' (agreed by 45.1%). Lower levels of agreement were expressed when responding to the statements 'People have to support their country even if the government is not always right' (41.6%) and 'Slovenia should contribute to reducing world poverty' (40.7%) (Table 15.2).

15.4 Rights of Refugees

The survey additionally examined commitment to cosmopolitanism and nationalism in relation to refugees. The study aimed to achieve an insight into how refugees appear in people's views. Do they acknowledge responsibility of state toward refugees? Do they recognise refugees as rightful political subjects? The results indicated that respondents generally express ambiguity concerning refugees' situations and that their opinions oscillate between at times conflicting nationalist, humanitarian, security and cosmopolitan concerns. This was mainly evident from respondents who largely agreed that 'Refugees are individuals, who need our protection' (agreed by 71.9%) and at the same time stated that 'Only those who are willing to accept the Slovenian way of life should be accepted' (agreed by 71.3%). While more than half of the respondents believed that 'The refugee crisis is primarily a security problem' (agreed by 55.1%), less than half of them thought that 'The refugee crisis must be approached with humanitarian actions (not by army or police)' (agreed by 43.8%). The absence of openness to other cultures and cultural diversity was manifested in the fact that only approximately one-fifth of respondents thought that 'Refugees bring cultural wealth' (agreed by 21.5%) and that 'Refugees should be given access to Slovenian citizenship' (agreed by 25.3%).

Furthermore, the prioritisation of nationals over non-nationals as a distinct nationalist tendency has been voiced through low levels of agreement with the standpoint that 'The rights of refugees are equally important as the rights of nationals' (agreed by 35.8%). On the other hand, respondents generally agreed that 'Refugees should only be allowed to stay for a temporary period until the situation in their country is settled' (agreed by 64.4%). A fairly unreceptive attitude was also identified in relation to economic migrants coming through the Balkan refugee route: respondents

Table 15.2 Public opinion on endorsement of cosmopolitan and nationalism values

	Strongly agree (%)	Agree (%)	Neither agree nor disagree (%)	Disagree (%)	Strongly disagree (%)
Members of my nation should have precedence over members of other nations	36.2	19.9	16.6	10.4	16.9
The distress of people in Syria personally worries me	23.7	27.6	25.4	10.2	13.2
If the existence of my country is threatened, the government can limit some basic human rights	23.3	24.0	21.5	12.4	18.8
I could never feel the same affiliation towards humanity that I feel toward my own nation	27.2	17.9	22.5	14.4	18.0
People have to support their country even if the government is not always right	27.8	13.8	18.2	17.2	23.0
Slovenia should contribute to reducing world poverty	16.4	19.7	25.8	13.5	24.6

generally agreed that 'Economic migrants have to be returned back to their home countries' (agreed by 71.2%). Less than half of the respondents supported the position that 'Refugees should be allowed to enjoy an equitable life in Slovenian society as soon as possible' (agreed by 41.2%) (Table 15.3).

Respondents generally disagreed that 'Refugees on their way to Germany should be prevented from entering the Slovenian state' (disagreed by 56.7%) and thought that 'All EU countries, including Slovenia, should share the burden on the principle of solidarity' (agreed by 69.3%). Less than half of the respondents held that the Slovenian 'Government should lead an "open-door" asylum policy' (agreed by 49.0%), while 26.3% said that 'Refugees should be removed from the country as soon as possible'. Almost one-third of respondents (32.8%) suggested that 'Other countries should provide for refugees' (Table 15.4).

If the government attempted to prevent entry into the Republic of Slovenia to all refugees, 19.8% respondents said they 'would oppose to the best of their ability' and 6.3% that they 'would resist strongly'. Nearly half of the respondents held that they 'would not feel good about it, but would not object (46.0%), while 28.0% of them 'would approve such measure'. Revealingly, from the list of issues that they find the most important in the light of the present refugee crisis, nearly half of the respondents chose the 'protection of Slovenian citizens' (48.6%), 38% opted for 'solving the situation in Syria, Afghanistan and other war zones', while only 11.4% of the respondents opted for the 'respect of refugees' rights' (Fig. 15.1).

Respondents were also asked which of the listed governmental measures they would support in the event that 10,000 refugees stayed in Slovenia. Again, commitment to cosmopolitan human rights goals ranked lower than the goals that serve national security and control. High agreement was evidenced in relation to 'Depriving free movement for all refugees, who cause civil disorder' (86.2%), 'Reinforcement of state border control' (supported by 70.2%), 'Increase of police and military jurisdiction' (supported by 57.2%) and 'Widening of the network of volunteers and public workers' (supported by 55.1%). On the other hand, respondents were generally not in favour of measures that would restrain civil liberties. Approximately one-third expressed support for 'Restraining refugees' right to privacy' (supported by 37.5%), 'Prohibition of public protest' (supported by 35.4%), 'Strict border control' (supported by 26.2%) and 'Media censorship' (supported by 25.0%). A low level of support was expressed in relation to 'Increase of financial resources for a safe and proper reception of refugees' (supported by 33.2%) and 'Refugee-friendly asylum policy' (supported by 36.4%) (Table 15.5).

As evident from the results, public opinion poll results display rather unreceptive attitudes toward refugees in terms of recognition of their rights and inclusion into society, let alone viewing refugees as equal counterparts to nationals. However, one must acknowledge that from a juridical point of view, the UN *1951 Refugee Convention* creates moral and legal obligations for state parties to provide shelter to foreigners in need of protection and thereby overcomes the legal gap of their lack of state rights, which would otherwise exist due to their non-membership. The right to seek and enjoy asylum in this respect becomes a decisive cosmopolitan category because it establishes a legal channel and constitutes political and legal standing for

Table 15.3 Public opinion on the rights of refugees

	Strongly agree (%)	Agree (%)	Neither agree nor disagree (%)	Disagree (%)	Strongly disagree (%)
Refugees are individuals, who need our protection	51.2	20.7	14.0	7.2	6.9
Only those who are willing to accept the Slovenian way of life should be accepted	37.1	19.3	19.1	10.2	14.3
The refugee crisis is primarily a security problem	35.0	20.1	18.4	12.9	13.7
The refugee crisis must be approached with humanitarian actions (not by army or police)	25.6	18.2	26.1	12.6	17.5
Refugees bring cultural wealth	9.6	11.9	19.8	18.6	40.0
Refugees should be given access to Slovenian citizenship	9.5	15.8	20.4	17.2	37.1
The rights of refugees are equally important as the rights of nationals	22.5	13.3	15.9	16.7	31.5
Refugees should only be allowed to stay for a temporary period until the situation in their country is settled	46.8	17.6	19.9	7.4	8.4
Economic migrants have to be returned back to their home countries	53.3	17.9	13.3	7.1	8.4

(continued)

Table 15.3 (continued)

	Strongly agree (%)	Agree (%)	Neither agree nor disagree (%)	Disagree (%)	Strongly disagree (%)
Refugees should be allowed to enjoy an equitable life in Slovenian society as soon as possible	20.6	20.6	20.9	15.0	22.9

Table 15.4 Public opinion on European and national asylum policy

	Strongly agree (%)	Agree (%)	Neither agree nor disagree (%)	Disagree (%)	Strongly disagree (%)
Refugees on their way to Germany should be prevented from entering the Slovenian state	17.4	9.4	16.5	16.3	40.4
All EU countries, including Slovenia, should share the burden on the principle of solidarity	51.0	18.3	12.8	8.0	9.8
Government should lead an 'open-door' asylum policy	27.2	21.8	24.6	13.9	12.5
Refugees should be removed from the country as soon as possible	20.0	6.3	22.9	18.2	32.7
Other countries should provide for refugees	18.0	14.8	28.1	13.7	25.4

refugees, paving a way to active membership and enabling individuals to regain their political and legal identity.

Despite this, the poll results evidence preference for nationalism over cosmopolitanism, manifested in the fact that refugees were not recognised as 'citizens of the world', as rights-bearing subjects to whom protection is owed, as one can understand the provisions of international law. This essentially indicates an absence of an effective cosmopolitan view which would potentially enable the recognition of their political and legal personality. What can be concluded from the results presented in this section is that the language of empathy, human rights, tolerance and cultural openness expressed at the level of principles and ideals does not enforce a cosmopolitan political standing, but, rather, following Gündoğdu (2015, 76), renders 'the subjects of those rights extremely precarious, as always dependent on the generosity and goodwill of compassionate others'.

15.5 Compatibility of Cosmopolitanism and Nationalism

As seen in the previous section, nationalism and cosmopolitanism work well together when their values are articulated in the form of general ideas and commitment to their values. Nevertheless, it could be assumed that cosmopolitanism represents a creed that offers argumentation for recognition of refugees' political status and rights attached to it, and that, on the other hand, nationalism, as an ideology giving preference to national community and nation-state, is consequently less inclined to respect refugees' rights.

From these starting points, an iterated principal factor analysis was performed on the questionnaire and five factors were extracted: (1) nationalism, which measured national pride and commitment to the values of nation and nation-state; (2) cosmopolitanism, which was tied to commitment to the values of human rights,

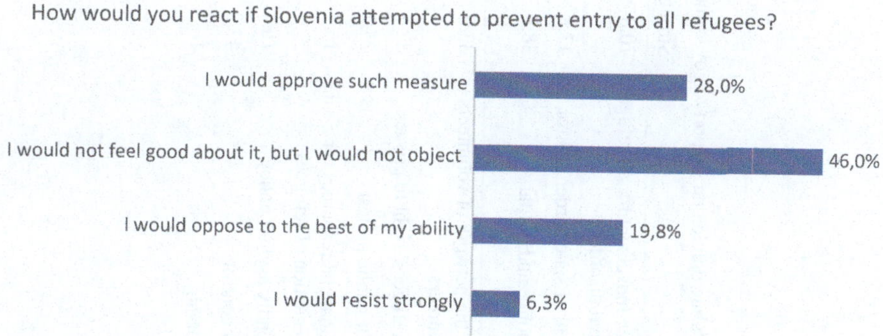

Fig. 15.1 Public opinion on preventing entry to refugees

Table 15.5 Public opinion on support to governmental measures in regard to reception of refugees

	Strongly support (%)	Support (%)	Neither support nor oppose (%)	Oppose (%)	Strongly oppose (%)
Depriving free movement for all refugees who cause civil disorder	70.8	15.4	8.6	1.4	3.7
Reinforcement of state border control	47.8	22.4	15.6	5.8	8.4
Increase of police and military jurisdiction	38.8	18.4	16.4	10.6	15.8
Widening of the network of volunteers and public workers	33.9	21.2	16.7	7.7	20.5
Restraining refugees' right to privacy	22.7	14.8	24.4	15.5	22.6
Prohibition of public protest	25.2	10.2	16.1	14.0	34.6
Increase of financial resources for a safe and proper reception of refugees	16.7	16.5	21.7	15.6	29.6
Refugee-friendly asylum policy	16.4	20.0	26.1	14.2	23.3
Strict border control	47.8	22.4	15.6	5.8	8.4
Media censorship	16.2	8.8	17.0	12.8	45.2

openness to cultural differences of empathy, coexistence with all the world's inhabitants and willingness to share one's resources on a global level; (3) humanitarianism, which consisted of claims of support and assistance to refugees and asylum seekers, humanitarian actions, supporting a humanitarian corridor and decent reception of refugees; (4) security related to the claims of the refugee crisis as a security problem, border control, imprisonment, increasing the competence of the army and the police, restricting movement, interfering with the right to privacy of refugee; and (5) inclusion, which was comprised of claims regarding the importance of refugee rights, access to citizenship, temporary residence, return of refugees, sharing of responsibilities for reception of refugees.

The analysis of the results confirmed that correlations for most of the concepts are statistically significant. Thus, it was established that the concepts of nationalism and cosmopolitanism predispose the endorsement of refugee rights. Participants who express greater support for the values of cosmopolitanism express greater support for the humanitarian treatment of refugees; they are more inclined towards the integration of refugees into Slovenian society, and fewer are in favour of security measures to tackle the refugee crisis. Likewise, the analysis confirmed that nationalism is negatively correlated with a humanitarian and inclusive approach to refugees, and positively correlated with security concerns. Participants who expressed greater support for nationalism values tended to be more inclined to support security measures and less inclined to accept and help refugees (Table 15.6).

Remarkably, the analysis also confirmed that the correlation between cosmopolitanism and nationalism is not statistically significant. Respondents who expressed high support for values of nationalism could also equally and simultaneously support the principles of cosmopolitanism. This is particularly interesting since it implies an implicit compatibility of cosmopolitan and nationalism values, which, however, in relation to refugees, reveals its real character. The findings moreover support the contention that nationalism and cosmopolitanism attitudes entail multiple dimensions, and that they are differentially related to rights of refugees.

Table 15.6 Correlations between concepts of humanitarianism, nationalism, security, inclusion and cosmopolitanism

	Humanitarianism	Nationalism	Security	Inclusion	Cosmopolitanism
Humanitarianism		−0.276**	−0.591**	0.769**	0.548**
Nationalism	−0.276****		0.484**	−0.407**	−0.058
Security	−0.591**	0.484**		−0.669**	−0.248**
Inclusion	0.769**	−0.407**	−0.669**		0.470**
Cosmopolitanism	0.548**	−0.058	−0.248**	0.470**	

**Correlation is significant at the 0.01 level (2-tailed)

15.5.1 Cosmopolitanism as 'Doublethink'

Is it possible that nationalism and cosmopolitanism are compatible and incompatible at the same time? Compatible at the level of ideas and incompatible at the level of practice? What does this mean in terms of our analysis of the relationship between nationalism and cosmopolitanism? It was indicated earlier that when analysing the interplay between nationalism and cosmopolitanism, a political dimension manifesting in a form of recognition of rights stemming from one's humanity must be acknowledged as one key element defining the complementarity of nationalist and cosmopolitan outlooks. For social sciences, concerned more with 'how things are' than with 'how things should be', this is a necessary twist, which offers an argument grounded in an empirical perspective.

Pursuing this perspective, it is necessary to identify principles as the ultimate rule, which manifest in political and social practices. We can clearly observe that many states across the globe tend to incorporate the idea of human rights into their policies, providing proof that cosmopolitanism can exist within policies and institutions. Missing, however, from such a view is more scrutiny examining what happens beyond what is manifestly visible—what are the rules upon which contemporary politics is ultimately decided? Is it cosmopolitan or nationalist principles that represent the ultimate criterion of political decision? To discuss this question, we turn to Schmitt and his well-known understanding of exception, which to him is more important than the rule, because it goes deeper than the clear generalisations inferred from what ordinarily repeats in the form of a rule: 'The rule proves nothing; the exception proves everything' (Schmitt 2005, 15). Moral cosmopolitanism, which manifests in repetition within state institutions, is powerless if it does not confirm itself also as the rule of exception. But, as has been noted by Agamben, among others, in the 'state of exception', i.e. when 'refugees no longer represent individual cases but rather a mass phenomenon [...]—all the solemn evocations of the inalienable rights of human beings notwithstanding—have proved to be absolutely incapable not only of solving the problem but also of facing it in an adequate manner' (Agamben 2008, 92).

In fact, even in ordinary circumstances, we somewhat tend to neglect that also 'cosmopolitan' nationalism is exclusive. Brubaker (2004, 141) offers an insightful argument when saying that civic or liberal nationalism is deemed inclusive for it is based on citizenship, which includes all citizens, regardless of their particularistic ethnic origin. However, as he points out, what is often ignored in such accounts is that citizenship itself, by its very nature, is an exclusive category and an extremely powerful instrument of social closure and that access to citizenship is everywhere limited, often on very anti-cosmopolitan grounds. In the words of Brubaker, citizenship shields prosperous and peaceful states from the great majority of those who, in a world without borders and exclusive citizenries, would seek to flee war, civil strife, famine, joblessness or environmental degradation (ibid.).

What can be deduced from Brubaker's observation is that the relationship between them is fundamentally antagonistic—namely, as understood by Laclau and Mouffe, antagonism is when 'the presence of the "Other" prevents me from being totally myself' (Laclau and Mouffe 2001, 125)—since pursuing cosmopolitan principles entirely makes nationalism impossible, and, vice versa, the existence of nations and nation-states is based on exclusion of non-members. In other words, nation-states exist when the principles of cosmopolitanism are adapted to their conditions of existence, and these are essentially related to border control, national membership, exclusion and population management. As Balibar (2004, 318) maintains, in the world of nation-states the difference between citizenship and humanity must in practice subsist in order for the 'people' to remain a political subject, a community of belonging, and not be dissolved into a multitude of individualities who are simply bearers of a demand to be governed by authorities of their choice and under their control, as it could be formulated by cosmopolitanism. Despite the antagonism between nationalism and cosmopolitanism, we saw that their relationship is defined by what George Orwell famously called a *doublethink*, that is, by the ability of holding two contradictory beliefs in one's mind simultaneously and accepting both.

15.6 Conclusion

Exploring the opinion of the Slovenian public concerning cosmopolitanism reveals that its principles are *a priori* understood as something good, positive, useful and moral, and cannot be investigated solely at the level of an abstract commitment. Normative claims about cosmopolitanism are supplied with social desirability concerns and attract a high level of agreement, although this does not confirm that people also give priority to its values in real-life circumstances. Regardless of high levels of support expressed in relation to cosmopolitan ideals, respondents at the same time expressed considerably higher levels of restrictive attitudes, prioritising security issues and national self-interest when asked about rights of refugees. The public opinion poll's results displayed rather unreceptive attitudes toward refugees in terms of recognition of their rights and inclusion into society, let alone viewing refugees as equal counterparts to nationals.

Seen from this is the preference of nationalism over cosmopolitanism, manifest in the fact that refugees were not recognised as rights-bearing subjects to whom protection is owed. The results presented in this chapter indicate that the language of empathy, human rights and tolerance is not sufficient to enforce cosmopolitan political standing and recognition of human rights of 'others'. Precisely for this reason, refugees are a potent subject in determining how efficient and far-reaching cosmopolitanism is when confronted with nationalism. Contrary to Nielsen (1999, 446), who states that to be a cosmopolitan is to identify and have a commitment to and a concern for all of humankind, it can be claimed that cosmopolitanism should be considered more far-reaching than that—cosmopolitanism is not only about a wide variety of forms of life, practices, art forms, languages, religions, cuisines, but essentially involves recognition of the political, legal and moral standing of an individual based on his/her belonging to humanity.

Finally, the results established that the concepts of nationalism and cosmopolitanism predispose the endorsement of refugee rights and at the same time indicated their multidimensional interrelatedness. Despite the fact that respondents generally express ambiguous views concerning the refugee situation, their opinions at times oscillate between conflicting nationalist, humanitarian, security and cosmopolitan concerns. From this perspective some principles of nationalism and cosmopolitanism have proven to have the ability to appear in one's mind simultaneously and be accepted regardless of their logical contradictions. As shown in the chapter, the relationship between cosmopolitanism and nationalism is not only complementary or contradictory but also antagonistic one, since consistent and unconditional implementation of cosmopolitan principles in fact runs counter to existence of nations and nation-states.

Bibliography

Agamben, G. (2008). Beyond human rights. *Open 15: Social Engineering, 15*(2008), 90–95.

Balibar, É. (2004). Is a philosophy of human civic rights possible? New reflections on equaliberty. *The South Atlantic Quarterly, 103*(2/3), 311–322.

Beck, U., & Sznaider, N. (2010). Unpacking cosmopolitanism for the social sciences: A research agenda: Unpacking cosmopolitanism for the social sciences. *The British Journal of Sociology, 61*(1), 381–403.

Beitz, C. R. (1999). International liberalism and distributive justice: A survey of recent thought. *World Politics, 51*(2), 269–296.

Breuilly, J. (1993). *Nationalism and the state*. Manchester: Manchester University Press.

Brown, D. (2000). *Contemporary nationalism*. London: Routledge.

Brown, G. W., & Held, D. (2013). *The cosmopolitanism reader*. Cambridge, UK: Polity.

Brubaker, R. (2004). *Ethnicity without groups*. Cambridge: Harvard University Press.

Chung, J., & Monroe, G. S. (2003). Exploring social desirability bias. *Journal of Business Ethics, 44*(4), 291–302.

Fine, R. (2009). Cosmopolitanism and human rights: Radicalism in a global age. *Metaphilosophy, 40*(1), 8–23.

Gellner, E. (1983). *Nations and nationalism*. Oxford: Basil Blackwell.

Gibney, M. J. (2004). *The ethics and politics of asylum: Liberal democracy and the response to refugees*. Cambridge: Cambridge University Press.

Gündoğdu, A. (2015). *Rightlessness in an age of rights: Hannah Arendt and the contemporary struggles of migrants*. Oxford: Oxford University Press.

Halikiopoulou, D., Mock, S., & Vasilopoulou, S. (2013). The Civic Zeitgeist: Nationalism and liberal values in the European radical right: The Civic Zeitgeist. *Nations and Nationalism, 19*(1), 107–127.

Hannerz, U. (1990). Cosmopolitans and locals in world culture. *Theory, Culture & Society, 7*(1990), 237–251.

Hastings, A. (1997). *The construction of nationhood: Ethnicity, religion, and nationalism*. Cambridge: Cambridge University Press.

Hobsbawm, E. J. (2007). *Nations and nationalism since 1780: Programme, myth, reality*. Cambridge: Cambridge University Press.

Ignatieff, M. (1993). *Blood and belonging: Journeys into the new nationalism*. New York: Farrar, Straus, and Giroux.

Kedourie, E. (1961). *Nationalism*. London: Hutchinson University Library.

Kendall, G., Woodward, I., & Skrbiš, Z. (2009). *The sociology of cosmopolitanism: Globalization, identity, culture and government*. Houndmills: Palgrave MacMillan.
Kohn, H. (1944). *The idea of nationalism: A study in its origins and background*. New York: Macmillan.
Kohn, H. (1965). *Nationalism. Its meaning and history*. Princeton, NJ: Van Nostrand.
Kymlicka, W. (2001). *Politics in the vernacular: Nationalism, multiculturalism and citizenship*. Oxford: Oxford University Press.
Laclau, E., & Mouffe, C. (2001). *Hegemony and socialist strategy: Towards a radical democratic politics*. London: Verso.
Marshall, T. H. (1950). *Citizenship and social class, and other essays*. Cambridge: Cambridge University Press.
Mau, S., Mewes, J., & Zimmermann, A. (2008). Cosmopolitan attitudes through transnational social practices? *Global Networks, 8*(1), 1–24.
Mazzini, G. (2009 [1832]). On the superiority of representative government. In S. Recchia & N. Urbinati (Eds.), *A cosmopolitanism of nations Giuseppe Mazzini's writings on democracy, nation building, and international relations* (pp. 39–52). Princeton, NJ: Princeton University Press.
McFarland, S., & Mathews, M. (2005). Who cares about human rights? *Political Psychology, 26*(3), 365–385.
Miscevic, N. (2018). Nationalism. *The Stanford Encyclopedia of Philosophy* (Summer 2018 Edition). In E. N. Zalta (Ed.). https://plato.stanford.edu/archives/sum2018/entries/nationalism/. Accessed September 21, 2019.
Nielsen, K. (1999). Cosmopolitan nationalism. *Monist, 5*(4), 446–465.
Pogge, T. W. (1992). Cosmopolitanism and sovereignty. *Ethics, 103*(1), 48–75.
Schmitt, C. (2005). *Political theology: Four chapters on the concept of sovereignty*. Chicago: University of Chicago Press.
Smith, A. D. (1991). *National identity*. London: Penguin Books.
Smith, A. D. (2003). *Nationalism and modernism: A critical survey of recent theories of nations and nationalism*. London and New York: Routledge.
Tan, K.-C. (2004). *Justice without borders: Cosmopolitanism, nationalism, and patriotism*. New York: Cambridge University Press.
Vertovec, S., & Cohen, R. (2002). *Conceiving cosmopolitanism: Theory, context and practice*. New York: Oxford University Press.

Barbara Gornik is a Research Associate at the Institute for Social Studies at Science and Research Centre of Koper, Slovenia. Her research interests are migration, nationalism and human rights, which she studies using the anthropology and discourse theory as basic theoretical framework to explain the implementation and interpretation of human rights within the knowledge/power nexus. She has published works dealing with asylum, refugees, unaccompanied minor migrants, international human rights law, erased residents of Slovenia, governmentality and anthropology of human rights. Currently, she works as academic co-coordinator of the Horizon 2020 Research and Innovation project 'Migrant Children and Communities in a Transforming Europe'.

Chapter 16
Volunteering for Change: Practicing Transborder Citizenship in Grassroots Volunteer Networks in Support of Refugees in Northern Europe

Lydia Maria Kirchner and Line Steen Bygballe

Abstract Taking as our point of departure the complex socio-political landscape in the wake of the arrival of a large number of refugees into Europe in 2015, this article analyzes the everyday practices of the grassroots volunteer networks that formed to support refugees in Berlin and Copenhagen. Based on ethnographic fieldwork conducted in 2017, and with theoretical inspiration from a *performative approach* to data collection and analysis, the chapter investigates the activities of the volunteers in the networks researched as enactments of *transborder citizenship*. It thereby builds on the concepts of *acts of citizenship* and *borderwork*. Exploring the multiple ways of performing transborder citizenship in the grassroots volunteer networks, the article argues that they function as platforms for negotiating and practicing alternative structures for political participation. They thereby point to questions concerning the realities, opportunities and challenges for cosmopolitanism on a civil societal level.

Keywords Volunteering · Grassroots networks · Transborder citizenship · Forced migration · Civil society · Northern Europe

16.1 Introduction

The words of the German chancellor Angela Merkel 'Wir schaffen das' ('We can do it') became emblematic of the German reaction to the more than one million refugees[1] arriving into the European Union during 2015, particularly from Syria, Afghanistan

[1] UNHCR defines refugees as: '[…] someone who has been forced to flee his or her country because of persecution, war, or violence. A refugee has a well-founded fear of persecution for reasons of race, religion, nationality, political opinion or membership in a particular social group' (UNHCR 2017).

L. M. Kirchner · L. S. Bygballe (✉)
European Ethnology, University of Copenhagen, Copenhagen, Denmark
e-mail: linebygballejensen@gmail.com

L. M. Kirchner
e-mail: lydia.m.kirchner@gmail.com

M. C. Jacobsen et al. (eds.), *Cosmopolitanism, Migration and Universal Human Rights*, https://doi.org/10.1007/978-3-030-50645-2_16

and Eritrea, as a consequence of years of wars and armed conflicts in the world (UNHCR 2015; Die Zeit 2015). In the context of a Europe in crisis in which the EU member states struggled with managing the reception of refugees, Germany took on a leading position in the attempt to find a common European solution. Germany's strategy at the time was to temporarily halt the enforcement of the Dublin Regulation[2] and to welcome the people seeking refuge (Thränhardt 2019). This resulted in more than 890,000 refugees arriving in Germany in 2015 (Eurostat 2016). Germany's initial approach stood in contrast to the reaction from the neighbouring country Denmark, where the strategy from the liberal-led government was characterised by tightening of regulations for refugees to achieve asylum and the reinforcement of border control (Politiken 2015; Udlændinge- og Integrationsministeriet 2016).

However, 'Wir schaffen das' echoed amongst parts of a polarised civil society in Europe (Hamann and Karakayali 2016, 96). Throughout Europe, citizens took a stance against the anti-refugee, right-wing movement that was rising, amongst others by finding ways to welcome and support the arriving refugees (Schiffauer et al. 2017; Toubøl 2015). Therefore, the 'summer of migration' of 2015 has also been characterised as 'the summer of welcome' (Karakayali and Kleist 2016).

In Denmark and Germany, thousands of people demonstrated their feelings of solidarity with the refugees arriving into their local communities (DR 2015a; Die Zeit 2015). In the form of grassroots volunteer networks, citizens amongst others started to take the matter into their own hands by welcoming and supporting refugees in their local contexts. Thus, in 2015 there was a growing and diverse landscape of grassroots volunteer initiatives that supported refugees in both Germany and Denmark. The plurality of small grassroots volunteer networks was especially salient in cities such as Berlin and Copenhagen.

Scholars across disciplines have increasingly been looking into the 'the summer of welcome' and the volunteer initiatives as a societal as well as a political phenomenon investigating it, amongst others, with respect to social movement theory (e.g. Toubøl 2015; Hamann and Piening 2017; Karakayali and Kleist 2016), (trans)national solidarity and identities (e.g. Rozakou 2016; Hamann and Karakayali 2016; BIM 2017; Schiffauer et al. 2017) and the (re)bordering of European space (e.g. Sandberg 2018; Helping Hands 2019). While much of the initial research on the grassroots volunteer initiatives built on empirical material from a national context, calls for studies that investigate the phenomenon from a comparative cross-border perspective have become louder (Karakayali and Kleist 2016, 6; Helping Hands 2019). The study underlying this article conforms to these endeavours by considering the phenomenon from a Northern European perspective.

Building on ethnographic research from Berlin and Copenhagen,[3] this article explores how the grassroots volunteer networks relate to European and global issues

---

[2]The Dublin Regulation determines which EU member state is responsible for processing the asylum applications. The Dublin Regulation states that usually the responsible member state will be the state through which the asylum seeker first entered the EU (EC 2017a).

[3]The research was carried out in the context of a M.A. thesis as part of the Master's program of Applied Cultural Analysis at the faculty of European Ethnology at the University of Copenhagen (Kirchner and Steen Bygballe 2017). The research was furthermore connected to the Helping Hands

on a local level. The article analyses the different scales at play in the daily activities of the grassroots volunteer networks, as well as the underlying rationales and motivations. This is done by using mundane, everyday life as an ethnological entrance point (Löfgren 2014). Thereby this article argues for an understanding of the grassroots networks as platforms for practicing *transborder citizenship.*

The research that underlies this article adopts a dynamic and situated understanding of scales such as the local, national, European or global context. This is in line with methodological endeavours within the social sciences to deconstruct rather than reproduce the static confinement of scales and border setting used in political and legal frameworks, in particular in connection to the nation state (Berking 2006, 9; Glick Schiller and Wimmer 2003, 576). Accordingly, this chapter takes inspiration from the approach of *methodological cosmopolitanism* that Ulrich Beck and Natan Sznaider introduce, amongst others, as a productive entrance point to overcome conceptual dualism and instead analyse how different scales are active simultaneously in practices on all social and political fields and levels, e.g. as transborder or transnational activities (Beck and Sznaider 2006, 9). Our understanding of the volunteering activities as practices of transborder citizenship borrows from two central concepts that are likewise following a dynamic understanding of scales, namely *acts of citizenship* and *borderwork.*

Citizenship is commonly framed as formal membership of a political community within which the citizen upholds certain rights and responsibilities (Glick Schiller 2005, 53). Regarding the complexity of its development in times of globalisation, citizenship as a theoretical concept has been dealt with by many scholars (e.g. Isin and Saward 2013; Glick Schiller and Wimmer 2003). Nina Glick Schiller and Engin F. Isin argue for a more flexible, multiple version of citizenship, broadening its traditional understanding as static membership of a nation state. Glick Schiller's understanding of the citizenship figure goes beyond legal definitions, to the subject of social and cultural citizenship, in regard to which she examines citizenship claims and practices from a transnational perspective (Glick Schiller 2005, 48, 56). Similarly, Isin directs attention to subjects claiming their rights and constituting themselves as citizens, disregarding their legal citizen status. He argues that this has begun to change our dominant figure of citizenship (Isin 2009, 368). The article follows Isin's suggestion for an investigation of the notion of citizenship through the term *acts of citizenship* and uses it to comprehend the actions in the grassroots volunteer networks as political acts.

The question of *what makes the citizen* is closely connected to a dynamic understanding of the concept of borders, being more than a demarcation line and constitutive of political space (Rumford 2008, 1). Border scholars such as Etienne Balibar and Chris Rumford argue that borders encompass an intrinsic ambivalence as they have both an internal and external function and thereby work as barriers for some and gateways for others (Balibar 2010, 315; Rumford 2008, 2). Rumford coined the term *borderwork* and argues that:

Research network and its research questions directed at investigating the everyday border work of citizens in Europe in support of refugees (Helping Hands 2019).

> [...] debordering and rebordering are no longer the exclusive business of nation-states, or even of the EU [...]. Borderwork is very much the business of citizens, of ordinary people. (Rumford 2008, 3)

In the light of the notion of borderwork, the chapter analyses how the volunteers are involved in constructing and contesting borders and thereby rearrange the question of who belongs as a citizen. The combination of the concepts of acts of citizenship and borderwork hereby allow us to comprehend the activities in the networks as enactments of transborder citizenship through the everyday negotiation of rights.

The situated, practice-based approach with respect to the activation and negotiation of scales allows for unfolding our empirical material in relation to realities, opportunities and challenges that the networks as platforms hold for the idea of cosmopolitanism. This is in accordance with the theme of this volume and with a focus on processes of *cosmopolitanisation*, as the cosmopolitan transformation of social structures, on the level of civil society (Beck and Sznaider 2006, 14).

16.2 Action as Reaction

The political reactions of Denmark and Germany, as outlined above, are emblematic of how EU member states during the 'summer of migration' were guided by different rationales ranging from the political right to the political left. The EU faced an existential crisis as it struggled to coordinate a common response (Krastev 2017, 22). As the migration flow laid a disproportionate amount of pressure on some countries, especially in Southern Europe, the Dublin Regulation broke down and national asylum systems all over Europe were challenged (Eurostat 2016). Temporary border controls were introduced at several of the EU Schengen borders (EC 2017a). Thus the motto of the EU 'United in diversity' was disregarded in favour of nation states turning their attention inwards (EU 2017). With this as a backdrop, during the 'summer of welcome' in 2015 many volunteer networks in support of refugees were founded or repurposed at grassroots level throughout Europe.

In the spring of 2017, we conducted ethnographic fieldwork in grassroots volunteer networks in Berlin and Copenhagen. We did initial research in eight networks and later focused our research investigations on four of them; *Venligbohus* and *Solbjerggruppen* in Copenhagen and *Moabit hilft* und *Wedding hilft* in Berlin. They were founded and run by local citizens in order to support refugees and were not connected to any political, religious or established aid organisations. We did 23 participant observations as well as auto-ethnography by volunteering in the networks and participating in their activities. In this context our field site was, on the one hand, made up of the physical platforms on which the network members engaged in everyday activities such as collecting and distributing clothes and sharing meals. On the other hand, it consisted of online forums, mostly on Facebook, that the networks used for organising activities and sharing practical or legal information relating to forced migration, amongst others. By actively engaging with the field sites we got in contact with the volunteers of the networks and conducted semi-structured interviews with 14 of them.

During our research we explored the rationales, structures and dynamics in the volunteer networks with a focus on the perspective of the volunteers. In this connection the volunteers make up the local citizens that founded or joined the networks on a quest to provide support to the arriving refugees. The group of the volunteers in both Berlin and Copenhagen encompasses a diverse group of people with regard to age and social, cultural and professional background. The term volunteer does not necessarily reflect the self-perception or ascriptions of the members of the volunteer networks. The way our informants framed their activities and role in the networks differed from person to person and from network to network (Kirchner and Steen Bygballe 2017).

One of our first enquiries was directed at the motives of the volunteers that triggered them into volunteering for refugees in the networks. From our data it emerged that our informants decided to volunteer as a reaction to one or a combination of three socio-political developments in 2015, namely refugee politics, media representations and societal mood. These triggers were invoked by our informants irrespective of the political response to the situation of their country and/or city, which, as outlined before, differed in Denmark and Germany.

The volunteers we spoke with explained that they found the treatment of refugees of their respective government as well as of the EU as a whole inadequate and inhumane. They perceived the precarious situation that the refugees were facing on their way to and in Europe as intentional from the side of the governments. The following quote from Nina,[4] a 23-year-old student of social work and a volunteer at the Berlin volunteer network *Moabit hilft*, underlines this reading of the political handling of refugees:

> You can clearly see, that this is politically intended that the people [refugees] […] are not doing so well, or however you want to put it. That just makes me upset. (Interview, 29 March 2017, Moabit hilft)[5]

The German volunteers we interviewed saw this political intention manifested e.g. in the placement of refugees in mass shelters and the deportation of Afghan refugees (Sueddeutsche Zeitung 2016; Tagesspiegel 2016). Our Danish informants instanced the tightening of refugee laws and governmental deterrents to prevent refugees from choosing Denmark as their country of refuge in this connection (Politiken 2015). As a reaction, our informants decided to counteract the perceived political hostility towards refugees on a national and European level with welcoming and supportive actions in their immediate local surroundings.

Another motivating force for our informants' move to action was how the events of 2015 were covered by the media. Both negative as well as positive representations of the situation became emblematic of the so-called 'refugee crisis'. In Germany and

---

[4]We have changed the names of the people we interacted with in the field, including our informants, to aliases in order to keep them anonymous.

[5]The interview was carried out in English.

Denmark these pictures were different and context-specific; however, concurrently they provoked our informants into volunteering.

In the Danish media, pictures of refugees walking on highways were widespread (Jyllands-Posten 2015). From this setting a picture of a man standing on a motorway bridge and spitting on the refugees walking below became (in)famous (Information 2015). Some volunteers in Copenhagen that we talked to explained that these pictures caused shock and frustration in them and thus moved them to react. Likewise, several of our informants in Berlin reacted to pictures of countless refugees waiting for days and weeks in front of the *Landesamt für Gesundheit und Soziales* (LAGeSo), the institution responsible for registering refugees in Berlin at the time, without being provided with basic necessities (Berliner Zeitung 2015).

On the other hand, pictures and stories that our informants perceived as more hopeful circulated in the media. This included instances of people welcoming refugees at the central station in Munich (Sueddeutsche Zeitung 2015) or giving refugees walking on highways a ride from the southern part of Denmark to the Swedish border, where many of them headed (DR 2015b). These events and their representation in the media sparked in our informants in Berlin and Copenhagen the motivation to act and be part of welcoming the refugees.

This can be considered in the light of the idea of 'imaginary spaces' that Werner Schiffauer develops with respect to the concept of transnational solidarity (Schiffauer 2006). He argues that big migratory movements and their representation, for instance in the media, have brought the realities of other people from different parts of the world closer to one's own life. This in turn influences who we solidarise with and wish to support (Ibid.: 171).

Closely connected to this motive is the third socio-political development that our informants reacted to, i.e. the polarisation of the mood in civil society in Europe that gained momentum in 2015. On the one hand, public manifestations of xenophobic, anti-refugee attitudes were on the rise (Foroutan 2016). On the other hand, the optimistic atmosphere surrounding the 'summer of welcome' was omnipresent. Our informants explained that they were facing a moral decision in this situation. Ina, a 35-year-old lecturer of linguistics, who was volunteering at *Solbjerggruppen*, explained it as follows:

> In connection to the refugee crisis I needed to make up my mind: 'Whose team are you on – of those that help or those that find it horrible or those that just sit back?' (Interview, 14 March 2017, Solbjerggruppen)[6]

Other volunteers explained that their motivation to volunteer was spurred by what some of our informants characterised as a refugee hype. They saw and heard about the many people helping refugees in the media and their immediate surroundings and wanted to be part of what they described as a positive feeling.

The 'summer of welcome' of 2015 stands for attitudes and (re)actions amongst some parts of European civil society that advocated for a more humane and tolerant treatment of refugees. In the polarised political landscape, our informants felt the

[6]The interview was carried out in Danish and translated into English.

urge to take a position *for* refugees, thereby acting *against* anti-refugee politics and sentiments. Across borders, in the two Northern European capitals of Berlin and Copenhagen the motivational frame for their action in this context was made up of the same three elements of refugee politics, media representation and societal mood. Acting on their beliefs and emotions, they chose to become engaged locally in supporting refugees.

16.3 Volunteer Acts as Strategies for Political Participation

In the quote from Birte, a 60-year-old retired administrative employee, she explained how her dissatisfaction with the political handling of the 'refugee crisis' triggered her to take action in her own life. For her that meant joining and becoming active in the volunteer network *Solbjerggruppen* in Copenhagen.

> I don't think that Europe is doing it well enough with the distribution of the unfortunate people who arrive to the continent. I don't think the solution is to build walls around us. I cannot change the politics in Europe and I cannot make changes in Danish politics in any other way than using my vote for elections. So, I feel that it is more meaningful for me to do something in my own life, so I don't go around being frustrated all the time about how things are. I have never been active with anything regarding politics or volunteering, but it was simply this refugee crisis that got me started. (Interview, 6 April 2017, Solbjerggruppen)[7]

As a grassroots network *Solbjerggruppen*, as well as the other networks we researched, is characterised by being small, loosely organised and follows a bottom-up approach. The members of the grassroots networks are made up of both volunteers that joined the network activities sporadically as well as volunteers that were active on a regular basis. The networks were formed around a variety of hands-on, everyday activities. In the beginning the activities focused on providing emergency help to the arriving refugees by collecting and distributing clothes and basic necessities. Thereby the volunteers helped the refugees with assistance that the nation states did not manage or did not want to supply. Also after the numbers of arriving refugees decreased, due to reinforced border controls and tightened refugee regulations (Eurostat 2019; EC 2017b) amongst others, the grassroots volunteer networks continued to exist. However, they shifted their attention to help the newly arrived people get settled in their respective societies.

Clothing banks, language cafés and communal dinners are some of the activities that built the framework for the network members to provide support, meet and interact in an easy and accessible way. The core of the networks was thus characteristically everyday activities with a hands-on character, such as folding clothes, chopping vegetables or helping out with homework. The volunteers we talked to in Copenhagen and Berlin highlighted that they found this practical way of helping especially attractive. According to our informants, like Birte, they experienced an

[7] The interview was carried out in Danish and translated into English.

urgency to do something, triggered by feelings of injustice and frustration. The grassroots networks provided them with a platform to channel these emotions into concrete action with often immediate results—for instance, having provided a young boy with a winter jacket or having taught someone a few words in Danish or German.

Although our informants were triggered into action by a frustration with how the political establishment handled forced migration to Europe around 2015, most of them framed their action as not political. For instance, Peter, a 34-year-old IT employee, contrasts his volunteering at *Venligbohus* in Copenhagen to political activities in the following quote:

> I like that it [Venligbohus] is practical and not political. (Interview, 7 April 2017, Venligbohus)[8]

Like Peter, most of our informants distinguished their action from what is commonly understood as political action in the context of representative democracies. This is also shown in Birte's quote at the beginning of this section. She explains how the common expression of political participation, i.e. voting, was not sufficient to alleviate her frustrations. Thus she decided to act and do something in her own everyday life instead.

To grasp the connection and congruence between the everyday as well as activist features of our informants' local engagement, we took inspiration from Sarah Pink's discussions of the potential of everyday life and activism. Pink positions the everyday as a powerful domain to examine with respect to actions for change, as it is '[…] where we make our worlds and where our worlds make us. Therefore, everyday life is a context of human creativity, innovation and change' (Pink 2012, 4). Considering the interplay of activism and everyday life, we thus analysed how volunteering as activism influences and conditions the everyday life of the volunteers and vice versa (ibid.: 5).

In order to access the underlying rationales and motivations of volunteering as everyday activism, we built on a performative approach to data collection and analysis (Mol 2002; Sandberg 2009). This directed our focus to the performed dimensions of the volunteer work in the grassroots networks, i.e. we directed our attention to what the volunteers *do* in addition to what they say. In her elaborations in *The Body Multiple*, Annemarie Mol underlines that when turning attention to how an object of analysis is enacted in a given context, it will emerge in its multiplicity (Mol 2002, vii).

In the light of the conceptualisations of the everyday and activism outlined, when considering the multiple performative qualities of the volunteering activities in the grassroots networks we came to understand them as *alternative* ways of engaging in (refugee) politics. On the basis of two empirical examples from the everyday activities of political participation in the grassroots networks, we will discuss how the acts of volunteering emerged to us as practices of transborder citizenship.

---

[8] The interview was carried out in English.

16.4 Enacting Forms of Transborder Citizenship

16.4.1 Dissemination of Legal Advice

At the time we carried out ethnographic fieldwork at the grassroots network *Moabit hilft* in Berlin, it was located near the *LAGeSo*, as the refugees came there to register for asylum and therefore had easy access to the house. In addition to benefiting from the everyday activities, we learned that many of the refugees who came to *Moabit hilft* received counselling regarding their asylum process. Counselling ranged from receiving information about the asylum procedure in general to preparing for the personal interview in the asylum process (BAMF 2016). Karin, a 42-year-old employee at a private company and active volunteer at *Moabit hilft*, told us that the refugees were often poorly informed about their legal rights and the procedures for seeking asylum and resident permits. As an example, she described how some refugees, who went to the embassy of their home country to get their passports renewed, lost their right to asylum and risked deportation. Karin therefore saw it as the responsibility of and a task for *Moabit hilft* to provide the refugees with necessary legal information. They did so by sharing a post on *Moabit hilft*'s Facebook group that originated from *Berlin hilft*, a network that acts as an information and networking platform for refugee initiatives in Berlin. The post included a link to an article on the homepage of *Berlin hilft* about the risks connected to renewing passports with respect to people with different residency status (Berlin hilft 2017). The post had the following text in German:

> Wer muss zur Botschaft, wer nicht und wer darf das gar nicht? Dass man mit Flüchtlingsstatus die Anerkennung bei Botschaftsbesuch gefährdet, wissen inzwischen ja sehr viele, aber immer noch nicht alle. Wir haben daneben aber auch alle anderen Fälle beleuchtet.[9] (Moabit hilft, Facebook post 25 April 2017)

Following the link to the article, it examined the different scenarios for renewing passports and visits to embassies for refugees and asylum seekers. Through sharing this post on Facebook and by encouraging others to share it, they aimed to reach as many people as possible with the information.

In this example, there are many interlinked borders at play. There are the borders of the home country of the refugees, manifested both by the passport and the embassy. There are the borders of Germany, where the refugees have applied or are applying for asylum or are currently living in asylum and as non-members, and thereby are deportable. Additionally, there are the borders of the EU, which the refugees crossed in coming to Germany. The example elucidates the complex legal pluralism which the refugees find themselves in, as their lives are shaped by more than one set of laws, social norms and values embedded within the interaction of people and institutions (Glick Schiller 2005, 75).

[9]English translation: 'Who has to go to the embassy, who doesn't and who is not allowed to? That you, when having a refugee status, risk your recognition by visiting the embassy, many but still not everyone is aware of by now. We also examined all other cases' [authors].

The support from the volunteers can be seen as a practice of borderwork as they help the refugees to stay in Germany through informing them of the risk of being deported by renewing their passport. Synnøve K. N. Bendixsen, who did research on how borders are constructed in the context of irregular migration to Norway, argues for seeing deportation as part of a governing process of drawing an ultimate line between members and non-members (Bendixsen 2016, 11). The practice of borderwork therefore navigates around the governing process, so the refugees can stay in Germany, although still as non-members, but nevertheless impeding deportation. Through sharing the post on Facebook the volunteers from *Moabit hilft* therefore performed a version of citizenship in which non-members of the nation state are included as transborder citizens (Rumford 2008, 11; Glick Schiller 2005, 48).

16.4.2 The Language Café

Solbjerggruppen in Copenhagen is located in an old, yellow villa in the district of Frederiksberg, where one of the main activities at the time of our research was the language café. This was a popular activity in all of the volunteer groups we researched. One of the reasons for this was that refugees often needed to learn the language of the country they arrive to, both in order to live and work and as an element towards getting a residence permit. In Denmark a refugee who is seeking a residence permit has to pass a Danish language test (Ny i danmark 2019). Thus, the language café functioned as a setting for supporting the refugees in doing homework for their language classes or just practising their language skills by talking with others. It was an easy way for volunteers to help out and if there was nobody who needed help, it still functioned as a cosy café for socialising.

Providing language support in the language café is a low-threshold, everyday activity that does not indicate any political beliefs. Yet the activity supports the process of expanding the borders of who can be included in society. In line with the concepts of acts of citizenship, the acts of volunteering can be understood as a way of performing transborder citizenship by helping refugees learn the Danish language to become a part of the society they live in. As a result, some of the refugees were able to pass their language tests, thus getting one step closer to overcoming the borders that keep them from being acknowledged as legal citizens. Bendixsen argues that refugees are met with many borders in the process of applying for asylum, in the form of events and meeting-points that they have to navigate in and around (Bendixsen 2016, 9). The language test can be considered one of these events. Despite not offering legal counselling in *Solbjerggruppen*, the volunteers were aware of how far along in the process of seeking asylum and residence permits the refugees were. This was visible in the language café, as they paid extra attention to those who had language tests coming up.

While doing our research in *Solbjerggruppen* we witnessed this process happening, when two young refugee women, Ariam and Zada, passed a Danish test and received a language certificate. Anja, a 56-year-old administrative employee and one of the active volunteers from *Solbjerggruppen*, posted a picture on the network's Facebook group congratulating the women (Facebook post, 22 June 2017, Solbjerggruppen). The picture showed the two women standing with their certificates, each holding a red rose. Many of the volunteers commented on the picture and congratulated the women on their achievement. The comments underlined how they 'did a good job' and stressed how they had 'worked hard for it'. The picture and the comments made clear how this was not only a success for Ariam and Zada, but for the whole network. This was seen as a joint effort, where the volunteers too had worked towards this goal through participating in the language cafés.

The example reflects how volunteers in *Solbjerggruppen* through their everyday practices enact low-key, bottom-up political activism which challenges a government that makes it increasingly difficult for refugees to live in Denmark. Doing so, the volunteers are not only claiming rights for the refugees, but they are also challenging and rearranging the borders of the nation-state notion of citizenship that they themselves belong to. By changing the focus from the question of 'who is the citizen' to 'what makes the citizen', this example illuminates the process of performing versions of transborder citizenship (Isin 2009, 383). This is done through enactments where the volunteers and refugees bring together different notions of state and citizenship developed across borders (Glick Schiller 2005, 76).

These two examples illuminate how the volunteers together with the refugees in both Berlin and Copenhagen enacted versions of transborder citizenship by contesting borders throughout Europe, and thereby also the existing norms and regimes of citizenship (Isin 2013, 20–21; Rumford 2008, 11).

16.5 The Volunteer Networks as Platforms for Engaging Locally on Global Issues

Building on comparative ethnographic fieldwork from Berlin and Copenhagen, this chapter analyzes the volunteering in grassroots volunteer networks in support of refugees as inhering aspirations for an alternative political order in which the question of justice and belonging is not confined to the country of birth. More precisely, we discussed how the volunteers in the networks enact forms of transborder citizenship that reflect a vision to restructure mechanisms of political participation and belonging. They do so for instance by disseminating legal information or teaching their language to others. We argue that they thereby test out alternative ways of how to be political in the form of everyday negotiation and by that means contribute to rearranging the question of belonging, challenging the borders of citizenship. In our research we have seen transborder activities in the different urban and national contexts of Berlin and Copenhagen. In locally rooted, independent grassroots networks we have observed the same tendency towards finding diverse ways to enact an alternative political order. This adds yet another transborder dimension to the activities in the grassroots volunteer networks.

This chapter underlines that former perceptions of the nation state as the frame for who we can relate to are not supported by the volunteers we talked to. Due to the increase of refugees in Europe and times of 'intense globalization', it seems that the scope of who our informants can relate to has changed (Glick Schiller and Wimmer 2003, 576; Isin 2009, 367; Schiffauer 2006). Enacting of transborder citizenship by our informants can consequently be said to entail a cosmopolitan vision of belonging and justice, i.e. one that goes beyond a nationalist and towards a global understanding of (political) membership and access (Beck and Sznaider 2006, 6). In this context they develop ways to navigate in a complex socio-political sphere regarding citizenship in the era of globalisation.

Our informants exhibited a frustration directed at both their national government and the EU with regard to the treatment of the refugees and to where the governments draw the boundaries of who to include and not to include in their community. Thus, as we argue in this chapter, in the networks they actively work together to overcome national and supranational (legal) borders. They, however, act within the national legal framework in an effort to expand it from within. They can be seen as following the measures put in place by the nation state that a language test of the national language is an integral element on the way to achieving access to additional rights. Yet the volunteers teach their mother tongue to people that are considered non-members in the national framing which can be seen as one way of providing them with the necessary tools on their way to (national) membership. Thus, they can be considered working towards the idea of what Balibar calls 'a cosmopolitical transformation of citizenship' (Balibar 2010, 320).

In the context of the enactment of a transborder citizenship, however, the legal frameworks of the state remain active and powerful. Also Nina Glick Schiller points to this aspect in the context of discussing the potential of transnational networks. She underlines that the role of the states prevail, which is why transnational platforms should not be equated to liberated social space (Glick Schiller 2005, 58). This aspect points to one challenge as well as the reality of the practice in the networks with respect to cosmopolitanism, namely the persistence of the power of the state that is for the most part continuing to execute laws on the basis of a nation-bound understanding of citizenship.

Nevertheless, in the light of the approach of methodological cosmopolitanism the transborder activities in the networks represent relevant analytical insights as they point to processes of cosmopolitanisation taking place 'from within' (Beck and Sznaider 2006, 9). This chapter aimed to contribute to understanding these processes of transformation in society and politics with respect to the everyday acts of transborder citizenship in grassroots volunteers networks for refugees in Berlin and Copenhagen.

References

Balibar, E. (2010). At the borders of citizenship: A democracy in translation? *European Journal of Social Theory, 13*(3), 315–322.

Beck, U., & Sznaider, N. (2006). Unpacking cosmopolitanism for the social sciences: A research agenda. *The British Journal of Sociology, 57*(1), 1–23.

Bendixsen, S. (2016). The refugee crisis: Destabilizing and restabilizing European borders. *History and Anthropology, 27*(5), 536–554.

Berking, H. (2006). Raumtheoretische Paradoxien im Globalisierungsdiskurs. In H. Berking (Ed.), *Die Macht des Lokalen in einer Welt ohne Grenzen* (pp. 7–24). Frankfurt: Campus Verlag.

Foroutan, N. (2016). Nationale Bedürfnisse und soziale Ängste. In M. Castro Varela & P. Mecheril (Eds.), *Die Dämonisierung der Anderen. Rassismuskritik der Gegenwart* (pp. 97–107). Bielefeld: Transcript.

Glick Schiller, N. (2005). Transborder citizenship: An outcome of legal pluralism within transnational social fields. In F. Benda-Beckmann, K. Benda-Beckmann, & A. M. O. Griffiths (Eds.), *Mobile people, mobile law: Expanding legal relations in a contracting world* (pp. 27–49). Aldershot: Ashgate.

Glick Schiller, N., & Wimmer, A. (2003). Methodological nationalism, the social sciences, and the study of migration: An essay in historical epistemology 1. *International Migration Review, 37*(3), 576–610.

Hamann, U., & Karakayali, S. (2016). Practicing Willkommenskultur: Migration and solidarity in Germany. *Intersections, 2*(4), 69–86.

Isin, E. (2009). Citizenship in flux: The figure of the activist citizen. *Subjectivity, 29*(1), 367–388.

Isin, E. (2013). Claiming European citizenship. In E. Isin & M. Saward (Eds.), *Enacting European citizenship* (pp. 19–43). Cambridge: University Press.

Isin, E., & Saward, M. (2013). Questions of European citizenship. In E. Isin & M. Saward (Eds.), *Enacting European citizenship* (pp. 1–18). Cambridge: University Press.

Kirchner, L., & Steen Bygballe, L. (2017). *Volunteering for change. A cultural analysis of grassroots volunteer networks in Berlin and Copenhagen.* University of Copenhagen. Master thesis.

Krastev, I. (2017). *After Europa*. Philadelphia: University of Pennsylvania Press.

Löfgren, O. (2014). The black box of everyday life, entanglements of stuff, affects, and activities. *Cultural Analysis, 13*(2014), 77–98.

Mol, A. (2002). *The body multiple: Ontology in medical practice.* Durham: Duke University Press.

Pink, S. (2012). The digital places of everyday life: Thinking about activism and the internet. In S. Pink (Ed.), *Situating everyday life: Practices and places* (pp. 1–14). London: Sage Publications Ltd.

Rozakou, K. (2016). Socialities of solidarity: Revisiting the gift taboo in times of crises. *Social Anthropology, 24*(2), 185–199.

Sandberg, M. (2009). Performing the border: Cartographic enactments of the German-polish border among German and polish high-school pupils. *Anthropological Journal of European Cultures, 18*(1), 107–128.

Rumford, C. (2008). Introduction: Citizens and borderwork in Europe. *Space and Polity, 12*(1), 1–12.

Sandberg, M. (2018). Moving the border. The everyday border work in/of the European Border Regime. In H. Alzheimer, S. Doering-Manteuffel, D. Drascek, & A. Treiber (Eds.), *Jahrbuch für Europäische Ethnologie Dritte Folge 13-2018* (pp. 49–58). Paderborn: Schöningh Verlag.

Schiffauer, W. (2006). Transnationale Solidaritätsgruppen, Imaginäre Räume, Irreale Konditionalsätze. In H. Berking (Ed.), *Die Macht des Lokalen in einer Welt ohne Grenzen* (pp. 164–180). Frankfurt: Campus Verlag.

Schiffauer, W., Eilert, A., & Rudloff, M. (2017). *So schaffen wir das - eine Zivilgesellschaft im Aufbruch: 90 wegweisende Projekte mit Geflüchteten.* Bielefeld: Transcript.

Thränhardt, D. (2019). Welcoming citizens, divided government, simplifying media. Germany's Refugee Crisis, 2015–2017. In G. Dell'Orto & I. Wetzstein (Eds.), *Refugee news, refugee politics: Journalism, public opinion and policymaking in Europe* (pp. 15–25). New York: Routledge.
Toubøl, J. (2015). Septembermobiliseringen af flygtningesolidaritetsbevægelsen. *Dansk Sociologi, 4*(26), 96–103.

Online Resources

BAMF (Bundesamt für Migration und Flüchtlinge). (2016). *Das deutsche Asylverfahren.* https://www.bamf.de/SharedDocs/Anlagen/DE/Publikationen/Broschueren/das-deutsche-asylverfahren.pdf?__blob=publicationFile. Accessed March 19, 2019.
Berlin hilft. (2017). *Passbeschaffung: Wer muss, wer sollte, wer darf, wer nicht?* https://berlin-hilft.com/2017/04/25/passbeschaffung-wer-muss-wer-sollte-wer-darf-wer-nicht/. Accessed May 9, 2019.
Berliner Institut für empirische Integrations- und Migrationsforschung (BIM). (2017). Solidarität im Wandel? Das Forschungs-Interventions-Cluster zum Thema Flucht und Solidarisierung. https://www.bim-fluchtcluster.hu-berlin.de/de. Accessed January 15, 2019.
Berliner Zeitung. (2015). *Bundeswehr-Soldaten registrieren Flüchtlinge im LAGeSo.* https://www.berliner-zeitung.de/berlin/landesamtfuer-gesundheit-und-soziales-in-berlin-bundeswehr-soldaten-registrieren-fluechtlinge-im-lageso-22315380. Accessed May 3, 2019.
Die Zeit. (2015). *Angela Merkel: In the eye of the storm.* https://www.zeit.de/politik/deutschland/2015-09/angela-merkel-refugees-crisis-chancellor/seite-4. Accessed June 7, 2019.
DR (Danmarks Radio). (2015a). *Over 34,000 danskere sagde 'Welcome to Denmark'.* https://www.dr.dk/nyheder/indland/over-34000-danskere-sagde-welcome-denmark. Accessed May 17, 2019.
DR (Danmarks Radio). (2015b). Danskere klar til at bryde loven: Derfor vil vi give flygtninge et lift. https://www.dr.dk/nyheder/indland/danskere-klar-til-bryde-loven-derfor-vil-vi-give-flygtninge-et-lift. Accessed May 20, 2019.
EU (European Union). (2017). *The EU Motto.* https://europa.eu/european-union/about-eu/symbols/motto_en. Accessed July 11, 2019.
EC (European Commission). (2017a). *A coordinated EU approach for temporary internal border controls.* https://europa.eu/rapid/press-release_MEMO-17-132_en.htm. Accessed February 1, 2019.
EC (European Commission). (2017b). *The EU and the migration crisis.* https://publications.europa.eu/webpub/com/factsheets/migration-crisis/en/. Accessed March 3, 2019.
Eurostat. (2016). Asylum in the EU Member States. Record number of over 1.2 million first time asylum seekers registered in 2015. https://ec.europa.eu/eurostat/web/products-press-releases/-/3-04032016-AP. Accessed June 9, 2019.
Eurostat. (2019). Asylum statistics. Asylum applications (non-EU) in the EU-28 Member States, 2008–2018. https://ec.europa.eu/eurostat/statistics-explained/index.php/Asylum_statistics. Accessed March 23, 2019.
Hamann, U., & Piening, G. (2017). Eine neue soziale Bewegung? *Rosa Luxemburg Stiftung.* https://www.rosalux.de/publikation/id/14864/eine-neue-soziale-bewegung/. Accessed June 14, 2019.
Helping Hands. (2019). *Helping hands research network on everyday border work of European citizens.* https://saxoinstitute.ku.dk/research/research_projects_and_networks/helping-hands-research-network-on-the-everyday-border-workk-of-european-citizens/. Accessed March 3, 2019.
Information. (2015). *Skræmmekampagnen virker.* https://www.information.dk/indland/2015/09/skraemmekampagnen-virker. Accessed May 13, 2019.
Jyllands-Posten. (2015). *300 flygtninge vandrer på sønderjysk motorvej.* https://jyllands-posten.dk/indland/ECE8006218/300-flygtninge-vandrer-p%C3%A5-s%C3%B8nderjysk-motorvej/. Accessed Marts 3, 2019.

Karakayali, S., & Kleist, O. (2016). EFA-Studie 2: Strukturen und Motive der ehrenamtlichen Flüchtlingsarbeit in Deutschland, 2. Forschungsbericht: Ergebnisse einer explorativen Umfrage vom November/Dezember 2015. Berliner Institut für empirische Integrations- und Migrationsforschung.https://www.fluechtlingsrat-brandenburg.de/wp-content/uploads/2016/08/Studie_EFA2_BIM_11082016_VOE.pdf. Accessed February 12, 2019.
Ny i Danmark. (2019). *Ansøg om permanent opholdstilladelse.* https://www.nyidanmark.dk/da/Du-vil-ans%C3%B8ge/Permanent-ophold/Permanent-ophold. Accessed March 3, 2019.
Politiken. (2015). *Støjbergs flygtningeannoncer kan nu læses i Libanon.* https://politiken.dk/udland/fokus_int/Flygtningestroem/art5588293/Støjbergs-flygtningeannoncer-kan-nu-læses-i-Libanon. Accessed June 25, 2019.
Sueddeutsche Zeitung. (2015). *Warum man Ängste zulassen sollte.* https://www.sueddeutsche.de/politik/gesellschaft-und-fluechtlinge-angst-zulassen-1.2644135. Accessed June 21, 2017.
Sueddeutsche Zeitung. (2016). *Warum Deutschlands größte Flüchtlingsunterkunft so umstritten ist.* https://www.sueddeutsche.de/politik/tempelhofer-feld-warum-deutschlands-groesste-fluechtlingsunterkunft-so-umstritten-ist-1.2839170. Accessed May 2, 2019.
Udlændinge- og Integrationsministeriet. (2016). *Information about the Danish border control.* https://uim.dk/nyheder/2016/information-about-the-danish-border-control. Accessed April 15, 2019.
UNHCR. (2015). *Over one million sea arrivals reach Europe in 2015.* https://www.unhcr.org/news/latest/2015/12/5683d0b56/million-sea-arrivals-reach-europe-2015.html. Accessed June 26, 2019.
UNHCR. (2017). *What is a refugee?* https://www.unrefugees.org/what-is-a-refugee/. Accessed July 13, 2019.

Lydia Maria Kirchner holds a bachelor degree in Social and Cultural Sciences from the European University Viadrina in Frankfurt/Oder (Germany) and a master's degree in Applied Cultural Analysis from the University of Copenhagen (Denmark). In her research, she has been focusing on how recent migration flows to Europe have led to negotiations in civil society of how to live together and be political in increasingly pluralised democracies. Currently, she is working as an evaluator and consultant in the areas of culture, education and migration in Berlin.

Line Steen Bygballe holds a bachelor degree in European Ethnology and a master's degree in Applied Cultural Analysis from the University of Copenhagen (Denmark). Her research interests include the influence of migration on political and democratic structures. As part of the interdisciplinary research network 'Helping Hands', her recent research activities have focused on practices of everyday borderwork in Northern European volunteer networks for refugees. She is working as a research consultant in Copenhagen.

Part V
Facets of Citizenship and Border Regimes

Chapter 17
Multi-Level Citizenship in Eastern European Internal and External Policies

Oleg Bresky

Abstract The chapter is devoted to the new institution of quasi-citizenship and the formation of a wide range of civic statuses. These statuses provide an incomplete number of civil rights but make it possible to overcome problems linked to the crisis of political participation and migration. The features of its development in Eastern Europe are analysed. Particular attention is paid to the establishment of the Polish Card and the institution of the 'compatriots' in the Russian Federation, and to the ways they are conferred and how they create the basis for legal and political participation. The chapter also analyses how the media image of the 'compatriot' institution was created.

Keywords Quasi-citizenship · Equality · Multi-level citizenship · Participation · Public order

17.1 Introduction

Citizenship is a category with many meanings that vary depending on the context. Thus, citizenship can be represented as a formal status that determines the position of a person in a particular jurisdiction. But such a formal notion of citizenship is complemented by other aspects of citizenship, which allows it to be presented as, for example:

- political participation (Pocock 1995)
- a national tradition (Brubaker 1998)
- evolution, revealing citizenship as a form of civil rights (Marshall 1950)
- an understanding of the theory of post-nationalism (Soysal 1994)
- cosmopolitan understanding (Turner 1990)
- the theory of deterritorialisation (Bauböck 1994).

O. Bresky (✉)
Vilnius, Lithuania
e-mail: oleg.bresky@hotmail.com

M. C. Jacobsen et al. (eds.), *Cosmopolitanism, Migration and Universal Human Rights*, https://doi.org/10.1007/978-3-030-50645-2_17

Real citizenship can only be understood as a result of an interaction between all of its possible aspects. Therefore, it turns out that citizens of the USSR and citizens of the medieval free city of Emden[1] are different, both in status and in their understanding of civic affiliation and participation in public affairs. Such a category as citizenship is not solid and stable, but subject to constant rethinking and redefinition. For this reason there are inevitably many types of citizenship, which creates the need for special approaches and methods for studying them. Most often, it is not enough just to consider the legal framework of citizenship; to understand this institution, it is necessary to turn to the practices of its implementation and its everyday usage.

So, is it then reasonable to define the different forms of participation and belonging to the public sphere in one single word? Does this use of the word 'citizenship' prevent us from understanding at all what a citizen is?

It is important to identify the difference between 'self' and 'citizen'. A citizen is not a person, not a 'self'. A citizen is a legal or political construct or status. This is better seen when we introduce a different category as the opposite of a 'citizen'—the 'non-citizen'. This word can be used to designate anyone who is not a citizen. With such a strong dichotomy between citizen and non-citizen, it is assumed that such a person, deprived of any positive status, is placed completely outside the public order, not being included in it. Therefore, this human can be characterised to the greatest extent precisely as a person with no external determinations. It was already felt by the Greeks, when they introduced the concept of a cosmopolitan, or atopos,[2] who had no social roots and determinations. Sophocles described such an 'atopos' in the Oedipus Rex. Oedipus is not determined by anything, but he is himself the cause of everything in his life. For this reason Oedipus is like a god. But what exactly would not allow such a person to be a simple element in the public order? Is he fully deprived of all rights? Is he excluded completely? How could such an unlimited person enter into social interactions?

Of course, a non-citizen is unable to change anything in his position himself, he cannot create his own status. Such a person cannot change his position without simultaneously changing the public space itself. The emergence in this space of a place for a 'non-citizen' redefines this space. Any unilateral actions by the person will not make him a participant in the public space. Moreover, such a public space can resist and be closed to such an outsider and undesirable element.

A non-citizen cannot be represented in the public order precisely because public order itself does not create a representation for the non-citizen. In other words, there is no place for non-citizens in a public order, such a place has not been created, and they are not able to create such a place themselves. The mechanism for the formation of such places is beyond their control and capabilities. A non-citizen has nowhere to go, because there is no place for him.

Thus, citizenship is a representation. But what are its constituents? What exactly does citizenship represent? A person? Or is a citizen, after all, a representation of a certain political order that allows an individual to enter a public space? The latter

[1]Emden—the native city of Johannes Althusius, the father of the principle of subsidiarity.

[2]See the interpretation of the *atopos* concept in Barthes (1978).

looks like a better explanation. Citizenship is part of the political system and order, an integral element of such an order. It assumes the existence of a certain place for a person that allows this person to participate in some processes within the public sphere at any time and within the limits of the citizen status. This explains why the balance between citizen rights and human rights is so sharply denoted in the modern world; they do not coincide, since they relate to different situations and create different problems. Human rights assume directly that their carrier is a particular person; citizen rights are elements in the legal construction under the heading of the 'citizen', and have only an indirect relation to the person. Their combination seems desirable, but the scale of the problem becomes obvious when we attempt such a combination, since it requires too much restructuring and changing. In any case, the very existence of citizenship implies that it is important to maintain the distinction between person and representation, which gives those people a chance who do not have the rights and status of a (full) citizen. The opposite situation blocks any chance for the person without citizenship to reach human rights, because the identification of the representation and the 'self' blocks any chance for the non-citizens to reach human rights.

We can observe this within the framework of citizenship itself, where modifications are possible, even within the same legal and political system. So, for example, citizens of Denmark or Belarus, who permanently live abroad, have a different legal status compared with citizens who live permanently in the country (*Consolidated Act of Danish Nationality*). Sometimes the difference in status between resident and non-resident citizens is significant, though citizenship is not lost. For example, citizens of Belarus living abroad cannot conduct business in Belarus and cannot buy landed property, but, on the other hand, they are not obliged to pay taxes and they are not obliged to serve in the army (*Law of the Republic of Belarus of June 2* 1993). Danish citizens permanently living abroad do not participate in national elections. And this restriction applies even to those who live in a different EU country.

At the same time, we can observe various modifications within the category of 'non-citizens'. 'Non-citizens' are a heterogeneous mass. So, there are simply 'foreigners', but there are also 'refugees', there are persons with permanent residence permits, there are foreigners who are family members of citizens of the host country, there are displaced persons, there are workers temporarily staying in the state. They all have different statuses. Non-citizens are not completely powerless; they may have a greater or lesser number of rights and obligations in relation to a foreign state. And it seems unavoidable that this state creates special statuses for them that allow them to be the subject of legal relations and they are thus not completely excluded from the public sphere.

So at the level of non-citizens, we see a variety of forms of exclusion from public order, or, conversely, their inclusion in public order; that is, within this category, we can find a number of modifications, sometimes very different and sometimes approaching forms of citizenship. It can then be assumed that there are many intermediate forms between the status of 'full citizen' and the status of 'absolute alien', and that pure forms as such do not exist. Intermediate forms create a situation in which 'non-citizenship' comes into contact with citizenship, and various modifications of non-citizenship are very close to modifications of 'partial citizenship'. It is therefore possible that citizenship and non-citizenship do not form statuses and states isolated from one another, but they contain various transitional forms.

State policies regarding citizens and non-citizens are carried out in order to include or exclude groups of non-citizens in the political and legal system of their country of residence. Thus, there is no consensus between states on this matter. This is due to the fact that citizenship is often understood as different phenomena and institutions.

For the integration of different approaches we should take into account the existence of the intractable problems connected to the usage of words and their meanings. What is 'incomplete citizenship'? Can we say that 'incomplete citizenship' is still citizenship? And if there is such a thing as incomplete citizenship, obviously, there can be incomplete non-citizenship, and both of these forms can occur at a certain point common to both of them. This concept comprises a wide range of statuses and positions of individuals. Moreover, such an approach is being implemented in public policies toward different groups of people. Modern migration raises the very issue of membership and its recognition (Cohen 2014).

After having argued the case for a continuous or non-dichotomous understanding of different citizenship statuses, we will examine in the next section the state policies aimed at integrating this kind of approach to incomplete membership. The forms of membership arising in this case are denoted by the term quasi-citizenship. We will in particular study modern developments in the form of the 'Polish Card' and the 'compatriots' institution in the Russian Federation. The ensuing section will be a sub-conclusion on the challenges posed by the notion of quasi-citizenship in relation to its growing importance at the international level. We will go on to consider EU citizenship as an example of multi-level citizenship. From the material presented here, we will finally conclude that there are two ways to multi-level citizenship, depending on how they relate human rights to citizen rights. When they are identified, we will see a weakening in participation and public responsibility, while understanding it as a process that revives civic life.

17.2 Quasi-Citizenship

Quasi-citizenship creates many problems of a theoretical and practical nature, related to the implementation of advanced constitutive principles: the principle of equality, justice, participation, deviance, absenteeism, civic education and education in general. The origin of the quasi-citizenship institution can be traced back to the situation where states had to decide what to do with children of migrants born in their host country. Can such children be expelled if the migrants themselves are subject to expulsion?[3] Another situation prompting the question of quasi-citizenship is the

[3] See the case of Zambrano (Case C-34/09 of the European Court of Justice).

integration of migrant groups already in the host country. If they cannot be granted full citizenship, what special status could these people then have?

In 1990, the Swedish political scientist Thomas Hammer proposed the use of a special term—'Denizen' (Hammar 1990)—in relation to workers who have been living abroad for a long time, where they were actually integrated into the local community, but did not have the status of citizens. He used this term to describe the situation of migrant workers in Northern Europe who migrated in the 1960s and 1970s for temporary employment but who, ten or twenty years later, are still living in the host country. From a legal standpoint, these immigrants are non-citizens, foreigners. But in fact they are not ordinary non-citizens. They came to another country temporarily but stayed in the country permanently. What is the actual status of immigrants who have free access to the labour market, equal rights in the social security system, who often have electoral rights at the local level, and enjoy protection from being expelled from the country? It would be a great simplification to enrol them in the general category of 'aliens' or 'non-citizens' (Hammar 1990).

But how exactly is quasi-citizenship introduced? This question also entails a series of other questions:

- For which kinds of persons is such an institution used?
- Which states introduce this status and why?
- Should they be resident in that state or can they be living abroad?
- What are the conditions for the acquisition of this status? How is it different from full citizenship?
- Can this status be lost again? Is it a transitional or permanent status? Who is the initiator of such a policy of quasi-citizenship? Is it the government or a group of people? Why is a certain group of foreigners considered closer to the host country's government or nation, and how is this justified for public opinion? How does the government provide for the integration of full citizens and quasi-citizens?

In the 1970s quasi-citizenship was created in three European countries: in the United Kingdom in 1971 (Commonwealth states citizenship—*British Nationality Act* 1981), in Greece in 1975 (Homogenies—*Greek* Law 1975/1991 *on aliens*), and in the Netherlands in 1976 (children of migrants—*Netherlands* Vreemdelingenwet 2000).

In 1981, France protected the rights of national minorities and migrants by 'Code de l'entrée et du séjour des étrangers et du droit d'asile'. In the 1990s quasi-citizenship was introduced in Austria (*Federal Law Concerning the Entry, Residence and Settlement of Aliens* 1997), in Italy (*Legislative Decree 25.7.*1998), in Greece again (*Law 2910/2001 Entry and Stay of Aliens in Greek Territory* 2000). A total of eight out of 15 'old' EU Member States apply the status of quasi-citizenship.

In Eastern Europe the quasi-citizenship institution was established in 1999, with the adoption of the Russian Federation Law of Compatriots (*Federal Law of the Russian Federation of May 24* 1999). According to this law, compatriots living abroad have the right to rely on the support of the Russian Federation in the exercise of their civil, political, social, economic and cultural rights.

Compatriots are always members of a particular community. Their relationship to the Russian Federation is managed by the government which unites the compatriots living abroad, coordinating the councils of compatriots and the committees of compatriots, which represent the interests of compatriots within the governing bodies of the Russian Federation.

These measures are carried out in a specific context. Citizenship is the central idea in constitutionalism. Citizenship is a result of the limitation of political power based on legal and moral reasoning. There is a presumption that all humans seek personal freedom and try to sell their labour on the market. Citizenship creates possibilities for the realisation of such intentions. Citizenship in Eastern Europe developed, however, from the foundation of the communist state. 'Where are you working?' was the crucial question about human life in Eastern Europe. The citizen is a worker first of all. The state provides a secure position for the 'workers' in exchange for their political loyalty. What forms of participation can this model of citizenship propose? It could be political, economic or cultural participation depending on the areas in which the civilian activities were developing. The functions of such citizens were reduced only to the ability to 'inhabit' a certain territory. Namely, it provides for a secure position of 'workers' in exchange for their political loyalty. In the 1970s and 1980s Zinoviev used another term 'населенцы'/inhabitants (Zinoviev 1976) to describe those who have the status of citizens, but who are unable to use this status and realise their political activities because there is no public space. Their functions were reduced only to the ability to 'inhabit' a certain territory and work in it.

The compatriots legislation was created within exactly this paradigm for the newly created nation, thus establishing a new form of citizenship—in order to expand the corps of loyal compatriots supporting the political community, but without any personal and direct participation in political matters.

In general, we can observe a continuation in the forms of public participation in Eastern Europe—with reduced political participation and increasing participation in the distribution of the gross national product—everything from providing jobs to collection of social benefits. Legal political participation of people in this context inevitably decreases, just as it can increase outside of the political order where lack of representation creates a non-formal movement of the 'intelligentsia' or the workers (Solidarnost, Poland). Such movements destabilise the official order even when they are passive.

Economic participation is inevitably accompanied by participation in culture, education, information and history. There is a kind of social citizenship corresponding to the nature of the consumer. Participation of citizens in the distribution of the gross national product exacerbates the issue of access for non-citizens and consequently of the creation of filtering mechanisms, injustice and exclusion effects supported by the citizens. This is the constitution of the closed society, composed of equal active members. We can observe such an effect worldwide regarding non-citizens who pretend to participate in the distribution of the national product. It is very interesting to see how such a situation repeats itself with the quasi-citizens and compatriots in Eastern Europe. They use mainly social rather than political rights and they join the citizens who are deprived of political participation. This kind of policy does not contribute to the emergence of full citizens, but rather to a precariat of people who have a status that is alienated from the political sphere. The modern state in Eastern Europe forms such a class of people inside and outside its territory and jurisdiction. The beneficiaries of such policies are not only poor people or suffering people. There are both rich and poor, citizens and quasi-citizens in respect of whom the same model of alienation is chosen.

On 3 September 2007, the Law regarding the Polish Card was adopted in Poland. (*Act of 7 September* 2007 *on Polish Card*). The law assists Poles living abroad in order to ensure and maintain their ties with the national cultural heritage. This law was adopted with respect to persons who are nationals of third countries. Therefore, the jurisdiction of Poland was broadened to include non-citizens of Poland. The law concerns the moral obligations of Poland in regard to Poles in the East, who lost their Polish citizenship in the past, as well as to those Poles who have never been Polish citizens but have a sense of national identity and seek confirmation of their belonging to the Polish people.

The law has a national ethnic orientation and extends the normal understanding of the Polish nation as existing within its borders, while replacing it with a fairly narrow ethnic base. The main criterion for attaining the status of the Polish Card is citizenship possessed by the applicant in the period 1921–1939, or a family relationship with Polish citizens in this period. In 2018 the legislation was changed. Only ethnic Poles from the East could now join the Polish nation through the Polish Card.

An important element in the development of these new models of citizenship is the way states make decisions regarding people in third countries who are not their citizens. On 7 April 2011, the Constitutional Court of the Republic of Belarus thus made the decision № P-258/2011 regarding 'The Position of the Constitutional Court of the Republic of Belarus regarding the Law of the Republic of Poland on the Polish Card'. The Constitutional Court of Belarus claims that the Law on the Polish Card challenges the constitutional order of Belarus and this will be the subject of the next section.

17.3 Challenges

The institution of quasi-citizenship changes the model of citizenship and the nation, and can significantly change domestic and foreign policy relations of the state. The formation of quasi-citizenship at the national level is more conducive to the establishment of a special international legal status of persons with the status of a quasi-citizens belonging to multiple jurisdictions.

Quasi-citizenship makes it possible to understand the different types of partial citizenship and their relationship to full citizenship. Often quasi-citizenship or permanent residency status is seen as a transition to full citizenship. However, even in this case, quasi-citizenship is a long-time status for the individual, and a permanent status for the state.

The growing importance of international law and human rights is also due to the fact that they contribute to the process of forming statuses that previously did not exist and which could not exist in a system of wholly sovereign states. Such statuses also contribute to the constitutionalisation of international law in which public order and public authority are associated not only with the individual but also with such legal statuses that are extraterritorial in nature and not necessarily related to a particular sovereign state.

17.4 EU Citizenship

European Union citizenship is also an example of multi-level citizenship related to the quasi-citizenship. It officially originated in 1992. At the time of the beginning of the European Union, there occurred a well-known theoretical deadlock, because EU citizenship is perceived and interpreted as an extrapolation of national citizenship. As a simple reproduction of national citizenship, it only multiplies the problems of nationality on the Union level. One should take into account that EU citizenship is a tiered citizenship, which also incorporates a quasi-citizenship type of status. If EU citizenship is perceived and interpreted as an extrapolation of national citizenship, it creates a well-known theoretical problem.

Since its introduction in the Maastricht Treaty, the European concept of citizenship has been criticised from different sides as either too weak or too intrusive. A. Weiner said in 1998 that the requirement of citizenship in the Treatise on the European Union is only a little more than a cynical exercise in public relations. Others emphasise that the case law of the Court of Justice of the European Union concerning European citizenship after 1998 exceeds the limits of Union law (Stasinopoulos 2011). Citizenship of the European Union is appealing to EU residents, even when compared with national law, since the law they can refer to with an EU citizen status relates directly to the Charter of Fundamental Rights (CFR) of the EU and not to the constitutional right of the Member States.

Often these rights are broader than national constitutional rights. Furthermore, the constituting documents of the EU change and expand the concept of citizenship, compared with national constitutional rights. In the category of rights holders we find not only the full citizens of EU Member States but also the citizens of other EU Member States (regardless of their place of residence), the citizens of states that are in transition to EU membership or associate partners of the EU, and third-country nationals in the EU territory, including migrants. The constituent documents of the EU lay the foundations for a new model of citizenship, allowing for the multi-level nature of citizenship and for citizenship with different statuses, scope of rights and responsibilities.

The right to have rights is no longer dependent on any national constitutional provisions or international treaties on human rights (with all the attendant difficulties associated with access to such rights); they are now due to the fact that there is a common EU citizenship, taking into account a combination of EU jurisdictions, national governments and international law. Simultaneously, the EU taken as the whole of the EU is not subject to the jurisdiction of the European Charter of Human Rights (European Parliament 2017).

Article 20 Treaty on the Functioning of the European Union (TFEU) leaves no doubt that citizens of the Union are citizens of the Member States. But this position is not indisputable. In the *Rottman* case (*Janko Rottman v Freistaat Bayern.* Judgment of the Court (Grand Chamber) of 2 March 2010. ECLI:EU:C:2010:104), the Court of Justice questioned this provision because it indicated that national citizenship also depended on EU law. In this case, a German citizen was faced with the threat of denaturalisation, which, most likely, would have deprived him completely of all kinds of citizenship. Rottman became a citizen of Bavaria and at the same time of Germany, and thereby lost his Austrian citizenship. Later it turned out that Rottman had concealed from the German authorities the fact that he had a criminal record in Austria. On this basis, Germany annulled the decision to grant citizenship to Rottman. He argued that denaturalisation, since it would also deprive him of Union citizenship, is an interference with his rights within EU law and it should therefore be limited by EU law.

As often happens in the practice of the Court of Justice, Rottman won in principle, although he lost in fact: the Court indicated that, indeed, national measures that result in depriving a citizen of the Union of his Union citizenship clearly fall under the scope of EU legislation and, consequently, are subject to judicial review in the light of rules and principles of EU legislation. However, the decision stated that such measures were not in themselves prohibited. They should only be taken in accordance with the principle of proportionality.

Another example is the case, *Thierry Delvigne v Commune de Lesparre Médoc and Préfet de la Gironde* (Judgment of the Court (Grand Chamber) of 6 October 2015. Case C-650/13. ECLI:EU:C:2015:648). Despite the existence of a democratically elected European Parliament since 1979, the relationship between the Parliament and the status of Union citizenship has been ambiguous, since the Parliament did not represent a community of Union citizens but rather 'a community of European nations, where these peoples are determined by the Member States and national legislation'. The Treaty of Lisbon changed this paradigm, affirming that the European Parliament is not a representation of the peoples of Europe, but rather of the 'Union citizen'. The connection between Union citizenship and the European Parliament thus became apparent, and perhaps it was only a matter of time before the Court concluded that Union citizenship rights contain an autonomous right to vote in parliamentary elections in Europe. This decision was made in the *Delvigne* case.

In *Delvigne,* a French citizen challenged the internal provisions of French law, which automatically and permanently deprived him of voting rights, including his right to vote and the right to run for elections to the European Parliament, after his conviction for murder and imprisonment for up to 12 years. Not being able to take advantage of subsequent changes in legislation that would limit the duration of the ban, he challenged the decision to exclude him from the list of voters on the basis of two provisions of the Charter of Fundamental Rights—Article 49 on the application of a lighter punishment subsequently established and Article 39 on the right to vote in elections to the European Parliament.

The Advocate General Pedro Cruz Villalón found that punishment for murder and, therefore, the question of applying a lighter sentence was a matter of national law. Therefore, the first question was outside the scope of Union law, and the Charter did not apply. The second question, however, concerned elections to the European Parliament after the changes in the Lisbon Treaty. Here, the General Counsel found that the Union did have a sufficient interest in a matter arising from the still unexplored competence contained in Article 223 (2) TFEU regarding the adoption of a single electoral procedure or general principles. Applying the 'law' contained in Article 39 CFR to the case under consideration, he found that the restriction imposed by France was proportionate and respected the essence of the law. The Grand Chamber of the Court also found that the Charter applied, but that French law was nonetheless a permissible restriction of the rights contained in the Statute. For the Court, this issue generally entered into Union law, but not as arising from an interest or uncontrolled competence, but rather from the obligation contained in Article 14 (3) of the Treaty on European Union (TEU) and in the European Parliament Elections Act 1976, that such elections will be 'universal and fair '. The question thus fell under the scope of Union law, and, therefore, the rights of the Charter applied. Article 39 CFR, in conjunction with the above-mentioned requirement contained in Article 14 (3), the TEU actually contained a specific right to vote in elections to the European Parliament, which were granted to the citizens of the Union. This right may be limited, but French law seems to be proportionate and does not affect the essence of the right itself.

Delvigne is an important judgement in terms of constitutional law and the political nature of Union citizenship. (See case C-300/04 *Eman and Sevinger v College van Burgemeester en Wethouders van Den Haag* EU: C: 2006: 545, [2006] ECR I-8055.) In particular, it contains important statements about the political rights of citizens of the Union, which are based on the provisions of the Charter and not on the national constitution. The Court found for the first time that Union citizens enjoy a specific and autonomous right to vote in elections to the European Parliament, as contained in Article 39 of the CFR. Note that due to the nature of this protection of fundamental rights in the Union, the judgement cannot rely on this provision and the right contained in it in order to ascertain that this issue falls within the scope of Union law, therefore, the reference to TEU Article 14 (3) to ascertain the jurisdiction. Fundamental rights are 'second order norms' in the EU legal order and apply only if another 'first order rule' of the essential law of the Union applies. Thus, traditionally, national legislation will be subject to revision according to fundamental rights based on Union law, if such a right operates 'within the law of the Union', and as a rule either exercising or departing from EU legislation. The basic EU rights alone cannot form the basis for a review in the absence of any other element of Union legislation. It differs from the right contained in Article 20 (2) (b) to vote in the European Parliament and local elections in another Member State. This right is simply a classic transnational right to non-discrimination, ensuring equal treatment of citizens of the Union residing in other Member States. Citizens of the EU did not strictly speaking have a right to vote in European Parliament elections as pure citizens of the Union without their relation the national citizenship. In *Delvigne*, the Court actually recognises such a right for the first time. Union citizenship achieves a truly political and supranational status, including the direct right to participate in the democratic life of the Union itself.

The third example of the implementation of quasi-citizenship is the case *Zembrano* (*Gerardo Ruiz Zambrano v Office national de l'emploi, ONE*, Judgment of the Court (Grand Chamber) of 8 March 2011. C-356/11. ECLI:EU:C:2011:124). The case concerns the right of EU citizens to reunification with third-country nationals (TCN) who are family members residing in another Member State. In particular, in joint cases C-356/11, C-357/11 O, S & L, adopted on 6 December 2012, the Court was asked whether a TCN could receive the right of residence step-by-step in the case of family relations with EU citizens. This issue is situated at the crossroads between EU citizenship, immigration law and the fundamental right to family life, and this issue turned out to be annoying for the Court.

In the *Zambrano* case, the Court ruled that the Colombian parents of two Belgian children born and raised in Belgium, not enjoying the right to free movement, cannot be denied permission to live and work if the effect is to deprive citizens of the Union of the genuine use and essence of the rights granted by their status as EU citizens. *Zambrano* effectively revised the scope of EU legislation, expanding its scope to a 'purely internal situation' and avoiding backward discrimination, abandoning the cross-border element normally required to initiate EU legislation.

However, the Court did not give any indication as to what the 'true pleasure/essence of rights' test may entail, with the exception of the mysterious reference to the above-mentioned *Rottman* case; it was merely noted that the internal situation was subject to EU law 'by its nature and its consequences'.

Zambrano was an example indeed of the external limits of EU law: the Court sought to avoid the unfortunate consequences of reverse discrimination by stretching—if somewhat strained—the scope of EU law. However, it lost its credibility in subsequent cases, creating an unbearable degree of uncertainty and ambiguity in the jurisprudence. The *Zambrano* case is very important, since the Court retreated into the regime governing the reunification of third-country nationals.

17.5 Conclusion

Two paths of multi-level citizenship development are possible.

The first identifies human rights and citizen rights. This path can significantly weaken the standards of citizenship and create a model of citizenship without participation and responsibility. Moreover, such identification weakens protection for noncitizens, since access to human rights is provided only through citizenship. In such a model, human rights conceived without any connection to citizenship are also transformed into an ideology, since it becomes a theory of human rights poorly connected with everyday practices. In this model, law is no longer measured by justice, since it is itself the measure of justice. Morality has only a limited impact, because it is no longer the process of creating normativity and becomes an external system of rules. Moreover, morality becomes inapplicable wherever human rights coincide with the rights of the citizen.

Citizenship associated with public order and identified with human rights is a mechanism for alienation of those who are not citizens. This situation leads to the exaggerated importance of security and guarantees in the field of citizen rights, since the greatest degree of security is concentrated within the framework of the institution of citizenship. The result is the redefinition of the dichotomy between 'public' and 'private'; or rather, this dichotomy is being destroyed, since the private and the public merge into the area where security is ensured.

As a result, citizenship is isolated from the principles that feed it—from the 'Self', from 'Dignity' and from 'Freedom'. The link between dignity and 'absolute independence' on the one hand and 'equality' in the framework of a separate community on the other presages the modern version of dignity, which is inextricably linked to inviolability or autonomy and equality. Citizenship does the work of democracy, and yet it overlaps significantly with the principle of human dignity. The Polish constitution makes this explicit: 'The inherent and inalienable dignity of the person shall constitute a source of freedoms and rights of persons and citizens.'

Instead, security becomes the main common value. Persons are going for their secure conditions. It is important to examine those question especially considering the modern problems of increasing migration, marginalisation of aliens and poor groups, as well as ethnic and religious minorities, workers searching for a job guarantee from state authorities, to minimise risks on the labour market. Full citizens are the beneficiaries of such a system. It can lead to their paradoxical deprivation in the political sphere because they are included in the social order in a negative manner, through their political exclusions. They transfer their political competencies to the modern state, becoming similar to the quasi-citizens and non-citizens who are not participants in the public sphere. This promotes the erosion of the social and civic life.

The second path of quasi-citizenship development is to consider citizenship as a process. The concept of citizenship comprises:

- the individual status
- the community representation
- the relationships between them.

Connections between them are dynamic. To understand the importance of citizenship it is not sufficient to consider the legal consolidation of a certain status, and the horizontal relationships between citizens, their relations with the state, as well as the relationship between citizens and non-citizens. This is precisely because the study of such phenomena involves a certain difficulty. Citizenship and other statuses can be explained not only as static institutions but also as processes (Wiener 1998). Citizenship as a process is not a solid form, but a stream which includes the formation of representation. In this perspective, civil society is an imitation of representation, since civil society only matters in the context of a particular environment—the political sphere, the state, the political power endowed with a sensible decision-making process. In this situation civil society enters into constant conflict with those representations that are formed by the state. Such a conflict revives the civic life which develops between the representation (citizen) and the human being (Self).

It must be emphasised that this kind of practice develops within the context of several important circumstances. It is important to see the differences between the 'Self' and the representation or legal status. Some of the freedoms and values belong only to the 'Self', not to the 'citizen'. At the highest level of self-awareness, the Self remains autonomous. It is the ground of the true freedom. Simultaneously, the lack of citizenship creates a state of the deepest poverty associated with a lack of public connections. Public institutions cannot resolve any issues of the Self, but they can include the person in public relations. What kind of communication do the models of citizenship provide?

Participation in the public sphere is always a call for the 'Self', which should find its place in the public system, and own moral ground for participation. This is a complex and difficult task. In this path the 'Self' can discover that citizenship can be a process, that dignity is not a 'right' or a state, but an action and a form of moral creativity.

Hannah Arendt wrote:

> Human Dignity needs a new guarantee which can be found only in a new political principle, in new law on earth, whose validity this time must comprehend the whole of humanity while its power must remain strictly limited, rooted in and controlled by newly defined territorial entities. (Arendt 1973)

Hannah Arendt supposed that participation in a political community is what makes human dignity meaningful; where people are members of a political community, they have the 'right to have rights'. Political community and participation in it is the necessary environment for the appearance of human dignity. On the other hand, the dignity of those who are outside of any political community, who are stateless, is nothing more than the 'abstract nakedness' that renders them vulnerable to tyranny. If, as Arendt says, dignity is the capacity to act within a political community, the jurisprudence of dignity fosters that capacity.

This second path for the development of citizenship opens up for the close cooperation and communication between people in their local communities, wherein the dignity, rights, the model of collaboration and participation and the image of the 'Self' appear. In this place the 'Self' finds its realisation and readiness to bring about a status in the broader public sphere, though subject to constant change.

Bibliography

Act of 7 September 2007 on Polish Card. Dz.U.2014.1187. https://www.msz.gov.pl/resource/9b224df2-9dd2-44c6-8489-38ae23b9035f:JCR. Accessed May 6, 2019.

Arendt, H. (1973). *The origins of Totalitarism*. New York: Harcourt Inc.

Barthes, R. (1978). *A lover's discourse, fragments*. New York: Hill and Wang.

Bauböck, R. (1994). *Transnational citizenship: membership and rights in international migration.* Camberley: Edward Elgar Publishing.

British Nationality Act 1981. https://www.legislation.gov.uk/ukpga/1981/61. Accessed May 6, 2019

Brubaker, R. (1998). *Citizenship and nationhood in France and Germany*. Harvard: Harvard University Press.

Code de l'entrée et du séjour des étrangers et du droit d'asile [C.E.S.E.D.A.] [Code of Entry and Stay of Foreigners and the Right of Asylum] art. L511–1, https://www.legifrance.gouv.fr/affichCodeArticle.do?cidTexte=LEGITEXT000006070158&idArticle=LEGIARTI000006335173&dateTexte=&categorieLien=cid, archived at https://perma.cc/2JK2-TQYX. Accessed May 6, 2019

Cohen, E. F. (2014). *Semi-citizenship in democratic politics*. Cambridge: Cambridge University Press.

Consolidated Act of Danish Nationality (of 2003, with an amendment in 2004) jf. lovbekendtgørelse nr. 113 af 20. februar 2003, med de ændringer, der følger af lov nr. 311 af 5. maj 2004. https://www.retsinformation.dk/Forms/r0710.aspx?id=28974. Accessed May 6, 2019.

European Parliament (2017) EPRS, EU accession to the European Convention on Human Rights (ECHR), July 2017. https://www.europarl.europa.eu/thinktank/en/document.html?reference=EPRS_BRI%282017%29607298. Accessed May 6, 2019.

Federal Law Concerning the Entry, Residence and Settlement of Aliens (Aliens Act 1997). https://www.legislationline.org/documents/id/6541. Accessed May 6, 2019.

Federal Law of the Russian Federation of May 24, 1999, No. 99-FZ 'About state policy of the Russian Federation concerning compatriots abroad'. https://cis-legislation.com/document.fwx?rgn=1407. Accessed 6 May 2019.

Greek Law 1975/1991 on aliens. *** . Accessed May 6, 2019.

Hammer, T. (1990). *Democracy and the nation state: Aliens, denizen and citizens in a world of international migration*. Aldershot: Avebury.

Law 2910/2001 Entry and Stay of Aliens in Greek Territory. Acquisition of Greek Citizenship by Naturalization and Other Provisions. https://www.refworld.org/pdfid/3b209fd54.pdf. Accessed May 6, 2019.

Law of the Republic of Belarus of June 2, 1993, No. 2335-XII 'On the procedure for citizens of the Republic of Belarus to leave the Republic of Belarus and enter the Republic of Belarus' / Закон Республики Беларусь от 2 июня 1993 г. № 2335-XII «О порядке выезда из Республики Беларусь и въезда в Республику Беларусь граждан Республики Беларусь. https://kodeksy-by.com/zakon_rb_o_poryadke_vyezda_iz_respubliki_belarus_i_vezda_v_respubliku_belarus_grazhdan_respubliki_belarus.htm. Accessed May 6, 2019.

Legislative Decree 25.7.1998, No. 286 on 'Consolidated Act of Provisions concerning immigration and the condition of third-country nationals. https://ec.europa.eu/migrant-integration/librarydoc/legislative-decree-2571998-no-286-on-consolidated-act-of-provisions-concerning-immigration-and-the-condition-of-third-country-nationals. Accessed May 6, 2019.

Marshall, T. H. (1950). *Citizenship and social class: And other essays*. Cambridge: Cambridge University Press.

Netherlands Vreemdelingenwet 2000 [Aliens Act 2000] (Nov. 23, 2000, as last amended effective Mar. 9, 2013), Overheid.nl, https://wetten.overheid.nl/BWBR0011823/geldigheidsdatum_26-03-2013. Accessed May 6, 2019.

Pocock, J. G. A. (1995). The idea of citizenship since classical times. In R. S. Beiner (Ed.), *Theorizing citizenship* (pp. 29–52). Albany: State University of New York Press.

Soysal, Y. N. (1994). *Limits of citizenship. Migrants and post national membership in Europe*. University Chicago Press.

Stasinopoulos, P. (2011). EU Citizenship as a battle of the concepts: Travailleur v Citoyen. *European Journal of Legal Studies, 4* (2, Autumn/Winter), 74–103.

The Decision of the Constitutional Court of the Republic of Belarus on April 7, 2011, № P-258/2011 On the position of the constitutional court of the republic of Belarus under the law of the Republic of Poland 'On the Map of the Pole'. https://www.kc.gov.by/print.aspx?guid=23203. Accessed May 6, 2019.
Thierry Delvigne v Commune de Lesparre Médoc and Préfet de la Gironde. Judgement of the Court (Grand Chamber) of 6 October 2015. Case C-650/13. ECLI:EU:C:2015:648.
Turner, B. S. (1990). Outline of a theory of citizenship. *Sociology, 24*(2), 189–217.
Wiener, A. (1998). *European citizenship practice: Building institutions of a non-state*. Boulder: Westview Press.
Zinoviev, A. (1976). *Зияющие высоты / Ziiaiuszczije visoty*. Paris: L'Âge d'Homme.

Oleg Bresky Ph.D. in Law, is Director of the Johannes Althusius Institute, and author of the monographs *From Transitology to the Theory of Borderland* (Vilnius, EHU, 2008) and *Locality: To the Grounds of Social Place and Space* (Vilnius, EHU, 2011)

Chapter 18
Citizenship, Post-Communism and the Age of Migration

Leif Kalev and Mari-Liis Jakobson

Abstract The chapter discusses the contemporary tensions within citizenship as a substantive concept, focusing on the effects of migration on citizenship and utilising both the theoretical debates and empirical studies. Focusing on the experience of post-communist citizenship, we study which aspects of citizenship appear most relevant and which kind of message this conveys for citizenship and human rights. In order to develop a sustainable arrangement for a meaningful citizen status and agency in the age of migration, we need to ensure citizenship as a legal and political foundational status embedded and enacted meaningfully by the people in practice and fostered by the interactive state institutions in a way that enlarges the power and capacity of the involved actors.

Keywords Citizenship · Migration · Post-communism · Globalisation · Democracy

18.1 Introduction

In the contemporary era of globalisation, the foundational institution of democracy and individual autonomy—citizenship—is facing new challenges on many fronts. As political upheavals in different countries (e.g. the financial crisis, European migration crisis, Brexit) have indicated, liberal democracy, hinged on an understanding of equality of citizens, representative democracy, separation of powers and numerous rights ensuring civilised and pluralist dialogue, has come under significant strains.

The concept of globalisation and its content is rather diffused, more concretely conceptualised in terms of its macro-level effects. In order to look at the present trends from a wider perspective, including citizens, we will scale our discussion

L. Kalev (✉) · M.-L. Jakobson
Tallinn University School of Governance, Law and Society, Tallinn, Estonia
e-mail: leif@tlu.ee

M.-L. Jakobson
e-mail: mljakobson@tlu.ee

M. C. Jacobsen et al. (eds.), *Cosmopolitanism, Migration and Universal Human Rights*, https://doi.org/10.1007/978-3-030-50645-2_18

down and focus on the effects of migration on citizenship as a foundational political status of an individual.

As Bauman (1998) has illustrated, globalisation has divided polities internally—into the better educated, progressive and mobile winners of globalisation, and the more traditionalist groups leading a more local life (even when migrating), who feel they have lost out on the benefits of globalisation. This prompts us to ask in which ways the fundamental normative understandings of citizenship (see e.g. Heater 1999; Delanty 2000) are applicable in the contemporary context, and how to support meaningful state–citizen relationships.

International migration is perceived as one of the key characteristics of contemporary globalisation (Waters 2001)—the receding boundaries of individuals' mobilities enhance an understanding of an increasingly interconnected world, while also making the social fabric more complex and creating new and spatially more complicated interdependencies and social and cultural practices. In this chapter, we will use the theories that capture the transformations of citizenship in the era of migration to gain an understanding of how globalisation processes more generally can influence citizenship.

In addition, we argue that the aspects of the current crisis of democracy in Western Europe can be attributed to the weakness of citizenship as individual political agency. In fact, many of the characteristics of citizenship in the so-called post-communist Central and Eastern European states can also be witnessed among the 'losers from globalisation' in the Western world. A more detailed insight into citizenship in the post-communist context can also help to interpret the possible future transformations in relation to democracy and human rights.

The chapter is structured as follows; first, we will start by outlining the institution of citizenship and introducing the key debates over its development in the age of migration (e.g. Castles et al. 2014). This is followed by presenting the key features of post-communist citizenship. The main discussion will focus on which aspects of citizenship appear most relevant in the practice of post-communist citizenship and what kind of message this conveys for citizenship and human rights in the age of migration.

18.2 Citizenship as a Substantive Concept

Citizenship is an institution for establishing and ensuring the autonomous status of an individual and relating him or her to state authorities and fellow citizens. Citizenship as we know it is a relatively new phenomenon. Historically, there has been no comparable legal and political position for common people in terms of status and agency, and they have been characterised as subjects (e.g. Heater 2004). Modern citizenship developed with the modern state, especially in its nation-making stage during the last two or three centuries (e.g. Raadschelders 1998; Pierson 2004). The transfer of sovereignty from the body politic of the king to the body politic of citizens is a major turning point in the history of Western democracy (Turner 1990, 211).

As an institution, citizenship conveys internal defining rules. In the modern form, it is expected to be unitary, meaning that all holders of the status should have full rights and obligations; sacred, meaning that citizens must be willing to make sacrifices for the state (or the community) that grants them citizenship; national, meaning that membership must be based on a community that is simultaneously political and cultural; democratic, meaning that citizens should be entitled to participate significantly in politics, and that access to citizenship should be open to all residents so that, in the long run, residence in the community and citizenship will coincide; unique, in that each citizen should belong to one and only one political community; consequential, meaning that citizenship must entail important social and political privileges that distinguish its holders from non-citizens; and individual, meaning it can only be possessed and exercised by individual human beings (Brubaker 1989; Schmitter 2001).

At the same time citizenship has many dimensions and is associated with different democratic normatives. It can be characterised as an ever-changing compromise between its internal contradictions, termed *aporias* by Huysmans and Guillaume (2013). One of these *aporias* is the tension between nationalism and republicanism. Initially, modern citizenship was a political and legal status largely legitimised by nationalist sentiments. In the words of Habermas (1999, 115): 'The nation is Janus-faced. Whereas the voluntary nation of citizens is the source of democratic legitimation, it is the inherited nation founded on ethnic membership (*die geborene Nation der Volksgenossen*) that secures social integration.' Alongside rule of law and liberal democracy, the nationalist component became substituted by constitutional patriotism. However, due to its formality, constitutional patriotism on its own has turned out to be rather difficult to legitimise, which has resulted in counter-reactions.

Citizenship is simultaneously constraining and enabling. As a constraint, it has classically been characterised by closure, enabling feedback in a bounded community, a polity (Brubaker 1992). Polity is the locus of citizen agency and membership, be it legal, political, social or other. Citizenship is also an instrument of inclusion and exclusion, creating a community of sentiment and developing its identity bases, i.e. marking the borders with others, and strengthening it with symbols, routines, rituals, division of rights and obligations, etc.

But citizenship is also an enabling concept, conveying the values of democracy, equality, empowerment and responsibility. General citizenship is the premise of modern democratic governance, says Tilly (1995), for whom democracy is the prime relationship between the state and the citizen. Citizenship rights enable citizens to stand up for their other rights (Skinner and Strath 2003). This is related to citizen agency, active and democratic citizenship, etc. (e.g. Crick and Lockyer 2010; Stoker et al. 2011) and, more broadly, to political and societal participation and membership as a lived practice and also to identity construction (e.g. Sicakkan and Lithman 2005). Citizenship is the status that makes members of the community equal, regardless of their income, education or descent, as it grants people equal rights to decide over the affairs of the general community and provides equal minimal social standing. As famously noted by Marshall (1992), focusing on citizenship is the alternative to Marxist world revolution.

18.3 Modern Citizenship Meets the Age of Migration

The past few decades are often called the age of migration (e.g. Castles et al. 2014). While migration as such is nothing new, it has been transformed by the development of global opportunities for fast travel and instant communication, human awareness and skills in using these, and the resulting change in lifestyles, activities and identities of many people (see e.g. Kivisto and Faist 2010).

This change has often been characterised as transnationalisation (see e.g. Pitkänen et al. 2012; Faist et al. 2013), a bottom-up development of cross-border practices and hyphenated identities, building up transnational spaces. Transnationalisation is often perceived as simultaneous with globalisation, albeit occurring on a geographically more limited scale (Waters 2001). It has also led to discussions on multiple citizenship (e.g. Kalekin-Fishman and Pitkänen 2006; Spiro 2016) and securitisation (Nyers 2009; Guillaume and Huysmans 2013; Bourbeau 2017). This reflects some of the key strategies citizens and state institutions use in this new environment.

The theories on how migrant transnationalisation is affecting citizenship can be divided into two camps: the expansionists and the erosionists (Kivisto and Faist 2007). The expansionists tend to claim that processes related to globalisation and international migration are building up new governance and practice arenas for citizenship, transforming citizenship identities into broader and more inclusive identities and also bringing new legal forms of citizenship to light. Expansionists see that transnationalisation ought to result in the spread of multiple citizenship, an, if not, then it could be substituted by either residential citizenship, providing immigrants with rights enabling civic and political participation in host country, or external citizenship, ensuring that emigrants can continue to be participant in their country of origin (Bauböck 1994). They also associate migration with the spread of a more cosmopolitan identity. For instance, Schlenker et al. (2017) have witnessed that numerous Swiss emigrants abroad have opted for a cosmopolitan citizenship identity. Often, migration is even depicted as a school of democracy. For instance, Perez-Armendariz and Crow (2010) have illustrated how migratory experience can be a process of political learning and even helps to ensure democratisation in the country of origin. Smith and Bakker (2007) have portrayed the political activation of Mexican emigrants in the United States, and portrayed their role in the political and economic development of their country of origin.

The erosionists, on the other hand, tend to be critical about how empowered transnational migrants can actually be, since they need to establish their presence in more than one country at a time, and point out that migration is often utilised as an exit strategy, people voting with their feet against government policy, rather than about using their voice and aiming to achieve change with their participation (Jakobson 2014). Often, migrants end up in a legally disadvantaged position, where their participation in politics in their home country becomes more difficult or they do not have a sufficient rights-based position enabling them to protect their rights in the country of destination (Smith 2003), as not all states are willing to allow dual, residential or external citizenship. In addition, some studies (e.g. Chang 2004;

Jakobson et al. 2012) indicate that a status of a migrant, which also means having to cope with everyday practicalities in multiple locations simultaneously, can wear out one's political agency and affect political participation opportunities negatively. Moreover, migrant experience does not necessarily develop a cosmopolitan or even a dual identity, but can also result in long-distance nationalism (Conversi 2012).

These two approaches appear to explain somewhat different migration-related phenomena. The divergences demonstrate the importance of context—e.g. the particularity of the transnational space, of the subjects themselves and how they practice citizenship, but are also subject to multiple tensions currently challenging the modern concept of citizenship and its critiques.

18.4 Contemporary Tensions in Citizenship

In terms of theory, the tensions within citizenship in the age of migration are well highlighted by Chandler (2012) who scrutinises the (neo)liberal-cosmopolitan and poststructural-biopolitical critiques of the territorial political community, focusing on their more radical tendencies.

In the (neo)liberal-cosmopolitan critique, the liberal democratic frameworks of political community have turned out to be unable to empower and protect minorities, the marginal and the excluded. The positive programme is to reach an external mechanism for enforcing cosmopolitan rights. The objective is to legitimise liberal policy frameworks without engaging with the electorate, who are seen as too egoistic or apathetic and distanced from liberal policy elites, and, under reflexive modernity, lacking commonality. This is based on the belief that progressive ends—such as the protection of human rights, international peace or sustainable development—would be more easily achieved without the institutional constraints of democratic accountability (Chandler 2012, 106). The democratic feedback mechanism in the liberal-cosmopolitan order would be played by civil society, which is often rather elitist (see e.g. Walzer 1998; Falk 1995; Kuper 2004).

The poststructural-biopolitical critique demonstrates that (neo)liberal-cosmopolitan discourse of rights and law merely enhances the power of liberal governance and ultimately advocates for a permanent state of exception for governments to do whatever they prefer, using the banner of global human rights if necessary (see e.g. Agamben 1998, 2005). However, their proposal to disengage from any type of power and their understanding of formal political and legal frameworks is not divergent from the (neo)liberal-cosmopolitans.

Thus, neither the (neo)liberal-cosmopolitans nor the poststructural-biopolitical critics ascribe any significance to citizen agency or the distinction between citizens and non-citizens. Instead, they claim that the world is ruled by a benign or oppressive power separate from citizens. There is no clue which orientation the power could take, except at best a vague (neo)liberal-cosmopolitan hope, not shared by the poststructuralists.

All of this is in clear contrast to the modern theories of citizenship, which depict the political community as a sum of individuals bearing equal rights and where the rule of law and the legitimacy of government is derived from the consent and accountability of rights-holding citizens. Without a formal focal point of accountability, there can be no political community, nor a framework binding and subordinating individuals as political subjects (Chandler 2012, 111–115).

The attenuation of politics and hollowing out of representation constitutes the collapse of any meaningful political community. Without the need to worry about the constitutive relationship between the government and citizen, political community becomes entirely abstract. There is no longer a need to formulate a political programme and gains supporters in order to challenge or overcome individual, sectional or parochial interests. 'Engagement between individuals no longer has to take a political or stable form: all that is left is ever-fluctuating (and ultimately impotent) networked communication' (Chandler 2012, 119).

In the practice of contemporary Western states, we see a tendency of redefining the roles of citizens in order to be functional for a neoliberal governance order (Newman and Clarke 2009) and the psychology and data-based steering of people to fit the prescribed roles (Jones et al. 2013; Bigo et al. 2019). The question of societal limits for whoever holds power has already become relevant.

18.5 Key Characteristics of Post-Communist Citizenship

After the fall of the Soviet Bloc, Central and Eastern Europe underwent two broadly simultaneous transformations adopting both democracy and market economy. In most countries of the region this was complemented by a third development: building up full-scale nation states as many smaller countries became independent of the fracturing Socialist amalgamations such as the Soviet Union, Czechoslovakia or Yugoslavia (Kuzio 2001). It is easily understandable that the state–citizen relations became a fundamental test of democratisation in this context (Przeworski 1995).

Very broadly we can summarise the post-Soviet development of citizenship policies and legislation in four main phases: (1) Soviet legacy up to 1990; (2) nationalising developments of 1990s; (3) the influence of international human rights and EU conditionality from the mid-1990s to mid-2000s; (4) developments during the membership in European Union after 2004 (or 2007 for Eastern Balkans). During this development the post-communist Central and Eastern European discourse on citizenship obtained several specific features that can be summarised into five main points (see i.e. Jakobson 2017; Berglund et al. 2013).

18.5.1 Historical Legacy of Elitist Governance and Limited Role for Citizens

After the Middle Ages, Central and Eastern Europe became the territory of various large empires (see e.g. Flora et al. 1999; Bideleux and Jeffries 2007) where there was no significant political role for common people and the status of a citizen was weak if it existed at all. Although the communist regimes after the Second World War were very different, the elite-controlled Soviet systems had little role for evolutionary bottom-up political agency and the status of a citizen remained weak. This meant the Western European, more broadly understood citizenship had little direct presence here (e.g. Agh 1994) and the mass social movements during the regime change soon gave way to a top-down decision making estranged from mass publics (e.g. Lauristin et al. 1997). This was to an extent modified but not changed by the accession to the European Union which consolidated democracy but was led and utilised by the elite (e.g. Kalev and Roosmaa 2012).

18.5.2 Rule-Based and Specifics-Oriented Definition of Citizenship

The notion of the relation between the state and the citizen is strongly altered in the Central and Eastern European context in comparison with the West: the content of citizenship is defined and dominated by state institutions, or top-down, rather than bottom-up, or by the demands from the citizens themselves (see e.g. Skinner and Strath 2003). Post-communist citizenship has been much affected by the Soviet legacy—the meanings associated with it and the policies that regulated it. First of all, Soviet citizenship was not about equality and rights or about democracy, but rather about restrictions and privileges allocated by the state and/or the party (Alexopoulos 2006). The state remains a dominant player in terms of content of citizenship to date (Greene 2012). In Soviet times passports (as well as all the other benefits) were strictly rationed. Movement was a privilege allocated by the authorities (Galasiński and Galasińska 2007). The post-communist states have also tended to adopt rather rigid rules of citizenship allocation (Liebich 2000). Citizenship policy also came to be securitised (Shevel 2009). The rigidity of rules is generally associated with discursive claims about state sovereignty. As the rules are specifics-oriented, the wider understanding of citizenship as a fundamental status of rights and foundation for democracy becomes veiled. Even voting in elections can be construed as performing a legally prescribed citizen obligation and not as a part of democratic citizen agency.

18.5.3 Instrumental Approach to Citizenship Practice

As a result, the post-communist perception of citizenship is rather instrumental, with people often looking pragmatically for more opportunities to alleviate their standard of living. State authorities are seen as barely comprehensible power that is distant from a citizen's everyday life and best avoided to escape excessive regulation and surveillance. In the Russian Federation, for instance, the social contract over citizenship is based on the 'exchange of political quiescence for prosperity' (Greene 2012, 135)—it centres, in other words, on renouncing political rights for social rights. In comparison with the Soviet times, however, the citizens are no longer offered direct goods for political quiescence; rather, they are presented with the economic opportunity to gather these goods. A similarly neoliberal disposition towards citizenship has also been identified in more consolidated post-communist democracies (Solska 2011). The rent-seeking character of the post-communist state–citizen relationship developed in accordance with the dominant survival values, including materialism, prioritising security over liberty and abstaining from political activism (Inglehart and Weltzel 2005).

18.5.4 National Communitarianism

While Western citizenship has much been built upon the civic tradition of defining a political community, the importance of the ethnic understanding is significantly more influential in Central and Eastern European states. Again, historical context plays a role. The nationalising states (Brubaker 1996, 2003, 2011) can both restrict the opportunities of minorities and expand citizenship to members of the co-ethnic community abroad (e.g. Dumbrava 2014). Even after transition in other fields was completed, citizenship policy was one of the domains which states regarded as their expression of sovereignty and nationhood (Pogonyi 2011). Post-communist states tend to adapt rather rigid forms of citizenship implementation. For instance, in 2000 only five post-communist states out of 27 allowed multiple citizenship (Liebich 2000). Thus the cohesion of society has been traditionally based on national communitarianism as opposed to liberal citizenship which refers to national cohesion and legitimacy being significantly constructed via appeals to language, historical events and traditions instead of a more *Gesellschaft*-type of solidarity between autonomous individuals as democratic and legal citizens. This is partly related to a Central and Eastern European understanding of nationalism and citizenship (see e.g. Gellner 1983, 1997; Brubaker 1992) but partly to the limited political space for commoners in an elite polity (e.g. Agh 1994). This makes regime legitimacy very vulnerable when tolerating multiculturalism, transnationalism or some other kind of openness as it is understood as failing or even betraying the nation.

18.5.5 Contradictions of Nostalgia and Turbomodernism

Both the elitist and populist legitimating discourses in Central and Eastern Europe have included appealing to some kind of imagined historical golden era or situation or feature to which to return, as well as heralding avangardism in market reforms, digital innovation and whatever is currently fashionably new. For example, Kuhl (2009) outlined three major discursive transitional logics in Estonian administrative culture: anti-Sovietism, continuation of statehood, turbomodernism—of which the last one is projected into the future. Turbomodernist discourses depict Estonia as a small and dynamic state, in juxtaposition with other post-communist states as well as the static 'old democracies'. Embedded in liberalism, turbomodernism turned Estonia into a fertile ground for abrupt economic reforms, and it furthermore weakened the state–citizen relationship by explaining the modest expectations of citizens towards the state as a provider of welfare. Turbomodernism is also a potential discourse to make the Estonian post-communist citizen receptive to new changes and transformations, including those imposed by transnationalisation. This will be reflected in contradictions between the rigid and nationalising currents of the nostalgic citizenship discourse and the relative openness and flexibility of turbomodernist citizenship discourse (Jakobson 2017).

The above-mentioned notions are also evident in the citizenship discourses among transnational Estonians residing in or commuting to Finland. While their self-identification is predominantly national (as opposed to various forms of postnationalism), they perceive their citizenship status mostly in instrumental terms, as EU citizenship gives them the freedom of movement. And while they perceive it important to be law-abiding citizens in Finland, their political citizen agency has been almost non-existent in both countries (ibid.).

We can draw three key conclusions from the above discussion. First, an understanding of citizenship as a foundational and substantive status for democracy is clearly weak in post-communist states. The narrow legal and specifics-oriented view has allowed citizenship to be more of a top-down instrument for governments. Second, post-communist citizenship is embedded in a rather instrumental and passive discourse and practice, oriented at the national community. This has greatly detached it from the relationship with democracy that has been intense in the modern Western European democracies. It also strengthens alienation supporting either marginalisation or emigration. This has been to an extent counterbalanced by appealing to national sentiments and pursuing a national community orientation. Renationalising citizenship by the governments can be moderate but also develop into more ambitious projects, such as in Hungary and Poland. Third, this way the interactive and positive understanding of the role of the government in ensuring citizenship and democracy will be substituted by a disenchanted distance from the top-down elite structures for redistribution. Through these developments the key elements of a citizen-oriented and democratic political system becomes dysfunctional and citizenship is hollowed of substance.

18.6 Ensuring Meaningful Citizenship

Several of the features of post-communist citizenship help to bring into light such aspects of citizenship that are foundational for the establishment and sustainability of the autonomous status of an individual citizen and a meaningful operation of democracy. We can bring out three key aspects.

First, there is a clear divergence between understanding citizenship as a foundational status of an individual (Arendt 1958; Marshall 1992) and as a set of top-down or contractual rules (Aleinikoff and Klusmeyer 2002; Dumbrava 2014). The former is based on the idea of constructing a meaningful and integral position of a citizen in the relevant legal, political and wider societal contexts. The latter is predominantly legal, much more concrete, even specific, and available for bargaining and top-down changes.

In the case that attention is focused on the latter, citizenship becomes arbitrary, top-down and not discursively ensuring a strong position of an individual. Thus, even civil and legal citizenship is not clearly ensured. The foundational status is based not only on somehow emerging rights and freedoms but the starting point of a sustainably autonomous individual enjoying rights balanced but also ensured by obligations. Of course, the existence of the foundational status is even more relevant for citizenship as a meaningful political status, be it legal (e.g. Dumbrava 2014) or substantial (e.g. Stoker et al. 2011).

Second, citizenship is also not just something that is stated or listed but is exercised, embedded in a societal context; it will be reproduced in the daily activities of people. This will make it alterable to changes, including subtle and evolutionary ones, and so keep it related to societal dynamics. This is in fact the way to mediate between the contradictions inherent in the concept of citizenship but also present in any other concept that is applied in social reality. This also allows sufficient flexibility for citizenship as an instrument of both inclusion and exclusion and through these establishing closure (Brubaker 1992).

Crucially, without embeddedness and evolution, there is no bottom-up mechanism for citizens for mutual motivation and empowerment, as well as a meaningful but peaceful test of their power as holders of significant autonomy. According to the performative view of public knowledge as the foundation of popular sovereignty (Chwaszsza 2012), people reproduce their status in the system based on constant observation and reflection of how others behave. Thus, the level at which an individual citizen acts as a part and representative of the (popular) sovereign is constantly reinterpreted, and this way the actual practice of democracy is established.

This is, of course, even more relevant for the quality of democracy that is largely based on citizen status and agency. Here, societally embedded and enacted citizenship needs an additional feature—the existence of at least some hope that it is possible to make life better by purposive common action. In the words of Habermas (2001, 60): 'The diagnosis of social conflicts transforms itself into a list of just as many political challenges only if we attach a further premise to the egalitarian institutions of rational law: the assumption that the unified citizens of a democratic community are able to shape their own social environment and can develop the capacity for action necessary for such interventions to succeed.'

Third, from a citizenship perspective, state authorities are not just legally mandated and sovereign top-down imposers evoking compliance. State institutions are seen as embedded in interactive and mutually constitutive relationships with citizenry, civic associations, companies and other societal but also inter- and trans-national actors. This provides the basis for the autonomy and agency of citizens being practically acknowledged by the state authorities. It also enables evolution (instead of just revolution) as the activities of the state institutions are not fixed but evolving in interaction with citizens.

Here the differences between redistributive and structural dimensions of state power are also highlighted. In the first, state institutions may redistribute the rights and obligations changing the rules and arrangements, and this is likely to be more beneficial to some and less so for others. But from the structural perspective, the state power is a societal resource that can be expanded by purposive action. In this positive dimension of power, the government can expand its authority by empowering citizens and other actors and may win out even by giving up some of its own powers or regulations as it gains a more capable citizenry and societal infrastructure to tap as an additional resource for political order and governing (Goverde et al. 2000; Kooiman 2003; Bell and Hindmoor 2009).

18.7 Conclusion

In order to develop a sustainable arrangement for a meaningful citizen status and agency in the age of migration, we are to find sufficient answers to the outlined three key challenges: how to (1) ensure citizenship as a legal and political foundational status, that is simultaneously (2) embedded and enacted meaningfully by the people in practice and (3) fostered by the interactive state institutions in a way that enlarges the power and capacity resource of the actors involved. This is relevant not only for individual autonomy but also more broadly for democracy and citizen-oriented governance.

The expansionist thinking about citizenship becoming post-national and being enacted or even celebrated as such in the context of migration may easily collide with the hollowing and alienating countertrends described by the erosionists (which, as noted above, are greatly at play in the context of post-communist transnationalism). However, this does not mean that citizenship as an empowering institution, which vests all members of the political community with equal rights, should be disregarded overall, as has happened in the (neo)liberal-cosmopolitan and poststructural-biopolitical critique of the nation-state-centred liberal democratic concept of polity. Without these, the so-called winners and losers of globalisation have the potential to step on rather different courses of political agency and the democratic and responsive government may well disappear. Based on the Central and Eastern European experience, we can say that the hope of side-lining citizen political status and agency in favour of an enlightened elite or the progressive power of radical activist networks is not fulfilled in practice and the internationally oriented elitism and instrumentalism can create a basis for strongly nationalising tendencies.

Substantive citizenship offers a practical basis to link citizens and state institutions together in a way that ensures and balances individual autonomy, social and political cohesion, and democratic and effective authority, and this way enables the alleviation of the currently strongly highlighted tensions of elitism and populism. Of course, these contingencies of normative ideals are articulated in the context of different political interests. In this sense, citizenship mostly offers resources for more moderate and cooperation-oriented political strategies.

In human rights discourse, there are also discussions related national citizenship and democracy as a human right (see e.g. Owen 2017) and also some approaches to citizenship and human rights as situated democratic practices (see e.g. Tully 2008). But citizenship also offers an understanding of the role of state institutions in proactive metagovernance oriented to a positive understanding of power as a resource, as well as the contingent and relational mutual construction of each other in state–citizenry interaction. Thus, the contextual and interactive aspects of citizenship may offer some fresh points of reflection also for human rights scholarship.

Bibliography

Agamben, G. (1998). *Homo sacer: Sovereign power and bare life*. Stanford: Stanford University Press.

Agamben, G. (2005). *State of exception*. Chicago: University of Chicago Press.

Agh, A. (1994). Citizenship and civil society in central Europe. In B. van Steenbergen (Ed.), *The condition of citizenship* (pp. 126–198). London, Thousand Oaks, New Delhi: Sage Publications.

Aleinikoff, T. A., & Klusmeyer, D. (2002). *Citizenship policies for an age of migration*. Washington D.C.: Carnegie Endowment for International Peace.

Alexopoulos, G. (2006) Soviet citizenship, more or less: Rights, emotions, and states of civic belonging. *Kritika: Explorations in Russian and Eurasian History*, *7*(3), 487–528.

Arendt, H. (1958). *The origins of totalitarianism*. Cleveland: The World Publishing Company.

Bauböck, R. (1994). *Transnational citizenship. Membership and rights in international migration*. Cheltenham, Northampton: Edward Elgar.

Bauman, Z. (1998). *Globalisation: The human consequences*. Cambridge, Oxford: Polity Press.

Bell, S., & Hindmoor, A. (2009). *Rethinking governance. The centrality of the state in modern society*. Cambridge: Cambridge University Press.

Berglund, S., Ekman, J., Deegan-Krause, L., & Knutsen, T. (2013). *The handbook of political change in Eastern Europe* (3rd ed.). Cheltenham, Northampton: Edward Elgar.

Bideleux, R., & Jeffries, I. (2007). *A history of Eastern Europe: Crisis and change* (2nd ed.). London, New York: Routledge.

Bigo, D., Isin, E. F., & Ruppert, E. (Eds.). (2019). *Data politics: Worlds, subjects, rights*. Abingon, New York: Routledge.

Bourbeau, P. (Ed.). (2017). *Handbook on migration and security*. Cheltenham, Northampton: Edward Elgar.

Brubaker, W. R. (1989). Traditions of nationhood and politics of citizenship. *States and Social Structures Newsletter, 9*(1989), 4–8.

Brubaker, W. R. (1992). *Citizenship and nationhood in France and Germany*. Cambridge, MS, London: Harvard University Press.
Brubaker, W. R. (1996). *Nationalism reframed. Nationhood and the national question in the New Europe*. Cambridge, New York: Cambridge University Press.
Brubaker, W. R. (2003). The return of assimilation? Changing perspectives on immigration and its sequels in France, Germany, and the United States. In C. Joppke & E. Morawska (Eds.), *Toward assimilation and citizenship: Immigrants in liberal Nation-States* (pp. 39–58). Houndmills, New York: Palgrave Macmillan.
Brubaker, W. R. (2011). Nationalizing states revisited: projects and processes of nationalization in post-Soviet states. *Ethnic and Racial Studies, 34*(11), 1785–1814.
Castles, S., de Haas, H., & Miller, M. J. (2014). *The age of migration. International population movements in the modern world* (5th ed.). Houndmills, New York: Palgrave Macmillan.
Chandler, D. (2012). The limits of post-territorial political community. In L. Beckman & E. Erman (Eds.), *Territories of citizenship* (pp. 100–122). Houndmills, New York: Palgrave Macmillan.
Chang, S. (2004). *Racial politics in an Era of transnational citizenship: The 1996 "Asian Donorgate" controversy in perspective*. Lanham: Lexington Books.
Chwaszcza, C. (2012). The practical conditions of the sovereignty of the people: The status of citizens in multilevel political organisations. In L. Beckman & E. Erman (Eds.), *Territories of citizenship* (pp. 81–99). Houndmills, New York: Palgrave Macmillan.
Conversi, D. (2012). Irresponsible radicalisation: diasporas, globalisation and long-distance nationalism in the digital age. *Journal of Ethnic and Migration Studies, 38*(9), 1357–1379.
Crick, B., & Lockyer, A. (Eds.). (2010). *Active citizenship: What could it achieve and how?* Edinburgh: Edinburgh University Press.
Delanty, G. (2000). *Citizenship in a global age. Society, culture, politics*. Buckingham, Philadelphia: Open University Press.
Dumbrava, C. (2014). *Nationality, citizenship and ethno-cultural belonging. Preferential membership policies in Europe*. Houndmills, New York: Palgrave Macmillan.
Faist, T., Fauser, M., & Reisenauer, E. (2013). *Transnational migration*. Cambridge, Malden: Polity Press.
Falk, R. A. (1995). *On humane governance: Toward a new global politics*. Cambridge: Polity Press.
Flora, P., Kuhnle, S., & Urwin, D. (Eds.). (1999). *State formation, nation-building and mass politics in Europe. The theory of Stein Rokkan*. Oxford, New York: Oxford University Press.
Galasiński, D., & Galasińska, A. (2007). Lost in communism, lost in migration: Narratives of the post-1989 polish migrant experience. *Journal of Multicultural Discourse, 2*(1), 47–62.
Gellner, E. (1983). *Nations and nationalism*. Ithaca: Cornell University Press.
Gellner, E. (1997). *Nationalism*. New York: New York University Press.
Goverde, H., Cerny, P. G., Haugaard, M., & Lentner, H. (Eds.). (2000). *Power in contemporary politics. Theories, practices, globalizations*. London, Thousand Oaks, New Delhi: Sage Publications.
Greene, S. A. (2012). Citizenship and the social contract in Post-Soviet Russia: Twenty years late? *Demokratizatsiya, 20*(2), 133–140.
Guillaume, X., & Huysmans, J. (Eds.). (2013). *Citizenship and security. The constitution of political Being*. London, New York: Routledge.
Habermas, J. (1999). The European Nation-State: On the past and future of sovereignty and citizenship. In C. Cronin & P. De Greiff (Eds.), *Inclusion of the other: Studies in political theory/Jürgen Habermas* (pp. 105–127). Cambridge, Maldon: Polity Press.
Habermas, J. (2001). *The postnational constellation. Political essays*. Cambridge, Massachusetts: The MIT Press.
Heater, D. (1999). *What is citizenship?* Cambridge, Malden: Polity Press.
Heater, D. (2004). *A brief history of citizenship*. Edinburgh: Edinburgh University Press.
Huysmans, J., & Guillaume, G. (2013). Citizenship and securitizing: Interstitial politics. In G. Guillaume & J. Huysmans (Eds.), *Citizenship and security. The constitution of political Being* (pp. 18–34). London, New York: Routledge.

Inglehart, R., & Weltzel, C. (2005). *Modernization, cultural change and democracy*. New York, Cambridge: Cambridge University Press.
Jakobson, M. -L. (2014). *Citizenship in transformation: Political agency in the context of migrant transnationalism*. [Doctoral dissertation]. Tallinn: Tallinn University.
Jakobson, M. -L. (2017). 'It all does not matter that much in the European Union'—Migrant transnationalism and the transformation of post-communist citizenship discourse. *Europe-Asia Studies, 69*(5), 754–770.
Jakobson, M.-L., Kalev, L., & Ruutsoo, R. (2012). Becoming postnational? Citizenship as discourse and practice among "transnationals." In R. Vetik (Ed.), *Nation-building in the context of post-communist transformation and globalization: The case of Estonia* (pp. 115–140). Frankfurt: Peter Lang.
Jones, R., Pykett, J., & Whitehead, M. (2013). *Changing Behaviours. On the rise of the psychological state*. Cheltenham, Northampton: Edward Elgar.
Kalekin-Fishman, D., & Pitkänen, P. (Eds.). (2006). *Dual citizenship as a challenge to European Nation-States*. Rotterdam, Taipei: Sense Publishers.
Kalev, L., & Roosmaa, L. (2012). Riikluse ülesehitamine. In R. Vetik (Ed.), *Eesti poliitika ja valitsemine 1911–2011* (pp. 25–66). Tallinn: Tallinna Ülikooli kirjastus.
Kivisto, P., & Faist, T. (2007). *Citizenship. Discourse, theory, and transnational prospects*. Malden, Oxford, Carleton: Blackwell Publishing.
Kivisto, P., & Faist, T. (2010). *Beyond a Border. The Causes and consequences of contemporary immigration*. Thousand Oaks: Pine Forge Press/Sage.
Kooiman, J. (2003). *Governing as governance*. London, Thousand Oaks, New Delhi: Sage Publications.
Kuhl, M. (2009). *Siirdeloogika juured. Acta Politica Estica, 3*(2009), 56–64.
Kuper, A. (2004). *Democracy beyond borders. Justice and representation in global institutions*. Oxford: Oxford University Press.
Kuzio, T. (2001). Transition in post-communist states: Triple or Quadruple? *Politics, 21*(3), 168–177.
Lauristin, M., Vihalemm, P., & Tallo, I. (Eds.). (1997). *Return to the Western World: Cultural and political perspectives on the Estonian post-communist transition*. Tartu: Tartu University Press.
Liebich, A. (2000). Plural citizenship in post-communist states. *International Journal of Refugee Law, 12*(1), 97–107.
Marshall, T. H. (1992) [1950]. Citizenship and social class. In T. H Marshall & T. Bottomore (Eds.), *Citizenship and social class* (pp. 1–51). London: Pluto Press.
Newman, J., & Clarke, J. (2009). *Publics, politics and power: Remaking the public in public services*. London: Sage.
Nyers, P. (Ed.). (2009). *Securitizations of citizenship*. London, New York: Routledge.
Owen, D. (2017). Citizenship and human rights. In A. Shachar, R. Bauböck, I. Bloemraad, & M. Vink (Eds.), *The Oxford handbook of citizenship* (pp. 247–267). Oxford: Oxford University Press.
Perez-Armendariz, C., & Crow, D. (2010). Do migrants remit democracy? International migration, political beliefs and behavior in Mexico. *Comparative Political Studies, 43*(1), 119–148.
Pierson, C. (2004). *The modern state*. London, New York: Routledge.
Pitkänen, P., İçduygu, A., & Sert, D. (2012). *Migration and transformation: Multi-level analysis of migrant transnationalism*. Berlin; New York, Philadelphia: Springer.
Pogonyi, S. (2011). Dual citizenship and sovereignty. *Nationalities Papers, 39*(5), 685–704.
Przeworski, A. (1995). *Sustainable democracy*. Cambridge: Cambridge University Press.
Raadschelders, J. C. N. (1998). *Handbook of administrative history*. New Brunswick, London: Transaction Publishers.
Schlenker, A., Blatter, J., & Birka, I. (2017). Practising transnational citizenship: Dual nationality and simultaneous political involvement among emigrants. *Journal of Ethnic and Migration Studies, 43*(3), 418–440.
Schmitter, P. C. (2001). The scope of citizenship in a democratized European Union: From economic to political to social and cultural? In K. Eder & B. Giesen (Eds.), *European citizenship between*

national legacies and postnational projects (pp. 86–121). Oxford, New York: Oxford University Press.
Shevel, O. (2009). The politics of citizenship policy in new states. *Comparative Politics, 41*(3), 273–291.
Sicakkan, H. G., & Lithman, Y. (Eds.). (2005). *Changing the basis of citizenship in the modern state. Political theory and the politics of diversity*. Lewiston, Queenston, Lampeter: The Edwin Mellen Press.
Smith, R. C. (2003). Migrant membership as an instituted process: Transnationalization, the state and the extra-territorial conduct of mexican politics. *International Migration Review, 37*(2), 297–343.
Smith, M. P., & Bakker, M. (2007). *Citizenship across borders: The political transnationalism of 'El Migrante'*. New York: Cornell University Press.
Spiro, P. J. (2016). *At home in two countries. The past and future of dual citizenship*. New York: New York University Press.
Skinner, Q., & Stråth, B. (2003). *States and citizens: history, theory, prospects*. Cambridge: Cambridge University Press.
Solska, M. (2011). Citizenship, collective identity and the international impact on integration policy in Estonia, Latvia and Lithuania. *Europe-Asia Studies, 63*(6), 1089–1108.
Stoker, G., Armstrong, C., Banya, M., McGhee, D., McGrew, A., Mason, A., et al. (2011). *Prospects for citizenship*. London, New York: Bloomsbury Publishing.
Tilly, C. (1995). *Citizenship, identity and social history*. Cambridge: Cambridge University Press.
Tully, J. (2008). *Public philosophy in a new key, Volume 2: Imperialism and civic freedom*. Cambridge: Cambridge University Press.
Turner, B. S. (1990). Outline of a theory of citizenship. *Sociology, 24*(2), 189–217.
Waters, M. (2001). *Globalization: Key ideas*. London: Routledge.
Walzer, M. (1998). [1991] The civil society argument. In G. Shafir (Ed.), *The citizenship debates: A reader* (pp. 291–308). Minneapolis, London: University of Minnesota Press.

Leif Kalev is professor of state and citizenship theory at Tallinn University. His research has mostly focused on citizenship as status and agency, the state as a democratic political community and the modes of its governance, transnationalism and globalisation, and the politics–policy nexus in citizenship, migration and integration. From 2012 to 2015 he worked at the Estonian Ministry of the Interior as deputy secretary general on public order and migration policy and as secretary general. Kalev has been a member of the European Consortium for Political Research (ECPR) Citizenship Standing Group since its foundation.

Mari-Liis Jakobson is associate professor of political sociology at Tallinn University and researcher at the Estonian national contact point for the European Migration Network. She holds a Ph.D. in politics and government from Tallinn University (2014). Her research interests relate to transnational citizenship and migration, in particular how the policies and politics of migration and citizenship shape citizenship as identity and practice. She has been a member of the European Consortium for Political Research (ECPR) Citizenship Standing Group since its foundation.

Chapter 19
Visa Restrictions as an Obstacle for International Development

Iryna Ivankiv

Abstract Entry visas are considered a sovereign prerogative of states; however, restrictive visa regimes create a considerable burden for migrants. It is argued that the economic benefits from a more liberal movement of people can outweigh the problems caused by increased migration. Additionally, from a human rights perspective, the presumption of innocence is discussed in conjunction with freedom of movement and limits of modern concepts of citizenship. The article aims at contributing to the discussion of visa regime liberalisation that can enhance international development and make it more sustainable.

Keywords Visa restrictions · Human rights · International development

19.1 Introduction

> The era of supposedly unprecedented mobility is only part of the picture, and is at the same time also an era of great, continued and enforced inequality in access to foreign spaces based on the principle of nationality.
>
> Eric Neumayer 2006

Modern social and economic relations require unification and clarification of the rules for international trade, transfer of goods and services. It is often ignored that this unification should also touch upon the freedom of movement for the labour force—human beings. Currently, 164 out of 193 (UN official website) existing states are members of the World Trade Organization (World Trade Organization official website n.d.). The states work on trade liberalisation agreements with each other and negotiate common satisfactory norms for trade. However, this leads to a situation when it is easier to transfer a car from one state to another than its driver. Some scholars argue that the majority of the world's population remains 'nationalised' and is dependent on passports, visas, residence, etc., and continues to live in a closed world 'trapped by the lottery of birth' (Neumayer 2006, 82).

I. Ivankiv (✉)
National University of "Kyiv-Mohyla Academy", Kyiv, Ukraine
e-mail: iryna.ivankiv@yahoo.com

M. C. Jacobsen et al. (eds.), *Cosmopolitanism, Migration and Universal Human Rights*, https://doi.org/10.1007/978-3-030-50645-2_19

Why do governments work hard on the facilitation of trade, but do not work even nearly as hard on the improvement of the migration conditions for people? One might provide many suggestions for why people are less desirable than cars, but when it comes to equality and respect for human rights, those arguments do not stand. In this chapter, the attempt is made to prove with economic data that visa restrictions not only violate fundamental human rights but also constitute significant obstacles for international sustainable development.

It goes without saying that travel and the ability to work, study and live in different countries is necessary. The restrictions which the majority of the world's population face in the form of visas constitute degrading treatment and violation of basic human rights and freedoms. The issue of sovereign power over borders and territory is controversial; hence, limiting access to the territory for aliens would be justified if applied on a personal basis. Justice and equal opportunities are basic for the development and the rule of law. This chapter argues that visa restrictions might lead to the violation of human rights and are contrary to the economic interests of states.

Basic definitions should be given to make the chapter consistent. The scholars of migration differentiate migration and mobility: migrants (migration) travel internationally and over long distances with the intention of settling at the destination, whereas 'movers' travel internally and for short distance without any intention to settle (Lucassen and Lucassen 2014, 6). For purposes of this research, this difference is not crucial, so the term 'migrants' would be used for both categories. However, where the difference needs to be underlined, the term 'mover' is used as described above.

I use the expression 'restrictive visa regime' for the situation in which a person needs to obtain a visa prior to the initiation of an international trip and, in order to obtain it, one needs to present evidence of trustworthiness and financial welfare.

According to the World Tourism Organization (UNWTO) (2013), visas serve for several functions, including to ensure security, control immigration and limit the entry, duration of stay or activities of travellers, generate revenue, apply measures of reciprocity, ensure a destination's carrying capacity and control demand. Security is often mentioned as the most important factor in implementing restrictive visa regimes.

The UNWTO also provides information that in 2012, more than two-thirds of the global population needs to obtain a visa before initiating an international trip, and only 18% of the world's population would not require a visa at all when travelling for tourism purpose (UNWTO 2013). In 2018, the Visa Openness Report UNWTO provided information that only 21% of the world population would not need a visa to travel (UNWTO 2018). These percentages result in concrete numbers for economies, e.g. in a loss in the tourist industry. Therefore, the tendency is that developing countries tend to have more liberal regimes for travellers (UNWTO 2018). Here the first contradiction appears: while the citizens of developed countries enjoy visa-free travel to developing countries, the citizens of the latter face major obstacles when travelling to developed countries. For example, in 2005 the President of Ukraine established a visa-free regime for many European states, including all states parties to the Schengen Agreement, but this step was not reciprocal and Ukrainian citizens continued to face various restrictions and violations of the European Union Visa Code, which was recognised by the European Commission (Economics.unian.ua 2012) up until June of 2017 when the visa-free regime for Ukrainian citizens was approved for short-term visits. It took 12 years to achieve conditional reciprocity in visa regulations because the visa-free regime was provided to Ukraine on specific conditions and with provisions that allow revoking it. (Schengen Visa Information 2019). It can also be called a 'negotiation chip in broader geopolitical games' (Czaika et al. 2018, 590), as lifting EU visas for Turkish citizens was described by the researchers.

Eric Neumayer states that the enhanced freedom of movement for citizens of certain states is achieved at the expense of decreased mobility for others. He quotes former Ukrainian President Leonid Kuchma, who said that the Schengen visa rules would 'replace the Iron Curtain with a different, more humane but no less dangerous Paper Curtain' (Neumayer 2006, 75). Lack of reciprocity is one of the main obstacles for travellers. It can be argued that this issue may constitute a violation of the principle of equality, proclaimed in many international binding treaties and soft-law documents. The citizens of higher-income states enjoy considerably more freedom of movement than those of the lower or low income. As mentioned by Neumayer: 'the average OECD citizen faces visa restrictions in travel to approximately 93 foreign countries, the average non-OECD citizen needs a visa to travel to approximately 156 countries' (Neumayer 2006, 78).

This state of affairs will be discussed from two standpoints: economic implications and human rights consequences of the visa restrictions for sustainable development.

19.2 Economic Implications

The widely supported opinion suggests that migration has a negative effect on the economy of the state of destination, where migrants tend to occupy the workplaces of natives, put additional strain on the social security system and increase criminality rates. However, 'well-managed immigration would generate demonstrable benefits for countries of destination as well as for immigrants and countries of origin – not least because of aging populations in EU member states' (MEDAM 2018). Based on statistical data, scholars argue that those opinions are no more than stereotypes, and are often not only proven wrong but also reversed (Caplan 2012; Wynne 2015).

The economic analysis shows impressive figures. Mark A. Wynne names visa restrictions 'the last frontier of globalization' and proves that its liberalisation will have the following effect on the global economy:

> [T]he global trading system is so integrated that the elimination of the remaining barriers to international trade in goods would only add 0.3 to 4.1 percent to global GDP. However, if all remaining barriers to international migration were eliminated, global GDP would be 67 to 147.3 percent bigger. (Wynne 2015, 4)

This possible growth of global GDP would impact different spheres, including tourism, academia, science, and international trade, which would benefit from the free movement of persons.

Joint research by the UNWTO and the World Travel and Tourism Council (WTTC) presented in May 2012 demonstrated that improving visa processes could have generated an extra US$206 billion in tourism receipts and created as many as 5.1 million additional jobs by 2015 in the G20 economies (UNWTO 2013). While these incomes are not small and could contribute to the global fight against extreme poverty, many states choose not to liberalise their visa regimes.

Lack of free movement of persons also influences the sphere of remittances. The money that migrants send back to some poorer countries as remittances can amount to 5% or more of GDP (Wynne 2015, 4). This figure is impressive; however, migrants send not only financial remittances but also ideas, know-how, business and social connections, which are called 'social remittances' (Migration Policy Centre team with the contribution of Peter Bosch 2015, 11). This human capital is often underestimated but is essential for sustainable development. It should be emphasised that through 'the social remittances channel, migration is thought to work for innovative approaches to solve development issues' (Migration Policy Centre team with the contribution of Peter Bosch 2015, 11). Crossflow of experience is beneficial for migrants and for natives because the knowledge and specific skills are shared and can be used by both parties. This would be especially important for higher-skilled migrants, who have unique experience. Restrictive visa regimes result in a change in the routes of the prospective migrants. Highly qualified professionals would rather choose a destination without the necessity of going through unnecessary bureaucratic procedures, which are also often humiliating. Consequently, the country of destination loses a possible source of innovation and development.

The popular myth says that migrants steal jobs from natives. Scholars and official reports prove a different point. Statistics show that countries with a larger percentage of foreign labour have lower unemployment rates. Bryan Caplan argues that lower-skilled migrants create a new market for the natives, providing them with services that they would not be able to afford otherwise (e.g. babysitting, house cleaning, care for elderly) (Caplan 2012, 7–9). He shows data that lower-skilled migrants would not be rivals for lower-skilled natives because these two groups have a significantly different background. Therefore, this scholar suggests that liberalised migration laws would be beneficial for the US economy, also mentioning the history of this state as being 100% composed of immigrants (Caplan 2012).

The recent European Migration Policy Centre report shows data that:

> [T]here is a negative correlation between unemployment and immigration, both because unemployment deters potential migrants and because immigration generates net employment. (Thibos 2014, 15)

Another benefit of legal migration is the increase in tax revenue, which is higher from migrants in the long run because they receive fewer or no social benefits compared with natives. Therefore, restrictive visa regimes, in reality, do not protect internal markets, but, on the contrary, form roadblocks for economic development.

19.3 Limits of Citizenship

It can also be argued that the factor of citizenship plays a crucial role from a person's development perspective, given the differences in the human development index. Mobility worldwide is mostly ensured in so-called 'regional free mobility clusters' (Czaika et al. 2018, 611). Theoretically, citizenship creates a bond between a person and a state, where the latter has a duty to protect human rights. Nevertheless, this bond can harm individuals when a state implements authoritarian practices, disregarding its duties towards its citizens. In such (rather widespread) cases, a state faces sanctions from the international community, which are targeted at those holding authority but backfire on the general population. Consequently, citizens become even more vulnerable, facing a violation of their human rights in their own country and having increased visa restrictions in other countries.

On the other hand, practices of granting citizenship for certain 'valuable' individuals are also widespread. The worlds of sport, art and academia have plenty of such examples. It is important to note that instead of implementing exclusive practices, generally less restrictive visa regimes would boost the creative potential of respective states, therefore contributing to development and making it more sustainable. The limits of citizenship are evident in the globalised world, where the bond between an individual and a state depends on possibilities to live a decent life and realise one's potential to the fullest extent. Otherwise, a change of citizenship or change of residence is always an option; the question is only whether such a change can happen in a legal and clear way or a forced, irregular one.

19.4 Human Rights and Moral Consequences

Since the adoption of the Universal Declaration of Human Rights in 1948, human rights discourse has officially become an international issue, introducing equal human rights standards for all. Many international organisations are now working on ensuring full respect for the human rights and development of the standards. Notwithstanding the efforts, the main actors in international affairs create major obstacles for the people to enjoy their rights and freedoms. Restrictive visa regimes prevent human beings from exercising their free will and install discriminative barriers for the freedom of movement. Being unable to move and choose where to settle, one often cannot fully enjoy other rights. The right to freedom of speech cannot be exercised in a repressive totalitarian state; the right to private life is undermined when homosexuality is considered a crime; the right to education is non-existent where it is prohibited for girls to study in schools; finally, the right to life is in great danger when capital punishment exists within an unfair and corrupt justice system. These examples show that, sometimes, for a human being the only solution to live a decent life is to migrate to another country. There is no universal obligation to fight against injustice in one's own country, so, since all states recognise the Universal Declaration of Human Rights, there should be a possibility to choose where and how to live one's life.

The Universal Declaration of Human Rights (art. 13) and International Covenant on Civil and Political Rights (hereinafter—the ICCPR) (art. 12) guarantee freedom of movement. Paragraph 3 of article 12 of the ICCPR states the following:

> The [...] rights shall not be subject to any restrictions except those which are provided by law, are necessary to protect national security, public order (*ordre public*), public health or morals or the rights and freedoms of others, and are consistent with the other rights recognized in the present Covenant.

In the human rights doctrine, national security, public order, public health or morals or the rights and freedoms of others have to be considered as consistent with democracy and the rule of law. Therefore, everyone should be entitled to freedom of movement within the country of residence, and abroad, as long as the actions of a person do not endanger the above-mentioned values.

Visa regimes, being the sovereign prerogative of the state, often violate the right to free movement and, more importantly, the presumption of innocence. The restrictions on the basis of citizenship violate the principle of equality, undermining the human rights values proclaimed by the Universal Declaration of Human Rights and supported by many binding treaties. Instead of viewing individuals as equal human beings, the states use the constructions of the 'useful migrant' or 'undesirable migrant', 'understood in putative economic contribution' (Geddes 2005, 787). Neumayer describes the difference between the desirable and undesirable migrants in a comprehensive way:

> Visa restrictions fulfil the double role of pre-selection and deterrence. Those who do not need a visa are regarded as desirable and low-risk visitors by default, those who need a visa and have been approved by the country's consulate or embassy abroad are regarded as not undesirable and not representing a great risk upon closer inspection, whereas those who need a visa and do not have one are denied access. (Neumayer 2006, 75)

The argument of whether a person is desirable is made based on a country's performance, political and economic situation, and position in the international arena. Visa-free regimes are negotiated at the state levels. The individuals are not treated according to their credentials, only on the basis of citizenship. Therefore, one has to prove his or her own 'desirability' and credibility every time he or she applies for a visa.

This situation creates a presumption of guilt, according to which a person needs to prove that the intended trip is of a legal nature and would be appropriately conducted without violation of the law. Frequently, an applicant for a visa is asked by consulates to prove something that does not exist, and hence cannot be proved or disproved. Restrictive visa regimes create a vicious circle, where to prove one's credibility and legal status a person has to seek out third-party intermediaries, which offer illegal services of document forgery or similar (Avdan 2012, 176). Prospective migrants or movers, who intended to be legal have to use third-party illegal services to cross the border and/or to work in the country of destination, and therefore violate the law because legal procedures are overcomplicated.

Contact with illegal facilitators of the visa process poses a threat to a person who can become involved in human trafficking or smuggling. As described by Nazli Avdan, restrictive visa regimes are intended to fight trafficking, but often give rise ‘to a demand for traffickers, as prospective migrants are forced to use illegal channels’ (Avdan 2012, 172). This scholar concludes that although visas are a significant deterrent against potentially dangerous entrants, human traffickers rely on forged documents and alternative methods to cross borders (Avdan 2012, 194).

The current refugee crisis, increased by populist and nationalist government policies, leads to imposing extremely restrictive visa regimes for citizens of many African nations, which basically prevents them from any legal way of migration to many European countries (De Haas 2008). Therefore, the prospective migrants end up being actual refugees or pretending to be such, even in those cases where they could have been eligible for a visa with a work permit. Instead of working and bringing economic growth to a host country, people become dependent on social services and create an additional burden.

Bryan Caplan, mentioned earlier, emphasises in his research that a work permit in the US is difficult to obtain, so some prospective migrants pay to third parties to be transferred to the country illegally, sometimes paying a quota of the work permit or even larger amount just to be transferred to the country and be held in virtual slavery (Caplan 2012, 10–11). The opinion that open procedures for anyone interested will be beneficial for states and migrants is worth considering. Moreover, international law against human trafficking imposes obligations on states to provide help and asylum to the victims, meaning that the taxes paid by the natives are spent on the victims. Consequently, overly restrictive visa regimes do not help taxpayers.

In so-called welfare states, social benefits for the natives often spearhead discussions related to migrants, who allegedly put additional burden on the state budget. The population in many developed countries is rapidly aging. Accordingly, the inflow of a young labour force is essential to maintain a high level of social protection. Mamta Murthi, Country Director, Central Europe and Baltic Countries (World Bank), compares the situation in Western Europe and in Central and Eastern Europe (CEE), which shows interesting tendencies. According to the presented data, the demographic situation in Western European countries, unlike in CEE, has improved over the last decades. The scholar names three reasons for this: the free movement of people within the European Union, the higher level of morbidity and ill-health in the CEE, and lower fertility in the CEE. Another view is the following: ‘Immigration is making Western Europe younger, swelling the ranks of those who earn and pay taxes there, while making Central and Eastern Europe older’ (Murthi 2015). The conclusion is obvious: if the high level of human rights standards is to be maintained, migration is essential and should be encouraged.

In the context of the European Union, unfortunately, even higher-skilled educated migrants or movers are often deliberately banned from entering the European Union space. According to the Migration Policy Centre: ‘too often bright students that have applied and that have been admitted to these programmes are prevented from participating because of a member state not issuing a visa’ (Migration Policy Centre team with the contribution of Peter Bosch 2015, 8). In our opinion, this practice is against the human rights standards in the area of the prohibition of discrimination and goes against the argument about the 'credibility' of the potential migrant. The problem lies in the absence of any remedy for this human rights violation because *de jure* the right to obtain a visa is not guaranteed by any human rights treaty, and therefore being denied an entry visa is not considered a violation of human rights. However, unsubstantiated denial may be considered discrimination on the basis of nationality.

The obstacles to international development in this particular situation are apparent and have far-reaching consequences. A young person would not be able to receive education; hence, society would lose the potential innovation of a highly skilled professional, and the person might be deprived of the chance for personal development. The right to sustainable development, as specified in article 1 of the Declaration to the Right to Development (A/RES/41/128) would also be violated when equal access to the achievements of human civilisation is precluded.

19.5 Conclusion

The above arguments prove that the economic effects of a liberal visa regime will contribute to the development of both societies, that of origin and that of destination. The heated political debate and lack of tolerance for migrants could be explained from a different standpoint. It has nothing to do with the economy, rather a profound complex of fear of 'the Other'. As Moris Farhi describes:

> Initially *The Other* is non-perceptual. At first, the host society, either smug or complacent or wary, disdains to give *The Other* a close look and, consequently, sees it as a being that has emerged 'from somewhere out there'. When later, economic and political turmoil erupts – as it always does – it is forced to scrutinise this being either subjectively, through ingrained prejudice, or premeditatedly out of political expediency. But it does so always with *The Other's* alien image branded on its mind. Thereafter, *The Other's* features can be drawn so that they reflect the host society's most problematic instincts, fears and prejudices. In effect, they are implanted and take control of the host's consciousness, to paralyse its reason and perceptions, to blind it to reality and suffuse it with any – or all – of its insecurities. (Farhi 2006, 67–68)

The constant fear of the Other makes people reject people who are different. Nevertheless, as Farhi also states, this treatment makes migrants become more inventive and hardworking, which eventually leads to acceptance and recognition (Farhi 2006). In a world in which we face 'space–time compression', one could not live in local terms because globalised society has an impact on the smallest local matters.

The economic data presented in this chapter is only a small portion of the existing economic and financial studies in the sphere. However, it is sufficient to prove the hypothesis that restrictive visa regimes are not helpful in terms of a globalised economy.

Broad understanding of the human rights doctrine provides some arguments in favour of the liberalisation of visa regimes as well as the argument that globalised societies require free movement for everyone, not only those born in the privileged states. Sustainable development cannot be achieved by some states at the expense of others. Governments should regard human beings as truly equal with the presumption of innocence and respect for human dignity.

Bibliography

Avdan, N. (2012). Human trafficking and migration control policy: Vicious or virtuous cycle? *Journal of Public Policy, 32*(03), 171–205.

Caplan, B. (2012). Why should we restrict immigration? *Cato Journal, 32*(1), 5–24.

Czaika, M., De Haas, H., & Villares-Varela, M. (2018). The global evolution of travel visa regimes. *Population and Development Review, 44*(3), 589–622. https://doi.org/10.1111/padr.12166.

De Haas, H. (2008). The myth of invasion: The inconvenient realities of African migration to Europe. *Third World Quarterly, 29*(7), 1305–1322.

Economics.unian.ua. (2012). *ЄК визнає системні порушення при видачі віз українцям і готова їх усувати.* https://economics.unian.ua/soc/673507-ek-viznae-sistemni-porushennya-pri-vidachi-viz-ukrajintsyam-i-gotova-jih-usuvati.html. Accessed April 24, 2014.

Farhi, M. (2006). All history is the history of migration. *Index on Censorship, 35*(2), 64–73.

Geddes, A. (2005). Europe's border relationships and international migration relations. *JCMS: Journal of Common Market Studies, 43*(4), 787–806.

Lucassen, J., & Lucassen, L. (Eds.). (2014). *Globalising migration history: The eurasian experience (16th–21st Centuries).* Brill.

MEDAM. (2018). *Assessment report on asylum and migration policies in Europe flexible solidarity: A comprehensive strategy for asylum and immigration in the EU.* https://www.medam-migration.eu/en/publication/2018-medam-assessment-report-on-asylum-and-migration-policies-in-europe-2/. Accessed March 15, 2019.

Migration Policy Centre team with the contribution of Peter Bosch. (2015). *Towards a pro-active European labour migration policy concrete measures for a comprehensive package.* https://cadmus.eui.eu/bitstream/handle/1814/35037/MPC_2015-03_PB.pdf?sequence=1. Accessed March 17, 2019.

Murthi, M. (2015). *In Europe, life gets shorter for some.* Brookings. https://www.brookings.edu/blogs/future-development/posts/2015/04/21-europe-aging-murthi. Accessed May 17, 2015.

Neumayer, E. (2006). Unequal access to foreign spaces: How states use visa restrictions to regulate mobility in a globalized world. *Transactions of the Institute of British Geographers, 31*(1), 72–84.

Regulation (EC) No 810/2009 of the European Parliament and of the Council of 13 July 2009 establishing a Community Code on Visas (Visa Code), https://eur-lex.europa.eu/legal-content/EN/ALL/?uri=CELEX:32009R0810. Access April 24, 2014.

Schengen Visa Information. (2019). *Ukrainians can now travel to EU Member States without a visa—Schengen Visa Information.* https://www.schengenvisainfo.com/news/ukrainians-can-now-travel-to-eu-member-states-without-visa. Accessed March 15, 2019.

Thibos, C. (2014). *Is what we hear about migration really true? Questioning eight stereotypes.* [online] Florence: European University Institute, Robert Schuman Centre for Advanced Studies, Migration Policy Centre. https://cadmus.eui.eu/bitstream/handle/1814/31832/Migration_Report_EUI.PDF?sequence=3. Accessed March 17, 2019.

UN General Assembly. (1986). *Declaration on the right to development: Resolution/adopted by the General Assembly*, December 4, 1986, A/RES/41/128 [online] Available at: https://www.refworld.org/docid/3b00f22544.html. Accessed July 8, 2019.

UN official web-site. (n.d.). Member states of the United Nations. [online] Available at: https://www.un.org/en/members/. Accessed March 15, 2019.

UNWTO. (2013). *Visa facilitation: Stimulating economic growth and development through tourism*. Madrid: UNWTO. https://www.e-unwto.org/doi/pdf/10.18111/9789284415175. Accessed March 17, 2019.
UNWTO. (2018). *Visa openness report 2018*. https://cf.cdn.unwto.org/sites/all/files/docpdf/2018visaopennessreport.pdf. Accessed March 17, 2019.
World Trade Organization official web-site. (n.d.). WTO members and observers. https://www.wto.org/english/thewto_e/whatis_e/tif_e/org6_e.htm. Accessed March 15, 2019.
Wynne, M. (2015). *International migration remains the last frontier of globalization. Economic Letter, 10*(2). https://www.dallasfed.org/assets/documents/research/eclett/2015/el1502.pdf. Accessed April 9, 2015.

Iryna Ivankiv works as a Senior Lecturer at the National University of 'Kyiv-Mohyla Academy'. She holds a master's degree in Law from the Yaroslav Mudry National Law University of Ukraine, and an LL.M. degree in Rule of Law for Development from the Loyola University in Chicago. In 2019, she defended her Ph.D. thesis on the rights of humanity.

Chapter 20
Citizenship, Open Borders and Human Rights

Mogens Chrom Jacobsen

Abstract For some, entry and citizenship are the reserved area of the state since the state is perceived as a historically created community within the free choice left over by a limited number of moral duties. Those denying the state such prerogatives apply end-result principles where the state is a historical accident with possible instrumental value. We will argue that conventional ideas about the burden of proof ignore this difference being thus biased towards these principles. These insights will enhance our understanding of how different conceptions of human rights conceive these matters.

Keywords Migration · Citizenship · Human rights · Rule ethics · Circumstantialism

20.1 Introduction

How do human rights cope with questions of citizenship and migration? The question is topical considering the current situation. We will not discuss how we should handle this situation, but rather consider the problematic philosophically, explaining how two different conceptions of human rights approach citizenship and migration differently. We consider this to be useful for a more practical approach to migration.

Before getting to the crux of the matter, we should relate the discussion of human rights to the philosophical discussion of migration and here mainly the discussion in Anglo-Saxon philosophy. We consider this discussion to be somewhat biased and at times confused, but our endeavour to show how it is biased and confused will clarify our point about human rights. We will attempt to do that with an analytical apparatus developed in the book *A Different History of Human Rights* (Jacobsen 2017, Chap. 1). This will be the subject of the first section, The Burden of Proof. In the second section, Two Models of Ethics, the offshoot of the first section should be a clearer understanding of the disagreement between those who consider questions of

M. C. Jacobsen (✉)
Nordic Summer University, Copenhagen, Denmark
e-mail: chrom.jacobsen@gmail.com

M. C. Jacobsen et al. (eds.), *Cosmopolitanism, Migration and Universal Human Rights*, https://doi.org/10.1007/978-3-030-50645-2_20

entry and citizenship the reserved area of the state and those who deny the state such prerogative. The first envisage a limited number of moral duties considering the state as a historical created community within the area of free choices left over by these basic duties. The others apply what Nozick calls end-result principles (Nozick 1980, 153 ff.) where the state is a historical accident with possible instrumental value. This fundamental difference is overshadowed by a particular conception of the burden of proof, and this conception is biased towards such end-result principles. In our opinion, even those who could benefit from a more correct view of the burden of proof seem to neglect this. In the last section, Two Attitudes to Citizenship, these insights should enhance our understanding of how different conceptions of human rights conceive these matters, because the eighteenth century declarations would belong to the first view, while the Universal Declaration of Human Rights (UDHR) from 1948 would belong to the second view. We will here find the same confusion since the International Covenant on Civil and Political Rights (ICCPR) seems to reiterate the first view even though it should be an implementation of the second view.

20.2 The Burden of Proof

Questions concerning the burden of proof are often raised in connection with discussions of immigration and citizenship (Dummett 2004, 117; Seglow 2005, 319; Miller 2008, 376; Wellman 2008, 119; Pevnick 2009, 146; Blake 2013, 103, 115, 118, 120). It is generally assumed that the burden of proof lies on the state who wishes to limit immigration treating immigrants differently from residents and citizens, or that liberty, in this case liberty of movement, is basic such that any deviation therefrom should be justified by special moral reasons. We will challenge these views, arguing that the basic situation is neither equality nor liberty, but a state of affairs without any duties at all, such that those believing that there are any duties should state their point. If we do not start out from this state of affairs, the discussion will be biased in favour of particular views.

Michael Walzer cites Bernard Williams for the view that 'goods should always be distributed for, "relevant reasons"' (Walzer 1983, 9). Walzer would connect 'relevant reasons' to social meanings rather than essential meanings, as he thinks Williams would do (Walzer 1983, 9; see also 88), However, they seem to disagree in some other respects as well. Walzer states that:

> Across a considerable range of the decisions that are made, states are simply free to take in strangers (or not) – much as they are free, leaving aside the claims of the needy, to share their wealth with foreign friends, to honour the achievements of foreign artists, scholars, and scientists, to choose their trading partners, and to enter into collective security arrangements with foreign states. (Walzer 1983, 61)

The fact that they are 'simply free' implies that they do not have to give relevant reasons for their choice. They can act in their own interest or according to whatever whim that might come to mind as long as they have taken care of the needy. The principle that Williams proposes suggests something else:

> … that for every difference in the way men are treated, a reason should be given: when one requires further that the reasons should be relevant, and that they should be socially operative, this really says something. (Williams 1973, 241)

Taken as it stands, although Williams is cautious about an indiscriminate use of the principle (it would seem that others are less scrupulous), and assuming that relevant reasons are morally relevant reasons, it would leave little room for 'simply free' choices. For any choice we make we should give a moral reason for why we treat this person (or this case) differently from another, which means a pervasive moralisation of our lives. Should we also give morally relevant reasons for choosing between strawberry and vanilla ice cream? Of course not, but two approaches seem possible. One would say that we are simply free to choose. This is not a moral choice at all. Some choices are morally indifferent. However, one could also say that this choice is not sufficiently significant to impact anything. If the strawberry ice cream had been organic, there might have been reasons for choosing it. But which impact? According to which standard should reasons be judged morally relevant? If the judgement should be made according to some kind of perfectionism or utilitarianism, it is easy to understand why we end up with this pervasive moralisation. Morally relevant reasons are then the way our choices impact perfection or utility, and most choices will impact these matters in some way. Sometimes the impact is insignificant, and we will apply some kind of triviality limit, but in principle no choice escapes moralisation.

The ice-cream example should highlight the idea of moralisation, but another example should show that at least some current ideas about what could be done are contrary to this principle. Take the case of recruitment of new personnel to a private enterprise (cf. Walzer 1983, 162, 136). It is generally admitted that an owner of an enterprise can favour his wife/her husband or some other person without any discrimination. It might not be wise, if these people are unqualified, but the owner can have his reasons. If the owner or his deputy wishes to employ the most qualified person, which is generally the case, they cannot reject a qualified person just because of this person's skin colour, religion, etc., since this would imply that these characteristics have less moral worth, which is morally wrong. However, employing one's spouse in order to build up the enterprise together does not imply any such thing. The owner has a simple free choice. He can employ anybody as long as he is not doing anything wrong. He is not obliged to justify why he is employing his brother rather than some more qualified and available person. According to this view, he could choose some person at random, if he wishes to. There is here a space of liberty; a liberty from morals. If you are a deputy or a civil servant, you are generally supposed to employ the most qualified person and cannot act on a whim. According to this view, you are not always obliged to give a morally relevant reason for treating this person or case differently. In this case, you will have to indicate some specific moral duty—for example, not to discriminate. With an all-encompassing duty like promoting perfection or maximising utility, the space of liberty becomes nearly non-existent.

The principle of the relevant difference can also be used to vindicate a radical conception of equality; a suggestion Williams also considers in the article cited above (Williams 1973, 243 ff.), but more famously championed by John Rawls. Rawls's basic intuition is that social conditions and natural capacities should not influence the distribution of social goods. These factors are arbitrary from a moral point of view. You have not merited them by any effort of your own (Rawls 1999a [1971], § 12–13, 17). From this basic intuition Rawls extracts his difference principle, saying that inequalities are justified if they favour the least advantaged persons (Rawls 1999a [1971], § 41–48), but Rawls only applies this principle to the fundamental structures of society (Rawls 1999b, 117). Joseph Carens has, however, ventured to apply this principle more generally and notably to questions of immigration. Carens thinks that the place where you were born or where you happen to live is arbitrary in this way. He compares the privileges of citizenship with the feudal privileges of the Middle Ages. Nobody has merited the place where they live, so ideally there should be open borders (Carens 1987, 251–252). An important purpose of the original position is to minimise the effects of contingencies such as birthplace and parentage on the choice of the principles of justice (Carens 1987, 256, 261). This would also seem to make it impossible for a business owner to employ his son or brother (because they were such). Being a son or a brother is not something you have merited by your own effort, and the effect of such a contingency should be minimised. It is, however, difficult to say how much simple free choice such a theory would allow, since it should only apply to the basic structure of the (world) society and not to individual morality. Nonetheless, one would think that an ordinarily accepted simple free choice to employ one's relative would not be allowed by Rawls's basic intuition. Carens would, however, have to explain when this basic intuition is applicable and why it is not always applicable (if it is not always applicable). If treating people differently merely because of birthplace and place of living is unjust, because these are contingent matters the privileged people have not merited, then it would seem that the only just way to treat people differently is made on the basis of merit. When we go to the cinema and choose one film rather than another, should we then do this on merit, always going to see the best film according to some idea about merit? The team behind one film is treated differently from the other, so should their effort not be appreciated according to their merit? Unless this idea gets a limited application, it becomes extremely moralising.

The different principles evoked above assume the existence of different kinds of duties, and if we ignore this point, they will be biased in favour of these duties. The same point goes for another argument for (mostly) open borders which takes its point of departure in the idea of liberty. Liberty is here taken to include liberty of movement. Since liberty is taken as the normal situation, we should indicate why this liberty should be restricted. Those in favour of border controls should indicate, why there should be such controls. Michael Dummett takes this line of argument. He believes that the burden of proof lies on those wanting to limit liberty (Dummett 2004, 117, 118). For him there are only two clear cases where this seems justified, and these are the case of genuine danger of overpopulation and the case of a very small population in danger of being submerged (Dummett 2004, 119). We will not discuss these reasons or others that might be invoked, but argue instead that they suppose an excessive presumption for liberty. Liberty is a complex notion. According to the consecrated analysis developed by Hohfeld (1920, 35 ff.), liberty can be a simple liberty or a right to liberty. In the first case, we are at liberty to do what we have no duty to do or to omit. Here we have an option we can choose to seize or not. However, having such a simple liberty does not confer on other people a duty not to interfere with our choice, whatever it is. If the sole duties in my moral system were to attend church services on Sundays and donate €1 to charity, then I would be free to take a walk in the park on a Monday (among many other things), but my moral system does not confer any duty on other people not to interfere with my promenade. If we included in our system a duty not to harm other people—that is, not to kill, injure and harass them—then we would have a right to walk in the park protected by a corresponding duty on the part of others not to bother us. Saying that someone has a right to liberty involves two things, then: there is no duty in that respect and others have a duty to respect this liberty. Our moral system is far from perfect, though; the liberty of one person could still in some respects conflict with the liberty of some other person, so we could instead stipulate that everybody should have as much liberty compatible with the same liberty for others. Here liberty could only be restricted by considerations of liberty, and this implies some kind of maximisation of equal liberty for all. This is a very strong presumption for liberty, and I do not think Dummett would argue anything like this. He would say that liberty is very important, but other moral concerns can limit it, so those who think that there are such moral concerns should then indicate what they are. What I think Dummett is overlooking is that moral concerns can enter in different ways.

Liberty of movement implies that we can move in the specified way or not, as we like. Normally, we should not enter other people's property, or enter restricted areas like natural reserves and military bases. We also have to move in particular ways according to the Road Traffic Act, etc. (cf. Miller 2014, 365). If we respect these duties, other people and the government should let us move around freely. They have a duty not to interfere with our movements. This right to free movement is restricted considerably by all sorts of moral concerns, and even minor moral concerns such as not trespassing on lawns in public parks can limit this right. However, we can move around in the public space and this should be as large as possible, but it is the public space of the state entity we are living in. The state entity should protect this liberty, because it is generally seen as its purpose to protect the rights of the inhabitants. When we speak about cross-border movements, the case is a bit different. We can move freely to the border and are free to cross it, and it is generally thought that the state entity we are living in should allow us to do that (right of emigration), but is the other state entity obliged to receive us (right of immigration)? Here we are speaking about a different duty falling on a different entity, at least as long as different state entities exist, and Dummett assumes this (Dummett 2004, 115), and it also seems to be the underlying assumption of the whole discussion about open borders. The different obligations of the two different state entities are the reason for the often noticed asymmetry between emigration and immigration (cf. Seglow 2005, 324–325; Wellman 2008, 135–136; Miller 2014, 367). So, speaking about the burden of proof, those who believe there is a right to immigration should indicate why the other state entity has a duty to protect this right. They could, for example, have a duty to succour people in need or some other duty. That the burden of proof lies on those who believe there are duties means that those who think that we have duties restricting our simple liberty should indicate what these duties are, but it also means that those who think that we have a right to liberty should indicate why others have a duty to respect this liberty. If we simply assume there is a presumption of liberty, then we simply assume that any liberty is a right to liberty and thus protected by a duty on the part of others, and this is an excessive presumption (cf. Bader 2005, 339; Miller 2008, 376; Wellman 2008, 135).

We assume here that rights are not primary, but that they depend on duties. Rights understood as permissions suppose an environment of duties. They are permissions because duties can forbid or command. That is how we say that everything that is not forbidden is permitted. Assuming there are no duties at all, then everything would be permitted. Rights can relate to duties in a different way, when duties are not conceived as rules but as particular actions which should realise some comprehensive end such as perfection. Here you have a duty to perfect yourself, but in some sense you also have a right to what is necessary for this perfection. If education is necessary for perfection, then you have a right to education. Even though you cannot strictly speaking say that rights depend on duties or the opposite, it seems as though we arrived at rights through duties, such that you have a right to the things necessary for perfection because you have a duty to perfect yourself. You do not have a duty to perfect yourself because you have the right to the things necessary for perfection. From these considerations we conclude that an unbiased approach to these matters must assume there are no duties whatsoever, and those who believe there are duties should indicate this and argue from this assumption. We cannot assume that all differences of treatment should have a moral relevant reason, because this excludes automatically that we have a space of liberty consisting of permissions where we have a simple free choice. We cannot assume that freedom should always be a presumption, because we would then assume that simple liberties are always protected by corresponding duties. Discussing migration and open borders, each position would have to indicate which duties they assume to exist, and argue for them and from them. This, I think, will emerge more clearly if we outline the contours of two different models of ethics.

20.3 Two Models of Ethics

The first model we could call a rule-based ethics (model one). This theory supposes a set of duties and lets us assume that these are very much those of the Decalogue. Simple rules such as ‘Thou shalt not kill’. So what is not actually forbidden or commanded by these rules is taken to be permitted. These rules do not say anything about the organisation of society, so those deciding to do so can get together and they have then a simple free choice about the form of government and the distribution of property. Having done this, there is no particular duty to let people enter their territory and share their wealth with others. In order to oblige them to do so, you would have to indicate the origin of such a duty, and the burden of proof would thus lie on you.

The modern discussion of migration seems, however, to assume that the burden of proof lies on those who wish to close the borders, and this make for a kind of odd discussion. We will suggest that Michael Walzer, David Miller, Christopher Heath Wellman and Michael Blake profess model-one theories of ethics and therefore they are not obliged to justify the refusal of entry considering the duties they accept, even though some of them think they are (Blake 2013, 103; Miller 2008, 376). The only one who explicitly objects to this burden of proof is Wellman (2008, 119–120).

Wellman clearly situates himself in the same model-one tradition by taking his point of departure in freedom of association. Just as individuals have a right to decide whom they will marry, a political community has a right to decide who they will associate with. States have a right to manage their own affairs, and for this there is no need of any elaborate justification. He refuses to attribute the burden of proof to states and rejects the notion of equality which is often behind this attribution. He accepts a natural duty to help others, but this does not necessarily imply receiving them on one's territory, since they can be helped in some other way with the possible exception of refugees (Wellman 2008, 109–111, 114, 119–121, 124–125, 128). Although Wellman rejects any necessity to explain why states can refuse entry to migrants on the basis of his general conception of what states are and what duties they have, he still seems to accept this burden of proof elsewhere, arguing that the interest of cultural continuity advanced by David Miller has to be weighed against other concerns, since he asks about how weighty such a right would be (Wellman 2015). He seems to assume that Miller has to justify such a right. Miller and Blake seem to suppose something similar, namely that the state has a duty not to open its borders, because of its duty of protection towards its own community, whether it is a specific national culture or a reasonable burden of protection (Miller 2008, 375; Blake 2013, 104). Miller assumes the existence of basic human rights and state entities would for this reason be under certain specific duties, but this would not make them responsible for equal opportunities for the whole world population.

> One answer *might* be that we should attempt to provide everyone with equal opportunities to pursue their goals in life. But another, equally plausible, answer is that we should play our part in ensuring that their basic rights are respected, where these are understood as rights to a certain minimum level of security, freedom, resources, and so forth – a level adequate to protect their basic interests, as suggested earlier in this chapter. These basic rights can be universally protected and yet some people have greater opportunities than others to pursue certain aims, as a result of living in more affluent or culturally richer societies. (Miller 2014, 367)

This fits in well with our model one. There are basic duties, and when these are fulfilled, the state entity has simple free choices to manage its affairs. Why does he then say that potential immigrants have a claim (desire) to be let in, and that we have to give good reasons to deny them entry? What he is actually doing here is what he did earlier on when he considered whether harmful consequences of migration would outweigh the value of freedom of choice or whether freedom of choice had sufficient weight to be a right (Miller 2014, 364). He is weighing the supposed claim of immigrants against the interests of the state. When you start weighing duties against each other, they become instrumental to something else according to which they are weighed. Miller does not say what this something is. Maybe it is the maximal satisfaction of total interests or something comparable. Why burden the state with this additional duty, when he could just fall back on basic human rights and vindicate the simple free choice of the state? Why have such things as basic human rights if he thinks that the important consideration was one of satisfying the maximal total interests? One would suspect that Blake is in fact doing the same thing as Miller, introducing other kinds of duties which evacuate the simple free choice of the state. We do not know why they do that, but maybe the whole discussion is so soaked with consequentialism that they do not even notice. These other kinds of duties belong, on our analysis, to the second model, and we propose to call this theory the circumstantialist theory.

Circumstantialism means that an action has to be judged according to how it furthers a complex goal in particular circumstances. Such a goal could be perfection or the maximisation of utility. Utilitarianism would then be a form of circumstantialism, at least if we take for granted David Lyons's demonstration that rule-utilitarianism will collapse into act-utilitarianism (Lyons 1965, cf. ch. III, 133, 144, 161). It is also criticised for its moralising effect. Sinnott-Armstrong gives the example of a person considering buying a pair of new shoes even though the old ones are still usable, and ask whether it would not be better on utilitarian grounds to give the money to charity, thereby saving somebody else's life. According to the common view, it is not morally wrong to buy the shoes, although it might be a good thing to donate the money to charity, but that is something supererogatory (Sinnott-Armstrong 2003). Williams calls attention to negative responsibility, since we, according to utilitarianism, are not only responsible for what we do, but also responsible for what we are not able to prevent. This seems a very strong infringement on individual integrity, since we would have to intervene in all sorts of situations in order to prevent them (Smart and Williams 1993, 87 ff.).

Even if perfectionism and utilitarianism are different in many respects, they seem to converge on circumstantialism and moralisation. They deploy a comprehensive goal and the question arises to what it should be applied: to a group, country or the whole of humanity. It seems that the burden of proof is here reversed. Those who want to restrict the application of the principle to a particular group are required to explain why it should only apply to this group. Here frontiers become relative to how they impact the comprehensive goal. If overall utility would be maximised by applying the goal separately to different state entities, then it seems that frontiers would be important. There are always considerations for and against, and one would have to balance different considerations. In a rule-based theory you are not balancing concerns. A rule has its scope of applications, it can be more or less general or it can be hierarchically subordinated to another rule in case of conflict. In this last case, the rule has to yield to some other rule, but it is not, strictly speaking, balanced against something else. This idea about balancing supposes that we can attribute a measure of value to each concern and, placed on each side of the scales, we can see which concerns are the weightiest. Nozick considers the difference between a theory according to which we should minimise 'the total (weighted) amount of violations of rights' and rights as 'side constraints upon the actions to be done: don't violate constraint C' (Nozick 1980, 28–29). The first view would balance moral rights against each other in order to reduce their total violation, while the second view forbids any violation of them. Wellman in his *Stanford Encyclopedia of Philosophy* article on immigration describes the objection against Miller's cultural argument in these terms: 'citizens have an understandable *interest* in maintaining cultural continuity, it remains an open question as to whether they have a corresponding moral right (and, if so, one might wonder about how weighty this right is)' (Wellman 2015). If the state entity has a simple free choice about entry, because it has no duty to let them in, and these free choices are generally conceived as protected, then it has a moral right, and according to what could you start weighing this right against something else? You simply have to show that it has a duty to do this, or that the whole construction yielding a simply free choice is wrong. The weighing of rights is possible when rights are an instrument to something else, as in Nozick's example, or when they are conceived within the utilitarian calculus, or as perfectionist rights serving perfection or some other end. It seems as if the discussion is so imbibed with consequentialism that those who would not seem to need this language are obliged to use it anyway. We can weigh the concern for migrants against the concern for the state, its inhabitants and its culture, but weigh it according to what? Here we come down to theory. If you speak the language of rights, the state either has a right to refuse entry or not. You will have to accept or reject this right; you cannot weigh it. If refugees have a right to entry, then the state has a duty to this and no right to refuse them entry. If you speak about weighing, you are in a different kind of theory, where things can be more or less important for something else. These two different approaches are also visible in how different conceptions of human rights view citizenship.

20.4 Two Attitudes to Citizenship

We have argued elsewhere that the eighteenth century declarations of human rights are based on a model-one ethics (Jacobsen 2017, Chap. 10), and we have also argued that the UDHR is based on a model-two ethics (Jacobsen 2017, Chaps. 12–13). One of the most influential declarations of the eighteenth century is the Declaration of Human and Civic Rights of 26 August 1789, and we will take this declaration as the paradigmatic case. It focuses on liberty in order to define a space immune from interference from fellow humans and the state entity. For this purpose, a specific number of rules lay down once and for all the duties which limit this space. The UDHR deploys, on the other hand, a perfectionist goal in terms of development of the human personality. The rights outlined in the declaration (or most of them) should be understood as being at the same time duties, since we have a right to what is necessary in order to perform our duty to develop our personality. From these two declarations emerge different attitudes to citizenship.

The 1789 declaration has several direct references to citizenship. Citizens are attributed rights to legislate, equal eligibility to offices (§ 6), free speech (§ 11), equally distributed tax (§ 13) and control of the administration (§ 14). However, the declaration also speaks about the rights of man. Those rights are liberty, property, safety, resistance to oppression (§ 2 and § 4), habeas corpus (§ 7), presumption of innocence (§ 9), freedom of opinion (§ 10) and freedom of speech (§ 11). This would suggest that there is a difference between the rights of man and the rights of citizens. It might seem odd that the right of free speech is both a right of man and a right of the citizen, but the insertion of the term 'therefore' indicates that the second part depends on the first: 'Any citizen may therefore speak, write and publish freely …' (§ 11). Citizens partake in the rights of man. Free speech has, however, a special importance for citizens participating in legislation, and for this reason it is also emphasised as a citizen's right. The decisive argument for considering these two rights as conceptually different can be found in the electoral law which was enacted shortly after the declaration (*Loi du 22 décembre 1789 relative à la constitution des assemblées primaires et des assemblées administratives*). Section II § 3 specifies that in order to qualify as an active citizen with voting rights one should be French or naturalised as such, be 25 years old, having one's residence in the canton for at least one year, paying direct taxes corresponding to the local value of three working days and not being a servant. Gender is not even mentioned here. It goes without saying that women were not active citizens. The question was debated at the time by Olympe de Gouges (*Déclaration des droits de la femme et de la citoyenne*, 1791), and other women disputing this exclusion.

Emmanuel-Joseph Sieyès is most likely the author of this distinction between active and passive citizens. In a text read to the National Assembly on 20 and 21 July 1789 and later published, Sieyès presents the distinction. He declares that all inhabitants enjoy the rights of the passive citizen—that is, the protection of their person, property and liberty. But they cannot all take part in the public power being reserved for active citizens. Women, at least in their present state, children, foreigners and non-taxpayers should not have any political influence. Only taxpayers (contributors to the public weal) are the real stakeholders in society (Sieyès 1789, 29–30; Mavidal et al. 1875, 256–261, notably 259). This view was disputed in the Assembly by Abbot Grégoire, Adrien Duport and Maximilian de Robespierre, but passed into law without much debate (Mavidal et al. 1878, 479). Since women, children, foreigners and servants clearly have human rights, then citizens' rights must be something different. Citizens, according to the 1789 declaration, must be active citizens in the sense of Sieyès and the electoral law.

The ICCPR more or less follows the same lead, reserving political rights to citizens (§ 25; note some protection for aliens—See General Comment No. 15). The UDHR would, however, have led to a different view. Article 15 states that 'Everyone has the right to a nationality' and that 'No one shall be arbitrarily deprived of his nationality nor denied the right to change his nationality'. In article 21.1 it is said that 'Everyone has the right to take part in the government of his country, directly or through freely chosen representatives'. Everybody has a right to political participation, but only in his own country, which would suppose that he has a nationality. Since everybody has a right to a nationality, everybody would in principle have a country. So everybody has a right to political participation somewhere. Stateless people would then constitute a violation of the UDHR. In the ICCPR the right to a nationality is absent. The Convention somehow ignores stateless people, since only citizens have a right to political participation. Without a right to a nationality, we cannot in principle assume that everybody is a citizen somewhere. This is somewhat surprising if the ICCPR should be considered as the implementation of the UDHR. In the UDHR, citizenship is essential as a part of human flourishing. How to implement this is a different matter. According to the UDHR, it is not enough to have a passport, but actual participation is necessary (General Comment No. 25). For people not living in their own countries, this is, of course, rather difficult. Perfectionism only considers what is necessary for human flourishing, and if political participation is thus necessary, then everybody should be able to participate somewhere. Perfectionism cannot distinguish between human rights and citizenship in the way the 1789 declaration does. In this last declaration, citizenship is not essential. Human rights can be assured without citizenship. It is, however, assumed that most people are citizens and their collective control of the political institutions should safeguard human rights for the inhabitants. In the UDHR, citizenship is a part of human rights because political participation is a part of human flourishing. In the 1789 declaration, human rights do not include the establishment of society and government. Communities are established by contract. The government should protect human rights, but not all humans are citizens, since society and government are purely contingent. Membership and participation cannot then be human rights.

20.5 Conclusion

In order to be unbiased, we should start out from duties. One should consider what kind of duties individuals and moral entities such as states have. If there are relatively few moral rules, a rather large space of simply free choice would follow, and it is very possible that questions of entry and citizenship would belong to this space or be subject to minimal restrictions. In any case, in order to make these questions moral, one should indicate which duties would make them so—for example, a general duty to mutual aid. If one thinks that morality is about realising a comprehensive goal, one would start from the other end, since such a duty tends to moralise nearly everything. Here we would have to weigh different concerns against each other in order to determine what would best realise the goal. We would then have to argue that the interest of the state in controlling entry and citizenship is more or less important than the interest of the migrants to move around. In both cases, the protagonists must state the duties they believe to exist, and they cannot assume any kind of duty. But that is what is actually happening when you automatically assume that one should justify the state's control of entry and citizenship. This is certainly not the case on the first view, if these matters are simply free choices. Thus, it is rather surprising that some authors feel obliged to take on the burden of proof, when one would expect them to adopt the first view. This would at least be an easier way to argue when someone believes that the state controls these matters. The same difference shows up when we speak about human rights. The French declaration of 1789 distinguishes human rights from citizen rights, and it is natural that it does so, since these eighteenth century declarations are born of a political philosophy which deploys the first view and leaves such matters as citizenship to be determined by the contingent communities which humanity has seen emerging through its history. The 1948 declaration starts from a different basis, making citizenship a part of human flourishing and something everybody should enjoy. Here state control on citizenship and entry is subject to external considerations about perfection, and state control should be judged on its instrumental value for the attainment of this goal.

Bibliography

Bader, V. (2005). The ethics of immigration. *Constellations, 12*(3), 331–361.

Blake, M. (2013). Immigration, jurisdiction and exclusion. *Philosophy and Public Affairs, 41*(2), 103–130.

Carens, J. H. (1987). Aliens and citizens: The case for open borders. *Review of Politics, 49*(2), 251–273.

Dummett, M. (2004). Immigration. *Res Publica, 10,* 115–122.

Hohfeld, W. N. (1920). *Fundamental legal conceptions as applied in judicial reasoning*. New Haven: Yale University Press.

Jacobsen, M. C. (2017). *A different history of human rights, second revised edition of three conceptions of human rights*. Paris: Les politiques.

Lyons, D. (1965). *Forms and limits of utilitarianism*. Oxford: Oxford University Press.

Mavidal, M. J., Laurent, M. E., & Clavel, E. (1875). *Archives parlementaires de 1787 à 1860, 1(8)*. Paris: Librairie Administrative de Paul Dupont.

Mavidal, M. J., Laurent, M. E., & Clavel, E. (1878). *Archives parlementaires de 1787 à 1860, 1(10)*. Paris: Librairie Administrative de Paul Dupont.

Miller, D. (2008). Immigrants, nations, and citizenship. *Journal of Political Philosophy, 16*(4), 371–390.

Miller, D. (2014). Immigration: The case for limits. In I. Cohen & C. H. Wellman (Eds.), *Contemporary debates in applied ethics*. Oxford: Wiley Blackwell.

Nozick, R. (1980). *Anarchy, state, and Utopia*. Oxford: Basil Blackwell.

Pevnick, R. (2009). Social trust and the ethics of immigration policy. *Journal of Political Philosophy, 17*(2), 146–167.

Rawls, J. (1999a). *A theory of justice* (Revised). Oxford: Oxford University Press.

Rawls, J. (1999b). *The law of peoples*. Cambridge Mass: Harvard University Press.

Seglow, J. (2005). The ethics of immigration. *Political Studies Review, 3,* 317–334.

Sieyès, E. J. (1789). *Préliminaire de la constitution : Reconnaissance et exposition raisonnée des droits de l'homme et du citoyen*. Versailles : Imprimerie de Ph.-D. Pierres.

Sinnott-Armstrong, W. (2003). Consequentialism. In E. N. Zalta (Ed.), *The stanford encyclopedia of philosophy*. https://plato.stanford.edu/archives/sum2003/entries/consequentialism. Accessed February 20, 2019.

Smart, J. J. C., & Williams, B. (1993). *Utilitarisme, Le pour et le contre, Le champ éthique no 30*. Genève: Editions Labor et Fides.

Walzer, M. (1983). *Spheres of justice, a defence of pluralism and equality*. New York: Basic Books Inc.

Wellman, C. H. (2008). Immigration and freedom of association. *Ethics, 119*(1), 109–141.
Wellman, C. H. (2015). Immigration. In E. N. Zalta (Ed.), *The stanford encyclopedia of philosophy*. https://plato.stanford.edu/archives/sum2015/entries/immigration. Accessed February 20, 2019.
Williams, B. (1973). The idea of equality. In *Problems of the self, philosophical papers 1956–1972*. Cambridge: Cambridge University Press.

Mogens Chrom Jacobsen is cand. mag. in philosophy and political science from Copenhagen University. His Ph.D. thesis on *Jean Bodin et le dilemme de la philosophie politique moderne* was published at the Copenhagen University Press in 2000. His habilitation thesis, *Three Conceptions of Human Rights*, was published at the NSU Press in 2011 (second edition, *A Different History of Human Rights,* Les politiques 2017). He is specialized in political philosophy and human rights.

The manufacturer's authorised representative in the EU is Springer Nature Customer Service Centre GmbH, Europaplatz 3, 69115 Heidelberg, Germany. If you have any concerns regarding our products, please contact ProductSafety@springernature.com

Printed and bound by CPI Group (UK) Ltd, Croydon, CR0 4YY
28/09/2026
02224073-0011